Seeds of Discontent

Seeds *of* Discontent

THE DEEP ROOTS OF THE AMERICAN REVOLUTION
1650–1750

J. Revell Carr

Walker & Company
NEW YORK

Published by Walker Publishing Company, Inc., New York

All papers used by Walker & Company are natural, recyclable products made from wood grown in well-managed forests. The manufacturing processes conform to the environmental regulations of the country of origin.

LIBRARY OF CONGRESS CATALOGING-IN-PUBLICATION DATA

Carr, J. Revell (James Revell), 1939–
Seeds of discontent : the deep roots of the American Revolution, 1650–1750 / J. Revell Carr.
p. cm.
Includes bibliographical references and index.
ISBN-13: 978-0-8027-1512-8 (hardcover)
ISBN-10: 0-8027-1512-5 (hardcover)
1. United States—History—Revolution, 1775–1783—Causes. 2. United States—History—Colonial period, ca. 1600–1775. 3. Great Britain—Colonies—America—History—17th century. 4. Great Britain—Colonies—America—History—18th century. 5. Colonists—America—History—17th century. 6. Colonists—America—History—18th century. 7. Social conflict—America—History—17th century. 8. Social conflict—America—History—18th century. 9. Territory and Dominion of New-England—History. 10. Louisbourg (N.S.)—History—Siege, 1745—Influence. I. Title.

E210.C367 2008
973.3—dc22
2008030318

Art credits: page 22, *Novi Belgii Novaeque Angliae*, courtesy of the Geography and Map Division, Library of Congress (G3715 169-.V5 TIL Vault); page 100, *Francis Nicholson*, attributed to Michael Dahl, courtesy of the Maryland State Archives (MSA SC 1621-1-590); page 151, courtesy of the Mount Vernon Ladies' Association; page 165, courtesy of James Eley of Globe Treasures; page 200, courtesy of Historic Northampton, Northampton, Massachusetts; page 227, *General John Bradstreet*, by Thomas McIlworth (oil on canvas, 30 x 25 inches, c. 1764), National Portrait Gallery, Smithsonian Institution (NPG.2007.5).

Visit Walker & Company's Web site at www.walkerbooks.com

First U.S. edition 2008

1 3 5 7 9 10 8 6 4 2

Designed by Rachel Reiss
Typeset by Westchester Book Group
Printed in the United States of America by Quebecor World Fairfield

To my family, friends, and mentors, who, over nearly seven decades, have encouraged and assisted me in my work.

Contents

Acknowledgments

A project such as this is the result of the efforts of many people over centuries. It could not have come together without the records left by diarists, journalists, archivists, and historians who created the record of those events of the past. They, many listed in the bibliography but many who remain anonymous, are owed a debt of gratitude.

In the present time, there are many organizations and people who have contributed to this book. B. A. (Sandy) Balcom and Kenneth Donnovan, historians at Fortress Louisbourg and the staff at the Louisbourg Institute of Parks Canada, were generous with their time and encouragement as this project took shape. At the American Antiquarian Society, Vincent Golden, John B. Hench, and Jaclyn Donovan were very helpful, as were Bill Fowler, Peter Drummey, and Rakashi Khetarpal of the Massachusetts Historical Society. I also want to specifically thank Gail Bretton and Denise Rankin at the Skidompha Library in Damariscotta, Maine; Don Simmons at the Firestone Library of Princeton University; Paul O'Pecko and the staff of Mystic Seaport's G. W. Blunt White Library; Cathy Williamson of the Mariners' Museum Library in Newport News, Virginia; George de Zwaan at the National Archives of Canada; Jennifer Kittlaus of George Washington's Mount Vernon Estate and Gardens; and Holly Smith of the Bostonian Society.

The following institutions and their fine staff members contributed significantly to this effort: the National Archives in Kew in the United Kingdom; the Caird Library of the National Maritime

Museum, Greenwich, United Kingdom; the Bowdoin College Library; the Massachusetts Archives; the Boston Public Library; the Houghton and Lamont Libraries of Harvard University; the New England Historic Genealogical Society; the Phillips Library of the Peabody Essex Museum; Historic Northampton; the Maine State Library; the Maine Historical Society; the Rhode Island Historical Society; the Connecticut Historical Society; the New York Public Library; the William L. Clements Library of the University of Michigan; the Maryland Historical Society; the Georgia Historical Society; the Maryland Archives; the Zimmerman Library of the University of New Mexico; the Meem Library of St. John's College; and the Santa Fe Public Library.

I also want to thank Abby More of the Department of Romance Languages at Bowdoin College for her help in recruiting George S. MacLeod and Violaine Delmas, who did a superb job of translating *La chute de Louisbourg,* the journal of Gilles Lacroix-Girard.

At Walker & Company, I have received encouragement, support, patience, and friendship from publisher George Gibson, who also provided astute editorial guidance. My editor, Michele Lee Amundsen, cheerfully did a thorough job and spotted many flaws and excesses, which when addressed made for a better book. George and Michele have been a joy to work with, and the rest of the Walker & Company team has demonstrated its professionalism.

My agent, Stuart Krichevsky, and his colleagues at SK Literary Agency continue to be a steady source of encouragement and guidance. Stuart is attentive amid the fast pace of his successful firm. Kathryne Wick and Shana Cohen carry out their work efficiently and with good humor that makes working with them a pleasure.

Several friends have been of particular help in this effort. Ruth and Lawson Willard eased the strain of overseas research by providing the most comfortable of homes away from home during several trips. Their friendship over the years is cherished. Two other literary friends have been particularly supportive, Nat Philbrick and Jamie McGrath Morris of the E/TL&DS.

Final thanks go to my family. I could not be more proud of Rev,

Geordie, Mieko, Lisa, Bud, Willow, and River or more thankful for their presence in my life. Special thanks go to Barbara, who worked tirelessly on the first edit of the manuscript and contributed significantly to this book.

J. Revell Carr
Santa Fe

Prologue

For Decades, The English Colonists along the east coast of North America had been enduring the increasingly oppressive rule of English kings and their heavy-handed and sometimes light-fingered representatives in the colonies who strictly enforced repugnant policies and added to their personal wealth at the expense of the colonists. The liberties the colonists had cherished as Englishmen had been eroded. In Boston, English "redcoats" manned the cities' fortifications and walked the streets to support the harsh governmental policies and suppress resistance. The Royal Navy was afloat in the harbor, adding its cannons to the intimidation. The people were enduring capricious taxation without representation. The tradition of electing a representative legislature had been suspended, and the charter of the colony, its "constitution," had been revoked. Free trade and commerce that had enabled Massachusetts and the other colonies to gain financial strength was being impeded and manipulated by Navigation Acts that favored the Crown and promoted the steady flow of income to the royal purse at the expense of colonial merchants and mariners.

These conditions extended to all the northern colonies, including Maine, Massachusetts, New Hampshire, the Plymouth Colony, Rhode Island, Connecticut, New York, and East and West Jersey. Similar frustrations existed in Maryland, Virginia, and the Carolinas farther south. However, it was in Boston that the seeds of discontent had been firmly planted, and it was in Boston where the colonists and the redcoats would first meet, gun barrel to gun barrel. When the tinderbox ignited in Boston, the flames of what would become a successful revolution spread quickly down the coast and engulfed all of England's colonies.

Remarkably, the year was not 1775 but 1689, and the hated king was not George III but James II.

The conditions in England's American colonies in the seventeenth century had deteriorated to the point that the colonists felt compelled to risk their lives in an attempt to right the wrongs they had endured and regain the freedoms they had enjoyed for decades. During a period of benign neglect in the first half of the seventeenth century, the nascent colonies established themselves and set up their own governance under the charters they had been granted or the guidance of colonial proprietors. With the English kings and Parliament preoccupied with more immediate issues at home, the colonies were left to struggle on their own and in the process developed a strong sense of independence. The political ordeal for the colonists began with the first of the Navigation Acts, which was imposed during the Interregnum and increased significantly after the Restoration of the Stuarts to the English throne in 1660. In the decades that followed, the increasingly onerous impositions of the Crown created deep resentment that led to revolution in the spring of 1689.

The cumulative effect of over one hundred years of British disrespect, mismanagement, and exploitation prepared the minds of the colonists for revolution. In 1815, John Adams, when reflecting on the Revolution wrote, "What do We mean by the Revolution? The War? That was no part of the Revolution. It was only an Effect and Consequence of it. The Revolution was in the Minds of the People." While Adams was referring to the fifteen years immediately preceding the Revolution, this book will reveal that the "Minds of the People" were gradually being shaped by events and British actions over the course of more than a century. Those events and actions led to the revolution in 1689 and ultimately to the Revolution in 1775.

CHAPTER 1

Liberties and Benign Neglect

T HE NEW WORLD GLEAMED as a land of opportunity for England and her European rivals in the late sixteenth century. The Spanish government had been sending ships, conquistadors, and missionaries to the Americas and the Caribbean for most of the century to establish their dominance in this region, while generating income in silver and gold to finance their empire and wars in Europe. The French government had sponsored exploration along the St. Lawrence River and its approaches and encouraged settlement in New France, hoping to reap huge profits from the fur trade. With its traditional rivals threatening to dominate the Americas, Queen Elizabeth of England and her advisers saw the strategic imperative of establishing English colonies in the New World. England's treasuries, however, had been ravaged by wars with Spain, and the government could not afford to finance risky colonial ventures. Imitating the method used by the French and Spanish, Queen Elizabeth and her government avoided the financial burden of colonization by outsourcing the task. The Crown awarded licenses to various groups of adventurers and speculators who were certain that wealth awaited them across the ocean. This method of establishing English colonies in America would allow for extraordinary autonomy in the early decades of colonization, and those who ventured to the North American wilderness would be rewarded with liberties inconceivable back in England.

With Queen Elizabeth's encouragement, men who were not averse to high risk formed themselves into companies and initiated plans for colonization. The earliest of these adventurous groups, the "West Country men," included some of the boldest adventurers in the realm, including Sir Francis Drake, Sir Walter Raleigh, and Sir Richard Grenville. In contrast with the daring reputations of its members, the West Country men announced three seemingly simple goals: to plant the Christian (Protestant) religion, to "trafficke" as merchants and traders, and to conquer. It was soon apparent that the Protestant English were less zealous than the Spanish Franciscans and French Jesuits with regard to "planting religion," but the economic motivations to traffic and conquer were powerful.

The first attempts to establish colonies in America were costly disasters. After early missteps, in the late 1580s Sir Walter Raleigh established a settlement at Roanoke, on the outer banks of what is now North Carolina. Owing to the need for ships to repulse the attack on England by the Spanish Armada in 1588, Raleigh was unable to secure vessels to resupply the 117 men, women, and children he had left on Roanoke. It was two years before Raleigh's supply ship, carrying Governor John White back to the colony, reached the site and the governor discovered that the colonists, including his daughter and American-born granddaughter, Virginia Dare, had vanished. All that White found were some ransacked chests of the colonists' belongings, including three of his own, and the word *CROATOAN* carved into a post. White wrote, "Of the same chests three were my owne, and about the place many of my things spoyled and broken, and my bookes torne from the covers, the frames of some of my pictures and Mappes rotten and spoyled with rayne, and my armour almost eaten through with rust; this could bee no other but the deede of the Savages our enemies at Dasamongwepeuk, who had watched the departure of our men to Croatoan; and assoone as they were departed, digged up every place where they suspected any thing to be buried: but although it much grieved me to see such spoyle of my goods, yet on the other side I greatly joyed that I had safely found a certaine token of their safe being at Croatoan, which is the place where Manteo was borne, and the Savages of the Iland our friends." Despite White's optimism that his family and the other settlers were safe, no trace of the 117 men, women, and children of the Roanoke Colony was ever found.

Elizabeth died childless in 1603, having established no viable English colonies. Her death ended the rule of the Tudors and ushered in the Stuarts, who would have their unsteady hands on the helm of England throughout the seventeenth century. Elizabeth's successor was James VI of Scotland, who obtained the English throne as James I through his descent from his great-grandmother Margaret Tudor. James I brought two questionable attributes with him to the English throne: a weakness for favoritism and an abhorrence of Puritans and other religious dissenters. As king, he was also head of the Anglican Church and used it to his political gain. Through church courts, James I found ways to prosecute and persecute religious dissenters.

James I realized that the need for English colonies in America was urgent: economically, politically, and strategically. The next attempt at colonization was the Jamestown settlement in Virginia, which was begun in 1607 under the auspices of the Virginia Company. Contrary to the enticing image of a land of plenty conveyed by the promoters, life in this wilderness was a deadly ordeal as disease, malnutrition, and conflicts with the natives took their toll. Despite the grim hardships of the New World, there were a number of positive economic, political, and religious motivations for Englishmen and -women to risk the perilous ocean voyage and rigors of life in the wilderness after arriving in America. England's population had grown enormously, from three million in 1500 to four million by 1600, and was destined to increase by another million by 1650. Opportunities for earning a living had not kept pace, and hundreds of thousands led lives of subsistence. As the sixteenth century neared its end, with the great majority of the English being rural village dwellers tending leased plots of land, a severe blow was dealt to these peasant farmers. The aristocracy accelerated a program known as "enclosure" to more efficiently use the land by "enclosing" and privatizing what had been common land used by the peasants and managing it more effectively. This was devastating for the subsistence farmers since much of the land they had used for centuries was enclosed. They lost their meager farms and much of the common land that had been open to them for grazing or hunting, creating a desperate group of people who would take any risk to find a better life and avoid the humiliation and slow starvation at home. For many of these, the siren song of the colonial promoters had great appeal. It was from among these dispossessed people and other adventurers that the early settlers for Jamestown were drawn. For some, their persistence ultimately paid off.

Of the first 104 Jamestown settlers, only 38 were still alive nine months after their arrival. While the Jamestown colonists struggled to survive, more settlers were recruited for this dangerous opportunity, but during the winter months of 1609–1610, the population was decimated from a high of 220 to a mere 60. The incredibly grim reality of this "starving time" was recorded by George Percy, who served as governor of the colony twice between 1609 and 1611. He wrote: "Now all of us att James Towne beginneinge to feele that sharpe pricke of hunger wch noe man trewly descrybe butt he wch hath Tasted the bitternesse thereof A worlde of miseries ensewed as the Sequell will expresse unto you in so mutche thatt some to satisfye their hunger have robbed the store for the wch I caused them to be executed. Then haveinge fedd uponn horses and other beastes as long as they Lasted we weare gladd to make shifte wth vermine as doggs Catts Ratts and myce . . . And now famin begineinge to Looke gastely and pale in every face thatt notheinge was spared to mainteyne Lyfe and to doe those things wch seame incredible As to digge up dead corpses outt of graves and to eate them and some have Licked upp the Bloode wch hathe fallen from their weake fellowes."

In addition to the attacks by the natives and starvation, the location of the Jamestown settlement, in a marshy area next to the James River, exposed the settlers to the ravages of malaria while their own poor sanitary measures brought on dysentery and typhoid. After enduring fifteen years of hardship, only two thousand of the approximately ten thousand settlers who had been brought to Jamestown remained alive. It was only when these first Virginians moved away from the river, improved sanitary conditions, established a system of individual landownership, and began the cultivation of the highly remunerative tobacco in 1616 that the colony gained viability.

Other potential colonists were found among disaffected middle-class Protestants, who believed that the Protestant Reformation, which had been so successful on the continent, had failed to fully mature in

England. For them, too much of the Catholic liturgy and customs lingered in the Anglican Church, England's official religion. Their task, to "purify" the English church, was formidable because the church and the monarchy were tightly linked. The monarch was the head of the church, and during the early decades of the seventeenth century, King James I used the church for his political gain. Some Puritans grew so frustrated that they split off from the church and created separate congregations. The Crown and the church hierarchy made it so difficult for these "separatists" that some left England for Protestant strongholds like the Netherlands in order to be able to worship freely.

As this religious turmoil developed, a bold promoter with extensive experience in the New World, Captain John Smith, explored the northern coast of North America and returned to England to tout its virtues. This region, which he called New England to create a sense of familiarity, appeal, and comfort, attracted the attention of the religious dissenters. One group of separatists, which had initially fled to the Netherlands, returned to England and in September 1620 boarded the *Mayflower* for the pilgrimage to this attractive new land. Favorable winds and currents—which would have taken them first south and then west across the Atlantic, before heading north with the Gulf Stream along the east coast of the New World to the northern reaches of the Virginia Company's patent—were not understood at the time. The *Mayflower*, with its sorry band of 104 settlers, simply beat its way against contrary winds toward the American shore. After this difficult two-month passage, the beleaguered Pilgrims found an austere and forbidding land that was, in fact, beyond the Virginia Company's northern limit. With winter upon them, neither they nor the *Mayflower*'s captain had the will and courage to return to sea and sail farther south. From their initial landfall on the tip of Cape Cod, they pushed on and established their settlement at Plymouth, on the shore of what would become Massachusetts, and New England had its first permanent English community. As with Jamestown, the Pilgrims found survival in this wilderness to be devastating, and half of the colonists died in that first winter. Describing that cruel period, William Bradford, who would be elected governor the following year, wrote, "But that which was most sadd & lamentable was, that in 2. or 3.

moneths time halfe of their company dyed . . . And of these in ye time of most distres, ther was but 6. or 7. sound persons, who, to their great comendations be it spoken, spared no pains, night nor day, but with abundance of toyle and hazard of their owne health, fetched them woode, made them fires, drest them meat, made their beads, washed their lothsome cloaths, cloathed & uncloathed them; in a word, did all ye homly & necessarie offices for them wch dainty & quesie stomacks cannot endure to hear named." By adopting some practices learned from Native Americans, the surviving Pilgrims planted crops the following spring. Several difficult winters followed, but in their first decade in America the Pilgrims succeeded in establishing their settlement and extricating themselves from the demands of the "investors" who had financed their voyage and colony. Plymouth began to thrive, and its Puritan "Pilgrims" had the homeland and the religious freedom they sought.

James I was succeeded by his son Charles I in 1625, just as the Pilgrims were beginning to feel firmly established. Although Charles I continued his father's heavy-handed suppression of religious radicals and use of the church for political leverage, his reign was plagued by his assertion of the "divine right of kings" and constant disputes with Parliament. His lavish spending on art and two ill-conceived wars early in his reign brought the legislators' criticism. He dissolved Parliament no fewer than three times in four years, and to the consternation of the people and their representatives, he married a French Catholic princess and secretly agreed to lessen strictures against English Catholics. Frustrated by resistance from the Houses of Lords and Commons, the king determined to rule without their council and without the tax revenues only Parliament could allocate. For eleven years he ruled alone, generating income through a number of creative impositions, fines, and fees of questionable legality.

Charles I recognized that the colonies in the New World were part of the solution to the problem of religious dissent. If he could facilitate the establishment of additional colonies, dissenters would leave English soil, the overpopulation issue would be eased, and it was even possible that the colonies, once well established, could generate income to support the king's lifestyle and political objectives. In 1629, a Royal Charter was granted to the Massachusetts Bay Company for the land bordering that bay from just south of the Charles River to just north of the Merrimack. The following year, a group of four hundred led by John Winthrop set off in four ships, determined to establish a Puritan colony and set an example of the godly life they envisioned. They established their colony at the mouth of the Charles, with Boston as the primary settlement. They were not immune to the rigors of the wilderness, however, and as had happened at Jamestown and Plymouth, many died during the first winter. When new settlers arrived the following year, some of the original settlers abandoned the colony to return to England, where the heavy, strict hand of King Charles I continued to demand conformity to the Anglican Church, which in turn motivated many others to join the "Great Migration" of Puritans to the New World.

Virginia and Massachusetts were established by charters issued to stock companies, which financed the colonies' development. However, when the Virginia Company, which had financed the Jamestown settlement, went bankrupt in 1624, King James I declared Virginia a royal colony in 1625 with a governor appointed by the king. In addition to the charter and royal colonies, proprietary colonies were awarded to powerful and influential individuals who often governed their colonies from the comfort of their stately homes in England. In 1632, Lord Baltimore, a Catholic and political ally of Charles I, was awarded the proprietary colony of Maryland. Lord Baltimore's rent for Maryland could be said to be nominal, as indicated by this note from Cecil Calvert, Lord Baltimore, which accompanied his first annual payment on April 23, 1633. The note read, "By a late grant of a Territory . . . called Maryland in America, passed onto me under the greate seale of England I am to pay his Matie [Majesty] every year on the Tuesday in Easter weeke at his castle of Windsor two Indian arrowes as a yearly rent for the said Territory. Wch Arrowes I have sent by this bearer my servand to be payd accordingly and I desire yir acquittance for the receipt of them so I rest."

Lord Baltimore's noble intention was to create a place where religious tolerance would allow Catholics to live alongside Anglicans and other Protestant sects, and the first ships carrying both Catholics and Protestants arrived in 1634 to establish the colony's capital at St. Mary's City. Few English Catholics took the opportunity to settle in

Maryland, however, and the majority of the earliest colonists were Protestant "refugees," many Puritans and Quakers from Virginia just to the south where the Church of England was dominant. With generous land grants, the colony of Maryland quickly took hold and began to flourish when tobacco, its primary cash crop, sold in England at many times the cost of production. Fifty years after the establishment of Maryland, William Penn became the proprietor of fifty thousand square miles just to the north—known as Pennsylvania, envisioned as a refuge for Quakers, a "peaceable kingdom" where European settlers and Native Americans could live in peace.

Some of the colonial settlements felt internal pressures and strife. The desire for more land motivated some settlers in the Massachusetts Bay Colony to carry their Puritan faith north into the economically marginal, primarily Anglican, coastal communities of New Hampshire and Maine, and by the mid–seventeenth century, Maine came under the control of Massachusetts. Religious differences drove others in the Bay Colony into the wilderness to establish colonies more suited to their religious practices, and dissenters like Roger Williams and Anne Hutchinson were packed off to the Narragansett Bay region. Other dissenters, as well as ambitious settlers who had no religious grievance but a desire for opportunity, followed them, and through their energy and hard work, the Narragansett settlement became Rhode Island, with its thriving commercial center at Newport on Aquidneck Island. Those who found the Puritan settlement around Boston too lax in its religious adherence headed to the fertile Connecticut River valley at Hart's Ford or settled in New Haven, on the north shore of Long Island Sound, and those settlements combined into the colony of Connecticut. Each of these new colonies eventually received its own charter.

While it seemed as if English colonization were proceeding smoothly from Maine to Virginia, other nations made claims in the region. Dutch entrepreneurs established several forts near the mouth of the great Hudson River in the early seventeenth century, and the Dutch West India Company was created to carry on trade with the Iroquois Indians and colonize the region. After Peter Minuit purchased Manhattan Island in 1626, the Dutch colony of New Netherlands took hold, its early years a time of loose control, loose living, and controversy. A land grant program offered large tracts of Hudson River valley land to those who would bring groups of settlers but failed to entice sufficient colonists until New Netherlands opened its doors to people from any nation, and New Amsterdam became a thriving settlement by early colonial American standards. A decade later, Swedish colonists hired Minuit to help them settle along the Delaware Bay and River one hundred miles to the south, but their colony lasted only fifteen years until the Dutch took it over.

During these years of early colonial settlement, England was enduring political and religious strife, which required the full attention of the king and Parliament. As a consequence, the American colonies enjoyed an exceptional amount of autonomy and developed a sense of entitlement to religious, economic, and political rights and self-government. Most colonies had elected assemblies that established laws, allocated lands, and levied taxes under the authority of their charters or proprietors. With England thousands of miles away and embroiled in internal conflict and continuing economic threats from the Dutch colony in addition to Native Americans uniting against the northern colonists, the new Americans exercised their "rights" of self-determination and began to develop a distinctive, "independent" character. In 1643, the New England Confederation was formed, with the Articles of Confederation reading, in part, "Whereas in our settling (by a wise providence of God) we are further dispersed upon the sea coasts and rivers than was at first intended, so that we can not according to our desire with convenience communicate in one government and jurisdiction; and whereas we live encompassed with people of several nations and strange languages which hereafter may prove injurious to us or our posterity. And forasmuch as the natives have formerly committed sundry Insolence and outrages upon several Plantations of the English and have of late combined themselves against us: and seeing by reason of those sad distractions in England which they have heard of, and by which they know we are hindered from that humble way of seeking advice, or reaping those comfortable fruits of protection, which at other times we might well expect. We therefore do conceive it our bounder duty, without delay to enter into a present Consociation amongst ourselves, for mutual help and strength in all our future concernments."

This unique early cooperative venture, which set aside traditional rivalries among colonies, with the exception of Rhode Island, came together based on the realization that the colonies had more strength working together. Without London's involvement, in 1644 the confederation established treaties with the French in Acadia, the area bordering Maine, and the Dutch in New Netherlands.

The crisis in England was predominantly political but had religious components. The king's actions brought the crisis to a boiling point by the mid-1630s, and Charles found himself engulfed in turmoil. When he attempted to impose the Anglican faith on the Presbyterian Scots, they rebelled. Four years later, in 1642, civil war erupted in England and Oliver Cromwell led the parliamentary side to victory in 1648. Charles I was tried on charges of treason, found guilty, and executed, and an act of Parliament interrupted the usual succession to the throne, which would have made Charles's son the third Stuart king. On January 30, 1649, the day of the king's beheading, Parliament prohibited the proclamation of a new king and a week later abolished the office of king altogether. The monarchy was abandoned, and England moved into a decade in which it was governed as a commonwealth under Cromwell's leadership. During this Interregnum, England struggled as military and other factions sought political power. Despite the turmoil around him, Cromwell realized the importance of the fledgling colonies and took the first significant steps to assert governmental control over them. Parliament passed the Declaratory Act in 1650, demanding that the colonies be subordinate to and dependent upon the English government and subject to laws made by Parliament. The Navigation Acts followed the next year, to control colonial trade and shipping. These acts posed the first threats to the liberties the American colonies had experienced during the first half of the century of colonization.

For the most part, the colonies, particularly those in New England, ignored these restrictive acts and relied on the authority granted in their charters for their laws and on the New England Confederation for their trade regulations. With no method of enforcement, England was unable to curb the colonial defiance. Two years later, Parliament was once again dissolved and Oliver Cromwell was given the reins of government as lord protector, but the turmoil continued. After

Cromwell's death, the nation was floundering and impoverished and needed stability and firm leadership. In the power vacuum, the army, led by George Monck, forced the Long Parliament to dissolve, and a newly elected Parliament invited Charles II to return from France to rule as king.

For the English colonies in America, the fifty-year period of benign neglect that had enabled them to establish their own systems of governance with bicameral, elected legislatures and elected governors in most colonies was about to end. The English men, women, and children who had risked so much to settle in the New World had endured great hardships but had also enjoyed liberties and opportunities unequaled in the mother country. A sense of independence and right to self-governance had become cherished components of the emerging American character. In the decades ahead, when those liberties were threatened, the colonists would rise in their defense.

CHAPTER 2

Seeds of Rebellion

CHARLES II, AFTER MORE THAN a decade in exile, eagerly accepted the opportunity to regain the throne and returned to London on May 29, 1660. Although the monarchy was restored, the early years of Charles's reign were fraught with disasters. In order to compete with the commercially successful Dutch, Charles took steps in 1663 to strengthen the Navigation Acts, which had been introduced during the Interregnum. In an attempt to curb Dutch enterprise, only English ships carrying predominantly English crews could trade with the English colonies. As the colonies were deemed to be English, their ships and sailors were participants, but colonial merchants were prohibited from hiring cheaper transportation in ships from other nations. A shipper could not load his cargo onto a readily available and inexpensive Dutch ship but would have to wait for a more expensive English or colonial vessel. Certain commodities were designated as "enumerated." These items, tobacco, rice, indigo, and sugar, could be shipped only to England, cutting off vast profitable markets from direct colonial trade. In addition, all European goods and commodities destined for the colonies had to pass through England in order to be taxed before they could go on to the colonies, adding significant cost to the desirable and often necessary foreign products.

A year after the Navigation Act of 1663, Charles II made the bold move of initiating a war with the Dutch and arbitrarily annexing the Dutch colony of New Amsterdam, using the rationale that John Cabot had previously claimed all the territory from Nova Scotia to the Delaware Bay for England in the late fifteenth century, a hundred years before Henry Hudson's claim for the Dutch. The king granted the new province to his brother, James, the Duke of York, who, eager to assert his ownership, sent a fleet to seize the colony by a surprise attack in September 1664. When the Dutch surrendered, the colony was renamed New York, and the only non-English colony between Maine and Carolina was eliminated. In that same year, the king awarded his brother the land between the Hudson and Delaware rivers, as the colony of New Jersey. The Duke of York, to advance his political strength, gave the colony to two English nobles, and New Jersey became East Jersey and West Jersey.

While the cost of the Dutch war put a huge strain on the resources of England, the country was visited by two more disasters. Bubonic plague, the Black Death, broke out in London in the spring of 1665. By fall nearly one hundred thousand, one fifth of the population, had succumbed in London, and the plague spread to other parts of the country. The following year, over 80 percent of London was burned in the Great Fire. The economic and human toll of war, pestilence, and fire was enormous, for the king, for England, and for her colonies.

The king saw the colonies and their trade as a potentially significant source of revenue and increased taxes on that trade. With the restrictions of the Navigation Acts, tobacco glutted the English market and the price plummeted to one quarter of its former value. A depression hit the Chesapeake region as taxes on tobacco soared, providing 5 percent of the Crown's income in the 1660s but crippling the economies of Virginia and Maryland. The depression in Virginia brought on the first rebellion against royal rule in the colonies. After the Restoration in 1660, with Virginia under the leadership of the royal governor, Sir William Berkeley, unrest had begun to develop. Berkeley was notorious for favoring an elite class of rich planters whose fortunes grew under his largesse. When the Navigation Acts and heavy taxes fostered the economic depression after 1665, small tobacco planters could not sustain their farms. Robert Beverley, in his

The History and Present State of Virginia, published in 1705, said, "Which taxes and amercements fell heaviest on the poor people, the effect of whose labor would not clothe their wives and children. This made them desperately uneasy, especially when, . . . they had no encouragement . . . : nor any certainty when they should be eased of those heavy impositions." As a result of the desperate state of the poor, the rich gentry acquired many of their farms. The dispossessed headed for the frontier to the west with the intent of acquiring land there. When trouble inevitably erupted between the new frontier settlers and the natives who were being swindled and pushed off their lands, the settlers appealed to Governor Berkeley to wage a war of annihilation against the Indians. When Berkeley refused, the settlers took action. The impoverished and now landless farmers volunteered to march against the Indians and claim the land for themselves.

Stepping into the role of leader of this band of volunteers was Colonel Nathaniel Bacon, "a gentleman of moderate fortune" who had arrived from England only a few years earlier. "He was young [29 years old], bold active, of an inviting aspect and powerful elocution. In a word, he was every way qualified to head a giddy and unthinking multitude." When Berkeley, who was related by marriage to Bacon, refused to grant him a commission to head the army and endorse his war against the Indians, a confrontation resulted. It was only through coercion from Bacon's armed force that Berkeley granted Bacon a commission as general. As soon as Bacon's army moved away from the capital of Jamestown, Berkeley, with the advice of the colonial assembly, issued a proclamation of rebellion against Bacon. One hundred years before Lexington and Concord, the English colonies in America experienced their first uprising against royal governance.

Bacon issued a "Declaracon of the People" in which he leveled eight charges against the governor and twenty of his supporters. In the document he said, "Of this and the aforesaid Articles we accuse Sir William Berkeley as guilty of each and everyone of the same and as one who hath traitorously attempted, violated and Injured his Majesties interests here . . ." With these words, Bacon positioned his rebellion against the injustices and favoritism of the royal governor but not against the king. Bacon and his men returned to Jamestown and forced Governor Berkeley to flee from the capital and take refuge on Virginia's eastern shore across the Chesapeake Bay. The rebels then burned Jamestown to the ground and looted the property of the governor's allies. Soon, however, Bacon fell ill with dysentery and died. The leaderless army dissolved into factions, and Berkeley, with the support of several heavily armed merchant ships that arrived from England, was able to regain control of the colony. More than twenty of Bacon's supporters were hanged as part of Berkeley's bloody retribution.

When word of the insurrection reached England, the king sent a regiment of troops to put down the revolt. By the time they arrived, Berkeley was in firm control, but for the first time, English soldiers were present in the colonies to enforce the power of the Crown. After having been governor for more than thirty years, Berkeley was called to England to account for his actions that had resulted in rebellion, but once in England, he fell ill and died. While Bacon's rebellion may have been a minor aberration, it was clear evidence that English colonists, with, as Robert Beverley wrote, "minds full of discontent," were prepared to risk their lives in rebellion against the authority placed over them. The rebellion also gave the king the opportunity to demonstrate his willingness to assert his authority in the colonies through the force of the English army.

The discontent that erupted into rebellion in Virginia was also simmering in nearby Maryland. A few years before Bacon's rebellion, the deputies in the lower house of the legislature drafted "The Publick Grievances of 1669," which protested the authority of the proprietor, Lord Baltimore, questioned his veto power, argued for relief for the poor, protested favoritism and privilege, and objected to "taxation without consent of the freemen." The response to this "seditious" list of complaints was curt, with the proprietor-controlled upper house of the legislature condemning the list and celebrating the paternalism of the proprietor. In August 1676, while Bacon was fomenting his rebellion in Virginia, two less charismatic Marylanders, William Davyes and John Pate, led a short-lived revolt of some sixty men in what became known as "the Affair of the Clifts." Their published list of grievances had a familiar ring and focused on taxes that they protested were too high and unequally heavy on the poor. After an armed but bloodless, confrontation with the local militia, the Maryland rebels fled to the north when the government sent troops against them. The revolt did not remain bloodless, as Davyes and Pate were captured, returned to the tall "clifts" of Calvert County where their revolt had begun, and hanged. This violent government response did not quell the discontent. Late that year, an anonymous document entitled *Complaint from Heaven with a Huy and crye and a petition out of Virginia and Maryland* was addressed to Charles II and rambled on in a crudely worded protest against Lord Baltimore. In the Complaint the author makes the charge, "And now pray where is the liberty of the freeborne subjects of England and owr priviledges in Maryland, the Lord proprietary assums and attracts more Royall Power to himselfe over his Tennants then owr gratious Kinge over his subjects in Engl^d, and therefore charge the Lord proprietary with Breach of Charter." The Complaint, which is full of anti-Catholic invective, argues for the removal of the proprietor and desires that the colony come under direct royal control. With the Catholic sympathies of Charles II, it fell on deaf ears.

In 1677, another rebellion against the enforcement of the Navigation Acts erupted in Carolina, just south of Virginia. John Culpepper led a group who overthrew and imprisoned the acting governor and customs collector, Thomas Miller. An independent legislature was convened, Culpepper was elected governor, and he governed for two years before Miller, who had escaped, brought charges of treason and embezzlement against Culpepper in England. Culpepper was never punished, but the Carolina proprietors reasserted their authority. The furor over taxation, interference with free trade, and heavy-handed rule by royal governors or proprietors in Virginia, Maryland, and the Carolinas in the 1670s was palpable.

One of Governor Berkeley's complaints to the Crown had been that while Virginia adhered to the Navigation Acts, they were at an economic disadvantage because "the New England men break through and . . . trade to any place that their interests lead them." In response to allegations such as this and to get a full picture of the response of New Englanders to the Navigation Acts, the Lords of Trade, the commission that had recently being put in charge of colonial mercantile policy, sent a spy to New England in June 1676. The English agent, Edward Randolph, received a cool reception in Boston despite his "cover" of carrying royal instructions to Massachusetts and investigating claims concerning the governance of Maine and New Hampshire. His report to the king that September confirmed the stories of New Englanders flouting the Navigation Acts and, significantly, of the independent attitude of Massachusetts. He told the king of his conversation with Massachusetts governor John Leverett, in which he reports, "He [Governor Leverett] freely declared to me that the lawes made by your Majestie and your parliament obligeth them in nothing but what consists with the interests of that colony, that the legislative power is and abides in them solely to act and make lawes . . . and that your majestie ought not to retrench their liberties . . ." This report and others from Randolph set the Crown and Massachusetts on a collision course and made Randolph a hated man in New England. Matters were further exacerbated when, in order to bring Massachusetts into line, Randolph was appointed the first customs collector for all of New England in 1678. He received the same resistance from the colonial government that had greeted his initial arrival two years earlier, and New England merchants continued to find ways to circumvent the Navigation Acts.

As the symbol of the monarch in residence in Boston, Edward Randolph applied himself rigorously to the task of bringing Massachusetts under royal control. He constantly urged the revocation of the Massachusetts charter, which the colonists insisted granted them broad autonomy. In 1683, legal action was taken to wrest the charter from Massachusetts, and the colony was asked to voluntarily submit its charter for *revision* or face legal action. Voicing the colonies' position in March 1683, Samuel Nowell, a prominent minister and magistrate, wrote, "By our Pattent we have full and absolute power to rule and governe, pardon and punish, etc.; by which always hithertoo we have judged ourselves free from appeals, and either we may finally judge of and determine all things, or else appeals ly in all cases, which will make the Government here to be a mere cipher." Nowell and others feared their colonial government was being stripped of its authority. The famous Boston minister Increase Mather was asked for his opinion as to whether the Massachusetts freemen should vote to submit to the revision, and his response, cast in appropriate religious terms, was firm. Mather said, "As the Question is now stated, . . . wee shall sin against God if wee vote an Affirmative to it. . . . If we make a full submission . . . we fall into the hands of men immediately. But if we do it not, we keep ourselves in the hands of God." Increase Mather's words won the day, and the freemen of Massachusetts rejected the submission, but to no avail. English retribution was swift. On June 4, 1683, the despised Edward Randolph submitted a list of seventeen "Articles against the Government of Boston." An English court, with strong allegiance to the king, began *quo warranto*—by what warrant or right—proceedings, which theoretically investigated the Massachusetts government and its claim to authority. The biased court revoked the charter, and in an instant this document, which the Puritans in Massachusetts cherished and treated as their constitution, was rendered null and void.

While the king worked to assert greater authority in the colonies, another serious concern, the monarch's religion, once again became an issue in England. While Charles II outwardly advocated the Anglican Church and made life difficult for Puritans and other dissenters, after his marriage to his Catholic princess, he suspended penal laws against Catholics. His strong Catholic sympathies were reinforced by his brother James' conversion to Catholicism in 1669. Charles and French king Louis XIV made a secret pact, known as the Treaty of Dover, in which Charles agreed to declare himself Catholic and ally with France against the Netherlands. That alliance never materialized, and Charles conveniently revived his support for Protestantism. To illustrate his newfound respect for his former Dutch enemies, he arranged for his Protestant niece Mary, James's eldest daughter, to marry the Dutch prince William of Orange. When it became apparent that Charles II would have no legitimate heirs, there loomed the prospect of a Catholic king if James assumed the throne. In the early 1680s, Parliament attempted to exclude James's succession to the throne, but on three occasions, Charles dissolved Parliament to protect his brother's right.

Confirming widely held suspicions, on his deathbed in 1685, Charles II converted to Roman Catholicism, and James, Duke of York and lord proprietor of the colony of New York, succeeded his brother, assuming the throne as James II. Immediately, he faced an insurrection challenging his right to the throne. The rebellion was easily put down, but this motivated James to strengthen his control by enlarging the army and placing Roman Catholic officers in command.

James needed financial strength as well as military and, like his brother before him, saw the colonies as a potential source of income. As the Duke of York, he had controlled and oppressed the Dutch colonists of New York. He dissolved their representative assembly and ruled strictly through his appointed governor, Sir Edmund Andros, an autocratic former soldier who was fiercely loyal to his patron. When he became king, James II sought to exert his control over the renegade colonists in Massachusetts and consolidate his power in the colonies. The king and the Lords of Trade revoked the charters of the other New England colonies and arbitrarily combined the New England colonies and eventually New York and East and West Jersey into a single, huge colony known as the Dominion of New England. This megacolony was first led by a Massachusetts-born opportunist, William Dudley, and then by the hated Edmund Andros. With his lieutenant governor, Francis Nicholson, and a carefully appointed council, Governor-General Andros was given sweeping powers in his Royal Commissions of June 3, 1686, and April 7, 1688, and was determined to enforce royal control. Having experienced more than half a century of relative independence and autonomy, the colonists reeled under the harsh treatment of the new administration.

Governor Andros, backed by English soldiers, established the seat of his Dominion government in the hornets' nest of Boston, while he posted his lieutenant governor and additional English troops in the rapidly growing commercial center of New York. Together with his loyal council, Andros began to systematically dismember colonial autonomy. With no colonial assemblies to interfere, he arbitrarily levied significant taxes to cover his huge salary and the costs of his administration and troops. Cutting to the core of colonial rights and concerns, he questioned the grants of land that had been made by the colonies and towns, and there was widespread fear that long-held land would be reclaimed. Andros envisioned creating a steady and perpetual flow of income for the monarch by reissuing land grants and applying high quitrents, land taxes producing income for the Crown, and the

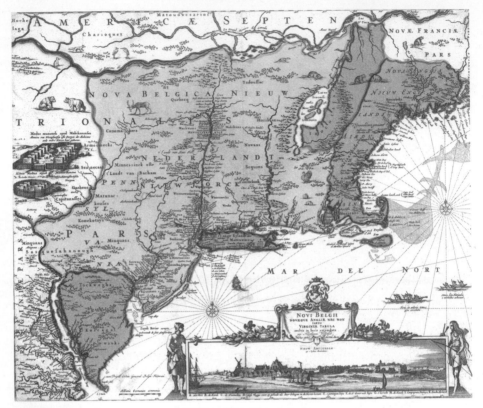

Map of the Dominion

colonists saw another tax burden eroding their often meager profits. To reduce the opportunity for opposition, traditional town meetings were restricted to one per year.

Empowered to appoint judges, sheriffs, and other officials, Andros filled those offices with people sympathetic to the new government and beholden to his patronage. When the Reverend John Wise led a protest in Ipswich, Massachusetts, against the quitrents and other tariffs, he and twenty-nine other protesters were arrested and given heavy fines and jail sentences. Wise was put in prison, fined the significant amount of £50 plus court costs, and stripped of his ministerial post. Also under the patronage of Andros, an Admiralty Court was established in Boston to rule on maritime issues and to strictly enforce the provisions of the oppressive Navigation Acts. Those who continued to smuggle or otherwise circumvent the acts experienced harsh penalties, and in the first year of the Dominion, six merchant ships were permanently confiscated.

In a particular affront to Massachusetts, which had been established as a Puritan colony, Andros brought with him an Anglican minister to establish the Church of England in Congregationalist Boston. No Anglican house of worship existed, so, to the great dismay of the Puritans, the governor asked to use the Congregational South Meeting House while an Anglican church was built. The response to the governor's request was negative, with congregation member Samuel Sewall recording in his diary, " 'Twas agreed that could not with good conscience consent that our Meeting House should be made use of for the Common Prayer worship." On receiving the rejection of his request, Andros simply commandeered the meeting house and then brazenly appropriated part of the public burying ground for the construction of the Anglican chapel. To the further frustration and economic detriment of the colonists, he terminated the practice of paying ministers' salaries out of town tax moneys, putting an added burden on the people, who now had to not only pay those taxes, but also fund this expense.

ONE OF THE reasons for creating the Dominion was the consolidation and coordination of the various colonial militias in order to better meet challenges and attacks from Native Americans and the French in Canada. The militia had been a fixture in the colonies from the earliest days, and all of the colonies, with the exception of Quaker-dominated Pennsylvania, organized militias during the seventeenth century. These armed forces were made up of the male citizens of the colonies between the ages of sixteen and sixty, who generally elected their officers and met for drills and military exercises on a regular basis, normally four times a year. Service was compulsory for nearly all, with exceptions for ministers, physicians, judges, college professors, sailors, and some others. The great majority of male colonists served in the militia, and each man was required to own and maintain basic military equipment, usually including a flintlock musket and a sword or hatchet. Without uniforms and with their mismatched weapons, the colonial militias gave the appearance of a motley rabble. Their military proficiency also varied enormously, as their elected officers were inconsistent in their understanding of military strategy and tactics as well as military discipline. Despite these deficiencies, the citizen soldiers of seventeenth- and eighteenth-century America were highly motivated defenders of "home and hearth." They formed the primary defense against native raids on the frontiers and pirate or privateer raids on coastal communities. In times of civil strife, they responded to the call of their fellow citizens. Now, however, under the tight rule of Andros, many of the colonial militia officers were replaced with newly arrived Anglicans, who were loyal to the governor but alien to their men.

In the fall of 1688, Governor Andros recruited an army of young colonials to wage a winter campaign against hostile Indians on the Maine frontier. As the winter months wore on, reports filtered back that the colonial soldiers were dying of disease and exposure. Suspicions rose that Andros had fabricated the war in order to lure large numbers of Massachusetts's youth away from the unrest brewing in the colony and to their deaths on a frigid winter campaign. The leaders of the colony expressed their frustration, writing, the "Army of our poor Friends and Brethren now under Popish Commanders . . . has been under such Conduct, that not one Indian hath been kill'd, but more English are supposed to have died through sickness and hardship, than we have Adversaries there alive; and the whole War hath been so managed, that we cannot but suspect in it a Branch of the Plot to keep us low."

The degree of the colonists' distrust of Andros became apparent when the governor began to negotiate with Native Americans. The Puritans feared that Andros was in league with the French and making secret agreements with the Indians to cede the American colonies to France, reflecting the great concern over England's Catholic king and his sympathies with the French. People in New England not only envisioned the loss of the precious liberties they had enjoyed for decades, but worse, they could see themselves as pawns in an international dilemma that could end with being forfeited to the hated popish French.

With the establishment of the Dominion, many of the colonists' rights vanished, particularly government through an elected assembly and the right of those assemblies to control taxation. Every colonist from Maine to Pennsylvania was affected by this assertion of royal authority. In the 1640s, the colonists had been willing to form themselves into the cooperative New England Confederation, but when the Crown imposed its Dominion of New England forty-three years later, the resentment was so strong that drastic measures were contemplated.

As James II took further steps to favor Catholics, anxiety increased in England. When his second wife, Mary, a Catholic and the daughter of Alfonso IV, Duke of Modena in Italy, gave birth to a son and heir apparent who was christened a Catholic, the destiny of England seemed certain. With over a century of religious turmoil, bloodshed, and martyrdom in defense of Protestantism, it was impossible for the English to face the return to the Roman Catholic faith.

CHAPTER 3

Revolution!

I T WAS A BRIGHT spring Thursday on April 18, 1689, when the
first American revolution began. Rising nobly at the head of King
Street was the focal point of political and commercial Boston: its
fine Town House. It was about to become the focal point of revolution.
The building had been a gift to the city from Robert Keayne thirty
years earlier, and the massive timber structure soared above the buildings around it. The ground level was a large open market defined by
fourteen substantial pillars that supported the building above. An enclosed staircase on the end of the building facing the harbor provided
access to the upper floors. On the upper floors, in addition to rooms
where merchants and the governing council met, there was a library,
also a gift from Mr. Keayne. Two cupolas crowned the building above
a balustraded observation platform.

The relative autonomy that the Massachusetts Bay Colony had enjoyed for more than fifty years had been snatched away, and three
years after the appointment of Governor Andros, the bold men of
Boston and the surrounding towns prepared to take up arms to expel
the king's governor and the other officials of the Dominion, which by
then included all the colonies north of Pennsylvania. Among the
most vocal opponents to the loss of Massachusetts's rights were Reverend Increase Mather and his son, Reverend Cotton Mather. They
were adamant that the old charter of Massachusetts be restored, and

toward that end, Increase Mather went to England in the fall of 1688 to plead the case. Once there, Mather published *A Narrative of the Miseries of New England, by Reason of an Arbitrary Government Erected There*, which began with, "That a Collony so considerable as *New England* is, should be discouraged, is not for the Honour and Interest of the *English Nation*; . . . Nevertheless, the whole *English* Interest in that Territory has been of late in apparent danger of being lost and ruined . . ." He went on to enumerate the excesses of Andros and the negative impact it all had on the colonists.

As Mather sailed for England, tantalizing bits of hearsay began to filter into Boston. Rumors spread that the Dutch prince William of Orange and his wife, Mary, the eldest daughter of James II and a Protestant, had been encouraged by Parliament to come to England and wrest the throne from the Catholic king James II. Before there could be any confirmation or refuting of the rumors in Boston, winter weather curtailed transatlantic voyages and, consequently, hard news.

The Dominion's opposition in Boston was emboldened in early April 1689 when a ship from the West Indies brought a document that confirmed that William of Orange had indeed arrived in England the previous November. There were further rumors of both the success and the failure of William's effort to gain the throne, but the people of Boston had no confirmation either way. Yet the revulsion felt over their status prompted the colonists into perilous action. As Samuel Mather recorded the mood of the time, when news reached Boston that William and Mary had landed in England, "Then a Strange Disposition entered in the Body of the People to assert our *Liberties* against the Arbetrary Rulers that were fleecing them." Mather went on to anticipate that disillusioned soldiers back from the fabricated war "would make a great Stir and produce a *bloody Revolution*."

For the "Body of the People" there was great danger. If they rebelled and failed, Governor Andros would surely have them hanged as traitors. If they rebelled and managed to bring down Andros and his government, they could still be branded as traitors if William failed in England and James retained the throne. The risks were high, and the lives of many Bostonians were at stake.

On April 18 that early spring Thursday, the people of Boston rose up against a formidable, militarily strong foe. Looming large in the harbor was the symbol of the king's strength, HMS *Rose*, a frigate with twenty-six powerful guns that was manned by more than two hundred officers and men. English troops garrisoned both "the Castle," the fort on Castle Island, which guarded the entrance to the harbor, and the less impressive position on Fort Hill rising above the defensive battery on the shore below, in the southern part of Boston.

As the day began, it was Governor Andros who was the primary object of the disaffection. He had hastily returned to Boston from the military expedition against Indians in Maine, the eastern war, and early that morning was holding a meeting in the Town House. Although the governor was aware of the unrest of the people and their efforts to have their old charter reinstated, he and his councillors were surprised by the sounds of the gathering armed force in the streets below. As Nathanael Byfield wrote in his eyewitness account that was published in London later that year, "Upon the Eighteenth Instant about Eight of the Clock in the Morning, in Boston, it was reported at the South end of the Town, That at the North end they were all in Arms; and the like Report was at the North end respecting the South end." The armed mobs gathering at both ends of the city converged on the Town House in the center. The group from the north end, led by Robert Small, a carpenter who had deserted from HMS *Rose*, seized the ship's irascible captain, John George, who was ashore. Andros could see from the leaded glass windows of the meeting room the throngs moving up King Street. Desperately, he and a few trusted colleagues bolted down the stairs and escaped from the Town House, hurriedly working their way through streets like Pudding Lane and Cooper's Alley, to gain the protection of the red-coated soldiers at Fort Hill.

The inflamed colonists seized the Dominion's powerful and hated secretary, Edward Randolph, several justices, the sheriff, and numerous other officials and led them off to jail. To be certain their captives remained secured, the rebels jailed the jail keeper and replaced him with a loyal ally, a bricklayer named Scates. When the mobs reached the Town House, they were frustrated at having missed their chance to snare Andros. By nine in the morning, as eyewitness Nathanael

Byfield recorded, "the Drums beat thorough the Town" to call out the militia, and using the signaling device atop Beacon Hill, the rebels alerted the townspeople and citizens' militias in the neighboring towns that the revolution had begun and they should prepare to join.

With the momentum in favor of the rebels, twenty companies of the militia took positions on King Street. Upstairs in the Town House, in the same room where the governor had met earlier, a group of leading citizens gathered to take control of the situation. Along with Reverend Cotton Mather, former governor Simon Bradstreet, and the brilliant political activist Elisha Cooke, there were others of high standing and respect in the community. The group was well prepared to assert their authority and, declaring themselves the "Council of Safety," assumed control over the colony. They prepared and read publicly a lengthy, formal declaration outlining, in twelve articles, their grievances against the Andros government. The declaration related the New Englanders' view of their status, saying, "It was now plainly affirmed, both by some in open Council, and by the same in private Converse, that the People in New-England were all Slaves, and the only difference between them and Slaves is their not being bought and sold." It went on to state their fear of attack by the French, saying, "We are informed that the rest of the English America is alarmed with just and great Fears, that they may be attaqu'ed by the French, who have lately ('tis said) already treated many of the English with worse then Turkish Cruelties." In the final article of the declaration, they declared their intentions with regard to Andros and his cohorts and their consummate fear. That article read, in part, "We do therefore seize upon the Persons of those few ill Men which have been (next to our Sins) the grand Authors of our Miseries; resolving to secure them, for what Justice, Orders from his Highness with the English Parliament shall direct, lest, ere we are aware, we find (what we may fear, being on all sides in Danger) our selves to be by them given away to a Forreign Power . . ."

At the same time they drafted the declaration, the fifteen members of the Council of Safety prepared a brief letter to Sir Edmund Andros in which they asserted that they were unaware of plans for the revolution but demanded his surrender. The letter read, in part,

"We judge it necessary you forthwith surrender and deliver up the Government and Fortification . . . promising all security from violence to your Self or any of your Gentlemen or Souldiers in Person and Estate: Otherwise we are assured they will endeavour the taking of the Fortification by Storm, if any Opposition be made." While an early part of the statement says that the council members were surprised and ignorant of the plans for revolt, it may have been disingenuous, particularly since Cotton Mather later told his son Samuel that the members of the council were prepared to step in if an uprising occurred and they may have already drafted the declaration. Nevertheless, it served the purpose of positioning the council as a stabilizing force amid the chaos.

In the harbor, the lieutenant of HMS *Rose* assumed command and ran out the ship's guns in preparation for battle. When word rippled through the city that a ship's barge from HMS *Rose* was speeding toward the fort to rescue Andros, rebel soldiers raced to the battery below the fort and captured the boat and its well-armed crew. Andros and about ten others were partway down the hill when they saw their escape plan foiled and retreated into the fort. As the large rebel force gathered below the fortress, the English soldiers who had retreated in the face of this army were reprimanded by their officers, and Samuel Prince recorded that one of the redcoats, who was actually a Dutch mercenary, said, "What the Devil should I fight against a tousand men?"

At the South Battery below Fort Hill, where several cannons faced the harbor for defense, the militiamen wrestled the heavy cannons around so they could fire on the garrison house. A tense confrontation ensued, and Samuel Prince wrote, "Had they within the fort been resolute to have lost their lives in a fight, they might have killed an hundred of us at once—being so thick together before the mouths of their cannons at the Fort, all loaden with small shot: but god prevented it." At that point, two representatives from the Council of Safety arrived at the fort and presented Andros with the letter demanding his surrender. Sequestered in the fortified garrison house atop Fort Hill, the aristocratic Andros summarily rejected the demand. The military power of the rebels was growing, however, and the message reached Boston that over fifteen hundred militiamen from the surrounding communities were assembled and ready to join the fray in Boston. Facing the artillery from the battery below and the growing crowd of hostile Boston militia and residents, who as the council's letter said were prepared to take "the fortification by Storm," Andros agreed to return to the Town House. He was escorted back and, once again in the chamber where his day had begun, faced the Council of Safety. Andros was haughty and belligerent when he entered the council chamber, but he was quickly subdued as "Mr. Stoughton first spake, telling him, He might be arrested and confined in comfort that night under heavy guard at the home of John Usher."

As the day of April 18 came to a close, with Governor Andros under guard, a key objective was accomplished when the English troops surrendered the fortified garrison house on Fort Hill and it was placed under the control of colonial troops led by John Nelson. Unfortunately, two large obstacles remained: The Castle was still in the hands

Governor Edmund Andros

of English soldiers, and HMS *Rose* lay in the harbor with her guns manned. As Samuel Prince related the situation, "The frigate, upon the tidings of the news, put out all her flags and pennants, and opened all her [gun] ports, and with all speed made ready for a fight, under the command of the lieutenant—swearing that he would die before she should be taken." However, Prince reports that the self-concerned captain George sent a message to the ship urging them not to open fire, saying "that if he shot one shoot, or did any hurt, they would kill him." Captain George was clearly eager to survive the ordeal; however, the lieutenant in command felt his duty, as Prince says: "But he [the lieutenant], not regarding that [plea of the captain], continued under those resolutions all that day."

That first night passed in relative peace, and the following morning Andros was approached on a key issue. Two colonels demanded that Andros order the Castle to surrender and delivered the ominous threat that if he refused, "he must expect to be delivered up to the rage of the people, who doubtless would put him to death." The colonels left him to consider his fate, and Andros soon acquiesced, realizing that the Council of Safety's "promising all security from violence to your Self" would not protect him if he refused to surrender the Castle. Obeying the order from Andros, the garrison at the Castle grudgingly surrendered and was taken into captivity, and the colonial militia occupied the Castle.

The rebels next turned their attention to the *Rose*, the last powerful English military presence in Boston. With the colonists in control of the Castle and its guns, it was going to be very difficult for the *Rose* to escape without being damaged and possibly sunk, since she would have to pass directly under the fortress. The lieutenant's defiance of the previous day remained firm. The Bostonians aimed every cannon from the shore batteries and armed merchant ships at the Royal Navy frigate, and a terrible fight seemed inevitable. Then the pragmatic and egocentric captain George inserted himself into the situation with an extraordinary plea. He said this entire situation was the fault of Edward Randolph and indicated that he did not want to fight. He expressed his hope that he would not be forced to surrender his ship since that would mean he and his crew would lose their wages. The ever pragmatic captain George then offered to neutralize his ship by sending all the sails ashore, taking down the topmasts, and sealing the gun ports. In that condition, HMS *Rose* could not maneuver to fight or escape. With bloodshed in the balance, this unusual offer was accepted, eliminating the final military challenge to the revolution.

The citizens were still agitated, and "the country people came armed into the town in the afternoon, in such rage and heat, that it made us all tremble to think what would follow." The subject of their rage was Andros, the symbol of the tyranny under which they had suffered. The crowd surrounded John Usher's home where the governor was being held, and as Samuel Prince documented, "nothing would pacify them but he [Andros] must be bound in chains or cords, and put in a more secure place, and that they would see done ere they went away, or else they would tear down the house where he was to the ground." Those in authority had little choice. Escorted by the surly crowd, Andros was moved to the garrison house at the fort, where he joined other prisoners including the commanding officer of the English soldiers, Lieutenant Colonel Ledget. The crowd's anxiety over the possible escape of their overthrown governor was well-founded. Nathanael Byfield confirmed the prudence of the move when he wrote: "We have also Advice, that on Fryday last towards Evening, Sir Edmond Andross did attempt to make an Escape in Women's Apparel, and passed two Guards, and was stopped by a third, being discovered by his Shoes, not having changed them." The creative, cross-dressing Andros had been foiled in his attempt to escape.

Immediately after the revolution and the capture of Andros, the rebels began to search for Joseph Dudley, the Massachusetts native, born and raised in Roxbury, who was viewed by most as a traitor. Dudley had been on Dominion business conducting a court at Southold on Long Island at the time of the uprising. Making his way back, he arrived in Newport, Rhode Island, learned of the uprising, and went into hiding at the home of a friend, a Major Smith in Narragansett. Clearly, Dudley's escape to Major Smith's was not done with as much secrecy as he would have liked, and a dozen young men from Boston had little trouble tracking him down and taking him to Boston and to

Joseph Dudley

prison. The somewhat disorganized Boston revolution had been surprisingly efficient and fortunately bloodless. The confrontation itself lasted only two days, and within ten days, the leaders of the Dominion were in custody.

CHAPTER 4

The Revolution Spreads

WORD OF THE REVOLUTION spread quickly to the other colonies. The yoke of oppression had been lifted by the arrest of Andros in Boston, and Dominion officials were taken into custody in Rhode Island, the Plymouth Colony, Connecticut, and New Hampshire. Yet as April turned to May, the rebels still couldn't be certain if there was a new ruler in England or if James II still reigned and would send troops to crush the bold rebellion.

In New York, the lieutenant governor of the Dominion, Francis Nicholson, struggled to keep control as disquieting information filtered in. Back on March 1, when Nicholson first received word through a confidential message from the governor of Pennsylvania that William, Prince of Orange, had invaded England the previous fall, he took extraordinary measures to keep this information from the people of New York. He knew that New Yorkers shared many of the resentments of the New Englanders and word of William's invasion could cause serious trouble. Nicholson called together the three members of the Dominion's council who were resident in New York, and they resolved "that for the prevention off any tumult and the divulging of soe strange news, The said letters [mail for other people that had been brought from England via Pennsylvania] be opened to see if they contained the same substance off England's being invaded, which was forthwith done . . ." Upon opening the private correspondence of the citizens of

New York, they saw that several of the letters did indeed contain the news of William's invasion, but that mail never reached the intended recipients, all in the effort of "the prevention of any tumult."

Nicholson was successful in keeping news of the invasion by William secret for over a month, but in late April, word of the revolution in Boston and William's invasion reached New York's Suffolk County on the eastern end of Long Island. On May 3, the freeholders of the county issued a declaration that threw in their lot with the Bostonians and cited "our Country of England's example for securing our English nations liberties and proprietyes from Popery and Slavery." Acknowledging that they had been subjected to arbitrary power, they acted for what they called their self-preservation. The freeholders proposed taking over all the fortification, including those in New York City and Albany, and throughout the colony people began to angrily voice their grievances against the rule of Andros. Just as it was for the people of Boston, there was great risk because it was still not known if the invasion of William had been a success.

Lieutenant Governor Nicholson wrote in mid-May that he thought he could have kept things "at peace and quiet . . . unless the seed off sedition had been blazed from thence [Boston] to some outward skirts of this province." He went on to describe how officials were being arrested on Long Island. With the revolution swirling in the outer reaches of the colony, Nicholson reported that an armed colonial force was headed for New York City on the pretext of defending the city from a supposed French attack.

Finally, on May 26, a full six weeks after the Boston revolution, news reached the colonies that the coronation of William of Orange and Mary, his queen, had taken place. In what they called the Glorious Revolution, the people of England had seen their Catholic king, James II, flee to France and the staunchly Protestant William and Mary ascend to the throne. Once confirmation of William and Mary's ascension to the throne reached New York, the tone of the complaints grew more bitter. In utter frustration, on May 30, Nicholson threatened "to fire the town about our ears" if the people continued their impudent behavior. The resistance of the people was soon galvanized, and the militia joined the popular uprising. On June 4, four companies of the New York militia were formed up in front of the city's fort, under the command of officers still loyal to the Dominion, and in the words of another loyal officer, "The soldiers . . . had been disobedient to the commands of their officers and in a rebellious manner left their said officer, went to the fort to side with Captain Leisler and committed insufferable insolences." The revolution in New York was now complete. A few days after the takeover of the fort, Nicholson was allowed to leave for England and the militia selected Captain Jacob Leisler as their leader. Leisler, a rabid Calvinist and anti-Catholic from Germany, had been a merchant in New York for almost twenty years. He quickly exerted firm control in New York, and before the summer was over, Leisler had been elected commander in chief.

Farther to the south, the proprietary colony of Maryland was also seething with unrest. There had been long-running friction between Lord Baltimore, the proprietor, and the majority of his colonists. The charter that had been given to Lord Baltimore by Charles I fifty years earlier was viewed as archaic by most of the colony's residents, as the proprietor wielded autocratic power. The frustration had fueled insurrections in 1659, 1676, and 1681, but these were suppressed because the proprietor had the backing of the Crown. However, as the 1680s progressed, criticism of Lord Baltimore grew and his critics in the lower house of the colonial assembly began openly to air their grievances. Lord Baltimore's Catholic faith and his blatant favoritism and nepotism were central issues. These complaints along with supporting evidence found their way to the King's Privy Council in 1681, and the council issued a stern reprimand to Lord Baltimore, accusing him of favoritism "toward those of the Popish religion" and saying, "Wee cannot but take notice thereof unto your Lordship praying and requiring you to cause the same if true to be speedily redressed." The Privy Council went on to direct that the proprietor demonstrate his confidence in his Protestant settlers by distributing arms and ammunition to Protestants as well as Catholics.

In addition to religious conflicts, Maryland was suffering severe economic hardships, since the price of its primary export, tobacco, had sunk to a penny a pound, a fraction of its earlier price. To combat what were described as most deplorable and calamitous conditions, the Maryland Assembly passed legislation encouraging the production and export of grain and meat that put the colony at odds with

Lord Baltimore

the Crown and its Navigation Acts. Exacerbating the economic crisis, Lord Baltimore in 1683 abolished the "Headright System" by which many in Maryland had acquired their land. Under this system, land grants were made to persons who either paid their own way to America or paid the transportation of others such as indentured servants. Five years later, the Crown, acting in concert with the proprietor, also tried to prohibit the exportation of bulk tobacco, and this added fuel to the discontent. With Lord Baltimore in England, his representative, William Joseph, castigated the Maryland Assembly when they resisted passage of the bulk tobacco bill. First Joseph urged the assembly to suppress and abolish "several heinous and habitual Crimes now most in Mode and use amongst the People as Drunkeness, Adultry, Swearing, Sabboth breaking, etc." After this insult to the people, he urged the passage of the tobacco bill and reprimanded the members of the assembly, saying it was unbecoming to question the king. After this arrogant attempt to quash debate and resistance, Joseph preached the gospel of blind obedience to the paternalism of the proprietor, ending with the threat that anyone who went against Lord Baltimore would be declared a traitor.

This heavy-handed treatment did not produce the desired effect, and one week later, on November 22, 1688, the lower house of the assembly listed its grievances. Among the eight serious complaints was the fact that tax collectors failed to follow the custom of payment in tobacco but demanded hard currency, which was extremely difficult to obtain. Additional charges included the levying of illegal fees, the impressments of men into the militia, the wrongful appropriation of winter food supplies from families and putting their lives in jeopardy, and, most seriously, the arbitrary arrest of people who were held without being informed of the charges against them. To their great frustration, the protest not only fell on deaf ears, but the lower house was summarily prorogued, having its meetings discontinued in an attempt to silence the discontent.

As 1689 dawned, Maryland was equally as tense as the colonies to the north that were struggling under the Andros regime. While the people of Boston were rising in revolution, the battle lines were being formed in Maryland. A colorful character, John Coode, emerged to lead the uprising. Coode had the courage, ambition, and political will to organize "an Association in arms for the defence of the Protestant religion and for asserting the right of King William and Queen Mary to the Province of Maryland and all the English dominions." Like their counterparts in New England, the members of this "Protestant Association" were acting on rumor and not confirmed fact that William and Mary had succeeded. When rumor turned out to be fact, the Maryland government still refused to proclaim the sovereignty of the new monarchs, waiting for instructions from Lord Baltimore in England. Coode and his Protestant Association were not prepared to wait. In mid-July, Coode and his troops moved to capture the seat of government in St. Mary's City. Arriving on July 27, Coode's men "marched down to the Citty of St. Marys to secure the Records [of Catholic domination]," There they found the proprietor's forces barricaded in the statehouse with their guns protruding from every porthole and window. Once again, as in Boston, armed colonists were gun barrel to gun barrel with the representatives of the king's government. The Protestants sent their demands for surrender of the garrison and the official records, and after two or three hours' parley, the building was surrendered. As in Boston, the tense moment of armed confrontation had passed without a shot fired and without bloodshed.

From the statehouse, the center of authority, the Protestant Association issued its declaration, which was distributed in the colony and also sent over to England. The declaration aired their grievances and justified their action in opposing the proprietor's government. The proprietary party found it difficult to raise troops to oppose Coode but did coerce a small band of men to join the fight. Confronted by Coode's large force that outnumbered the proprietor's loyalists four to one, the loyalists surrendered at Lord Baltimore's plantation on August 1. Three and a half months after the revolution in Boston brought down Governor Andros, the revolution in Maryland was complete. Within a month, a convention of newly elected delegates was held, and John Coode and the other leaders of the insurrection turned over their control of the colony to the new government.

THE ASCENT OF William and Mary to the English throne had profound effects on England, her American colonies, and Europe. In the discussions that preceded the offer of the throne to William and Mary, Parliament obtained promises that marked the end of the royal abuses of power that had been experienced under earlier Stuart kings. The final agreements, which emerged as English law, would place significant constraints on future kings and ensure that Parliament played a central governing role in the future. Beginning as a Declaration of Rights and materializing as a Bill of Rights, it affirmed the role of Parliament as the legislative body and sole taxing authority, along with the plan for regular parliamentary elections and parliamentary control over the king's expenditures. The Crown was not allowed to suspend laws made by Parliament or impose taxes. The monarch could not interfere with elections and could not maintain a standing army in times of peace without the authority of Parliament. Additionally and significantly, all Catholics were excluded from the English throne. This was a watershed moment for England, her Parliament, and her future kings and queens who would have to swear to their Protestant faith.

With the coronation of William and Mary confirmed, there was renewed hope that the old charters of the colonies would be reinstated and life would return to the days of self-rule and relative independence, thousands of miles from England and her political machinations. However, the ramifications of this drastic change did not produce the results that the colonists anticipated. In a pattern that would be repeated time and again in subsequent decades, the Crown's officials who had been accused of wrongdoing in the colonies were exonerated. Edmund Andros spent nine months in custody in Boston before being returned to England, and he faced thirty-one charges brought against him by the colonists. The English court failed to find him guilty of any charge, in a clear affirmation of the sovereign rights of England over the colonies. Others who had been held prisoner in Massachusetts, including the hated Edward Randolph and Joseph Dudley, were also returned to England to face charges and were also acquitted. The lieutenant governor of the Dominion, Francis Nicholson, who had been allowed simply to leave New York, faced no charges whatsoever. It was a bitter blow to the revolutionaries, when their just grievances against the oppressive leaders of the earlier regime were dismissed and they were let off without punishment. It signaled once again to the colonies how little power they had when dealing with the government and king in England.

Unlike the New England colonies, New York and Maryland, Virginia had not participated in the rebellion and remained a royal colony. To the consternation of the American colonists, the new royal governor of Virginia was Sir Edmund Andros, who was rewarded for his loyalty to the king, despite that king having been deposed. Maryland, where John Coode had led the successful revolt, actually experienced significant change. The protests against the proprietor had been heard, Lord Baltimore's proprietary rights to govern were taken away, although he retained his property and his right to revenue, and Maryland became a royal colony. Edmund Andros also held the distinction of being the royal governor of Maryland, as did Francis Nicholson at a later date, as a reward for his loyalty in New York. Maryland also saw the "rehabilitation" of another enemy of the Massachusetts colonists,

Edward Randolph. As surveyor general of His Majesty's Customs, Randolph not only worked as an agent for Lord Baltimore to see to it that he retained as much of his revenue as possible, but also continued his role as spy, reporting back to England on the state of politics and the economies in the colonies he visited. Bearing testament to the colonial attitude toward Randolph, he said in a letter to the auditor general of the revenue, William Blathwayt, "I expect you shall receive Articles against me from Maryland because I was diligent in prosecuting my seizures. Mather and the New England agents misrepresented me to those of Maryland and some of them have been so weak as to give them creditt."

In New York, the impact of the rebellion was felt for two years. Acting Governor Leisler created enemies among the colony's elite who had benefited from favoritism during the Dominion. When William III appointed a new royal governor in 1691, Leisler refused to turn over the fort in New York to English troops. A battle ensued, at least one person, Josias Brown, was killed, and Leisler retained the fort. When the new governor, Henry Sloughter, arrived two days after the battle, Leisler and some of his supporters finally surrendered and were arrested. The future for Leisler was bleak since the newly appointed chief of the council of New York was Joseph Dudley, the hated former officer of the Dominion. Like Andros and Nicholson, Dudley was rewarded for his loyalty to the Crown with this New York appointment. He was named president of the court in Leisler's trial on charges of treason and murder for his battle with the English troops. Although Dudley was hardly an unbiased individual, the trial of Leisler and nine others moved forward. Two of the accused were acquitted, but after determining that Leisler had no authority to name himself acting governor, the court found the rebel leader and seven of his supporters guilty. With excessive zeal, the court sentenced the eight to be hanged, disemboweled, and decapitated and their bodies quartered.

After more than a month of turmoil following the sentencing in New York, with many sympathetic to Leisler, Governor Sloughter acted to remove the focus of the discontent and ordered the execution of Leisler and his son-in-law, Jacob Milborne. On May 16, 1691, Jacob Leisler and Jacob Milborne were hanged, and while their heads were

Statue of Jacob Leisler

severed from their bodies, the rest of the grim sentence was not carried out. The other six convicted with Leisler and Milborne were eventually given reprieves. The revolution in New York had ended in a bloody scene that made Leisler into a martyr in the eyes of many New Yorkers.

Although Massachusetts was spared the bloody reprisals witnessed in New York, the disappointment in William and Mary's response to the rebellion made in their name was palpable. The exoneration and "rehabilitation" of Andros, Nicholson, Dudley, and others was a sound rebuke to the leaders of the rebellion. Massachusetts was clearly not going to have its charter of 1629 restored, and lengthy negotiations were needed before a compromise was reached. Ultimately, the people of Massachusetts lost their right to elect their own governor, and a royal governor was imposed upon them. They did, however, retain their elected assembly, which held responsibility for expenditures, including the fractious issue of the governor's compensation and, importantly, taxation. Only Connecticut and Rhode Island were left unaffected with their old charters and sense of independence intact. As the dust settled on the revolution in America, the colonies were all still English, with the mother country exerting slightly less onerous control than under the Dominion, but significant control nevertheless.

In a preview of what would occur almost a century later, the colonists had demonstrated that they had the courage and fortitude to stand up against authority when their liberties were at risk. The key point of the revolution of 1689 in England's American colonies was that it was against the tyrannical rule of the Dominion and the monarch who had imposed it. Emphatically, it was not against England. The economic, psychological, cultural, familial, and emotional links to England were still too strong for the colonists to consider independence. The Boston Committee of Safety in their initial declaration carefully framed the argument that the revolution was in the name of William and Mary, hoping that the rumors of their ascent to the throne would become reality and that the new monarchs would be sympathetic to their American colonies. These hopes were not fulfilled, and the colonists were quickly presented with a new challenge: proving their loyalty by entering into an English war against the French.

CHAPTER 5

Proof of Loyalty

O NLY WEEKS AFTER THE end of the revolution, the English
colonies began to be drawn into a series of European conflicts.
With William and Mary on the throne and England and the
Netherlands allied against the French, the national rivalries would
reach across the Atlantic, and the French in Canada, with Indian allies, would be pitted against the English North American colonies.
Since the question of their future charters had not yet been addressed,
the colonists recognized, when England declared war on France in the
summer of 1689, that it was necessary for them to demonstrate their
loyalty to England and the new monarchs.

In his new role as king, William was in the ideal position to oppose French expansion in Europe, and he joined the Netherlands and
the German League of Augsburg to form the Grand Alliance against
the French king, Louis XIV. The Grand Alliance declared war on
France in June 1689. Despite being a small, asthmatic man plagued
with a consumptive cough, William was a courageous soldier who personally led his men in battle. In America, this conflict, known as King
William's War, marked the first time in which the North American
colonies were drawn into a European war. The period of colonial iso
lationism was over, and a new era, one in which the French, English,
and Spanish colonies were expected to join in support of their respective mother countries, had begun. War was declared less than two

months after the rebellion in Boston and while the subsequent upris-
ings in the other colonies were still under way. Consequently, in the
midst of the uncertainty of their position and governance, the English colonies were not prepared to immediately initiate action against
the French. Each of the English colonies had an improvised government; for example, Leisler acted on behalf of New York, and Simon
Bradstreet, the last Massachusetts governor before the Dominion,
was in control there and abiding by their original charter until they
were instructed otherwise. However, fearing attacks from the north,
the English colonies began to discuss some form of unified action.

Unfortunately for the English settlers on the frontier, the Canadian governor, Count Louis de Frontenac, an experienced military
man, acted more quickly. By early 1690, he had a plan in place for
devastating raids, intended to terrify and intimidate the New England and New York settlers. The Indian tactic of well-planned swift
surprise attacks was adopted and refined by Joseph-François Hertel
de la Fresniere. Captured by the Iroquois at the age of nineteen, Hertel had taken advantage of his two years in captivity to learn their
language, absorb their culture, and study their native tactics before
he escaped. By the time of King William's War, the respect he had
gained through his leadership of surprise raids against hostile Indians earned him the nickname "the Hero" among his contemporaries,
and he was given command of similar raids against the English.

Frontenac's scheme was to use Hertel's tactic of surprise attacks in
three locations along the northern frontier of the English colonies.
Jacques Lemoyne de Sainte-Helene led the first group against New
York. Realizing that Albany was too well defended, they chose the little village of Schenectady as an easier target. It turned out to be even
easier than expected when the French discovered only two snowmen
on watch and the gate of the stockade open. At dawn on February 9,
1690, they overwhelmed the village of Schenectady in a surprise attack against the unsuspecting community. An eyewitness, Robert
Livingston, recorded the gruesome attack in his journal, saying, "The
bloodthirsty people [the French and their Indian allies], then, to accomplish their evil purpose, . . . divided themselves into three troops
and . . . the full wrath of God was poured out over us . . . they attacked
simultaneously at the signal of a gun. They first set fire to the house

of Adam Vroman, who when he offered resistance was shot through the head . . . his wife . . . opened the back door, whereupon she was immediately shot dead and devoured by the flames. . . . His eldest daughter . . . had her mother's child on her arm . . . whereupon [one of the invaders] . . . took the child from her and taking it by the legs dashed its head against the sill of the house, so that the brains scattered over the bystanders . . ." The grim narrative continued, describing the flight of underclothed women and children into the freezing night and their deaths, the capture of many, and the ultimate release of the women, children, and older men so that only twenty of the men were marched north as prisoners.

The final tally included sixty people murdered, with forty houses and twenty-two barns filled with cattle destroyed. When news of the attack reached nearby Albany, Mayor Peter Schuyler expressed the shock of the people, writing, "The Cruelties committed at said Place no Penn can write nor Tongue expresse."

To the east, Hertel and a band of sixty men, half French and half Indian, launched the second attack against Salmon Falls near Portsmouth, New Hampshire. William Vaughn and Richard Martyn made a report to the governor of Massachusetts, saying, "The enemy made their onset between break of the day & sunrise—when most were a bed & no watch kept neither in fort nor house they presently took possession of ye fort to prevent any of ours doing it & so carried all before them by a surprize, none of our men being able to get together into a body to oppose them, so that in the place were kild & taken between fourscore & 100 persons, of which between twenty & Thirty able men, the fort & upwards of twenty houses burnt, most of the Cattle burnt in the houses or otherwise kil'd which were very considerable . . ." More than thirty were killed in the attack on Salmon Falls, and fifty were taken captive. Not only was the brutal attack a complete success, but Hertel also managed to lay an ambush for the pursuing militia from Portsmouth. His tactic was successful, and having defeated the militia, Hertel's force with their captives slipped away into the depth of the wilderness.

While part of his force headed north with their captives, Hertel and others of his men joined the third French contingent of four hundred French and Indians under command of Sieur de Pontneuf that had been sent against settlements in Maine. The large force laid siege to the small fort at Falmouth, Maine, on Casco Bay. After four days of attack, the fort's captain, Sylvanus Davis, negotiated a surrender to secure the safety of the surviving men, women, and children. Once the surrender was made, however, the French could not control their Indian allies, who killed many of the wounded and took others captive, including Captain Davis, who was taken as a prisoner to Quebec.

The colonists resented the fact that their new king had drawn them into this war but would not spare troops to help protect his colonies. Forced to act in self-defense, Massachusetts mounted a retaliatory attack under the dubious leadership of the Maine-born Sir William Phips, a man of questionable integrity and violent temper. Phips, originally from a Maine outpost near the Kennebec River, moved to Boston as a young man. With little education, he found work as a shipwright. On the waterfront, he was inspired by tales of sunken Spanish treasure ships and organized treasure-hunting expeditions with the backing of his family connections. Although he failed on his first expedition, he recovered a vast fortune of more than £250,000 on the second, which he took to his investors in England. James II awarded him a knighthood for his success, and when he returned to Boston with his title and wealth, he also carried a royal appointment as provost marshal general of the Dominion of New England. His reception by the other officials of the Dominion, who treated him as an uneducated adventurer, was so offensive to Phips that he soon returned to England to complain. There he became friends with Increase Mather, who was lobbying unsuccessfully for the return of the Massachusetts charter. Fortunately for Phips as an officer of the Dominion, he was still in England when the revolution of 1689 occurred, since he would probably have been arrested with the likes of Andros and Dudley had he been in Boston.

A month after the revolution, Phips returned to Boston and, having been heavily influenced by Increase Mather, joined Mather's North Church. The wealthy Sir William soon became recognized as a leading citizen. He was a tall man, with a forceful, adventuresome personality, and he seemed the ideal person to lead the assault on the French capital of Acadia, Port Royal, on the Bay of Fundy shore of Nova Scotia. Phips and his small army were eager to avenge the attacks on Schenec-

tady and Salmon Falls when they set off in seven ships. When they arrived at Port Royal on May 9, they found a dilapidated fort with no
guns mounted and defended by only 72 men who were no match for
Phips and his 736 New England militiamen. After the French accepted
terms of surrender, which promised that the settlement would not be
molested, the duplicitous Phips reneged and brutalized the settlement.
The "journal" of the Phips expedition reported, "We cut down the
cross, rifled the Church, pulled down the High-Altar, breaking their
images." His looting and destruction were not restricted to the popish
monument; as the journal said, they "kept gathering Plunder both by
land and water, and also under ground in their Gardens." Phips was
personally accused of taking the French governor's silver forks and
spoons, plus his wigs, shirts, garters, and nightcaps!

Feeling he did not have enough men to leave as a garrison at the
fort, he forced the Acadians to swear allegiance to William and Mary

William Phips

and placed a Frenchman in charge. Phips departed for New England content with his victory, naively expecting the French to honor their oath of allegiance when he had not honored his assurances at their surrender. Not surprisingly, the French were soon back in control of Port Royal and rebuilding the fort.

Five months later and brimming with confidence, the northern colonies prepared to send an expedition against New France despite the fact that they had no military or naval support from the mother country. Representatives of Connecticut, Massachusetts, New York, and the Plymouth Colony were called together by Massachusetts governor Bradstreet and agreed upon a plan offered by Jacob Leisler, who was still acting governor of New York. A land army would be sent from Albany to attack Montreal and draw troops away from the defense of Quebec, the capital of New France, while an amphibious force would sail from Boston and make its way up the St. Lawrence to attack Quebec. The ambitious plan was complex and depended on effective communications and coordination. As the land force headed north under the command of Connecticut's Fitz-John Winthrop, smallpox broke out among the troops. When only a fraction of the expected Indian allies joined the group, Winthrop was forced to abandon the campaign and turn back. News of this disaster reached Boston a week after Phips's amphibious force had departed. Ignorant of this turn of events, Phips sailed on at a leisurely pace, despite the approach of winter weather and an outbreak of smallpox among his troops. On October 6, the thirty-four ships of the colonial fleet anchored near Quebec. When Phips sent an envoy ashore to demand the city's surrender, the governor, Frontenac, would not dignify the demand with any answer other than, *"Non, je n'ai point de réponse à faire à votre général que par la bouche de mes canons et de mes fusils."* (I have no reply to make to your general other than from the mouth of my cannons and muskets.) With defiance from the French, Phips's depleted force of twelve hundred men waded through icy water onto the north shore of the St. Lawrence River, two miles east of the city. The St. Charles River, which they would have to ford under fire, lay between them and Quebec. Phips prematurely positioned his warships to bombard the city in support of his troops when they eventually attempted to cross the river, and Frontenac immediately engaged the ships in an artillery duel.

Phips expended much of his powder in a prolonged and futile exchange, while his troops ashore shivered in the damp cold. During the five-day fiasco, Phips realized that under the experienced leadership of Governor Frontenac, and reinforced with troops from Montreal, Quebec was an unattainable goal. He ordered the troops to return to the ships, and in frantic disarray, they hastily reembarked, abandoning valuable artillery pieces to the French.

The fleet withdrew out of range of the city's guns, repaired the damage they had caused to the ships, and, humiliated, headed down the St. Lawrence. Disease continued to take its toll, and several ships were wrecked in storms as the expedition groped its way home in defeat. The pride and enthusiasm of the New Englanders had taken a serious blow, and the luster of the reputation of Sir William Phips had dimmed considerably. Massachusetts had been counting on the plunder taken from Quebec to pay for the costly expedition. When this was not available, the Massachusetts government printed the first paper money, called "bills of credit," to be issued in the western hemisphere, to pay the disgruntled surviving soldiers and sailors.

Despite the failure of the Quebec campaign, Phips was determined to try again and went to England to garner support for the effort. He found the Crown and Parliament absorbed in other issues, including the status of Massachusetts and its charter, which the Reverend Increase Mather had continued to negotiate. The final compromise provided for an elected assembly but an appointed royal governor, and Mather suggested a member of his congregation as a candidate for that position. The resilient Sir William Phips returned to Massachusetts in May 1692 without the support for another Quebec attack, but with a far greater personal prize, the appointment as the first royal governor of the colony of Massachusetts. His arrival and the perspective on his appointment are recorded in the records of Salem, Massachusetts: "May 14th. Sir Wm. Phipps arrived with a new Charter from William and Mary, dated the preceding Oct. 7th. This Charter constitutes Massachusetts, Plymouth, Maine and Nova Scotia one Province, of which Wm. Phipps was appointed Governor by their Majesties. Thus the hope, which the Colonists of Massachusetts had cherished, in some degree, as to the confirmation of their first Charter privileges, was disappointed." Phips, who had risen from the most obscure beginnings, had reached the pinnacle of power and seemed destined for success.

Phips had returned to Massachusetts at the height of the famous witch-hunting mania, and he quickly put an end to it. His firm hand and decisive actions, which occasionally rose to physical violence when his wishes were challenged, were also brought to bear on a vital issue that threatened the liberty of many men in the colonies: impressment. While some men volunteered for naval service, there were never enough, particularly in time of war. Impressment, which had been in existence since the era of King John in the thirteenth century, was the standard method throughout England for supplying the men needed for the Royal Navy. Led by an officer, a gang of sailors would sweep through a coastal community and "press" the men they rounded up into naval service. Men were snatched from merchant ships or dragged from streets and dwellings, forced onto navy ships, and sailed off to all parts of the globe. They often had no chance to communicate with family or friends before sailing, and some never returned home.

The service into which the victims of the press were forced was often brutal and hazardous. Life on the ships of the Royal Navy of the late seventeenth century was harsh, with poor food, constant danger from the perils of the sea or combat, and the looming discipline of the lash. Wages were low, and accumulated wages were often withheld, sometimes for years, in order to discourage desertion. English naval vessels visiting colonial ports in North America were plagued by desertions, since life in the New World had appeal to many sailors who were dissatisfied with their naval service. Some colonial merchant shipmasters enticed sailors to desert with promises of better conditions and higher pay. The need to find and capture deserters or press replacements into service was a constant challenge for English naval officers. The press was a feared but accepted evil in England until 1833. As an indication of their early attitude of independence, the American colonists strongly felt that the press applied only to England and not to America.

The catalyst that first brought government attention to the issue of impressment in the American colonies was a particularly egregious incident that took place in Boston a month after the arrival of Governor Phips. Twice in the middle of the night during the last weeks of June 1692, doors in Boston were pounded open by the press gang from HMS *Nonesuch*, a new English frigate of thirty-six guns. The gang was led by the ship's captain, Richard Short, and it was not English deserters or even colonial sailors who were rousted violently from their beds, but two members of the Massachusetts Assembly. The first was residing at the Green Dragon, a tavern that would later become famous as the meeting place for American revolutionaries. John Tomson was pulled from bed and hauled down the stairs. As Tomson approached the bottom of the stairs, he reported, "The Captain came up towards me calling me several ill names . . . and that he had a good mind to Slatt out my brains." The astonished and insulted Tomson was hauled through the streets for some distance and then was simply cast aside to make his way back to his lodgings.

Ten days later, Short and his gang were again on the prowl and broke down the door of Caleb Chaphin's house, where Assemblyman Peter Woodbury was staying. Woodbury later testified, "Richard Short . . . broak open the door upon me and came to the bed, and struck me three or four blows with his cane . . . he struck me eight or ten blows more and broke open my head, so I lost much blood." He was then hauled out along the road for one hundred yards before he, too, was abandoned. These two men were clearly not seamen, and their treatment was more likely a reflection of Captain Short's contempt for Massachusetts and its assembly, which had tacitly endorsed the 1689 rebellion. However, it demonstrated the arrogance of the Royal Navy and the brutality of the press. It was also a precursor of the contempt for the "provincials" that many in the English military would demonstrate in the decades that followed, which fostered serious resentment among the colonists.

The two assemblymen, Tomson and Woodbury, took their complaints to Governor Phips, who confronted Captain Short on the waterfront. Each man ridiculed and insulted the other, and their encounter escalated into a full-fledged brawl between the short-tempered governor and the belligerent naval captain. After several blows were exchanged, Phips struck Short down with his cane. Exercising his authority as not only governor but also vice admiral, Phips had Captain Short removed from command of the *Nonesuch*, establishing an important precedent for the action of later colonial officials. Short was shipped back to England for disciplinary action, but the response of the Admiralty was the same as that of other English authorities dealing with legal complaints from the colonies. As with the exoneration of Andros, Nicholson, and Dudley, no legal action was taken against Captain Short. He was, however, recognized as a liability by the Royal Navy and never again held command. In revenge, Short lodged charges against Phips, which when added to a number of others against the volatile governor created sufficient cause for the King's Privy Council in England to recall him. On arrival in England on January 1, 1695, Phips was arrested but released on bail provided by English friends. Seven weeks later, while preparing his defense, Sir William Phips died.

Although impressment in the colonies had gotten the attention of the authorities in England, abuses continued on the North American mainland and in the English "sugar islands" of the West Indies. It was not, however, the rights of the sailors that ultimately brought action. Mariners were generally viewed as a low sort and definitely as second-class citizens. They had a reputation for violence, drunkenness, and loose living. The image of the swaggering Jack Tar, reeling around the waterfront from one sordid establishment to another, stayed with sailors for centuries. Because of this reputation, they were given little standing in the community and little regard when it came to individual rights. The English authorities, therefore, responded not to the sailors' grievances, but to the complaints of powerful merchants who were losing not only profits, but also too many men to the press. The English Board of Trade issued a regulation that required English captains to obtain permission from the respective colonial governor before conducting a press in his colony. Government officials in England thought that the real problem lay not with impressment, but with the rough and demanding actions of the captains in the Royal Navy, and that if responsibility were shifted to the colonial governors, the problem would be defused. This perception was wrong, since the colonists cherished their freedoms and detested any arbitrary breach of those liberties. The ominous cloud of impressment hung over the colonies for another 125 years, and there would be numerous abuses. For the English colonists in America, the contentious issue of impressment became a major cause of friction, discontent, riot, and death.

As the 1690s wore on, so did King William's War, and attacks continued back and forth along the frontiers of New England and New York. The last major French attack was made on July 15, 1696, against the stone fort at Pemaquid. The French asserted that their territory of Acadia began at the Kennebec River, fifteen miles to the west of Pemaquid. After only a few shots were fired, Captain Pascoe Chubb surrendered the fort, which the French then demolished.

Small raids continued to plague the frontier region; however, in the spring of 1697 an unlikely heroine emerged from the brutality of King William's War. Hannah Dustin, a woman of about forty and the mother of eight, was at her home near Haverhill, Massachusetts, with her week-old infant and her nurse, Mary Neff, when a group of Abenaki natives attacked the farm. Dustin's husband, who had the other children with him in the fields, was able to hold off the attackers while he got his children to safety. However, he could do nothing to prevent the capture of his wife, the newborn, and Neff. Cotton Mather recorded the events, the terrible beginning of the captives' march, and the fate of Hannah's newborn, "but ere they had gone many steps, they dash'd out the brains of the infant against a tree; and several of the other captives, as they began to tire in the sad journey . . ." With their captives, the Indians retreated to the north, rendezvoused with other tribe members, and then split up to continue the march in small groups.

Six weeks into their trek, Dustin's party was camped on an island in the Merrimack River. On the night of March 30, when the five adult Indians and seven children were asleep, Hannah Dustin, Neff, and another captive, seventeen-year-old Samuel Leonardson, who had been captured at Worcester the previous year, took bold action, "a little before break of day, when the whole crew was in a dead sleep, one of these women took up a resolution to . . . take away the life of the murderers by whom her child had been butchered. She heartened the nurse and the youth to assist her in this enterprize; and all furnishing themselves with hatchets for the purpose, they struck home such blows upon the heads of their sleeping oppressors." Dustin, Neff, and Leonardson then set about the grim task of scalping their

Statue of Hannah Dustin

victims. Dustin's primary motivation for her attack was escape and retribution for the loss of her child, but there was also a "scalp bounty" of £50, which the government offered to encourage the colonists and militia to actively engage in the war against the natives. Fifty pounds was the annual salary for a village leader such as the minister, so it was high motivation. After she and the other two captives made their way more than sixty miles back to Haverhill and received their bounty money in exchange for their grotesque trophies, Hannah Dustin rejoined her family.

Her life, however, was changed, as her escape was widely celebrated. As Mather wrote, "But cutting off the scalps of the ten wretches, they came off, and received fifty pounds from the General Assembly of the province, as a recompence of their action; besides which, they received many 'presents of congratulation' from their more private friends: but none gave 'em a greater taste of bounty than Colonel Nicholson, The

Governour of Maryland, who, hearing of their action, sent 'em a very generous token of his favour." In an otherwise dismal war, Dustin became the symbol of the courageous frontier woman. Eventually, two statues would be erected to commemorate her ordeal, escape, and heroism.

Five months later, the exhausted European combatants agreed to end the conflict with the signing of the Treaty of Ryswick, in which the parties essentially exchanged all their military gains. The northern colonists had experienced the economic deprivations of war, the terror of attack, and the significant loss of life in frontier raids and military expeditions, yet they had nothing to show for this near decade of insecurity and sacrifice. The futile nine-year war had cost fortunes, sacrificed thousands of lives, and produced nothing but consternation. The French and English strategies initiated in King William's War would be used in three colonial wars that followed.

During the turbulent seventeenth century, strain between England and her colonists developed to the point of revolution. England had become a constitutional monarchy while her colonies struggled to maintain the liberties and freedoms they had experienced in the early decades of settlement and had salvaged in the wake of the Glorious Revolution.

CHAPTER 6

War Returns

L ATE IN THE SPRING of 1702, the English naval sloop HMS *Swift* arrived in Boston with the news that England had declared war on France and Spain, shattering the peace created by the Treaty of Ryswick, which had lasted only five years. When King William died on March 8, 1702, after a fall from his horse, the throne reverted to his wife Mary's sister Anne, the Protestant younger daughter of James II, because Mary had died childless in 1694. Immediately, there developed a threat from Louis XIV because of his interference in the succession to the Spanish throne. Louis's actions convinced Queen Anne, in the first months of her reign, to revive her predecessor's Grand Alliance and declare war on the Catholic countries of France and Spain.

It seems hard to imagine that the issue of who acceded to the throne of Spain could bring warfare to the New World, but it was an issue of vital concern to England, Spain, and France, and their colonies in America were drawn inexorably into the crisis. At the core of the issue was religion and European alliances. As the new century dawned, the Spanish king, Charles II, was dying without an heir. The European powers initially seemed content to let the transition follow its own course, but shortly before his death in 1700, the Spanish king designated Philip of Anjou as his successor. For England, this had an ominous portent. Philip was the grandson of England's avowed enemy, Louis XIV of France, and the prospect of Catholic France and Catholic Spain coming together in a powerful family, religious, and political alliance brought great concern. For a time, there was hope that this would not develop when Louis indicated that the two countries would not interfere with English commerce and that France and Spain would not merge into one European nation. However, by 1701, France and Spain were working in concert on the continent, with French troops entering the Spanish Netherlands. Tensions rose when, on the death of the deposed English king James II, Louis supported the claim to the English throne of James's son. England saw nothing but villainy in the actions of the French king and would have been further alarmed had she known that Louis had a clear French strategy in America. Louis expressed his intention, in May 1701, to have the French territories in Canada and Louisiana encircle the English colonies and block English expansion beyond their east coast settlements. All these events were propelling the European rivals into a new war after only five years of peace. Louis may have thought that the new and untried queen of England wouldn't stand up to his activities, but he misjudged, and she launched the War of the Spanish Succession. As with King William's War of the Grand Alliance, this war spilled over to the colonies, where it was known as Queen Anne's War.

Ironically, the first shots fired by Massachusetts's soldiers after this declaration of war were not against the French or the Spanish, but against the English Royal Navy vessel that brought the news of war, the *Swift*. Once again the issue was impressment. As the *Swift* prepared to depart Boston on July 14 and return to England with dispatches from the colony, Captain Robert Jackson realized that because of desertions, he needed half a dozen additional men. *Swift* was a small ship that carried a crew of about forty men and only two cannons and two swivel guns in her forty-eight-foot-long-by-sixteen-foot-wide hull. She was Captain Jackson's first command, following service as a lieutenant in six ships over the preceding eight years. He felt the power and stature of his new position, despite the small size of his ship. Jackson was a rough character, in language, manner, and appearance, as he stalked the streets of Boston on a wooden leg with his press gang to fill the vacancies in his crew. His trouble began when he failed to apply to the authorities for permission to press men into service, as a policy that had been enacted during the latter part of King William's reign and had recently been confirmed by Queen Anne.

Jackson's first victim, Edward Storey, was an experienced English mariner, but not one of his deserters. Storey had been master's mate in HMS *Gosport* when he learned of his father's death and an inheritance. Captain Crofts of the *Gosport* released Storey from service so he could return to England and claim his estate. The mariner was boarding at the home of Sarah Lambert and Sarah Fair until he could sail for England, working his passage on board the ship *Samuel.* As Lambert and Fair described in their legal deposition, "On Monday morning the 13th of July, Capt. Robert Jackson . . . came to their house and the said Captn. ran up the stairs into the said Story's Chamber, his men following him and said unto the said Story, you are the man for me & ordered his men to lay hold of him and carry him on board, and they hurried him away and carried him on board the said ship *Swift* . . ."

Still short of men, the following day the desperate Jackson and his gang swept through the ships at anchor in the harbor and at noon came alongside the ship *Union*. The only person aboard was the cook, John Gullison, who told how Captain Jackson came alongside the *Union* and ordered Gullison into his boat. When Gullison asked permission to extinguish his cooking fire, Jackson refused, and as Gullison testified, "threatening me if I would not come into the boat he would break my head and run me through," and then demanded, "Come into the boat and be damned you sorry son of a whore!" Fearing for his life, the cook promptly got into the *Swift*'s pinnace. When another sailor, William Best, returned to the *Union* an hour or more later, "he found the ship on fire without any person on board." Without Best's quick action, "the ship would in a little time by means of the said fire, have been consumed." With continued threats and profanity, Jackson next snatched fifteen-year-old Woodward Tay, who was the only person on board the *Elizabeth*. Having risked the *Elizabeth* by leaving her completely unmanned, he continued on to the *Goodspeed*, a coasting vessel, and Jackson's next victim, William Rowland. With these three and several men he had taken from other ships, including the *Lambe* and the *Orange Tree*, Jackson had his ship's complement and prepared to set sail. For the impressed men, their lives had changed in a moment. With threats of violence and death, they had been snatched from their vessels, leaving their ships in peril. The liberty of these men had been taken, and if they sailed away in the *Swift*, there was no assurance that they would ever return to New England.

News of this unauthorized press spread quickly, and several merchants whose ships had lost men sought the highest authority. The governor was in New Hampshire, but Lieutenant Governor Thomas Povey, who had been appointed to his post by the queen only on April 11 of that year, was authorized in the governor's absence "to Execute and perform all and singular the powers and directions contained in the said [governor's] commission." It was not only the plight of the pressed men and their loss of liberty that motivated Povey to act, but the negative economic impact of the press as it jeopardized the enterprise and benefits of the colony and Crown in preventing the departure of the merchant ships owing to their lack of crew.

Povey acted quickly. With several leading citizens, the Reverend Christopher Bridge, Samuel Lillie, and Joachim Addis, as witnesses, he went alongside HMS *Swift* and confronted the cantankerous Jackson with the fact that "the said Captain had impressed several men belonging to Merch't Ships without any order or Warrant [contrary to the instructions of the queen] and therefore thought fit to order him . . . to release the men." Jackson was belligerent and confident as he refuted Povey's claim of authority and said he would not obey his orders or release the men. When Povey told Jackson not to pass the fort on Castle Island until he had complied, Jackson challenged Povey to sink him. With the outcome of this tense test of wills in the balance, Povey's boat cast off and headed for the Castle.

The lieutenant governor was an experienced soldier and former captain in the Queen's Regiment of Foot who had been placed in command of the fort as a collateral assignment to his primary role. Within moments of his arrival there, the *Swift* approached and, as Povey testified, "I ordered the Gunner to fire one Gun athwart her forefoot to stop her, which he performed, and the said ship thereupon cast anchor." Povey ordered the fort's lieutenant, Nathaniel Holmes, to go to the ship and reiterate the order to release the men. According to Holmes's description, "Captain Jackson catcht up a Musquet, cockt it and presented it at me and said, God damn my blood if I do not shoot you through the head, you dog, if you come nigh my ship." Holmes went no closer, but he conveyed Povey's order, which was refused. Povey sent several others to talk with the belligerent captain, but to no avail.

The captains of three of the merchant ships that had lost men to the press had rowed out to the *Swift* and were commiserating with their men from their small boat, which they had moored to the sloop's anchor buoy. They heard Captain Jackson shout orders to prepare to sail. Lieutenant Holmes shouted from the fort, warning the three merchant captains to stand clear, and then ordered the ship to not make sail. The sloop was clearly getting under way, with two topsails and her fore course set, when Holmes warned Jackson that he had orders to sink him. Jackson, apparently feeling that the provincial gunners were incapable of hurting his ship, replied, "Kiss my arse, you dog. Fire and be damned." Holmes ordered a shot fired, and the cannonball passed through the rigging and cut a main brace; but the ship, with Edward Storey, the impressed former master's mate of HMS *Gosport*, at the helm, kept moving, swept faster by the ebbing tide. Holmes warned again, and more coarse words came from Jackson, who left the quarterdeck and went into the cabin just before the skilled colonial gunner from the fort fired his third shot. This time the cannonball tore through the ship at deck level just behind the mast, where it shattered several timbers and the top of the capstan, where men were laboring to bring the anchor into position to be catted. One sailor lay dead, and five others were wounded. When the captain reappeared on deck, ranting at the fort, the clear-thinking Storey "left the helm, ran to the Capstan, took hold of one of the parts of the [anchor] Cable about the same [capstan], surged it, and the anchor ran again to ye ground." The dead man, one of those pressed that day from the *Lambe*, lay with half his body torn away, but further carnage had been prevented by the initiative and quick action of Storey. The ship now lay at anchor directly under the lethal guns of the fort, and the irate captain Jackson had no recourse but to face his tormentor, Lieutenant Governor Thomas Povey.

The marshal of the Admiralty was sent to bring Captain Jackson to

Povey's lodgings in the garrison house on Fort Hill, where a number of members of the colonial council were assembled to participate in the hearing. When the furious Jackson arrived, Povey reviewed the events for which he blamed Jackson. As Povey recounted, "Capt. Jackson came up towards me in a violent manner, Saying you are a murderer . . ." As the loud argument continued, other members of the council attempted to speak and ameliorate the situation, but they, too, met with profanity and physical threats from Jackson. Confronted by these threats of violence, Povey, who temporarily carried the naval authority of a vice admiral, relieved Jackson of his command of the *Swift* and placed him in the custody of the marshal of the Admiralty until he could be transported back to England to face the consequences of his actions.

The pressed men were released, and after a brief delay for repairs, HMS *Swift* left for England. Povey did not send Jackson home in his former ship, fearing that the captain still held influence over the

The Castle in Boston Harbor

crew and the new commander. As the *Swift* passed south of Ireland on August 18, the French privateer *Duc de Bourgoyne* attacked her. Knowing she was no match for the formidable eighteen-gun Frenchman, *Swift*'s new captain, John Brookes, attempted to outsail the privateer and escape. The privateer was fast as well as powerful, however, and fired into the *Swift*, shooting away the topmast, cutting up the rigging, killing Captain Brookes, and forcing the ship's surrender. It is ironic to think that had Jackson not been relieved of command in Boston, he might have been the one to fall in with the French privateer in this fatal encounter.

It seemed certain that Jackson would be appropriately punished when he was returned to England, along with the sworn "affidavits and evidences" from Thomas Povey and twenty-two other witnesses to the events. However, in a pattern that had been seen before, the English Admiralty, with obvious contempt for the colonials who witnessed and experienced the abuses, turned a blind eye to Jackson's actions. Within a matter of months, Jackson was rewarded with command of a larger warship, the brigantine HMS *Fly*. Perhaps the Admiralty should have paid closer attention to the colonial complaints and the conduct of Jackson, since nine years later Jackson was convicted in a court-martial and dismissed from the service.

With incredible audacity, and in direct response to the complaints of colonial merchants on behalf of their impressed mariners, the colonial forces at Boston's Castle Island had fired on one of Her Majesty's warships, inflicting damage, wounds, and death. At the heart of this incident was the issue of impressment and the instructions that Queen Anne had sent to her colonial governors. The fact that such instructions existed bears testament to the significance of impressment in the minds of the colonists. The decades immediately ahead would see numerous impressment disputes, and the sailor killed on board the *Swift* would not be the only impressment-related death.

To establish his authority, Povey had quoted the instructions from Queen Anne in his deposition in the *Swift* case. These instructions clearly gave Povey the authority to stop Captain Jackson and demand the release of those impressed without the required application to the governor. However, for the colonials the situation was still perilous. The feared and arbitrary press still existed, the Royal Navy press gangs conducted them, and the only difference was that a governor had given the activity his blessing. The horror for a sailor homeward bound into Boston—looking forward to returning to his family and friends, being plucked from the deck of his ship and forced into the dangerous life on board a warship—loomed large in the minds of sailors. The problem increased for the merchants who saw the threat of the press impacting them and, therefore, the economies of the colonies. Outward-bound ships often alerted inward-bound vessels that a press was being conducted, and sailors took ship's boats and fled to shore before entering the harbor. Merchants complained that in some circumstances, ships had been lost because of the lack of enough sailors to handle them. Ports like Boston, where the Royal Navy was certain they would find experienced mariners, found that ships avoided them and used lesser harbors away from the press. This, of course, foiled the press gangs but also deprived Boston of commerce while enhancing other ports. In addition, since press gangs took people from local coasting vessels that supplied Boston with needed goods and materials, particularly firewood, the city was threatened with deadly shortages, including fuel for winter.

The instructions from the queen also placed a heavy burden on the governors, who had to walk the delicate line between serving their queen and keeping the colonists in line. The governors, who owed their positions to the Crown's royal appointments, had to support the monarch. To the colonists, they became the villains who were resented by the people. In rare circumstances, such as with Povey and the *Swift*, the governor could appear as a hero to the merchants and sailors, but had Captain Jackson applied to Lieutenant Governor Povey for a warrant, Povey would have had to, as Queen Anne's instruction stated, "take care that Her Ships of War be furnished with the number of Seamen that may be necessary." Jackson would have gotten his men, and Povey would have been the villain.

Captain Jackson might have been treated very differently by the new governor, an ambitious man sympathetic to the royal prerogative, rather than the militant, firm lieutenant governor. For almost a year the Massachusetts Council had governed on its own as the governor's position remained unfilled, but in April 1702, the new queen made her appointment: one that would be a crude affront to the people of Massachusetts. The new governor was Joseph Dudley, the man who had temporarily been governor of the Dominion of New England prior to the arrival of Andros and who continued to serve the hated Dominion until the rebellion. Now, a decade later, this native New Englander, carrying the burden of his collaboration and Dominion involvement, was sent to be the leader of Massachusetts and New Hampshire.

Dudley and his lieutenant governor, Povey, had sailed for Boston three weeks before war was declared and arrived on June 11, 1702, to assume their new assignments. With the popular attitude toward him being one of dislike and distrust, Dudley's task would be challenging under any circumstances, but racing across the Atlantic was HMS *Swift*, carrying the expresses officially informing Dudley and the colony that they were at war. The arrival of this news compounded the difficulty of Dudley's assignment.

Now, it was Governor Dudley who would have to lead New England in Queen Anne's War. However, it was not in New England, or against the French, that the first battles of this new war were fought. In the fall of 1702, South Carolina's governor, James Moore, aggressively and overconfidently led a force of nearly one thousand Carolinians and allied Indians against the Spanish in Florida to capture the Spanish fortress at St. Augustine. The siege lasted six weeks, while Moore waited in vain for additional cannons and naval support he had requested from the Royal Navy base at Jamaica. It was the Spanish, however, who sent reinforcements, not the English. With the people of St. Augustine secure inside their impregnable Castillo de San Marcos, the Carolinians saw no chance to capture the fort, but only burned the buildings outside the fortress walls. Moore then burned his fourteen ships to prevent their capture by the Spanish offshore and took his discouraged men overland back to Carolina in failure, embittered and betrayed by the lack of English naval support.

The anguish and pain of King William's War a decade before was still sorely felt in the northern colonies, and they were not quick to rush to war in support of the political maneuverings in Europe. New York and the Five Nations of the Iroquois had enjoyed a beneficial alliance during King William's War, but the Iroquois received nothing from England in compensation for the nearly two thousand lives they lost in the war. They were therefore disinclined to involve themselves again in the wars between the French and English, and in 1701, they made a treaty with the French assuring that the Iroquois would remain neutral in any future conflict. When war broke out the following year, New York had the neutral buffer of the Iroquois between its colony and French Canada and hoped that if they did not take the war north into Canada, the French would not bring the war south into New York.

New England was in a very different situation from that of New York. The preponderance of the fighting during King William's War had been in New England, and the nerves of all involved—the French, the New Englanders, and the Indians allied on one side or the other—were raw. All had vivid memories of death, deprivation, and terror in the earlier war. Consequently, there was no desire for war in the early summer of 1702, and it appeared for a time that perhaps New England could maneuver to stay out of the European war. Joseph Dudley, despite his negative image among the colonists, had a reputation for being skilled in negotiations with the native tribes. Soon after his arrival, he opened discussions with the eastern Abenaki tribes that ranged across Acadia and northern New England, hoping to establish a neutrality agreement similar to the one that protected New York. The governor of New France, Louis-Hector de Callière, and his ministers in France initially saw advantage in such neutrality but were alarmed by the progress Dudley had made in placating and potentially winning over the eastern Abenakis. Late in the summer of 1702, Callière received specific orders to initiate warfare in New England. With his forces limited, and with the comparatively heavily populated New England outnumbering his settlers twenty to one, Callière sought to entice the Abenakis into the war to bolster the French side. The French missionaries had been hard at work with the Native Americans in the region of the St. Lawrence, and many had converted to Catholicism. However, an appeal from Callière, linked to the shared Catholic faith of the French and the Indians, failed to persuade the Abenakis to join the French.

When Governor Callière died in 1703, he was replaced by an experienced soldier and administrator who had been in Canada for over fifteen years, Philippe de Rigaud de Vaudreuil. The new French governor quickly developed a plan to undermine Dudley's efforts and draw the Abenakis into alliance with France. He assembled a force of French officers and men and loyal natives at Chambly, between Lake Champlain and the St. Lawrence River. His concept was that if this force raided New England settlements and the New Englanders killed Indians, the Abenakis would come into the war on the side of the French.

Dudley was making progress with his peace negotiations with the Abenakis when an incident threatened to destroy his efforts. An English settler was killed by an Abenaki, and in revenge, the English killed an important Abenaki who was related by marriage to the French nobleman Baron de Saint-Castin. To defuse the situation, Dudley called a peace meeting for June 20 in Casco, Maine. Dudley, other New Englanders, and representatives of four Abenaki tribes, the Androscoggins, Kennebecs, Pennacooks, and Penobscots, attended this conference. Dudley opened the conference by saying, as recorded by the contemporary historian Samuel Penhallow, "that as he was commissioned by the Great and Victorious *Queen of England*, he came to visit them as his *Friends* and *Brethren*, and to reconcile whatever Differences had happened since the last *Treat*." With this introduction well received, the native spokesman, Simmo, replied "that they aimed at nothing more than *Peace*; and that as high as the *Sun* was above the Earth, so far distant should their Designs be of making the least breach between each other." While the conference resulted in a treaty, there were several very disturbing elements that foretold further trouble. To celebrate the treaty, both the English and the Indians fired volleys from their muskets. In eyewitness Penhallow's words, "The *Indians* desired the *English* to fire first, which they readily did, concluding it no other than a Complement; but so soon as the *Indians* fired, it was obser'd that their Guns were charged with Bullets." It was suspected and later confirmed that the Indian plan had been to attack the English, but that could not be done since their leaders were so intermingled with the English under the meeting tent that they could not attack without killing their own leaders. Despite the concern over the true intent of the Indians, the English remained at Casco for some days, waiting supposedly for a particularly important Indian leader to arrive. The English left before this stalling tactic resulted in disaster and a band of two hundred French and Indians could arrive and slaughter the English representatives. These were incidents through which, Penhallow reflects, "the matchless Perfidy of these bloody Infidels did notoriously appear."

However, there had been more "perfidy" afoot at the conference. Concealed within the group of 250 Native Americans were two Frenchmen disguised as Indians who had been sent by Governor Jacques-François de Monbeton de Brouillan of Acadia to assassinate Joseph Dudley. The French were certain that if Dudley was killed at the peace talks, the New Englanders would immediately retaliate against the Abenakis and the French objective of luring the Abenakis into the war against the New Englanders would be accomplished. The plot was foiled when one of the assassins was caught and confessed. Dudley appeared to be successful in resolving the Abenaki issues, and the treaty assured their neutrality.

When de Brouillan's plot to assassinate Dudley failed, he hatched another, forging a letter that appeared to be from Queen Anne to Governor Dudley, which the French governor made certain would make its way into Abenaki hands. Some of the natives believed the letter, which endorsed a plan to lure Abenakis into a trap, get them drunk, and then slaughter them. Instability was artfully introduced into the peace process by this intrigue. Another event added to the instability. Prior to the peace conference, the Abenakis had asked for French help in avenging the loss of the baron's Indian relative. In response, Governor Vaudreuil sent the French and Indian force that he had assembled at Chambly to Maine. It was this group that had arrived at Casco just after the English had left. When they arrived, the Abenakis told them that they had come to terms with Dudley over the Castin incident and planned to remain neutral. Several Mohawks in the group from Canada told the Abenakis that since they had come all that way, it was too late, and they would attack the Abenakis if they tried to remain neutral. This coercive threat from the Mohawks, combined with the doubt planted by de Brouillan's forged letter, which still infected the minds of some of the Abenakis, set the wheels in motion to bring about war.

CHAPTER 7

Terror

AS THE FIRST RAYS of sun streamed across Maine on the morning of August 10, 1703, bands of heavily armed warriors were concealed in the woods surrounding a number of coastal frontier settlements. Some were French officers like Alexandre Leneuf de la Vallière de Beaubassin, an experienced soldier and naval officer, and Jean-Baptiste Hertel de Rouville, son of "the Hero" who had perfected the technique of the organized raids that were about to be launched. Others were French cadets and soldiers from the Troupes de la Marine, the French "regulars" in New France. The rest were native fighters, about 180 from tribes loyal to the French and 300 newly allied Abenakis. In total, the group numbered more than 500, and all, except for the Abenakis, were from the force Vaudreuil had gathered at Chambly. Their objective was not simply to attack individual hamlets, but to launch simultaneous, coordinated attacks across a swath of the Maine frontier, striking terror into the settlers of all the outlying communities of Maine and Massachusetts. More than a year had passed since the arrival of HMS *Swift* with the news that England, France, and Spain were at war, during which New England had managed to remain free of serious conflict. That was about to change.

For the people of the settlement of Wells, about twenty miles up the Maine coast from the New Hampshire border, everyday life was a constant challenge. The community consisted of nearly one hundred dwellings spread out along several miles of the coast road. The buildings, most of which were on the north side of the road, ranged from crude log cabins to small houses and included several fortified "garrison houses" that served as places of retreat for the population in times of attack. Eleven years earlier, the Storer garrison house at the east end of Wells had been the scene of Captain James Converse's valiant and successful defense when he and thirty men held off three hundred to five hundred French and Indian attackers who besieged the garrison house for four days. Behind the houses of Wells, an area of partially cleared land functioned as pasture, and beyond this clearing stretched hundreds of miles of dense Maine forests. Across the road were the settlers' farm plots and beyond that salt marshes and the sea. The people sustained themselves with the cattle and sheep they pastured, the produce they farmed, and the natural abundance of birds and fish from the marshes and nearby waters. Wells was isolated and vulnerable, necessarily self-dependent, and exposed to the difficulties of harsh winters. In 1700, the community was proud of its newly rebuilt church, which replaced one torched during an Indian attack during King William's War.

August 10, 1703, began as a typical summer day for the residents of Wells. Women responded to the needs of their families and homes, while most men ranged farther into the fields and marshes to tend crops or gather sustenance from nature. One woman who was not involved with her normal routine that morning was the wife of Thomas Wells, who was in her house in the throes of labor, about to add another infant to the family, which already had two small children. Aware of his wife's urgent need for assistance, Thomas Wells had headed off to get the midwife. In her state of pain, Mrs. Wells was unaware of the subtle movements emerging from the tree line and stealing across the pasture.

The French commander, Beaubassin, had chosen a time for his attack when families were divided, going about their work. He and more than one hundred attackers silently approached a number of the houses simultaneously. The morning exploded in violence when the native attackers burst into the undefended Wells home and swiftly killed the pregnant mother and her two children. Their neighbors, Joseph Sayer and his entire family, were also surprised and slaughtered. In other homes, valiant but futile defenses were mounted. Some adults and older children were spared: to be taken to Canada as valuable prisoners. The old, those pregnant or weakened by recent childbirth, and small children, who would not be able to keep up with the pace of a fast withdrawal and forced march through the wilderness to Canada, were summarily killed. The small children of Samuel Hill's family were murdered and the rest of the family marched off to the north. Some residents had time to flee to the fields or woods. Among them was the family of blacksmith Stephen Harding, who first sent his wife and child into the relative safety of the farm fields while he stayed at the house to assess the threat. When four Indians attacked, he managed to escape, find his wife and child, and hide with them in the woods throughout the day and through the night. The following day, they made their way to the security of Joseph Storer's renowned garrison house. There, Harding found his stunned neighbors, who justly feared for their missing friends and family members, including the Storers' eighteen-year-old daughter, who had been captured. The raid on Wells ended as quickly as it had begun, and when the shocked survivors assessed their grim losses, they realized that numerous houses had been burned and thirty-nine residents killed or taken prisoner. Those who were captives faced the torture of lost loved ones, the exhausting march through hundreds of miles of wilderness to Canada, and the bewildering prospect of being owned by their native captors.

The Wells attack was just one of several launched that day. The natives and French soldiers attacked a stone fort near Saco that had been built ten years earlier by James Converse, who had led the 1692 defense of the Storer garrison. While those within the fort were able to hold out, those outside the structure suffered greatly. Eleven people from the community were killed, and twenty-four were taken prisoner. Just to the east, at Spurwink, twenty-two were killed or captured. Several fortified garrisons were successful in withstanding the attacks, but in other locations such as Purpooduck Point, known today as Portland's Spring Point on Cape Elizabeth, the slaughter continued. The men of Purpooduck were off fishing, and in their absence twenty-five women and children met their deaths and eight were taken off to captivity. A few miles farther along the coast at Casco, the site of Governor Dudley's peace conference only seven weeks earlier, warriors from the various raiding parties assembled to attack the fort. The fort's commander, Major John March, and three of the older men from the fort were lured out by the appearance of three seemingly unarmed and peaceful Abenakis carrying a flag of truce. As Penhallow records, "At first he slighted the Message, but on second thoughts went out to meet them; they seeming to him but few in number, and unarmed: However he ordered two of three Sentinels to be ready in case of Danger." March's suspicion was well placed, "for no sooner had they saluted him, but with Hatchets under their mantles they violently assaulted him." Other hidden Indians sprang into action and struck down March's companions. March, who was known for his strength and courage, held his own, until ten men from the fort, led by a Sergeant Hook, came to the rescue. March, Sergeant Hook, and his men gained the safety of the fort, where an additional twenty men stood by in defense of the bastion. The sobering reality of a siege soon became apparent as hundreds of French and Indians led by Beaubassin arrived with a small navy, which included a sloop, two shallops they had captured in their earlier attacks, and numerous canoes. Besieged by land and harassed from the sea, the defenders withstood the assault for six days. Just when it seemed likely that the attackers would prevail, Captain Cyprian Southack of the small Massachusetts warship the *Province Galley* arrived and opened fire on the French and natives. With no defensible positions, and with their little "navy" shattered or captured, the French and their allies disappeared into the forests and with their captives headed back to Canada.

In those few days in August in the area around Casco Bay, the French had accomplished their goal. The Abenakis had been lured out of their neutrality and into open warfare with the New Englanders, and now the colonies of France and England in North America were fully engaged in Queen Anne's War.

The shocking news of those August attacks, in which approximately 150 New England settlers had been either killed or marched off as prisoners, brought rapid retaliatory action. In September, the New England authorities sought to motivate the populace to wage war on the natives. As a preview of the brutality that lay ahead from both sides of the conflict, "The *General Assembly* being sensibly affected with the state of matters, and dispos'd to a Vigorous prosecution of the

War, enacted, That *Forty Pounds* should be given for every *Indian Scalp*, which prompted some, and animated others to a noble Emulation."

It was not simply the scalp bounty that motivated the reprisal attacks that followed the August raids in Maine. Numerous additional Abenaki raids were launched while Beaubassin, his troops, native allies, and their captives made their way north. In an attack on Berwick, the Indians were repulsed, which according to Penhallow "so enraged those Wretches, that at their return they executed their revenge on *Joseph Ring* . . . whom they fastned to a Stake and burnt alive: barbarously shouting and rejoicing at his cries." In another attack, the barbarity was reversed when the Indians attacked a dwelling in Haverhill, Massachusetts, home of the famous Hannah Dustin, the "heroine" of King William's War. In this instance another heroine emerged, when a pregnant woman hurled boiling soap at her attackers, scalding one of them to death. With exceptional tolerance, the Indians spared the woman's life, but her child, born during the march north, died. A year later, the woman was ransomed and returned home.

Motivated by the need for revenge and to a degree by the scalp bounty, English settlers planned a number of retaliatory raids. One of those who went on the offensive was a victim of the initial attacks, John March from the fort at Casco. After an earlier force of 360 New Englanders found only a deserted native settlement near Saco, Maine, March, who had been promoted to colonel, led a marginally successful follow-up attack. March and his group killed six Abenakis and captured an equal number. Another military adventurer, Captain Edward Tyng, led a daunting winter assault and returned with five scalps. However, these were small successes, and those New Englanders seeking retribution of the August attacks and the raids that followed faced the great frustration of guerrilla-type warfare, where the enemy attacks and then vanishes. Unable to take revenge on the specific enemy who carried out the original attacks, the avengers took the fight to whomever they could find. This furthered the animosity and perpetuated the cycle of attack and revenge.

Taking advantage of the increasing hostilities during the fall of 1703, the French set in motion a plan they had developed to attack

New England settlements far from Maine. The force assembled at
Chambly was originally gathered to attack settlements in the Connecticut River valley but had been diverted to Maine. After the brilliantly
executed August 10 attacks, the group returned to Chambly to plan
their next foray. This time, command was given to Lieutenant Jean-
Baptiste Hertel de Rouville, who at thirty-five was a veteran of many
successful attacks and one of the most experienced French military
leaders in Canada. Like his father, he spoke several native languages,
understood both the rigors of wilderness warfare and the character of
his native allies, and was revered by the men who served with him. In
his early twenties, he had accompanied his father on his successful attack on Salmon Falls during King William's War and later gained valuable combat experience in numerous other engagements, including the
defense of Quebec during Phips's inept attack and the recent Maine attacks with Beaubassin. His talents and experience made him the logical leader for the next expedition. The plan, which called for a large
force of over three hundred to make their way south in the dead of winter to surprise and attack New England communities, required commitment and great stamina on the part of the participants. The logistics
involved in mounting and sustaining such a force as it made its way
through 230 miles of wilderness was daunting, but Hertel de Rouville
welcomed the opportunity to lead a dedicated, well-disciplined force on
this attack.

The Connecticut River runs south from Canada through northern
New England, forming today's border between Vermont and New
Hampshire, then through Massachusetts and Connecticut, essentially
bisecting those colonies. With the fertility of this valley and the ease
of transportation the river provided, it was a natural area for colonial
development. In Connecticut, communities had been established at
the mouth of the river where it enters Long Island Sound and farther
up the river at Hartford and Wethersfield. In Massachusetts, the communities along or near the river marked the western frontier in the
early eighteenth century. Springfield had been established in 1636 after a smallpox epidemic had wiped out the villages of the native
Agawams and Woronocos who had planted crops in the area for over a
century. Twenty years later, Northampton was settled fifteen miles
upriver from Springfield, and a few years later, Hadley came into

Jean-Baptiste Hertel de Rouville

existence on the east side of the river. In 1703, the northernmost out-
post of the New England settlement on the Connecticut River was
Deerfield, and it was this little hamlet that lay directly in the path of
Hertel's intended expedition.

Unlike the village of Wells, which was strewn along several miles
of the Maine coast, Deerfield was planned as a compact community
along the undulating Deerfield River just east of the Connecticut, in territory the Indians called Pocumtuc. The settlers in this part of the wilderness in the early 1670s came from the older communities to the south
and from the Boston area. Their new home sites were neatly laid out on
either side of a mile-long central road. Beyond this core were common
lands for pasturing and communal growing of wheat and corn. Deerfield appeared destined to quickly become a thriving New England
town. Within only a few years, however, the conflict between the New
England settlers and the natives known as King Philip's War was rag-
ing throughout New England and, naturally, along the Connecticut.

The sparse population of Deerfield beat back several attacks, but after losing half the village's men in one ambush, the community was abandoned as indefensible.

After the defeat of the natives in King Philip's War, settlers returned to Deerfield. By the late 1680s, the community had gained strength and once again showed promise when King William's War plunged the weary residents of the Connecticut valley into a new war, this time an international conflict. Threatened from the north by the French and their native allies, Deerfield constructed a palisade barrier, which enclosed ten houses and included a number of small temporary shelters for settlers whose homes were outside the palisade. The fortification proved prudent, as it enabled the inhabitants to withstand a native attack in 1694. Sickness, crop failure, and native ambushes beyond the village took their toll, however, and the residents once again considered abandoning Deerfield. Peace following the Treaty of Ryswick in 1697 gave Deerfield a new opportunity to firmly establish itself. Since the mid-1680s, Deerfield had benefited from the presence of a respected minister, John Williams, who was married to the niece of the famous reverend Increase Mather. Born in Roxbury near Boston and a graduate of Harvard, Williams gave the community a sense of stability and attracted new settlers. As the 1700s dawned, Deerfield had grown to over 40 families, and Reverend Williams's congregation numbered over 250.

When hostilities erupted with the August attacks in Maine, Deerfield was an exposed and vulnerable frontier outpost. England would spare no soldiers to defend her remote colonial settlements, so the task fell to the colonial militias and the settlers themselves. When international conflict was brought to North America, it was the militia that bore the brunt of the fighting. Without the presence and ready response of the colonial militias, the whole of the English colonial enterprise would have been exposed and would surely have failed.

Queen Anne's War brought danger to the colonies, and after rumors of an impending attack on Deerfield reached the residents in the spring of 1703, they once again looked to its physical defenses and the militia for protection, as they had in the previous war. By the summer, Lieutenant Colonel Jonathan Tyng, the brother of Edward Tyng, who had led the successful reprisal raid after the Maine attacks, received another warning specifically mentioning the force gathered at Chambly and predicting attacks in Maine and along the Connecticut River. The Deerfield residents hoped that the war could be avoided and that they would benefit from the neutrality agreement established with the Iroquois to their west, but precautions had to be taken in response to these threats. Governor Dudley decided to establish a garrison within the palisade of Deerfield and manned it with twenty-five militiamen drawn from the larger communities in the region. No attack on Deerfield materialized that summer, although the news reached them of the brutal August 10 attacks in Maine. Further warnings came during the fall, but again there were no attacks, and the residents grew complacent as rumors failed to develop into actual confrontations. As winter blanketed the region, the residents began to focus more on their fight for survival in the harsh climate rather than a fight with an enemy that traditionally shied away from the hardships of winter expeditions and attacks.

For Hertel de Rouville and his force gathered at Chambly, the winter weather provided the opportunity for surprise, despite the "intelligence leaks" that had engendered the earlier warnings. All of his officers, including three of his brothers, were born in Canada, and they and the rest of his soldiers had wilderness experience. The native contingent at Chambly consisted of Indians from along the St. Lawrence who were loyal to the French. There were Hurons of Lorette just north of Quebec, Iroquois from La Montagne next to Montreal, and Mohawks of Kahnawake on the south bank of the St. Lawrence across from Montreal. While they were paid for their service, they were also motivated by the potential of acquiring captives, who were valuable assets. The captives could be put to work within the Indian community or they could be traded within the native culture, sold to the French, or ransomed back to the English. As with most military operations of that time, the victors anticipated "plunder," the valuable property of their conquered enemy. In this case, the most valuable plunder was human.

When Hertel and his men moved south, they rendezvoused with groups of Abenakis and Pennacooks who joined the formidable French and Indian force. While prisoners were of value to them as well, they had a more fundamental incentive to participate: continued vengeance for the losses in earlier Indian wars and the numerous frontier battles, including those in Maine. The cycle of attack and counterattack that had Indians scalping settlers and New Englanders scalping Indians had poisoned their relationship and made these Abenakis and Pennacooks willing participants in Hertel's Connecticut River campaign.

Hertel's full force numbered between 250 and 300, including approximately 50 Frenchmen. A winter expedition of this magnitude had special challenges. It would be impossible to hunt or forage for enough food because hunting would force the group to split up and the sounds of their muskets might alert New Englanders also hunting in the wilderness. To keep the group together and focused on its objective, it was necessary to bring ample food. On the march south, each man carried his weapons and ammunition, a pack with spare clothing, and food supplies, and they made their way through the winter depths on snowshoes. They carried extra provisions and supplies on dogsleds and man-drawn sledges to a point about twenty-five miles above Deerfield. From that point, they moved on with only what they carried.

By late February, the people of Deerfield had endured the worst of the winter without attack, and it seemed as if all the warnings were unwarranted. The extra militia troops were still there, crowded into the houses of the residents. Some of the inhabitants, whose houses lay outside of the protective palisade, still spent their nights in the crude, temporary hovels within the fort, while others had relaxed their guard and stayed in their homes beyond the walls. By this time, Deerfield had approximately forty homes, seventeen of them within the palisade. The fortification itself was old and weakened, but the eight-foot-tall barrier offered the best protection available. On the evening of February 28, the residents of Deerfield retired for the night knowing that they had alert sentries on watch. They had no idea that a large enemy force had moved silently into the woods about two miles north of the village and had settled down to await the sleepy hours just before dawn, when they hoped the sentries would not be so keenly alert.

Hertel's scouts reported that there were sentries on watch, but they also brought back news of great significance. The winter winds had built up a snowdrift on the northeast side of the palisade, providing a simple pathway into the palisaded village. As the last hour of darkness neared, the sentries either gave up their duties or fell asleep. As one Deerfield resident noted with resentment, "The enemy came in like a flood upon us; our watch being unfaithful;—an evil, the awful effects of which, in the surprisal of our fort, could bespeak all watchmen to avoid, as they would not bring the charge of blood upon themselves." With no guards to sound the alert, the French and Indian force moved quickly over the snow and up the drift, then dropped silently down into the enclosure. Still no alarm was raised, and seemingly at random the attackers dispersed and prepared to assault individual homes. Suddenly, with fierce cries and the crack of gunfire, the attack was announced and doors were battered open.

One of the larger homes, that of Reverend Williams, was an obvious and early target. Williams, his wife, Eunice, and seven of their eight children were in the house, along with his two black slaves and two militiamen who were lodged there. In Williams's published account of his ordeal, he recorded the first terrifying moments after the attackers had entered his house: "Returning toward my bedside for my arms, the enemy immediately broke into the room, I judge to the number of twenty, with painted faces and hideous acclamations. I reached up my hands to the bed-tester for my pistol . . . Taking down my pistol, I cocked it, and put it to the breast of the first Indian that came up; but my pistol missing fire, I was seized by three Indians, who disarmed me, and bound me . . ." In the frantic chaos, Williams and his wife watched in horror as two of their young children—John, who was six years old, and Jerusha, only six weeks old—were slaughtered, along with Parthena, the family's female slave. Amid the confusion, Lieutenant John Stoddard, commander of the soldiers garrisoned in Deerfield, who had lodged upstairs, escaped barefoot out a window and made off in the darkness to alert the nearby town of Hatfield. The Williams family—Reverend John, wife Eunice, and five of their children—were now captives.

The scene was repeated in other houses. Defenders were killed, some women and children were murdered, and others were captured. A few managed to flee into the night, hiding or seeking refuge in the fortified garrison house of Jonathan Wells that lay to the south of the palisade. Within the walls were two other fortified houses just to

Reverend John Williams

the north of Reverend Williams's home, one belonging to Ensign John Sheldon and the other to Sergeant Benoni Stebbins, who had been captured by the Indians years before but escaped. These secure dwellings had layers of brick between the outer and inner sheathing, making the walls bulletproof. In the midst of the attack, Sheldon left his home, despite its fortification, and raced to the garrison house of Captain Jonathan Wells, outside the palisade to the south. The stout front door of the Sheldon house kept the attackers at bay and the inhabitants safe inside until the Indians chopped a hole in the door and shot Hannah Sheldon as she sat on her bed. The attackers then discovered that the back door was more vulnerable and gained entry. The slain Hannah Sheldon was spared the terrible sight as the Indians "seized Mercy Sheldon, a little girl of two years, and dashed out her brains on the door stone." Defenseless, three Sheldon children and their sister-in-law were taken prisoner. The garrison house of Sergeant Stebbins proved to be more formidable and well defended.

In the confusion of the initial assault and perhaps because it was recognized as a well-fortified dwelling, this house was ignored. By the
time the raiders focused on it, the seven men, four or five women, and
numerous children who were barricaded inside the house had had
time to prepare their defenses. Despite numerous assaults by the
raiders, the Stebbins house held out. The defenders killed a number
of attackers, among them a French officer. They wounded many others, including the expedition's leader, Hertel de Rouville. While all
the others in the Stebbins house survived the attacks and attempts to
set fire to the house, Stebbins himself was killed.

The slaughter amid the mayhem may have seemed random, but
there was some method to the murders. The men who fought back
and threatened the attackers were often slain, but the women and
children had potential value as captives. There were random excruciating deaths as the French and Indians set fire to numerous houses
and other shelters in which settlers were hiding and trapped.

After more than two and a half hours, the battle waned and Hertel
de Rouville anticipated that the neighboring towns were now aware of
the assault and would be sending men for a counterattack. He began
the withdrawal, taking his men and the captives northward to the site
where they had spent the night and left their packs and snowshoes.
Some of the attackers stayed within the palisade, looting houses of
valuables, torching structures, and continuing the attack on the stub-
born Stebbins house. Preoccupied, they were unaware of a force of
thirty to forty men who had arrived on horseback from Hatfield and
Hadley. When these troops charged into the palisade through the
south gate, the surviving Deerfield men rallied and joined them. The
remaining attackers fled to the north, the New Englanders racing after them. Hertel de Rouville was with the bulk of his force and the
captives. Although wounded, he quickly laid an ambush just as he had
seen his father do at Salmon Falls thirteen years earlier. The retreating Indians led the eager militiamen into a trap in which thirty
Frenchmen suddenly came out of hiding and fired point-blank at the
New Englanders, who were forced to retreat, stunned and in disarray.
Nine militiamen were killed and others wounded in this "Meadow
Fight."

Both sides then stepped back from the combat, and Hertel organized his force to start their withdrawal toward Canada, over two hundred miles away through the snow-covered wilderness. The French and Indians had lost ten men and had twenty-two wounded among them. Deerfield had been devastated. Half the population was either killed or captured. Forty-one had been slain in the village fighting, 9 had died in the Meadow Fight, and the attackers were heading north with an incredible 111 captives. In Deerfield, the militiamen regrouped and assessed their options, which were grim. They could follow the large group heading north, leaving their own villages stripped of defenders. They all knew, however, that if they managed to catch and attack Hertel and his group, the captives would be executed. By the following day, over two hundred militia had made their way to Deerfield, a force nearly equal to that of the attackers, but they were faced with the cold reality that pursuit would put them and the captives in significant danger. A warm rain began to fall, the first sign of spring, and the deep snow turned soft. The men concluded that pursuing the French and Indians in the slush was impossible, and they headed for their own towns. A small group of Deerfield men trailed the retreating attackers and their captives in hopes of finding captives who had escaped or been left along the trail, but what they found simply added to their misery.

The forced march north was an ordeal of unfathomable magnitude. While struggling to make their way on narrow, snow-packed tracks, the captives were in constant fear. They witnessed the brutal efficiency with which those who could not keep pace were summarily dispatched with one blow of the hatchet. First, three-year-old Marah Carter was killed. Some of the Indians, recognizing the value of their young captives and probably with a degree of compassion, "carried our children, incapable of traveling, in their arms or on their shoulders." Then, during the first night's encampment, Reverend Williams's male slave, Frank, was arbitrarily killed by Indians apparently drunk on rum taken from Deerfield. The next morning, after one New Englander had managed to escape, Hertel told John Williams to inform the others that if further escapes were made, the remaining captives would be burned at the stake. The captives knew this was no idle threat, since instances of such burnings were well-known. The march north then began in earnest, with the captives overseen by their respective owners. The pace was fast, too fast for Eunice Williams, who had been separated in the line of march from her husband and children for most of the time since leaving Deerfield. Reverend Williams was forced to march near the head of the column, but on the second day of the march he was allowed a brief time with his wife, who was weakened by childbirth only six weeks before. John Williams recorded his wife's poignant words: "My wife told me her strength of body began to fail, and that I must expect to part with her; saying she hoped God would preserve my life, and the life of some, if not all of our children with us . . ." Reverend Williams was then told to return to his position at the head of the column. The group moved on and was forced to wade through a fast-running, frigid, waist-deep small river and then climb up very steep, mountainous terrain. Williams, exhausted by the climb, was permitted to rest by the side of the trail, and he asked each of the others as they passed by for a report on his wife. Finally, he heard that while crossing the river, his wife had fallen in over her head, and shortly after, one of the Indians "slew her with his hatchet at one stroke . . ."

Eunice Williams's body was one of the gruesome discoveries of the Deerfield men who followed the retreat. Out of respect for their minister, they carried his wife's body back to Deerfield for burial.

The march progressed, and on successive days two children were killed, followed by the execution of a woman, then by the murder of four more women. After four days, the group reached the site of their abandoned sledges. A disagreement among the natives was resolved by a redistribution of ownership of the captives, and the group pressed on. Some of the children who could not keep pace were hauled on the sledges, while the natives continued to carry some of their young captives on their backs. After covering ninety miles, at the junction of the White River and the Connecticut, the captives had another blow to their virtually nonexistent morale: The force divided into smaller groups, and anguished family members were separated. Mary Brooks, a pregnant young woman among the captives, demonstrated the faith and stoicism with which the captives faced their trials. On March 7, a week into their forced march north, she came to Reverend Williams and asked for his blessing. She had injured her ankle the day before, making it difficult for her to keep pace with the march. She anticipated that she would be killed but told Williams that she did not fear death. Mary Brooks was killed later that day. The historian Francis Parkman observed that while these executions were brutal, they were also swift and saved the weak, who could not keep up, from the slow torture of starvation and exposure if they were abandoned in the wilderness. Nevertheless, the suffering of the captives and their fortitude is awesome to contemplate. The exhausting ordeal lasted six weeks. Of the 111 who began the trek, 89 reached Canada.

The attack on Deerfield was the most successful of the numerous raids during Queen Anne's War. Because of its magnitude and impact, it riveted the attention of English colonists throughout North America. In New England, it immediately prompted calls for greater protection from the French and their allies. There was resentment that despite their efforts to avoid being drawn into the queen's European conflict, they were immersed in it with no support from English soldiers. The English settlers faced brutal attacks by natives who were led by professional French officers and augmented by professional French soldiers of the Troupes de la Marine. Without the support of professional English officers and troops, the resentful English colonials had to depend on their brave but often inadequately trained and armed militiamen. Deerfield stood as the symbol of French and Indian brutality and was the pivotal event at the beginning of Queen Anne's War that would galvanize public opinion among the New Englanders and cement the relationship between the Abenakis and the French.

CHAPTER 8

Retribution

As THE DEERFIELD CAPTIVES MADE their grim march through 250 miles of snow-covered wilderness to Canada, there were cries for retribution throughout New England and frustration that revenge could not be taken against those who had carried out the raid. Many of the terrified colonists were ready to leave for safer places such as Boston, and the government felt it was critical to discourage this exodus. To keep the remaining families from deserting the frontier settlements, many were informed that they would forfeit their title to property if they left. To provide additional security for these settlements in the absence of help from the mother country, colonial men, mostly young and without families, were drafted from the militia into the active duty colonial force, and within five months of the Deerfield attack, nearly nineteen hundred Massachusetts men were stationed in communities along the frontier. However, these were defensive actions, and the call was for offensive action that would punish the French and their Abenaki allies.

The governors of the northern colonies pressed for an attack on Port Royal, Nova Scotia, and Quebec to eliminate the French in North America. England, absorbed in her European campaigns, would not support the colonial request for troops and ships to accomplish that task, and the colonists were forced to rely on their own resources for smaller acts of retribution. Massachusetts chose Colonel Benjamin Church, a distinguished Indian fighter and veteran of King William's War, to lead a punitive raid along the coast of Massachusetts, Maine, and the Bay of Fundy. On May 15, ten weeks after the Deerfield attack, Church's force of 550 colonists and friendly Indians set sail in their small armada of fourteen transport ships and thirty-six whaleboats, escorted by three colonial warships. Resting in isolated coves during the day and sailing or paddling the whaleboats at night to surprise their enemy, they moved east along the coast and successfully raided numerous locations, killing and capturing a number of French and Indians. They proceeded to a rendezvous with their escorting warships at Mount Desert Island, where they captured two French officers who had plans for a campaign against New England. While still at Mount Desert, they received orders to proceed to Port Royal, where they hoped to seize French supply ships. Finding no ships upon their arrival, but intimidated by the strength of Port Royal's rebuilt fort, the colonial force turned its attention to Minas, a less well-defended French community at the head of the Bay of Fundy. The town was laid to waste, its buildings and fortifications burned, and its inhabitants taken as prisoners. Numerous other small settlements along the shores of the bay were similarly destroyed. Colonel Church then sent a message to Governor Vaudreuil of New France, in which he specifically mentioned the barbarities against women and children in Deerfield and told the governor that if such acts continued, he would bring a thousand Indians to commit similar atrocities on the settlers of the French frontier. On July 4, Church held a council of war with his officers to discuss the possibility of an attack on Port Royal, which they knew was prepared for that eventuality. Although they had suffered the loss of only six men, the colonial troops were fatigued and restless, and the decision was made to return to Boston, where some celebrated their success but others lamented that more had not been accomplished. In a lengthy report to Governor Dudley, Church wrote of avenging the brutalities inflicted at Deerfield, saying, "But I ever looked on it, a good providence of Almighty God, that some few of our cruel and bloody enemies were made sensible of their bloody cruelties, perpetrated on my dear and loving friends and countrymen . . . as they had been guilty of, in a barbarous manner at Deerfield . . ." Despite the disappointment that more punishment had not been administered to the French and their Indian allies, the Massachusetts Assembly officially thanked Colonel Church, then sixty-five. The feelings of revenge secured by the destruction of the French settlements were satisfying, but the greatest accomplishment of the expedition was the capture of over one hundred prisoners, roughly the same number of settlers taken from Deerfield. Those prisoners became valuable bargaining chips in negotiations with Canada.

During the remainder of 1704 and through most of 1705, there were periodic, isolated ambushes and occasional skirmishes, but losses were generally kept to one or two people. While there were no significant attacks on the New England frontier, there was great concern for the plight of those settlers who remained captive. Some were taken to native villages, while others were traded or sold to the French, who also put them to work. A few, like Reverend Williams, were recognized as persons of stature, with potential significant value in future prisoner exchanges. Many received kind treatment from sympathetic French, and there seems to have been relatively little abuse of those who remained with the natives. The one experience that was common to all the captives was the dogged attempt by the Jesuits to convert them from their Protestant faith to Roman Catholicism. Over the several years that the captives remained in Canada, most of the adults, including (to no surprise) Reverend Williams, resisted this pressure, but young people, separated from family members who had either been killed or sent to other parts of Canada, were the most susceptible to the new faith that was offered. Ultimately, twenty-two of the Deerfield captives converted and remained in Canada, most with French husbands. At least seven, including Reverend Williams's daughter Eunice, stayed with the natives, married, and made their lives there.

In 1705, discussions for a prisoner exchange began between Governor Dudley and Governor Vaudreuil, and New Englanders learned that the French held 117 of their fellow colonists and 70 were in the hands of the Indians. There was great hope that an exchange could be quickly and easily made, since the New Englanders held approximately 150 French prisoners. The issue was complex, however, because intertwined with the prisoner exchange was the broader concept of a potential neutrality treaty, which Governor Vaudreuil had been authorized by France to entertain. An intense period of negotiations between the

French and colonial governors was further hampered by suspicions of
private profiteering and political maneuvering. Dudley initially sent
two Deerfield men, John Sheldon and John Wells, to Quebec, along
with Captain John Livingston from Albany, who had mercantile connections in New France. Vaudreuil agreed in principle to the idea of a
general prisoner exchange but added several conditions in his response,
which he had taken to Dudley by Captain Samuel Hill, who with his
family had been captured during the August 1703 attack on Wells.

Before receiving Dudley's reply, the French governor, as an apparent show of faith, allowed Livingston, Sheldon, and Wells to leave
with a token of five captives. They were "escorted" by Vaudreuil's personal envoy, Captain Augustin Legardeur de Tilly, Sieur de Courtemanche, who was, in fact, on an intelligence-gathering mission. One
of Vaudreuil's conditions, the release of a notorious French privateer
who had ravaged New England's seaborne commerce, posed enormous
problems for Dudley. With Boston merchants vehemently opposing

Governor Philippe de Rigaud de Vaudreuil

the release of the privateer, Dudley offered a treaty and cessation of hostilities while negotiations were continued. Courtemanche, after gathering intelligence about New England's strengths and attitudes, fell ill while in Boston. He consented to be transported to Quebec by sea, which presented the New Englanders with a prime opportunity to gather intelligence of their own on the navigation of the St. Lawrence and the defenses of the approaches to Quebec.

The man chosen to command the voyage to Quebec was a thirty-seven-year-old Scotsman and opportunist, Samuel Vetch. With him on this voyage were Captain Samuel Hill, returning to join his family still being held in Canada, and Governor Dudley's eighteen-year-old son, William. They arrived in Quebec on September 6, 1705, and although Vaudreuil rejected Dudley's suggested prisoner exchange treaty, he was open to the broader neutrality offer proffered by Vetch and the young Dudley. When Dudley and Vetch arrived back in Boston in late November, they had only eleven former captives with them, and rumors began to race through the colony that they had actually used the voyage to conduct trade for their personal gain. These accusations broadened to include suspicions of Governor Dudley, whose credibility was always in question and who had a reputation for enhancing his position whenever possible. There were accusations that Vetch and the Dudleys had actually planned for the return of only a few prisoners in order to have an excuse for a further trip and more personal gain. Under this suspicion and without the ability to meet Vaudreuil's demands in the neutrality agreement draft, Dudley attempted to revitalize the prisoner exchange by sending Captain William Rouse, a New England privateer and merchant, to Port Royal with forty-seven French prisoners. He returned with only seventeen New Englanders but later secured eight more. Again, there was suspicion that Rouse, like Vetch, had been conspiring with Governor Dudley to carry on trade under the guise of prisoner negotiation.

Time was running out for a truce, and Dudley sent Ensign John Sheldon of Deerfield to Quebec in early 1706 in yet another attempt to extend the neutrality negotiations and continue the efforts for prisoner release. Finally, Vaudreuil had had enough of the procrastination, and the fragile truce shattered. Once again, the frontier settlements of New England were subject to the terror of ambushes and raids. Sheldon continued his efforts toward prisoner exchange, and in August 1706, he arrived in Boston with forty-four captives whose release he had secured. That same month, political pressure increased on Dudley when the legislature indicted Rouse "For Trayterous Correspondence with the Enemy," and the assembly then issued a proclamation "to apprehend all such as were suspected." Captain Vetch and several others were arrested, but with Dudley's help the charges were reduced from the capital offfense of treason to the lesser charge of high misdemeanor. By reducing the charges and allowing a legislative rather than a judicial trial, Dudley saved his friends from the possible death sentence. The case was appealed and the convictions of Vetch and Rouse overturned by authorities in London, much to the frustration of those in Boston. Penhallow aired the concern over these nefarious acts when he wrote, "How far these unhappy Measures tended to increase our Troubles, is Obvious to an impartial Eye, if we consider how they suppl'd the enemy with Powder, Shot, Iron Nails and other Materials of War."

While popular sentiment increasingly went against Governor Dudley, he sought to placate some of his critics by making one more attempt to obtain the release of the remaining prisoners. This time he acceded to Vaudreuil's demand and offered the release of the French privateer Pierre Maisonnat, who was known by the nom de guerre Captain Baptiste. However, by meeting this demand, Dudley further alienated the influential merchants who had suffered significant losses to the privateer. Dudley's willingness to release Baptiste advanced the process, but the final stumbling block was that the French, who did not attempt to exert sovereign control over the natives in their region, had trouble gaining the release of the prisoners still held by the Indians. Additional efforts were made, and finally, on November 21, 1706, fifty-seven New England captives, including Reverend John Williams of Deerfield, arrived in Boston. The grateful Williams later dedicated his published account of his ordeal to the governor. However, owing to the length of the negotiations and the allegations of self-interest and trading with the enemy, Dudley's reputation was damaged and his position was more tenuous than ever.

Queen Anne's War continued to plague the colonies with discord. The English were engaged in warfare in Europe and on the high seas as well, and the hated issue of impressment was brought back into focus. In 1706, as captains in the Royal Navy continued their press-related abuses in New York, one entrepreneurial commander, Captain Niles of the frigate *Triton's Prize*, made a profitable business of impressment, infuriating the New York governor, Edward Hyde, Lord Cornbury. The angry governor wrote to the Lords of Trade on October 3, 1706, describing how Captain Niles impressed more men than he needed and "afterwards for certain considerations disposes of some of them to some merchantmen then going out from this port." With merchant masters desperate for sailors to man their ships, they played into the hands of Captain Miles, who literally sold the sailors he had impressed. The governor attempted to stop this outrageous practice and the confrontations that ultimately ensued. Lord Cornbury further warned the Lords of Trade of the growing discontent, saying, "The people are not willing to be pressed under the pretence of the Queen's service when there is no need of it." The merchants of the city, who could not find sufficient sailors to man their vessels, were frustrated and suffered economically. The sailors would not come to man the merchant ships for fear of being impressed from them. The abuses of these Royal Navy captains took on a particularly egregious tone when Captain Miles released one of his midshipmen and set him up as a franchise in the business of pressing men and selling them.

The governor was caught in the middle, as he sought to control the Royal Navy officers and placate the merchants ensuring the continued prosperity of New York. He warned the Lords of Trade of the consequences of this impressment, writing, "If suffered, [impressment] will be the ruin of this place." As the governor attempted to stop this outrageous practice, he ordered Captain Miles not to move his ship. When the captain disobeyed the order, the governor threatened to fire on HMS *Triton's Prize* in what would have been a repeat of Lieutenant Governor Povey's action in Boston four years earlier. A deeper crisis was averted when Captain Miles died after a brief, four-day illness. This, however, prompted additional controversy and confrontation. With the death of Miles, his first lieutenant, Lieutenant Wilcock, should have been elevated to command, but the captain of the other frigate in New York, Captain Fane of HMS *Lovestaff*, attempted to take control and have his first lieutenant, Lieutenant Davis, put in command of *Triton's Prize*. When the governor ordered Lieutenant Davis to relinquish his assumed command, Davis threatened a "warm reception" for soldiers sent to arrest him. Eventually the governor prevailed, but the antipathy that developed between the Royal Navy officers and the colony of New York was palpable.

As a result of the enmity that grew out of the confrontations between the merchant masters and the Royal Navy, Captain Fane was so embittered that he publicly declared "that he hates the whole province and everybody in it and that if he met with a New York vessel at sea and in distress, he would give her no assistance." The colonials felt used and abused by these high-handed captains of Her Majesty's Navy.

News of these confrontations reached England, and Parliament received conflicting reports from the Admiralty, which saw impressment in America as a necessity, and from the Board of Trade, the body that had replaced the Lords of Trade in 1696, which saw the damage being done to the lucrative colonial commerce. Unexpectedly, and to the great consternation of the Admiralty and the desperate captains of the navy, Parliament passed "An Act for the Encouragement of Trade to America." With the queen's approval in 1708, the act became known as "the Sixth of Anne" or "the American Act" and contained language that appeared to finally settle the issue, to the great benefit of sailors in the colonies and of English and colonial merchants.

Among the provisions of the Sixth of Anne was the following: "that no mariner or other person who shall serve on board or be retained to serve on board any privateer, or trading ship or vessel, that shall be employed in any part of America, nor any mariner or other person, being on shore in any part thereof, shall be liable to be impressed . . . unless such mariner shall have before deserted from such ship of war." Here, in this act of Parliament, was the solution to the problem and a victory for the independent-minded colonials.

It was remarkable that the act was passed in the midst of a war. However, as lawyers and politicians parsed words and looked for loop holes, naval commanders disregarded the act or searched for ways to circumvent it. There was growing resentment of English authority and greater regard for the individual rights of sailors, despite their generally low social status. The concept of the individual's right to life and liberty grew in colonial consciousness, and incidents involving impressment were among the clearest examples of abuse of those rights.

IN 1707, AT the time that England began the impressment study that resulted in the Sixth of Anne, the New England colonies continued to suffer from small raids along the frontier and losses at sea, and the legislature reinstituted the grisly incentive of scalp bounties. To counter the attacks by French privateers on New England's fishing and merchant ships and prevent the French from supplying the Indians with weapons of war, it was deemed essential to carry out another attack on the base of those operations at Port Royal and wrest it from the French. Once again, Governor Dudley appealed to England for men and ships to assist, and once again the critical support the colonies needed was denied. Frustrated by England's refusal to assist her beleaguered colonies, the New Englanders again resolved to take on the task alone. Massachusetts raised two regiments, the Red and the Blue, consisting of 936 men, and New Hampshire and Rhode Island contributed an additional 140 men. Colonel John March, who had led the gallant defense of the garrison at Casco during the August 1703 attacks, was selected to command this expedition, and he gathered the troops at Nantasket, seven miles east of Boston, where they embarked into twenty-three ships. They sailed on March 13, 1707, escorted by the small warship belonging to Massachusetts, the *Province Galley*, and the one English contribution to the effort, the frigate HMS *Deptford*. March and his regimental commanders, Colonel Francis Wainwright and Colonel Winthrop Hilton, led a force that was military in name only, because the majority of the men had been drawn from the militias throughout the colonies and had little training or tolerance for military discipline.

After a two-week voyage, the fleet passed through the gut that formed the entrance to Port Royal's basin. Lieutenant Colonel Samuel Appelton landed 350 men from the Red regiment on the north shore of the bay, a few miles from the community and the fort of Port Royal. Colonel March, with 700 men from the combined regiments, landed on the south shore, and in a classic pincer movement, the two forces

advanced toward the fort. Anticipating the attack, the French had men
lying in ambush, but those on the north shore were clearly outnumbered and after minimal resistance retreated to the fort. To the south,
Acadia's governor, Daniel d'Auger de Subercase, commanded 200
French soldiers, who waited until Colonel March and his force were
in the midst of fording the Allen River before they opened fire, putting the New Englanders on notice that there was serious opposition.
With the odds four to one against him, however, Subercase found the
combat too intense, had his horse shot out from under him, and retreated to the fort to prepare for a siege.

The New Englanders advanced and began to dig into position in a
broad crescent before the fort, but constant arguments among the inexperienced officers undermined what semblance of discipline existed, and the attacking force was soon in chaos. The one professional
English officer, a military engineer named Rednap, refused to take
the lead and reportedly said he would not "venture his reputation
with such ungovernable and undisciplined men and inconstant officers." Rednap and Captain Stuckley of HMS *Deptford* might have exerted a stabilizing influence on the mob assembled at Port Royal, but
there was great animosity between English officers, who generally
held the colonial forces in contempt, and the colonials, who had little
tolerance for the arrogant English military professionals. The campaign was ripe for failure.

The New Englanders learned from French deserters that a force of
five hundred manned the fort at Port Royal and its forty-two cannons.
They also learned that an equal number of reinforcements were supposedly on the way. The contemporary historian Penhallow recorded
the frustration with the professional English military officers on board
HMS *Deptford*, "Whereas if the Officers on board her Majesty's Ship
had been true and faithful, matters had succeeded to good advantage.
But instead of pressing on, they did rather clog and hinder the Affair."
Several days of indecision followed before the order was finally given to
destroy the buildings outside the fort, prior to reboarding and abandoning the effort. The American colonials' frustration was evident as they
complained that they could have taken the fort without firing a shot by
simply starving the French into surrender. With their debilitated
commander, Colonel March, who had lost the respect of not only the

English officers but the colonial troops as well, the discouraged force departed Port Royal in failure.

Instead of returning directly to Boston, the fleet stopped in Casco, where a message was sent to Governor Dudley to report on the fiasco and request further orders. During the time they waited for his reply, a number of disillusioned men deserted and made their long way back home. Dudley refused to accept the defeat and ordered another assault. He sent another frigate and a hundred reinforcements, not nearly sufficient to make up for the number of desertions. Compounding the leadership problems, Dudley sent three members of the provincial council to advise Colonel March, none any more professional than he.

Weakened and demoralized, the force set off for Port Royal once again. Upon arrival, they learned that French reinforcements had indeed materialized, including the daring young privateer Captain Pierre Morpain, who had earned a fierce reputation by taking a serious toll on New England shipping. Morpain, his ship, and his sailors proved to be formidable. A token New England force was landed and a few skirmishes took place over the period of a week before the New Englanders reembarked and the defeated force sailed back to Boston, where the embarrassment of failure and outrage at the cost of the expedition fueled demands for courts-martial. The bickering, infighting, and posturing among the English and colonial officers continued to the point that it was impossible to bring charges against anyone, but publicly Colonel March was the subject of ridicule and bore the burden of failure. New England's bold attempt to strike back at the French failed miserably, and the confidence of the colonies to act independently of significant English support was shaken.

There was better success in defense along the war's land frontier. Hertel de Rouville, the commander of the Deerfield attack, led a group of 160 French and Indians against Haverhill in 1708, where the raiding party found strong resistance. There were 30 militia soldiers stationed in Haverhill when de Rouville's forces slipped into the village just before dawn. The raiders were discovered, and a fierce fight ensued. The French managed to kill 16 and take several others captive but were forced to hastily retreat when New England reinforcements arrived. In the woods, 60 militiamen, in an ambush reminiscent of those laid by de Rouville's father at Salmon Falls and by de Rouville after the Deerfield attack, awaited the retreating French and opened fire at point-blank range. Ten raiders, including de Rouville's brother Rene, died and the remainder of the attacking force had to abandon their gear, plunder, and captives to make their escape. The following year, de Rouville had his last opportunity for a large raid against the New England frontier. His target was once again Deerfield. The town, however, had been alerted to expect an attack, and de Rouville and his force of 40 Frenchmen and 140 natives were foiled in their attempt to draw the defenders out of the stockade into an ambush. Only a small force of 10 Deerfield defenders went forth on horseback into the trap. Two were killed, but with Deerfield still well defended, de Rouville was again forced to turn north in failure. The defensive network along the frontier proved to be effective.

The war that had begun in 1702 was now in its seventh year, and despite the high cost in lives, homes, and financial resources, the New Englanders had gained nothing. They had only the most minimal English support from the frigates based in Boston, and even this contact between the colonials and the English officers fueled their mutual animosity. It seemed likely that nothing would change and the indecisive war would stumble on, continuing to take its toll on the New Englanders, who bore the brunt of the attacks and mounted most of the retaliatory expeditions. If success was to be achieved and the French driven out of Canada, it would require the commitment of the English government and English military forces, and that seemed unlikely.

CHAPTER 9

The British Are Coming?

IN 1709, WITH QUEEN ANNE'S WAR in a stalemate, hope was re-vived for a major attack on New France with English assistance. The persuasive progenitor of this endeavor was the controversial Samuel Vetch, who after his conviction in Boston of trading with the enemy went to England, where his conviction was overturned. He then turned his efforts toward convincing the British, as they were now called after the establishment of Great Britain in 1707, that it served the nation well to expel the French from Canada. Vetch re-cruited another key player for this adventure in the person of Fran-cis Nicholson, who had been lieutenant governor of the hated Dominion and subsequently governor of both Maryland and Vir-ginia. In July 1708, "Col. Vetch . . . laid a plan of the whole Country [entitled 'Canada Survey'd'] before some of the chief Ministers of State . . . and . . . obtain'd a promise for sufficient Forces both by Sea and Land, for the Conquest of *Canada*." Finally, the pleas of the colonies had been heard and their lone battle against the powerful French and Indian forces was going to be joined by the professional British military.

The approach Vetch and Nicholson proposed was the same as had been suggested by Jacob Leisler and used in Phips's failed attempt in 1690, in which a land army would move up through New York and at-tack Montreal, drawing troops away from Quebec, while an amphibi-

Samuel Vetch

ous force sailed up the St. Lawrence to attack the capital city. The persuasive powers and political connections of Vetch were formidable, as
was his ambition. He not only obtained the queen's approval for his
"Glorious Enterprise," but was also given the rank of colonel and the
promise of the governorship of Canada when he successfully completed his plan.

The shrewd pair of Vetch and Nicholson arrived in Boston in April
1709 aboard HMS *Dragon*, determined to whip up enthusiasm for
this undertaking and prepare for the arrival of the British ships and
troops. They carried "her *Majesty's* Royal Commands and Instructions to the *Governors* of the several *Provinces*, to furnish their required Quota's."

The first critical task was to convince New York to finally abandon
the neutrality they had enjoyed while New England endured brutal
frontier warfare. In this effort, Nicholson's old connections with the
New York aristocracy and Vetch's connection by marriage to the

Francis Nicholson

famous Livingston family cleared away the resistance. Then they addressed the vital issue of recruitment. As part of his proposal, Vetch had offered to recruit 2,500 colonial soldiers to join 4,000 British regulars and six British warships in the attack. With the assurance of significant British involvement, and with the promise that "To such as should offer volunteers, they presented a good Firelock [musket], Cartouch-box, Flints, Ammunition, a Coat, Hat and Shirt; with an assurance of her Majesty's Princely Favour unto all such as should distinguish themselves," the colonials rallied to the call. While 1,000 colonial soldiers were to come from Massachusetts, the majority of the colonial troops were to be recruited from the colonies to the west and south. The 1,500 men needed for the attack on Montreal were enlisted from New York, New Jersey, and Connecticut, and although the Pacifist Quakers in Pennsylvania refused to send troops, they supported the campaign with £3000. Colonel Nicholson was in command of this army, which assembled in Albany for the push north. In June, after Nicholson sent an advance party to secure their line of march to the head of Lake Champlain, the troops labored to cut roads through the wilderness. They erected three protective fortifications and established advance storehouses filled with the necessities to support the campaign.

In Massachusetts, there was great enthusiasm among the Protestants for this crusade against the Catholic French, and they successfully recruited more than the thousand men required for the effort that would be undertaken on the sea. Throughout June, July, and August, the assembled army drilled and waited, while requisitioned transport ships swung at anchor. As September approached, Nicholson's men began to fall to disease, yet the waiting continued. Vetch wrote to Lord Sunderland, warning that if the ships and British troops did not arrive, "it would be the last disappointment to her Majesty's colonies, who have so heartily complied with her royal order, and would render them much more miserable than if such a thing had never been undertaken." Appealing again for the ships, ten days later he wrote, "I shall only presume to acquaint your Lordship how vastly uneasy all her Majesty's loyal subjects here on this continent are."

By mid-September, the crushing realization hit home: The British were not coming. Even before official notification arrived, Vetch, Nicholson, the colonial leaders, and the thousands of ready troops were appalled and disgusted by Britain's apparent failure to support this effort. Everyone in the northern colonies was affected, not only the troops. Families struggled to maintain their farms and businesses while the men were away on duty on the shores of Lake Champlain or in Boston. Both merchants and consumers felt the financial impact of the trade embargo, instituted to ensure the secrecy of the operation, and the enormous cost of military mobilization touched every taxpayer. The direct cost to the governments of Massachusetts, Rhode Island, and New Hampshire was more than £46,000, the equivalent of more than $1.75 billion in the year 2000. Word from Great Britain that the expedition had been "laid aside" finally arrived in October, and the colonists learned that the British troops intended for North America had been diverted to Portugal. Astonishingly, that decision had been made in London by the end of May, and the thoughtless British authorities had failed to send the message until August, and then it was sent on a ship that had other stops to make on its way to America. Samuel Penhallow expressed the discouragement felt throughout the colonies, saying, "When our Expectations are at the highest, things come to nothing."

The discontent with Britain's high-handed disregard for the colonial effort was widespread. Samuel Vetch's reputation was badly scarred, but he convened a meeting to discuss future options. Representatives from Massachusetts, Connecticut, Rhode Island, and New Hampshire attended, but New York, New Jersey, and Pennsylvania boycotted the meeting. Hopes and dreams for the expulsion of the French lay in ruins, and only a true optimist and entrepreneur could find something positive in the rubble. The dogged determination that emerged from this meeting was remarkable. To make the most of the disastrous situation, the governors resolved to use the forces gathered in Boston for a new attack on Port Royal. All that was needed was the participation of the British naval vessels that were already on station in the colonies. The British captains refused to join the effort, however, and once again the colonies felt betrayed.

When Colonel Nicholson carried an appeal to the Crown for an expedition against Port Royal but not Quebec the following year, Queen Anne gave her sanction to the scaled-down proposal and the news was sent to Boston with the expectation that the British ships and troops would arrive before the end of March. Nicholson was to command the expedition, and Samuel Vetch was to serve as his adjutant. This time, however, wary of the British and the Nicholson/Vetch team, the Massachusetts Legislature took no steps to recruit troops for the campaign. As before, March, April, May, and June passed without the arrival of the ships. Their reticence seemed well-founded, until Colonel Nicholson arrived on July 1, 1709, with several British warships and a regiment of Royal Marines.

With the presence of British ships and troops in Boston and the command from the queen, frantic efforts to raise and equip the colonial contingent began in earnest. Skeptical militiamen who had participated in the previous year's fiasco were offered a month's pay in advance, a uniform coat worth thirty shillings, and a queen's musket, which they could keep as their own. The New Englanders responded, and by mid-September, although late in the season for such an undertaking, all was prepared. Francis Nicholson was appointed "General and commander in Chief." A farewell dinner was held at the Green Dragon tavern for Nicholson, Vetch, and the other leaders of the expedition. Four hundred British marines and 1,500 colonial soldiers embarked, and the impressive flotilla of more than thirty ships sailed from Boston on September 18, 1710.

Only six days later, the people of Port Royal witnessed the arrival of five of Her Majesty's warships, the Massachusetts warship the *Province Galley* under the able command of Cyprian Southack, two dozen transports, two hospital ships, and several support vessels. With a clear memory of the disorganized debacle of the New England attack two years earlier, Governor Subercase was prepared to test the mettle of the invaders. The force again landed on both sides of the bay as they had in 1707, with Vetch and two regiments on the north, and Nicholson and two colonial regiments, along with the Royal Marine regiment, on the south, where the fort stood. That night a British bomb ketch moved into position and hurled seven mortar shells over the fort's wall and into the midst of the demoralized defenders. The New Englanders had drilled daily for months during the previous summer and were now joined by the British naval force and four hundred British marines. It quickly became clear to Subercase that this was a different army from that he had turned away in 1707. The attackers methodically went about setting up their advanced entrenchments a mere four hundred yards from the fort and prepared their artillery for a siege. During the several days of this preparation, the fort suffered the steady assault from the British bomb ketch. As Penhallow records, "Our *Bomb-Ship* came up again, and threw thirty six Shells into the fort, which put them into such an amazing Terror."

In stark contrast with the foul treatment Sir William Phips gave the French when he violated the terms of surrender at Port Royal in 1690, this engagement was conducted with punctilious courtesy. After three days of bombardment, under a flag of truce, a French officer brought a message to Nicholson, in which Governor Subercase informed him that the bombardment had distressed several ladies in the fort, and he requested that they be able to leave the fort and be housed in safety by Nicholson. Nicholson sent one of his own officers with a response, in which he agreed to care for the ladies, "for the queen, my royal mistress, hath not sent me hither to make war against women." Sensing that he was dealing with a man of honor, Subercase replied with an offer of surrender, "to prevent the spilling of both English and French blood." The cannonading on both sides continued for another day before a firm truce was established, but in just over a week, the British and New England forces had obtained the surrender of their nemesis. On October 5, the colonial troops marched to the gate of the fort, where Governor Subercase surrendered the keys to General Nicholson. Retaining their muskets, the French troops marched out with their banners flying and saluted Nicholson as they passed between the ranks of the New Englanders and British marines formed on either side of the gate. Nicholson's force then entered the fort, hoisted the British flag, and changed the name of the community to Annapolis Royal, in honor of Queen Anne. As a final courtesy, the British and New England officers gave a breakfast party to entertain the ladies who had been so distraught during the attack.

With this nicety behind them, attention turned to practical matters. As part of the surrender, the French officials and soldiers were transported to France in English ships. Samuel Vetch achieved his ambition and was made governor of Acadia, which included Nova Scotia and the mainland area to its north, since the loss of Port Royal meant the loss of the entire region. The French settlers were allowed to stay, provided they swore an oath of loyalty to Great Britain. Two hundred British marines and 250 New Englanders were left to garrison Annapolis Royal, while the rest of the New Englanders returned to Boston, this time in triumph. Finally, for the 10,000 residents of Boston and the rest of the colonists there was a major military success. The curse of earlier campaigns and embarrassments was lifted. The hornets' nest of Port Royal, which had served as the base for the French privateers that played havoc with the fishing and commercial maritime activities of the northern colonies, had been eliminated. In its place, Great Britain had acquired a vast new colony and strategic control of the northeastern American coast, including the critical approaches to the St. Lawrence.

Buoyed by this success, General Nicholson returned to England to revive the case for the conquest of all of New France, and his persuasive arguments fell on the receptive ears of the ministers of the newly elected Tory government. They were eager to earn the successes that had evaded their rival Whig Party predecessors and supported Nicholson's proposal before the queen. Permission was granted for another Canadian campaign, to once again employ Leisler's traditional two-pronged attack against Montreal by land and Quebec by sea. Nicholson returned to Boston on June 8, 1711, and a meeting of the northern governors was quickly convened in New London, Connecticut, to receive the orders from the queen and organize their side of the expedition.

This time there was no agonizing wait for the British forces. On June 25, the signal came from Castle Island in Boston harbor that ships were in sight. Sweeping into the harbor were no fewer than fifty British ships, fifteen of them warships. The commander in chief of the expedition was Sir Hovenden Walker, recently knighted and made rear admiral of the White Squadron. The army component of Walker's command consisted of more than five thousand regular British soldiers under the command of newly promoted brigadier general John Hill. This arrival of British soldiers and sailors instantly doubled the population of Boston and presented both a challenge and an opportunity. To delude French spies in England, the expedition had taken on only enough supplies for a normal foray to the Mediterranean rather than the larger amount, which to spies would indicate an expedition to North America. By the time of their arrival in Boston, there was an urgent need for food to feed the soldiers, who were to encamp on Noodles Island in the harbor, and the six thousand sailors aboard the fleet's vessels. Seeing an opportunity to earn back some of the revenue lost in 1709, some colonial merchants exploited the British. Nevertheless, the colonials realized the importance of preparing this force quickly, and it was noted, "It's surprising to think how vigorously this Expedition was forwarded, while at *Boston* . . . For in less than a month the whole Army was supply'd with ten weeks Provision, and all other Necessaries that were wanted."

During the month required for provisioning, an additional problem developed in the form of the desertion of hundreds of British soldiers and sailors who were attracted to life in the colony. Admiral

Walker accused the people of Boston of encouraging and harboring them, prompting the Massachusetts Legislature to pass an ordinance forbidding such action and levying fines and imprisonment for violation. The ill will that developed fueled long-lasting antipathy between the colonials and the English military. One British artillery officer, Colonel King, expressed his disdain for the colonials, writing to Secretary of State Henry St. John on July 25, 1711, "You'll find in my Journal what Difficultyes we mett with through the Misfortune that the Coloneys were not inform'd of our Coming two Months sooner, and through the Interestedness, ill Nature, and Sowerness of these People, whose Government, Doctrine, and Manners, whose Hypocracy and canting, are unsupportable . . ." He went on to advocate a return to the concept of the Dominion when he said that unless the colonies were brought under one government, "they will grow more stiff and disobedient every Day." The perception of the New Englanders as an independent people was noted by both the governor of New York and a French writer of the time, who wrote with extraordinary clairvoyance that if Canada fell, the American colonists "will then unite, shake off the yoke of the English monarchy, and erect themselves into a democracy."

Despite the harsh words of Colonel King, the colonial troops were raised, and less than a month after the arrival of the British, the campaign got under way. Nicholson led the forces moving north from Albany, and Colonel Samuel Vetch was in command of the two regiments of colonial troops that sailed from Boston in colonial ships accompanied by the British fleet. It appeared that a well-coordinated military expedition was in progress, but there was a severe lack of experience in the senior leadership of the British forces. Admiral Walker's career had been marked by both success and failure, and he had never held such broad responsibility. The army commander, General Hill, owed his recent promotion to political leverage, as he was the queen's cousin and the brother of Abigail Masham, the queen's closest friend, who enjoyed enormous influence over the queen and her politics.

The fleet made its way along the coast, around Cape Breton Island, and into the Gulf of St. Lawrence without mishap, but the admiral now faced the challenge of the St. Lawrence River. None of the British naval captains had navigated this river, and the admiral was reluctantly depending on the French pilots who had been bribed into service. He was also traumatized by the pilots' tales of ice closing the river and wrote later in his published journal of the expedition, "That which now chiefly took up my thoughts, was contriving how to secure the ships if we got up to Quebec: for *the ice in the river freezing to the bottom* would have utterly destroyed and bilged them as much as if they had been squeezed between rocks." He went on to record the horrors he envisioned if his fleet were trapped in the ice, writing, "I must confess the melancholy contemplation of this [had it happened] strikes me with horror . . . locked up by adamantine frosts . . . in a barren and uncultivated region; great numbers of brave men famishing with hunger, and drawing lots who should die first to feed the rest." The newly minted admiral was wavering as he faced the challenges of large-scale command and the St. Lawrence. Curiously, they had among them an experienced person who had made numerous trips up and down the river while negotiating prisoner exchanges five years earlier. Although not a mariner, Samuel Vetch knew the river well and offered to sail ahead of the fleet and alert them to dangers. The fretful Admiral Walker rejected his service, making a critical mistake.

The fleet had been in fog in the wide St. Lawrence for two days when a fierce storm came upon them, yet the obstinate admiral refused the advice of the French river pilot and, with their exact position uncertain, ordered the fleet to head north. At about ten-thirty on the night of August 22, shortly after making the fateful decision, the admiral retired to his cabin. Two hours later, he was again called on deck in his nightclothes to witness the disaster he had caused. The fleet was bearing down on breakers. They were on a dreaded lee shore, with a gale of wind and unseen current forcing them toward destruction, the lead ships already foundering. Hovenden's fleet was in a perilous state. A significant number of his transports were being smashed on the shore, and sailors and soldiers were dying.

Those ships that had room to execute the dangerous maneuver of wearing ship, turning with their sterns to the wind, were able to claw their way off the lee shore. For those that had to anchor, the wind fortunately eased around two o'clock in the morning, and most of the fleet was able to sail out of harm's way. Eight transport ships and one supply vessel had been dashed on the shore, however, and 705 soldiers,

200 sailors, and 35 "camp-following" women and children perished in this catastrophe. The scene on the shore was one of utter devastation, with bodies strewn among wreckage, supplies, personal possessions, and the cannons of the transports. The fleet cruised in the area for two days in an effort to retrieve survivors and salvageable equipment. Fortunately for the New Englanders, none of the wrecked transports was carrying colonial troops, and only one New Englander perished in the disaster.

Although the majority of his force remained intact, the fearful admiral abandoned the objective of Quebec. The alternative of an attack on the French in Newfoundland was considered, but the British commanders, Walker and Hill, who could see their careers foundering in this debacle, decided to cut their losses and head back to England. This "retreat" left the colonists to conclude that the senior officers lacked commitment to the cause and the colonies were not worth risking their careers. Ironically, after the admiral's departure from his flagship back in England, the seventy-gun ship of the line HMS *Edgar* exploded, killing over four hundred sailors. It came as some surprise to the colonists that both the admiral and the general escaped official censure. Samuel Penhallow once again gave voice to the suspicions of a cover-up and the colonists' disgust, writing, "Upon this disaster the whole Country (and indeed the nation) was alarm'd, and many Censures and Jelousies arose . . . If the *Admiral* was in fault wherefore was he not call'd to an Account? Or why did not the *General* to vindicate himself, lay a Remonstrance before the Council Board?" The answers to Penhallow's questions in the early eighteenth century, as now in the twenty-first century, are in the power of the ruler and the political influence of those close to the head of state. With his relation to the queen and his sister's political influence, General Hill received honors and a new command. Admiral Walker's naval career was less secure. Initially, he was also given a new command, but when the Tory Party left office, the Whigs remembered the disaster in the St. Lawrence, and Walker was dismissed from service.

The joy and satisfaction of success at Port Royal was tainted by the dismal failure of this massive campaign against Canada. The man who was most furious over the disaster and withdrawal from the St. Lawrence was Francis Nicholson, who had argued for years to secure the British force to conquer Canada. The news of the disaster reached him as he led his force toward Montreal. His violent reaction created a near comic scene as he impetuously tore off his wig, threw it to the floor, and stamped on it. He and his disillusioned troops then destroyed the fortifications they had built and retreated to Albany, where the disgruntled force was disbanded and the colonies still had the French menace looming over them.

THE FALL OF 1711 was relatively uneventful on the New England frontier, and late in the year peace negotiations began in Utrecht, Holland. The process took months, and there was anxiety among the colonists over the terms of the peace. Their fear was that the sole significant accomplishment of this North American war, the capture of Port Royal and Acadia, would be for naught, and it would be forfeited as the belligerents negotiated the exchange of their land conquests and the gains of both sides were neutralized. As the balance of power was argued at the negotiation table, the discouraged colonists awaited their fate, being determined by others thousands of miles away in Utrecht.

CHAPTER 10

Peace and Preparation in French Canada

THE DISASTROUS WITHDRAWAL FROM the St. Lawrence after the abortive campaign against Quebec in 1711 marked the end of significant North American involvement in Queen Anne's War. While negotiations for a cease-fire were being held during the first half of 1712, there were sporadic minor but unnerving ambushes and attacks along the New England frontier. Ironically, the last significant Indian attack of this war occurred in the same village where the war had begun a decade earlier, Wells, Maine. The natives attacked during a wedding, and in the fight several of those in attendance were killed and the groom was captured. The father of the groom was able to ransom his son at the huge cost of £300, the equivalent of six years' salary for the community's minister.

In August, a truce was signed and the first steps toward peace were taken. Consumed by two European wars for twenty of the preceding twenty-five years, North America had paid dearly in lives and resources. As the European parties settled down to negotiate the final treaty in Utrecht, the future of Port Royal and Acadia, the only British conquest in North America, hung in the balance. During the months of negotiations, it became clear that King Louis XIV eagerly wanted to reclaim Acadia, and his negotiators offered the British the West Indian islands of St. Christopher, St. Martin, and St. Bartholomew in exchange. When this was rejected, other inducements were offered, including the rights to the lucrative Newfoundland fisheries. The British stood their ground and refused to relinquish Acadia, but they did offer one concession. East of the Acadian peninsula of Nova Scotia was Cape Breton, a nearly deserted four-thousand-square-mile island of great hills, inland seas, and marshland, which seemed to have little economic or agricultural potential. It was left to the French as a token presence on the Atlantic, and time would demonstrate that the island had exceptional strategic value.

The Treaty of Utrecht, signed on April 11, 1713, addressed the key issues that had drawn Great Britain and her colonies into war. Britain agreed to recognize Philip V as the rightful king of Spain, provided he relinquish any future claim to the throne of France. Spain ceded the strategic islands of Minorca and Gibraltar in the Mediterranean to Britain. Spain and France agreed that they would remain separate and not form one large Catholic country. Louis XIV agreed to recognize Queen Anne as the legitimate monarch of Great Britain and accept the Protestant succession to that throne. They also made another curious concession: This provision was called the *asiento*, and it gave Britain monopoly rights to import forty-eight hundred African slaves annually into Spanish colonies in the New World for the next thirty years. This was a deplorable yet highly profitable contract for the British, and it was embellished by what seemed to be a minor addition. Spain was highly protective of trade with its American colonies, and other nations, like Great Britain, were excluded from all aspects of the lucrative trade. As part of the *asiento*, the backers of the slave trade could send one ship each year, laden with British products, to sell directly in this exclusive market. This was a crack in the wall protecting Spanish colonial trade, and over the years the British would attempt to drive a wedge into that crack.

In addition to the provisions that primarily affected Europe, there were several of great importance to the American colonists. France recognized the British claim to the vast Hudson Bay region and ceded Newfoundland and Acadia to Britain. The French retained the rest of Canada and Cape Breton Island, Île St. Jean, and several smaller islands in the Gulf of St. Lawrence. The French also acknowledged that, at least for their part, the Iroquois nations were English subjects. Short of eliminating the French entirely from North America, it

appeared that significant benefits had accrued to the northern
colonies. Prime among these was the acquisition of Acadia. They assumed that this opened Nova Scotia, and the mainland territory to the
north, to British settlement and that eastern Maine was also undis-
puted British territory. However, Article 12 of the Treaty of Utrecht
defined Acadia vaguely as "with its ancient boundaries," which left
ample room for future dispute and controversy. The New Englanders
envisioned a prosperous era of peace. Their fishing and merchant fleets
could ply their trades without the fear of French privateers swooping
down from Port Royal, and garrisoned outposts could control frontier
areas so New Englanders could expand their settlements without the
terror of attacks. However, the character of the French Acadian settlers, the old Indian alliances, the Catholic religion of the eastern Indians, and the lack of clearly defined boundaries in the treaty created
numerous points of conflict.

The French assumed that their colonists in Newfoundland and
Acadia would simply move to Cape Breton, which the French called
Île Royale. There were only a few hundred French settlers on Newfoundland, mostly fishermen and their families situated around the
fort in Placentia. The French government would not allow them to
stay when it became British territory, and in 1713, arrangements were
made to transport them to Cape Breton. When a similar plan was proposed for the French in Acadia, only a few hundred of the twenty-four
hundred Acadians agreed to go. They had been on their rich agricultural land for generations and had endured the periodic political
changes as Port Royal passed back and forth between the French and
the English. Acadia was the only home most had known, and they
wanted to stay if they could continue to worship as Catholics. This was
a serious setback for the French, who envisioned the transformation of
Cape Breton into a thriving French outpost. It was also a quandary for
the British, who had to weigh the risk of having two thousand French
citizens residing on British land against the benefits of a population
that would keep Acadia's fertile lands productive and supply a labor
force when needed. When it became apparent that there would be no
British or American plan to recruit new British settlers for Acadia, the
authorities in Annapolis Royal, the former Port Royal, resigned themselves to the reality of living with this potentially hostile population.

The eastern Abenakis were quick to acknowledge the truce when it was instituted in 1712 and, being exhausted by the constant warfare, opened their own peace negotiations with Governor Dudley. Representatives of Massachusetts and New Hampshire met with representatives of the eastern tribes at Portsmouth, New Hampshire, on July 11, 1713, three months after the European signing of the Treaty of Utrecht. At that meeting, a treaty was signed by Dudley, twenty New England councillors, and eight Native American representatives. In the agreement, the Indians agreed to acknowledge their past hostile acts and "confess our hearty and sincere Obedience unto the Crown of Great Britain." With these two treaties, the War of the Spanish Succession was ended, as was Queen Anne's War in North America, and there was hope that an era of peace lay ahead.

Just a year after the treaties were signed, the issue of succession to the British throne came to the fore when Queen Anne died without an heir. In order to ensure a Protestant succession, the "Act of Settlement" passed by Parliament in 1701 designated Sophia, the electress of Hanover in Germany and granddaughter of James I, to succeed Anne. In the event of her death, the crown would go to her Protestant heirs. Sophia had, in fact, died two months before Queen Anne, and the British government bypassed more than fifty Catholics with stronger claims to the throne to acknowledge Sophia's German son, George Lewis, as King George I. He was an odd fit for the role, as he spoke German and French but very little English. During his reign, he frequently returned to his native Hanover and depended on the ministers of his cabinet to govern: an unusual situation, but one that nominally gave Great Britain the Protestant ruler most Englishmen wanted.

In the New World, the experienced French governor Vaudreuil was in a position to advance the stature of Canada. He had developed ambitious initiatives to extend French influence westward to Lake Superior, impede New England settlement east of the Kennebec River in Maine, and increase immigration to New France. During the negotiations at Utrecht, the British diplomats had made a key mistake when they failed to insist that Cape Breton remain unfortified. This gave the authorities in France and Governor Vaudreuil the opportunity they needed to exercise his final initiative: the establishment of

Cape Breton as France's well-fortified stronghold on the Atlantic coast of North America.

There were four strategic objectives for the settlement of Cape Breton. The first was to establish a center from which resident fishermen, and the hundreds who would come seasonally from Europe, could easily access the abundant fishing grounds, bring their catch to shore, and process it for later shipment to world markets. Of equal importance, despite the peace that was in place, was to develop a strong military base to assert French rights over the island and provide a base from which French naval vessels could protect access to the St. Lawrence and keep open the supply lines for New France. A third purpose was to create an entrepôt, a port where ships returning to Europe from the West Indies or the Pacific could stop, trade, transship their cargoes, refit, and prepare for the passage back across the Atlantic, aided by the Gulf Stream that flowed past Cape Breton on its way to Europe. Most important, the French wanted a base to replace Port Royal, from which the French navy and privateers could descend upon colonial and British fishing and merchant vessels if and when war broke out in the future.

The creation of a strong military presence on Cape Breton began with the arrival of two ships. One, from Quebec, carried the hero of the Deerfield attack, Hertel de Rouville, and fifty handpicked soldiers experienced in frontier life. The second ship, the *Semslack*, had sailed from France, bringing supplies and a few officers and men who had been among the Acadian forces idling in France since the fall of Port Royal in 1710. Joseph de Monbeton de Brouillan, known as Saint-Ovide, who enjoyed an admirable reputation as a military leader, was in command of this combined military force as the king's lieutenant for Cape Breton. Saint-Ovide had first been assigned to Plaisance in the French portion of Newfoundland in 1692 when his uncle was its governor. Over the years he participated in a number of successful military operations, but he achieved his greatest success with an ambitious and daring attack that he conceived and carried out. The stronghold of British Newfoundland was at St. John's, which, with its narrow harbor entrance, was easily defended from seaborne attacks. With 164 volunteers, Saint-Ovide made the arduous sixty-five-mile march overland from Plaisance to St. John's and, before dawn on New

Year's Day 1709, led his men in a surprise attack. They quickly crossed the open ditch and, under erratic fire from the alarmed but disorganized British, threw up scaling ladders, achieved the ramparts, and quickly captured St. John's, with only three of his men killed and eleven wounded. On orders, Saint-Ovide destroyed the British fortification after loading the valuable British cannons, gunpowder, and other supplies onto the frigate *Venus*, which had been hovering offshore in support of the expedition. In recognition of his achievement, Saint-Ovide was awarded the Cross of Saint-Louis.

Under Saint-Ovide's command, the two ships explored and assessed the potential harbors along the Cape Breton coast and reported back, "In the year 1713 and the 2nd day of September, we . . . have seized and taken possession of the Island of Cape Breton, situated in the entrance to the Gulf of St. Lawrence . . . and after having visited all the ports in the said Island of Cape Breton which have been indicated to us, we believed and decided that we could not make a better choice for the present than that of Port St. Louis, formerly known as English Harbour, in which port we have this day landed the troops, the munitions of war and provisions . . ." The militarization of Cape Breton had begun, as had "Francification," since Harve a l'Angois was renamed after the French patron saint, St. Louis.

The fine deep harbor of Port St. Louis was large enough to accommodate a fleet of five hundred ships, and although drift ice blocked the entrance to the port in winter, the harbor itself did not freeze. A promontory on the northeast side and a sweeping peninsula to the southwest defined the entrance to the harbor. In addition to the almost 100 soldiers and their equipment, they landed the settlers who had been displaced from Plaisance. This anxious group consisted of 116 men, 10 women, and 23 children. To prepare for the winter that was fast approaching, the soldiers set about cutting wood for fuel and the construction of shelters, and the fishermen began to work the abundant fishing banks nearby. Within two months, 31 fishing crews from Newfoundland joined the initial settlers, swelling the civilian population to 300. With this many people in addition to the soldiers to shelter and feed, the preparations for winter were frantic.

As the cold weather descended on Cape Breton, King's Lieutenant Saint-Ovide departed for France on the *Semslack* to make reports to the ministry. The governor-designate of the island colony, Philippe de Pastour de Costebelle, had remained in Plaisance, Newfoundland, where he was among the last to leave in 1714. The settlers and soldiers in Port St. Louis were on their own as the drift ice closed off the harbor. As with so many nascent colonies, the first winter was an ordeal for the group, and the competent captain Hertel de Rouville was a stabilizing factor for everyone throughout the difficult winter months. With only the most primitive shelters, inadequate supplies, and insufficient food, suffering was widespread. To survive, the settlers slaughtered their precious cattle during the long, bitter winter. It was a full six months between the departure of Saint-Ovide and the arrival of the first supply ship in May. This vessel, the *Hercule*, fought its way through the drift ice for three weeks before reaching the haggard, desperate settlers, who had killed and consumed nineteen of their twenty-one cows. Although not of vital importance to

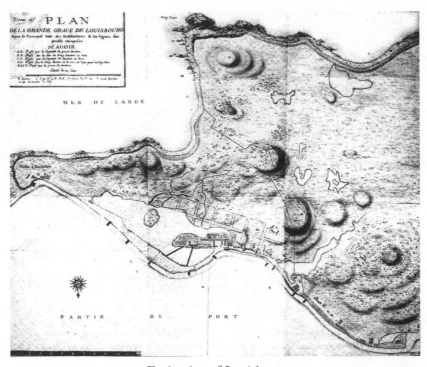

Early plan of Louisbourg

the inhabitants of Cape Breton, the *Hercule* brought the news that their monarch, Louis XIV, had changed the name of their settlement. As Port St. Louis, it carried the name of the patron saint of France, but the aged, egocentric king thought it more appropriate that it carry his name, and the site became Louisbourg.

Just over a year later, on September 1, 1715, the Sun King, Louis XIV, died of gangrene, having been on the throne of France for sixty-seven years. There was no question of who would succeed him but a significant question as to who would rule. The new king, Louis XV, the great-grandson of Louis XIV, was only five years old. In three years, four older heirs with precedence over him had died, and fate had put a child on the throne of France. The will of the late king, which designated his illegitimate son the Duke of Maine to rule as regent, was immediately challenged. Louis's nephew Philippe, the Duke of Orléans, succeeded in persuading the Parliament of Paris to declare the king's will null and void, and he was appointed regent. Within a period of fourteen months, the leadership of France and Great Britain, two of the strongest nations in the world, had changed. While nominally still ruled by their kings, others governed both countries: the regent in France and the Whig ministers in Great Britain.

Despite carrying Louis XIV's name, Louisbourg had been only tentatively designated as the site of the primary settlement on Cape Breton, and there was still discussion as to whether Port Toulouse on the east coast or Port Dauphin on the southwestern would be better. De Rouville and others, including the highly respected French military engineer Jean-François de Verville, made careful studies over a two-year period, weighing the merits and advantages of each site against the others. In 1717, it was finally recommended that Louisbourg would indeed be the best to serve as the commercial, administrative, and military center of Cape Breton. It was closer to the fishing grounds than the other possible sites, and the harbor provided miles of shoreline on which the fishermen could set up their fish-drying flakes. Positioned at the approach to the Cabot Strait, the body of water between Cape Breton and Newfoundland, which gave access to the St. Lawrence River and Canada, Louisbourg would put French naval vessels in the ideal position to defend this critical waterway.

Ships homeward bound for France could simply follow the Gulf Stream up the North American coast and stop in Louisbourg before making the Atlantic crossing, and its position was ideal for sending raiders against the New England fishing fleets and British and American merchant ships that would pass by on their way to Britain. The decision was made. When Governor Costebelle died in 1717, Saint-Ovide replaced him and governed the city rising in the wilderness until 1739. The legendary young privateer Pierre Morpain was appointed port captain for Cape Breton in 1716, and over the next three decades, he oversaw the French government's interests in maritime activities on the island colony.

The people of Louisbourg gained confidence that their community would thrive, as they established their lives and homes on the rugged coast. By the time their new king, Louis XV, turned seven years old, there were over eight hundred residents and soldiers in Louisbourg. The majority came from the abandoned Newfoundland settlements three hundred miles to the east, including three hundred fishermen who established their homes along the southern and western shores of the harbor, separate from the strategic center of the community, which was on the tip of the peninsula, on the southwest side of the harbor entrance. The population swelled as administrators, craftsmen, merchants, and additional soldiers arrived to begin the transformation of the crude colonial outpost into the most formidable fortress in North America and a thriving and sophisticated French community.

While hoping for a period of peace and the prosperity that fishing and trade would bring to Louisbourg, preparations were made for the next war, which they knew was inevitable. The French minister of marine, Count Pontchartrain, who had responsibility for the defense of Cape Breton, argued forcefully for the first military appropriation for Louisbourg, saying, "The English are well aware of the importance of this post, and are already taking umbrage in the matter. They see that it will be prejudicial to the trade, and that in time of war it will be a menace to their shipping, and on the first outbreak of the trouble they will be sure to use every means to get possession of it. It is therefore necessary to fortify it thoroughly. If France were to lose this Island the loss would be an irreparable one, and it would involve the loss of all her holdings in North America." Through the power of these prophetic words, the funding for Fortress Louisbourg began to flow.

In 1717, the engineer Jean-François de Verville sketched the initial concepts for the fortifications of this stronghold. He envisioned a classic European fortress developed from the design concepts of the most celebrated military engineer of the era, Sébastien Le Prestre de Vauban, who had died ten years earlier. Two hillocks, about one thousand feet inland from the tip of the peninsula, would form the foundations for two massive bastions, one honoring the king and the other the queen. Between the King's Bastion and the Queen's Bastion would stretch a thirty-foot-tall masonry wall. This wall would also extend from the King's Bastion north to the edge of the harbor, where it would terminate with a demibastion honoring the dauphin. The wall would extend from the Queen's Bastion southeast to the ocean, where another demibastion honoring the princess would mark the terminus. The naming of these fortifications after members of the royal family was fanciful, since at that time, with the king being only seven years old, there was no queen or dauphin or princess. In front of the wall, a swamp stretched for two miles, creating a formidable natural barrier. The engineers and military strategists theorized that this impassable quagmire would render an attack from the landward side impossible. A complex of defensive embankments and wide, deep ditches in front of the bastions and walls would stall any force foolish enough to attempt to cross the swamp, making them easy targets for the fort's defenders firing from the safe cover of bastions and parapets. Further batteries and fortifications would be built along the side of the city facing the harbor. Behind this impressive array of fortifications, the urban center of Louisbourg would develop on an orderly grid of streets laid out by the engineer.

Because land attack seemed highly improbable, the planners of Louisbourg envisioned an attack by sea as the only way an enemy could seriously threaten the new French stronghold, and de Verville's design called for the protection of the harbor and its entrance by four batteries, equipped with the most powerful cannons. Two of these batteries, the Dauphine Battery and the Battery la Grave, were part of the city itself. The Royal or Grand Battery, supplied with the most powerful cannons and located on the inner shore of the harbor a mile north of the city, could demolish anything afloat within the harbor. The Island Battery facing the narrow entrance to the harbor could fire point-blank at any vessel with the temerity to attempt to enter.

Construction of the fortress began in 1719, but the ambitious project was fraught with difficulties and took twenty-five years to complete. Spring came late and winter arrived early, making for a short construction season. Vast quantities of stone had to be imported from France. Because the Acadians had chosen to remain on their lands in Nova Scotia and there was a lack of a resident labor force, workers also had to be imported. There were great delays in decision making, as instructions came from France, requiring months of transatlantic travel. A profound complication was the divided government the French had established in New France and on Cape Breton. Instead of a single senior official, three powerful administrators, the governor-general, the intendant in Quebec, and the bishop of Quebec, governed New France and were often rivals and at odds. This division of authority, intended to provide a system of checks and balances, made governance inefficient. A similar situation existed on Cape Breton, where, with no appointed religious leader, two officials were charged with the administration of the colony. The governor of Cape Breton had authority over the military, naval, and maritime commerce, and his counterpart, the *commissaire-ordonnateur*, was the civil administrator, in control of the distribution of supplies, maintenance of the king's storehouses, operation of the hospital, and administration of the justice system. Together, the two men made grants of land and maintained order within the colony. This system added frustration and periodic chaos, both on Cape Breton and in France, where the Marine Ministry, which oversaw the colony, would often receive conflicting requests and opinions from the two administrators. It was under this system that the engineer, de Verville, would begin the transformation of his designs from drawings on vellum to actual stone and mortar.

The labor for the massive construction project came from two sources. Two French-based construction firms, first Michel-Philippe Isabeau and later François Ganet, arranged for the immigration of craftsmen with specialized skills as stonemasons, carpenters, and blacksmiths. The enormous undertaking required many laborers to carry out the directions of the engineer and the master craftsmen, but such a force was nonexistent on Cape Breton. To fill this void, the soldiers garrisoned at the fortress were expected to provide the muscle. Most of the troops assigned to New France were part of the Compagnies Franches de la Marine, which provided troops not only for the colonies, but also to guard naval facilities and serve as "marines" aboard naval vessels. For Louisbourg, special companies of men were recruited who wore the uniform of the Compagnies Franches but were not a full part of that organization and were intended for service exclusively in Louisbourg. A captain was assisted by a lieutenant and an ensign, who were in turn supported by several cadets and noncommissioned officers, who led each company of forty-five men. The unique aspect of the assignment to Louisbourg was that these soldiers were expected to work as laborers in the building of the fortress they would defend and were given the incentive of separate wages. This opportunity for extra pay aided in the recruitment of men for these companies. With the workforce in place and the arrival of finished cut stone from France, serious work commenced in 1720. The King's Bastion was to be the centerpiece of the entire complex, a citadel fortified on all sides, containing the most impressive of the king's buildings.

Within the citadel would be found the crowning glory of Louisbourg, the Château St. Louis, a stone building 360 feet long, with a cellar, two full stories, and a spacious attic, all under a steep slate roof. An arched gateway in the central block gave entrance to the parade ground. Above the entrance was the armory, built to contain 850 muskets. Above this, a spire on top of the clock tower and belfry soared to eighty feet in height and could be seen for miles in all directions. This was the longest building in North America at that time. The governor's sumptuous private and public apartments were in the south wing. The King's Chapel, which also served as the parish church for the city, was on the south side of the central block. The north side was intended as apartments for the *commissaire-ordonnateur*, the civil administrator, but no one holding that position ever took up residence there. The north wing contained the barracks for the troops in the garrison. The space between the building and the outer walls was the parade ground. Facing the grid of streets on which the city's buildings would be built was a defensive ramp known as a glacis, which was mounted with sharpened stakes, a moat, and a bascule drawbridge, so if invaders overwhelmed the city, the self-contained citadel could be sealed off and defended as a last stand or until relief arrived.

The next project was the Dauphin Bastion to the northwest. This included the primary land entrance to the city, with stout gates, a drawbridge, and the Dauphin Battery, from which guns could sweep the harbor. As the work continued, the builders became aware that the mortar, made from local limestone and sand, was inferior. Heated in kilns to produce quicklime, the limestone was then mixed with sand to create the mortar, but the sea sand was not adequately leached of its salts and the mortar would not dry properly. The damp weather and winter freezes allowed water to penetrate the stonework, where the resulting ice forced the stones apart and caused serious damage. The workers were constantly repairing what they had built, while still trying to advance with new construction.

With the setbacks, it was clear that more laborers were needed, and additional troops arrived in Louisbourg as the years of construction went on. The first mercenaries, fifty soldiers from what was known as the Regiment de Karrer, arrived in 1727, changing the composition of the troops at Louisbourg significantly. The Swiss colonel François Adam Karrer had signed a contract with Louis XV to provide troops for service in Louisiana, Martinique, Saint-Dominique, and Louisbourg. The majority of the troops in this regiment were Swiss or German, but the ranks included men recruited from other European countries as well. In addition to different nationalities, these troops brought religious diversity to the Catholic community, as most of the Karrer troops were Protestants. Despite periodic points of friction, the foreign troops served well throughout the 1720s and 1730s. They stood guard within the fortress, performed other military duties, and contributed to the construction force. By the 1740s, the Karrer force had tripled to 150 men, which constituted approximately one quarter of the garrison at Louisbourg.

Work on the fortifications continued for twenty-five years. Fearful that the fragile peace would collapse at any time, priority was given to those aspects of the defenses that would give the community the maximum security. In addition to the King's Bastion citadel, construction work focused on the Island Battery controlling the entrance to the harbor and the Grand Battery that dominated the harbor itself. The Island Battery was completed after a decade of work, in 1731, and the massive Grand Battery in 1733. Once these emplacements were fully functioning, the officials felt that the town was protected from its most logical threat, an attack from the sea. During the 1730s, they turned their efforts to completing the network of walls and bastions that would protect the town from an unlikely land attack. The gargantuan task stretched into the 1740s, and the Château St. Louis, the enormous building at the heart of the citadel, was not completed until 1743.

The fortress plan called for the orderly development of the community within the walls, and forty-five blocks were laid out between wide streets, which ran east and west, north and south. The northern limits of the town were defined by the harbor's edge, while the other sides were defined by the fortifications. The waterfront area along the harbor developed as the vibrant center of maritime activities, where cargoes were landed and shipped, merchants negotiated, captains and sailors enjoyed their time ashore, and the inns and taverns did a lively business. At the west end of the waterfront, nearest the town's primary land entrance, the Dauphin Gate, the first large city block housed various official government functions, including the artillery storehouse, the forge, the king's bakery, an expanded armory, and the magnificent king's storehouse. Eventually, large, privately owned commercial warehouses and other maritime structures would face the harbor and facilitate the transfer and storage of goods involved in the flourishing commerce of the community.

Stretching back up the streets from the waterfront, the increasing population built the homes, shops, and businesses that transformed the rough fishing outstation into a thriving and sophisticated entrepôt. The structures varied in form and construction, reflecting the increasingly stratified social order of the community, which resembled the "three estates" of France's ancien régime: the nobility, the clergy, and the people. With its distance from France, however, Cape Breton had a somewhat more flexible social structure, with more opportunities for an ambitious individual to advance in society. At the head of the social order were the governor and the *commissaire-ordonnateur*, whose birthdays were celebrated as civic holidays. Others among the upper level of Louisbourg society were the top government officials, such as the engineer and the port captain, the military officers, some of whom were minor nobles, and the most successful merchants of the community. Most of these people attempted to live the lifestyle of the upper classes in France, dressing in the latest fashions, with fine fabrics, elaborate powdered wigs, and makeup. Their homes were well-furnished and substantial structures of stone or heavy timber-frame construction, with accommodations for their families, servants, and sometimes African or Indian slaves.

The next level of society included the successful entrepreneurs, merchants, fishing proprietors, senior members of the religious orders, and lower-ranking civil administrators, who might aspire to the highest level but did not yet qualify. Their attention to fashion was less than that of the upper class, and their homes, though mostly of timber-frame construction, were less grand. It was relatively easy to advance by business success or marriage, and shopkeepers, tavern owners, small-scale fishing entrepreneurs, minor traders, and merchants could easily move up in Louisbourg society, as could the skilled blacksmiths, cabinet makers, stonemasons, shoemakers, and noncommissioned officers of the garrison troops who shared this class. At the lowest rung of the social ladder were the workers, the soldiers, construction laborers, employees in shops and taverns, servants, slaves, and many of the fishermen.

Most of the fishermen lived in simple homes with garden plots outside the walls of the city along the three miles of harbor shoreline that stretched west from the Dauphin Gate along the most densely populated "suburb," known as the fauxbourg, then northeast to the upper reaches of the harbor. Their homes were usually of piquet construction, which consisted of walls formed by standing small posts upright, side by side in a trench, and then chinking the space between the posts with clay and straw. A coat of lime and mortar sealed the outside with a smooth white surface. The houses were made weather tight by a sod, thatched, or shingled roof. This simple construction style was also found within the walls of the fortress, as homes for the lower classes or utilitarian outbuildings of the more well-to-do.

The appearance of Louisbourg by the early 1730s was that of a prosperous small coastal town in France, with a range of handsome structures dominated by the government buildings built of stone with slate roofs. By 1730, the hospital of the Brothers of Charity, with one hundred beds, a chapel, and other facilities, dominated the center of the city. Diagonally across the street, in the center of the block, was the school of the Sisters of the Congregation of Notre Dame, who arrived in 1727. Despite the presence of three religious orders in the small community, deliberate efforts were made to limit the religious influence on the administration of the town. The bishop of Quebec was far away, and no high-ranking priests were present in Louisbourg, so secular leaders were able to minimize the intrusion of the church in their operations. Because the people worshipped in the King's Chapel of the citadel or the chapel of the hospital, no parish church was ever built. Consequently, the people were spared the tithe tax that was normally imposed to support church activities. There was no religious representation on the Louisbourg Conseil Supérieur, the governor's advisory body, and religion was given a secondary role to defense and commerce.

Trade was supposed to take place only with France and her colonies in the West Indies and New France, but practicality influenced trading patterns. The supply of needed materials from France took great periods of time and was erratic, and residents of Louisbourg were well aware of readily available supplies nearer at hand, in New England and British-controlled Acadia. The French colonists who had stayed on their fertile farms in Acadia when it was ceded to Great Britain found it natural, though technically illegal, to supply food to the settlements of Cape Breton. Farther to the west, enterprising New Englanders saw peacetime as an opportunity to make financial gains by trading with their former enemies. Ignoring the strictures of the Navigation Acts, numerous New England merchants established lively and rewarding trade with Louisbourg, and in some years more than fifty New England vessels traded there. They supplied timber, flour, cloth, and some manufactured goods in exchange for sought-after molasses, indigo, and other French products that arrived in Louisbourg from Martinique and other French ports in the West Indies. The ministers in France wanted to discourage this trade, preferring that the colony be supplied directly from France, but they recognized that the difficulties of this long-distance supply would periodically create shortages that could be remedied by trade with the English colonies. Many in Louisbourg, including Governor Saint-Ovide and Port Captain Morpain, found ways around the government restrictions and enhanced their wealth by trading with the British colonies. The New England traders, captains, and sailors who visited Louisbourg during the 1720s and 1730s were keenly aware of the growing power of this French fortress and the possibility that it could easily become the home port for French privateers and naval vessels should war erupt again. The opportunity of making money through supplying the needs of Louisbourg was too tempting, however, and they were willing to take the risks of illicit trade for the financial benefit.

As the 1740s approached, Louisbourg was reaching its full development. A lighthouse, the first in Canada and only the second in North America, had been built of stone on the promontory opposite the Island Battery and guided ships to the harbor entrance. Within the city, seven of the original forty-five city blocks were eliminated in order to extend the fortifications completely around the community. Dwellings, businesses, and government buildings occupied all of the full blocks within the fortified city, and a thriving economy enabled energetic men and women to support their large families and in many instances gain wealth and social stature. A steady flow of ships during the spring, summer, and fall brought news, fashions, the latest literature and music, and a diverse transient population to this provincial outpost. The success of Louisbourg as an entrepôt gave it a level of sophistication and style that belied its remote location. The French had spent a fortune transforming a barren peninsula into a classically fortified community that could withstand assault, protect a vast harbor and the vessels within it, and dominate the region militarily. They had cleverly used the decades of peace to establish a strong fishery, create a vibrant port, and build an indomitable base for future military operations when war returned.

CHAPTER 11

Fragile Peace and Salutary Neglect in British America

THE PEACE THAT FOLLOWED the Treaty of Utrecht allowed the French in North America to construct the magnificently fortified Louisbourg to both defend the access to the St. Lawrence and act as a base for offensive actions in future wars. For Great Britain's North American colonies, no serious efforts at fortification would be undertaken, and the focus would be on agricultural and commercial development and the prosperity that would bring. Curiously, in their relations with the mother country, the British colonies would experience the identical pattern of the seventeenth century, with the same result: revolution. The seventeenth century was a period of immigration and growth within the colonies, with benign neglect during the early part of the century because England, her Parliament, and her kings were absorbed in issues at home. There was then an awakened interest in the economic potential of the colonies and the imposition of harsh restrictions, which caused animosity among the colonists and ultimately led to the revolution of 1689. In the eighteenth century, Britain's American colonies would expand through immigration, enjoy a degree of autonomy owing to the policy of salutary neglect, and then feel the sting of restrictions, abuse, exploitation, and oppression that would lead, once again, to revolution.

After twenty-five years of war, the coming of peace in 1713 gave

Britain and France an opportunity to refocus their energies and resources. Great Britain's challenge was to reduce her massive national debt and revitalize international commerce. Her new Germanic king, George I, went through a turbulent first six years, as factions within the Whig Party vied for power. The collapse of a scheme through which the South Sea Company would retire the huge national debt incurred during the decades of war brought down the leadership of James Stanhope and Lord Sunderland and brought Robert Walpole to the role of first lord of the Treasury in 1721. In his position at the Treasury, Walpole became the unofficial "prime" minister since that position did not officially exist. Just as the English had been absorbed in the crisis between their monarchs and Parliament in the early decades of the seventeenth century, they were preoccupied by financial disasters in the early decades of the eighteenth. One of the greatest opportunities for economic growth was through trade with the English colonies in America, and Walpole had two options. The first was to clamp down hard on the colonies by enforcing strict adherence to regulations such as the Navigation Acts and imposing additional laws and taxes on the colonies to generate income for the Crown. Considering the rebellion of the colonists when strong-arm tactics had been applied earlier, this seemed like a risky option, and at that time there was no way Britain could muster the military power needed to force the colonies into compliance with onerous regulations. Walpole followed his favorite principle of *quieta non movere*, literally "don't move settled things," but more colloquially "don't rock the boat" or "let sleeping dogs lie." He pursued this better option under a policy of "salutary neglect," which called for lax enforcing of the strictures on the colonies and letting them mature and thrive in an atmosphere of comfort and encouragement, so they would be enthusiastic partners in Britain's success. In the early eighteenth century, there was hope that the English colonies could once again enjoy the liberties and satisfaction of self-government that they had experienced a century before and be a place where opportunity and prosperity would beckon a steady flow of immigrants to stimulate growth and realize the American potential. This policy worked for twenty-five years, and, reflecting back on that period, Edmund Burke in addressing the House of Commons on the subject of reconciliation with the colonies in 1775 said, "When I know that the colonies in general owe little or nothing to any care of ours, and that they are not squeezed into this happy form by the constraints of watchful and suspicious government, but that, through a wise and salutary neglect, a generous nature has been suffered to take her own way to perfection; when I reflect upon these effects, when I see how profitable they have been to us, I feel all the pride of power sink, and all presumption in the wisdom of human contrivances melt, and die away within me." Burke clearly saw that the application of regulations had undermined the beneficial prosperity that had developed in the earlier period.

Circumstances for the lower classes in England had changed since the seventeenth century, however, and the issues that prompted English families to take risks in the New World were no longer strong incentives. After decades of immigration and war, the population crisis had eased, agriculture flourished and produced more jobs as well as food, and life was more comfortable. People were needed in the expanding manufacturing trades, as well as the army and navy required to protect the growing empire. As the immigration of English settlers to America diminished, the colonies encouraged the immigration of new groups. One new source was the Scots, who were able to immigrate to the English colonies with full rights as citizens as a result of the union of Scotland and England in 1707. Highlanders, Lowland Scots, and even the Ulster Scots, who had fled hardships in Scotland for opportunity in Ireland, became a significant part of the growth of American colonies, particularly in the Carolinas, Pennsylvania, and the Mohawk Valley of New York.

Another source of fresh energy and manpower for colonial expansion was the region of the Rhine, where some of the same incentives for the English immigration in the seventeenth century, limited opportunity and religious persecution, motivated people from the numerous German principalities to seek a better life. Some Germans had settled in Pennsylvania in the 1680s, and when stories of their success reached family members and friends, the lure increased. From the late 1720s, there was a steady flow of Germans making their way across the Atlantic and settling primarily in Pennsylvania, where they found others who spoke their language and perpetuated their customs. Many of the Germans could not afford the cost of their passage, so they entered into indentured servitude, a difficult but honorable arrangement through which an individual would work for a prescribed number of years, normally seven, to repay the cost of the trip to the New World, after which they would be "free." The work was often hard field labor, and there was some abuse of these workers serving in bondage. A more humane form of indenture was developed by Germans going to Pennsylvania, which enabled entire families to immigrate and be indentured together without fear of separation and ultimately be released from their servitude. During the first half of the eighteenth century, the population of Pennsylvania grew fivefold to 120,000, the bulk of this growth coming from these new immigrants.

Ownership of land and political rights were reserved for English citizens, and the disenfranchised foreign immigrants chafed under these limitations. When the issue threatened to cut off the flow of immigrants needed for colonial growth, a perceptive Parliament passed the Plantation Act in 1740 and provided a path to citizenship. After seven years of residence, a communicant of any Protestant sect who paid a small fee and swore allegiance to the king of England could become a citizen. This opened the door for great opportunity, and the flow of needed immigrants continued.

While voluntary immigration increased in the early eighteenth century, two forms of forced immigration added to the mélange of the population developing in America. One group was English criminals. After the end of Queen Anne's War, thousands of soldiers were demobilized. The flooded job market offered no employment for these war-hardened men, and many turned to crime to survive. At that time in England there were 160 offenses for which a death sentence could be awarded. The crime wave that followed the military demobilization crowded jails and created a crisis for the government, which faced a potential bloodbath of executions. The novel solution was to equate a period of servitude in the colonies to the death penalty and transport prisoners across the Atlantic. Often the term of this forced indenture was long, lasting more than a decade, and the work and treatment especially hard. The majority of the convicts were taken to the Chesapeake region, where they served their time as virtual slaves at hard labor in the tobacco fields. Broken by their work and unskilled, most convicts failed to make successful lives after their indentured servitude was completed. There were exceptions such as Anthony Lamb, who had been an apprentice instrument maker in England prior to his involvement in a robbery. Instead of the death penalty, he was sentenced to a six-year indenture in Virginia, after which Lamb made his way to New York, where he became one of the early American instrument makers. Such success was rare, and the great majority of released convicts became a permanent underclass.

The other group of forced immigrants, by far the largest, was Africans wrenched from their homes and transported across the Atlantic for lives of servitude. Their prospect was far grimmer than that of the convicts, and in most cases, the slavery of the Africans was a life sentence. The preponderance of Africans who made the Middle Passage in the eighteenth century were sold into servitude in the West Indies, but about 20 percent were carried to the English colonies in North America, where the majority labored in the tobacco and rice plantations from Maryland to the Carolinas, although every colony permitted slavery. In the southern colonies, a plantation usually had a number of slaves, and some degree of identity and community could be sustained amid the brutality. In the northern colonies, most slaves were found in the growing cities, where they worked as servants and laborers. There they were fewer in number, more isolated, and more alone. The slaves were part of the growth of America in the first half of the eighteenth century and reluctant but significant contributors to the emerging American character.

With slavery firmly established in the southern colonies, a curious experiment attempted to break the pattern in the early 1730s. James Oglethorpe proposed a new colony, to be located between the Carolinas and the Spanish colony of Florida. It was to be a utopian environment where large plantations, rum, lawyers, and slavery were prohibited and where poor English Protestants could find opportunity and a new life growing valuable crops on small farms. Despite the financial assistance of well-meaning supporters, including Robert Walpole, the noble scheme unraveled very quickly. Many of the first one hundred settlers died of disease, and the survivors, and those who followed, could not be coerced to work for the common good. Responding to the unrest of the early settlers, Oglethorpe lifted the prohibitions on large landholdings, rum, and lawyers during the first decade of colonization, but he held fast on the issue of slavery. In 1739, he wrote, "If we allow Slaves, we act

against the very Principles by which we associated together, which was
to relieve the distressed." The landowners responded angrily by saying
that through the prohibition on slaveholding, Oglethorpe had protected
the landowners from themselves and forced a life of hardship and limited financial success. Clearly, the formerly disadvantaged Englishmen
and their families, who had been provided with their transportation,
basic tools and equipment, and provisions for a year upon arrival, perceived that the good life that others in the colonies to the north enjoyed
required the ownership of slaves. Within a few years, the experiment
was given up, slavery was introduced in 1751, and Georgia became the
last British Crown colony on the eastern seaboard of North America.

Internationally, the establishment of the new British colony between the Carolinas and Spanish Florida created new strain between
Great Britain and Spain, as both nations claimed the land. For those
on the "front lines" there were tense, armed confrontations, but hostilities were avoided when Oglethorpe met with the Spanish representative, Captain Don Pedro Lamberto, under luxuriant tents on
Jekyll Island in 1736. With diplomatic courtesies, the two men negotiated and, as Oglethorpe reported to the Georgia trustees, Don Pedro
preferred to leave the determination of boundaries to the royal courts
in Europe. For the moment, the southern frontier remained peaceful.

As the first waves of the post-Utrecht immigration began, some
coming to the most populated colony, Massachusetts, sought to capitalize on the new peace and settle in Maine and the Acadian lands beyond
the Kennebec River that the New Englanders felt had been ceded to
Great Britain through the treaty. The newcomers headed to this northeastern frontier, where they found a region seething with tension, as
the French and Abenakis disputed the land claims. To achieve a settlement at Utrecht, the definition of Acadia had been left vague when it
became clear that if France and Britain attempted to argue out the
boundaries, the entire agreement would unravel and the nations would
be once again at war. Neither country wanted or could afford a renewed
large-scale conflict, so they left the ambiguities and created an unstable
and potentially volatile situation along the northern frontier. The New
Englanders pushed east of the Kennebec River and built small forts to
assert their claims. The Abenakis, despite having signed a peace agreement with Governor Dudley, felt this expansion was a violation of their

Colonel James Oglethorpe

territory. Taking advantage of this friction, the governor of New France, Vaudreuil, enlisted the aid of French Jesuit missionaries among the Abenakis to foment small-scale warfare. The most active of these Jesuits was Father Sébastien Rale, who at the age of thirty-seven in 1694 had founded a mission for the Abenakis at Norridgewock on the Kennebec, sixty miles inland from the coast. Rale's appetite for war and his influence over the natives were exhibited early on when he informed Governor Vaudreuil that his Indians would be "ready to take up the hatchet against the English whenever he [Vaudreuil] gave them the order." The governor accepted the offer, and the Abenakis participated in the August 10, 1703, raids on Wells and other Maine settlements, igniting the hostilities of Queen Anne's War.

In the aftermath of that war, Father Rale saw it as his duty not only to minister to his Abenakis, but to inspire their resistance to New England expansion. The tensions on the Maine frontier were growing in violence. In 1717, Governor Samuel Shute, who had replaced Dudley

as the Massachusetts governor, called a meeting of the Abenakis on
Arrowsic Island on the Maine coast at the mouth of the Kennebec
River. He seemed to have been successful in convincing the Abenakis
to allow English settlers into the region; however, behind the scenes,
Rale was still at work fomenting trouble. From correspondence between Vaudreuil and the French government in 1720, it is clear that
the government was giving orders to arm the Indians and have them
act as surrogates for the French. The conflict widened as deaths resulted from Indian raids, and in January 1722, the frustrated Governor Shute sent a force of one hundred men under Colonel Thomas
Westbrook to attack Norridgewock and capture the troublemaker
Rale. The missionary was alerted and fled to safety, but Rale's church
and the village, which was almost empty because most of the Indians
were off hunting, were ransacked. As Governor Shute pondered how
to deal with the escalating crisis, Rale's Abenakis took their revenge
for the January attack by launching their own attack on Brunswick
and the Merrymeeting Bay area of Maine. The cycle of attack and revenge had begun once again, and New England was at war.

This time, however, the war would not be nation against nation,
but a localized conflict that began when Governor Shute declared
war on the Abenakis on July 25, 1722. It quickly became apparent
that the old animosities between the elected, representative assembly
of Massachusetts and the royally appointed governor would complicate this war. The assembly had stymied Shute's earlier attempts to
placate the Abenakis with gifts and inexpensive goods to be sold at
trading posts. With the declaration of war, the assembly sought to
control the prosecution of the war, which brought them into direct
conflict with Shute. In frustration, the governor, with virtually no notice, left Boston to take his complaints to London, and the governance
of the colony fell to Lieutenant Governor William Dummer, and the
war became Dummer's War. As a native New Englander, Dummer
had a slight advantage over Shute, but his earlier support of the governor put him at odds with the assembly, and in a confrontation Dummer had to yield since the assembly controlled the finances. While this
manifestation of colonial resistance to royal authority played out, the
Indians' hit-and-run raids that had characterized early wars plagued
the frontier.

The inaction of the Massachusetts authorities in early 1723 emboldened the Indians, and the conflict began to spread. A Penobscot Indian attack on the fort at St. George in eastern Maine, led by the Jesuit Father Lauverjat, was repulsed. Far to the east, the Micmacs in Nova Scotia attacked the English fishing community at Canso, just across the narrow strait from Cape Breton; and to the west, Indians near Rutland killed the Protestant minister Joseph Willard. Finally, in the fall, the New Englanders went on the offensive, with Colonel Westbrook leading a force of 230 men against the Penobscots. They achieved little, however, and were able only to burn Lauverjat's home and church and the nearby Penobscot village when they found them deserted. By the following year, 1724, the supremely patient Dummer had won the confidence of the assembly, and an attack was planned that was intended to decapitate the French-inspired Indian resistance. Over two hundred men moved against Norridgewock and the incendiary Rale. The attack was accomplished with complete surprise: "The *Indians* were under amazing Terror . . . They immediately betook themselves to flight, and in running fell on the very muzzles of our Guns that lay in Ambush." The Indian settlement was easily overrun, and more than eighty were killed in the fight or drowned trying to escape. With the scalp bounty in place, Penhallow reports: "The number of the dead which we scaplt, were twenty six, besides Mounsieur *Ralle* the *Jesuit*, who was a Bloody Incendiary, and Instrumental to most of the Mischiefs that were done us." While it had been the intention to capture Rale alive, he fought the New Englanders and was killed by Lieutenant Benjamin Jacques and later scalped.

While the attack at Norridgewock was a tactical success, it failed in the strategic objective of demoralizing the native opposition. On the contrary, Rale's death was seen as martyrdom by the French and the Catholic Indians, and Vaudreuil capitalized on the moment to broaden the war to include the western Massachusetts frontier. Lieutenant Governor Dummer accused Vaudreuil of being the instigator, through his agent Rale, of the war between the New Englanders and the Abenakis. When the French governor denied the charge, Dummer, basing his response on letters to Rale that had been captured at Norridgewock, laid out the evidence that Father Rale was as much a military leader and incendiary as he was a religious leader. Dummer then sought to neutralize the criticism of the killing of Rale by pointing out the recent killing of a minister in Rutland, then part of New Hampshire, who had no military affiliations and whose scalp had been taken in triumph to Quebec.

As raids along the frontier continued, the British government failed to confront the French with the complex issue of their culpability. The French wisely declined to officially protest the death of Rale, and the British, conscious of the resistance Shute had experienced from the Massachusetts Assembly, turned a blind eye to the conflict in New England and the strain on those colonies. Once again, the New Englanders were left to cope, without the support of the mother country. Early in 1725, several expeditions, led by Captain John Lovewell, moved into northern New Hampshire to avenge an Indian attack on Dunstable, Massachusetts, a village on the New Hampshire border. After two somewhat successful incursions, Lovewell organized a third foray. The New Englanders encountered a large, fierce band of Pigwacket Indians led by their chief, Paugus, near the shore of what would become known as Lovewell's Pond. The bloody encounter lasted a full day and took a heavy toll on both sides, with both Lovewell and Paugus killed. At night, both sides retreated and the New Englanders straggled back to Dunstable. The futility of this battle, indecisive and costly to both the New Englanders and the Indians, was symbolic of the entire frustrating war. The following year, the Abenakis initiated a peace conference with Dummer, and after three years of strife, a treaty was signed in Boston. Peace had finally returned to New England. The French with their peace-loving chief minister, Cardinal de Fleury, and the British with their equally peace-minded first minister, Robert Walpole, had kept their distance during this period of intercolonial strife, and their policies prevented the localized warfare from spreading throughout the colonies and across the sea.

By this time, Robert Walpole had been first lord for four years, and his choice for secretary of state for the Southern Department (which included the American colonies), Thomas Pelham-Holles, Duke of Newcastle, had been in office for a year. The policy of salutary neglect pursued by these two officials allowed the colonies to steer their own course for the next fifteen years, during which the reasoning that minimal intrusion into colonial affairs would provide the best chance for colonial and British economic success began to pay dividends. The ports of New York and Philadelphia prospered as the rich lands surrounding those centers produced abundant crops. With the growth of the population, the flourishing of urban areas, increased commerce, and related financial success, the colonists were becoming consumers of more luxurious British goods rather than the basics of their earlier subsistence lifestyle.

NEW ENGLAND WAS still the most densely populated region of the country in 1730, but the middle Atlantic colonies from New York to Pennsylvania were fast nearing the population of New England, and those from Maryland to the south had already exceeded it, primarily through the rapid growth of slaveholdings. The colonies were on a positive economic path, but one of the first and leading cities was experiencing difficulties. Boston had endured the crisis over its rejection of Governor Shute, who never returned to Massachusetts after his departure at the beginning of Dummer's War. They had continued their resistance when the new king, George II, appointed William Burnet as governor in 1727. The resistance focused on the governor's salary, which was controlled by the Massachusetts General Court. To demonstrate their authority, the salary was made on a year-by-year basis rather than being set permanently, as the governor sought. The message from the governing general court was clearly, "Behave yourself or we will cut your income." In addition to this continued political tension, the region experienced a blight on its wheat crop, necessitating the importation of wheat from the middle colonies, and Parliament repealed its subsidy on "naval stores," including timber and pine tar, which severely impacted Boston's previously profitable timber trade and associated industries. To add to the difficulties, there were smallpox outbreaks in 1721 and 1730, which killed almost two thousand people. During these outbreaks, ships avoided Boston and found new and profitable harbors in the region and in other colonies. Boston's growth was stunted. The population of Boston in 1730 was sixteen thousand, and it would remain at this level throughout the remainder of the colonial period as rival cities to the south grew and expanded.

When Parliament became aware that large quantities of molasses were being imported directly into the colonies from sources other than the British sugar islands in the West Indies, the policy of salutary neglect was suspended and a new Navigation Act imposed. Distillers throughout the colonies used molasses to make rum, which was consumed at the astonishing rate of four gallons a year for every man, woman, and child in the colonies. Assuming that the consumption by females and children was substantially less that of men, it was clearly an important aspect of life for the men in the colonies. Distilleries exported over one million gallons per year in addition to local consumption, so the commodity had a serious impact on the balance of trade. To force the colonial distillers to give up their inexpensive Spanish, French, and Dutch molasses and purchase the British variety, a huge tariff was imposed on foreign molasses through the Molasses Act of 1733. In Boston, where there were twelve distilleries, the impact rippled through the economy, affecting the distillers, the taverns, the shipping industry, and the trades that supported them. Suffering economically from these setbacks, the creative Boston merchants turned to their traditional practices of subterfuge and smuggling to avoid the burdens of the Navigation and Molasses Acts, putting them in conflict with Britain once again.

One of the avenues for this subterfuge was trade with Louisbourg. From the earliest days of settlement on Cape Breton, the merchants of Boston and other New England ports saw trade with the isolated French outpost as an opportunity and a way to offset other losses. With resupply from France difficult, the New Englanders found a ready market for timber, livestock, and produce. The first settlers and soldiers had reached Louisbourg in 1713, and the following year, no less a figure than the king's lieutenant and future governor Saint-Ovide purchased the complete cargoes of four New England merchant ships. Soon there was a steady flow of goods and materials carried by New England ships east to Cape Breton. In addition to the food, livestock, and construction materials being sold in Louisbourg, the New England ships themselves were available and were frequently purchased. Those ships that did make the return voyage carried molasses, rum, indigo, contraband French-made goods, and coal from the mines of Cape Breton.

There were English officials like the governor of Nova Scotia, Samuel Vetch, and his successor, Francis Nicholson, who recognized this commerce as aiding and abetting the French in their development of Cape Breton. In response, the government in Massachusetts passed tepid, ineffectual restrictions, but the trade continued. In the early 1720s, Governor Shute attempted to force stronger legislation through the Massachusetts government, but their resistance to him was so blatant that the Massachusetts House of Representatives refused to act on his bill on the absurd premise that they knew of no one trading with Cape Breton. Throughout the 1720s, the trade continued despite nominal efforts on the part of the British and French governments to limit or eliminate the trade. The French government wanted the benefits of trade with Louisbourg to accrue to the merchants of Nantes, La Rochelle, Bayonne, Saint-Jean-de-Luz, and other French ports and issued edicts in 1717 and 1728 to control the trade. However, they had to face the reality that the colony might not survive if it couldn't acquire urgently needed items from nearby New England. The French king had opened a loophole in 1722 by allowing trade in livestock, lumber, and other items when there was a pressing and indispensable need, and the traders on both sides took full advantage of this throughout the period. By this time, Saint-Ovide was governor and he was clearly involved in and a defender of the trade with New England. French merchants, who perceived that they were losing business to the illicit trade, registered numerous complaints against the governor, but the trade continued.

The New Englanders developed some creative and complex procedures to avoid the appearance of violating the Navigation Acts. Ships were sent on triangular voyages between New England, Louisbourg, and the French West Indies, with New England and French captains alternating for the different legs of the voyage. Through this ruse, the New Englanders sought to bring contraband goods past the Crown's customs officers without question. In many instances, trade was carried on quite openly, with customs officials like John Jekyll in Boston advising the merchants on how to circumvent the law. As New England and Boston in particular felt the hardship of economic decline and the sting of the Molasses Act of 1733, there was an acceleration of trade with Louisbourg. Fewer than a dozen ships traded there each year in the early 1730s. That commerce increased to thirty-two ships in 1733, and for the next decade, there was an average of fifty New England ships per year trading with the French fortress. The most prominent merchants in Massachusetts were significant participants in this trade. The William Pepperrells, father and son, were from Kittery, Maine, but they conducted much of their business through Boston. They had been active in trade with Louisbourg as early as 1721, not only trading with Cape Breton, but sending ships through Louisbourg to the French islands of the West Indies and to France herself. Peter Faneuil, another famous Boston merchant of the time, had such an extensive Cape Breton trade that he set up an agent in Canso, just across the narrow strait from Cape Breton. The agent could move easily between Canso and the Cape Breton communities of Port Toulouse and Louisbourg to conduct Faneuil's business. There was no question that the products Faneuil traded for were contraband: sugar, molasses, rum, sweetmeats, cotton cloth, cocoa, wine, brandy, and silk. These were precisely the products that were supposed to pass through Britain and be taxed before arriving in New England, but Faneuil's trade continued and grew in the 1730s. In correspondence with Governor Saint-Ovide, Faneuil learned of severe shortages at Louisbourg in 1737 and recognized a choice opportunity to acquire rare commodities and make a fine profit. He invited Peter Warren, a rising Royal Navy officer and ambitious and astute businessman stationed in Boston, to partner with him in a venture. Six years earlier, Warren had married Susannah DeLancey, of a prominent Huguenot family in New York. With his strong credentials and his marital ties to the colonies, Faneuil was pleased to involve him in the project. To meet Saint-Ovide's food needs, Faneuil and Warren sent a ship loaded with food to Louisbourg. In exchange, they wanted cash, molasses, and rum—not just any rum, but "Cape François" rum, which could be acquired only from the former privateer and Louisbourg port captain Pierre Morpain. The trade turned out to be a very successful venture for Faneuil and Warren.

The irony of this trade was that the shortsighted and pragmatic New Englanders, as they transported tons of timber and building materials to Louisbourg over three decades, were supplying the material to build the massive fortress they would have to besiege in the near future. Even more ironic was the fact that the New England merchant William Pepperrell and the British naval officer Peter Warren would lead the forces besieging Louisbourg, the city they helped to build and supply, while Pierre Morpain would lead the defense of the French city.

During the 1730s, while commercial trade with Cape Breton was thriving, there was another trade being practiced in the colonies that would help prepare the colonists for a trying period ahead. The practitioners of this trade were evangelical ministers who would revive the Protestant religion and heighten the awareness of the threat posed by Catholicism as practiced by the Spaniards to the south and the French in Canada to the north and Louisiana to the west. As the colonies matured and the strain of rugged life in the wilderness evolved into a more comfortable life in the growing cities and on successful farms and plantations, the vitality of colonial Protestantism faded. There were periodic evangelical revivals, such as those conducted by Reverend Solomon Stoddard of Northampton, Massachusetts, during his sixty years on the pulpit, but they were local events. Reverend Jonathan Edwards took the spirit and fervor of his grandfather Stoddard's revivals and ignited a movement that swept through the colonies, from Georgia to Maine, known as the First Great Awakening. When the movement lost some momentum in the mid-1730s, Edwards put pen to paper and wrote *A Faithful Narrative of the Surprizing Work of God*, which when published in Boston and London became an immediate sensation that inspired many revivals.

One person who read and responded to *A Faithful Narrative* was a young charismatic Anglican minister in England, George Whitefield. He first took his mission to the poor working people of England and Wales who were often left out of the traditional Anglican service. With his natural sense of the theatrical, he drew crowds too large for churches and halls. Though small in stature, he had a bold voice that carried to vast crowds at outdoor services and converted thousands. Whitefield's brilliant success at home prompted him to take his ministry to America, where he began his sensational tour in the newest colony, Georgia. For two years, from 1739 to 1741, he traveled throughout the colonies, preaching his message of salvation with a drama that enraptured his audiences and won many friends, among them

Philadelphia printer and publisher Benjamin Franklin. Publishing Whitefield's simple, clear tracts was a way for Franklin to increase his income, but the messages found their way to thousands of readers, and the energy and vitality of the Protestant faith in America was revived. This renewed faith would help motivate the colonists when they were called upon to face the Catholic Spanish and French on the battle-fields in the years ahead.

During the twenty-five years that followed the Treaty of Utrecht, the French took advantage of the era of peace to prepare for the next war. They continued their close relationship with the Indians of northern New England and used their influence to foment trouble be-tween the Indians and the New Englanders whenever possible. They pushed west into the Great Lakes and established outposts down the Mississippi. They worked to develop their colony of Louisiana, which when linked to French Canada in the north encircled and inhibited the expansion of English colonies. During the same period, the En-glish government, seeking peace and nonconfrontation with both the French and their own colonies, followed the policy of salutary neglect. No American cities were fortified like Louisbourg, and the mercantile orientation of the British government and in its American colonies put the focus on immediate prosperity. As the 1730s came to a close, that mercantile focus was about to bring Britain into a war with Spain that would inflict pain and suffering on every British colony in North America.

CHAPTER 12

Captain Jenkins's Ear

I
T IS DIFFICULT TO comprehend that Captain Robert Jenkins's ear, or more precisely the loss of it, could initiate a decade-long conflict that would spread around the globe—from Madras in the East Indies to Cuba in the West Indies, from the Netherlands to Florida, from Cartagena in South America to Louisbourg in North America—but that was indeed the case. Driven by arrogance, overconfidence, and greed, the war faction in Great Britain's Whig Party convinced Robert Walpole and Parliament to enter a war of choice. They envisioned that their enemy would flee at the sight of English might, or at least submit after token resistance, but this was a terrible miscalculation that cost thousands of English and American lives.

After several decades of peace under the agile political leadership of Robert Walpole, there was a faction in his Whig Party that felt England's commercial and imperialistic goals could be advanced through war with Spain. They knew that a direct attack on the Iberian Peninsula would bring France to the aid of her Catholic neighbor and present a formidable challenge to British naval and military forces. The Spanish holdings in the West Indies were another matter, however, and it was felt that if Britain had a sound reason to go to war with Spain, and confined hostilities to Spanish holdings across the Atlantic, France would not enter into the fray. For over two hundred years, Spain's colonies in the West Indies and South America had supplied a

143

steady flow of riches, and the wealth of these colonies and the opportunities for commerce with them were a tempting prize that awaited
those bold enough to seize them. For more than a decade, British merchants had been fuming over the high-handed and rough treatment
they, their ships, and their sailors had received from the Spanish, who
sought to protect their trade monopoly within their colonies. The root
of this friction lay in the *asiento*, the provision of the 1713 Treaty of
Utrecht that gave Britain a thirty-year monopoly on the importation
of African slaves into Spanish colonies and permitted the South Sea
Company to send one ship each year to sell British products directly to
the Spanish colonies. As the years passed, other British merchants and
mariners attempted to penetrate that protected trade and gain access
to the lucrative market. Captain Robert Jenkins was one of those.

Jenkins and a number of other British merchant captains conducted
illicit trade with the Spanish colonies by either bribing Spanish colonial officials or smuggling outright. To establish nominal control over
the illicit trade, both the British and the Spanish governments agreed
that their ships could be stopped and inspected if suspected of conducting illegal trade. The Guarda-Costa efficiently and sometimes brutally
carried out this task on behalf of Spain, and in the early 1730s, twenty-
five British ships were taken in five years. The Spanish dealt violently
with English mariners caught in the contraband trade, and in 1731, the
captain of the *Rebecca*, Robert Jenkins, was accused of smuggling contraband goods and the Guarda-Costa meted out summary justice by
separating Jenkins from his ear. This event received little notice in
Great Britain at the time, but as the decade proceeded and 1737
brought the seizure of eleven British ships, British indignation soared,
fueled by the press, the merchants, and the Whig war faction led by
William Pitt. Suddenly the insult to Jenkins years earlier had new rel-
evance. Conveniently, he had preserved his severed ear, and in the fall
of 1738, Robert Jenkins made a sensational appearance in Parliament.
In relating the humiliating experience in the *Rebecca* seven years earlier, he described his ordeal at the hands of the Guarda-Costa's captain
Fandino. Jenkins then brought forth his pickled ear and said, "Gentlemen, after mangling me in this manner they threatened to put me to
death. I expected it, and recommended my soul to God, but the revenge
of my cause to my country."

A frenzy of nationalistic pride ensued, with calls to avenge this and other abuses, and momentum built behind Pitt and his desire for war with Spain. Walpole, however, continued to work for peace, and through his ambassador to Spain, Sir Benjamin Keene, an agreement was worked out to resolve a number of issues between the two countries. The Convention of Pardo called for Spain to pay Great Britain £95,000 in compensation for Spanish excesses, and it briefly appeared that war had been averted. When Spain refused to pay until her counterclaim for £68,000 in back payments owed by the South Sea Company was made, all of Walpole's efforts to retain peace proved futile and events spiraled out of his control. In mid-May 1739, the *asiento* was suspended, and a month later, King George II authorized privateering against Spanish shipping. On October 23, 1739, war was formally declared, and throughout the country the news was greeted with celebrations and the pealing of bells. The people of Britain had been keenly following the debate and were aware of the insults their nation had endured. They were ready to avenge the abuse their mariners had experienced, and after decades of peace, the War of Jenkins's Ear began.

Across the Atlantic, equal attention had been paid to the escalating tensions with Spain. When privateering was authorized in June 1739, the colonists were quick to respond. Even before the formal declaration of war, they mobilized their maritime resources: ships, shipyards, and sailors. The colonial governors granted "commissions of marque and reprisal" so that individuals and syndicates of private citizens could fit out, arm, and man small warships and send them to sea to capture Spanish vessels and harass Spanish settlements. In addition, colonies sent their government-owned vessels, such as the Massachusetts *Province Galley* under the command of Captain Edward Tyng, to defend the colonies against Spanish retaliation. The Tyng family had been active in the battles with the French and Indians, and now Captain Tyng would "defend" the colonies through swift "offensive" action. During the last four months of 1739, the colonies sent sixteen privateers, manned by over one thousand sailors, in pursuit of the Spanish.

While privateers began taking their toll on Spanish commerce, colonies like tiny Rhode Island were enhancing the navies. Within a few months of the declaration of war, the General Assembly of Rhode Island voted to build a new vessel for the defense of the colony. The keel for this 115-ton brig was laid on March 26, 1740, and in a remarkable thirty-six working days, the *Tartar* was launched. She carried twelve carriage guns and an equal number of swivel guns mounted on her bulwarks. The governor, Richard Ward, clearly saw her dual role as a defender of the colony and "a privateer able to fight a hundred men on her deck and ready for all emergencies." *Tartar* would join thirty-two other colonial warships in prosecuting the war at sea during 1740. These ships would make a significant contribution to the war effort.

By the time the War of Jenkins's Ear was declared, Great Britain had naval assets in place to swiftly bring the war to Spanish holdings in the Americas. Earlier, a brash, ambitious Royal Navy captain bragged that with six ships he could capture the well-fortified city of Porto Bello on the east coast of Panama. This was a tempting target not only because of its commerce, but because it was a base from which the detested Guarda-Costa operated. Captain Edward Vernon was tapped to make good on his boast, and in July he was promoted to vice admiral and sent to the West Indies with eight ships under his command. While he waited in Jamaica for confirmation that a state of war existed with Spain, he took fresh supplies and 240 infantrymen aboard. When he received the authority to move against the Spanish, he detached two of his ships for other duties, so he could attempt to live up to his prediction that Porto Bello could be taken by only six ships. In his flagship, HMS *Burford*, Vernon set off for Porto Bello with his remaining five ships. His orders required only that he attack and burn the ships in Spanish ports like Porto Bello, but Vernon thought he could do more, and at dawn on November 21, his ships boldly entered the heavily fortified harbor of Porto Bello, where the one hundred cannons of Fort San Filipe loomed on the port side of the harbor entrance. The British ships fired furiously at the fort and the secondary battery below, while sailors and marines landed to capture the battered fortress. Under the powerful naval cannonade, the defenders fled the fort two hours after the attack began.

While they had been primarily engaged in the attack on Fort San Felipe, the British fleet was also under fire from the Castillo Santiago,

Vice Admiral Edward Vernon

another fort on the opposite shore and deeper in the harbor. With San Felipe under the British flag, full attention was given to Castillo Santiago. All through the day the battle raged, as British cannonballs smashed into the fort and some carried past it, into the town and the governor's residence. As night fell, the bombardment ceased and Vernon prepared to resume the assault in the morning. His audacity and force made that unnecessary as a white flag appeared above Castillo Santiago at dawn, and later that day, the governor and head of the Guarda-Costa surrendered the city. News of this first great victory in the War of Jenkins's Ear raced back to England and the American colonies, and Vice Admiral Vernon became an instant hero. Poems and tributes appeared in the press, and medals were struck to commemorate the glorious event. Vernon had demonstrated what had been widely touted, that the Spanish were no match for British might and would flee or quickly surrender.

On the North American mainland, Georgia, the newest English colony, bordered directly on the Spanish colony of Florida, providing an obvious point for conflict to erupt. British authority rested in the founder of the colony, Colonel James Oglethorpe, an inexperienced military man and member of Parliament who was eager to take the offensive. Even before the declaration of war, Oglethorpe gathered a force of Scottish rangers from his regiment augmented by friendly Creek, Chickasaw, and Yuchi Indians and set off to avenge the death, at the hands of the Spanish, of two unarmed Georgia colonists. The force headed up the St. John River, where they encountered much the same experience Vernon had in Porto Bello. Oglethorpe's force found little resistance from the Spanish as they fled from their remote outposts and two small Spanish forts less than twenty miles from St. Augustine. As tempting as it was to press on with an assault on St. Augustine, Oglethorpe knew that he needed a more substantial force and the assistance of the Royal Navy to accomplish that goal. During the spring of 1740, with the temporary rank of general, he assembled a force of Georgians and Carolinians, and while the Royal Navy blockaded access to the St. John River, Oglethorpe's troops advanced on the Spanish fort at St. Augustine. His plan called for his force to attack from the north, while men and artillery from the British offshore fleet crossed the shallow bar and approached the city from the east. Unfortunately for the British-led force, the shallow water kept the naval vessels beyond the effective range of their guns, and the clever Spanish succeeded in positioning heavily armed shallow-draft vessels inboard of the bar to prevent the landing of troops. With that aspect of his plan foiled, Oglethorpe then sent a patrol of 135 soldiers and Indians to harass and distract the Spanish. Overconfident, these troops made the mistake of sleeping in a battered former Spanish stronghold, Fort Moosa, without keeping sentinels on watch. On the night of June 14, the Spanish sent a raiding party silently out of the city, and taken by surprise, Oglethorpe's patrol was slaughtered. At least seventy-two men were killed and many others captured.

The British forces realized that they faced a more formidable and courageous foe than they had anticipated. To their further discouragement, a week after the massacre, they learned that seven small Spanish ships had eluded the Royal Navy blockade and resupplied the city, enabling St. Augustine to hold out indefinitely. Confronting the futility of his situation, the disgusted Oglethorpe raised the siege and his disheartened force made their way home. For the colonists drafted into the failed expedition, there was resentment that the Royal Navy had been unable to participate in the initial plan and had failed to completely blockade the city. There was also friction between the colonial soldiers and Oglethorpe's British Regiment. In truth, it was Oglethorpe's poor planning and incompetence that resulted in the failure. On the eve of a major escalation of war, the British authorities had to balance the triumph of Vernon at Porto Bello against the failure of the colonial and British forces under Oglethorpe at St. Augustine as they considered the future of the war. The war planners in Great Britain had long felt the necessity to use colonial troops in the war against Spain. In fact, the war was "sold" to Parliament on the premise that a substantial colonial force would be raised to augment the British troops who would be sent from England to fight in the West Indies and in Spain's holdings in Central America and northern South America. Encouraged by Vernon's victory at Porto Bello and enticed by the potential for rich plunder from Spanish cities, Britain's North American colonies responded to the call to form an "American Regiment."

The term *American* had been used casually before this time, often in reference to "British Americans," but this reference to an American Regiment was the first broad recognition of the distinct breed that had developed along the east coast of North America. When official news of the war reached the Americans in the fall of 1739, they echoed the enthusiasm of the British with ceremonies and celebrations. In Boston, the militia formed up on King Street, where they had assembled in 1689 in the midst of revolution, but this time it was to hear the official declaration of war. The troops and citizens of Boston listened intently as the declaration was read from the council chamber balcony of the New Town House, the handsome brick structure that replaced the wooden building destroyed in the fire of 1711. In Boston and throughout the colonies, the news was greeted with cheers, the firing of cannons and muskets, bonfires, and many toasts made with the beer and rum that was liberally distributed.

It was curious that there was enthusiasm for a war that did not directly affect the great majority of Americans. There was little concern that their homes, families, and livelihoods would be threatened by the Spanish so far to the south. They were aware of the depredations of the Spanish on colonial shipping, however, and were happy to see Great Britain flexing her muscles after such a long period of peace and, to some, appeasement. Enthusiasm for the war remained high, and three months after the declaration of war, the Duke of Newcastle, in his capacity as secretary of state for the Southern Department, issued a call for His Majesty's subjects to enlist for the "glorious expedition" to the West Indies. Although Vice Admiral Vernon had argued that British naval power alone could carry out an effective campaign, crippling Spanish commerce and naval power in the West Indies, he was overruled. The government determined to amass a significant land army of British and American soldiers, under the command of the experienced and respected Lord Cathcart, and have this force join Vernon and his fleet to prosecute the war. Cathcart raised six new marine regiments, which were to join two veteran army regiments and fifteen hundred troops already in the West Indies, to make a British force of over eight thousand soldiers. To this it was hoped the American Regiment of at least three thousand men would be added.

In an astute political move, Colonel Alexander Spotswood, who had been in the colonies for many years and had served as lieutenant governor of Virginia, was designated commander of the American Regiment and, most significantly, second in command of the entire land army, with the rank of major general. This was an honor to the Americans and recognition of Spotswood's initiative a decade earlier, when he suggested that a force of Americans could take Havana. Before recruiting began, however, Spotswood died and his responsibilities were distributed. Command of the American Regiment was given to the lieutenant governor of Virginia, William Gooch, with the rank of colonel. The responsibility of second in command of the land forces, British and American, went to Brigadier General Thomas Wentworth, who had gained Cathcart's respect as an administrator and organizer of the new British regiments. It was recognized that the successful recruitment of the American Regiment would require American officers, since it was doubtful that significant numbers would enlist to fight under the direct command of British officers, generally perceived as arrogant. At the same time, the British military could not imagine the colonials performing adequately under colonial officers, so a compromise was struck. The American colonel, William Gooch, would lead the American Regiment, and each company would have an American captain and one American lieutenant. The lieutenant colonels, majors, and additional company lieutenants would be regular British officers. In general, the American company captains were young men from prominent families, and most had experience in the colonial militia. Among these officers was Lawrence Washington from Virginia, who was a bit atypical of the colonial company captains. When his mother died, his father remarried and began a second family. With the birth of his half-brother George, Lawrence was sent off to England to be schooled at Appleby-in-Westmorland. When he returned to Virginia in 1738, Washington brought a level of sophistication, gained from his time in England, that few of his contemporaries possessed. This polish would serve him and the American Regiment well in the difficult years that lay ahead.

To oversee the sensitive recruitment process in America, Cathcart sent his adjutant general, Colonel William Blakeney, and gave him

Lawrence Washington

thirty blank commissions to secure the necessary company captains. It was hoped that thirty colonial gentlemen, commissioned as captains, could each raise a company of one hundred men to complete the regiment of three thousand. Blakeney was surprised by the response. With a sense of youthful invincibility, a hunger for adventure, dreams of rich Spanish booty, and visions of the glories of war that Vernon had so easily won, the companies in the northern colonies filled quickly. In several colonies, men who anticipated commissions as captains successfully raised companies but were then disappointed. With only thirty commissions to distribute throughout the colonies, there were not enough available for all the companies raised. While "certificates," which would be converted to field commissions by Cathcart, were offered to the captains, only a few were accepted, and at least twelve companies were disbanded. This meant that through shortsightedness, the British lost the services of twelve hundred men: four hundred from Massachusetts, four hundred from Connecticut, two hundred from New Jersey, and one hundred each from New Hampshire and Rhode Island.

In the mid-Atlantic colonies, recruitment efforts were not as successful as in New England, and incentives were offered to fulfill their quotas. In Pennsylvania, release from indenture was offered to those who enlisted, and property owners complained bitterly as their servants left them. In Maryland, debtors were offered their release from prison, and old slaves, who were of little value, were enlisted by their owners, who were happy to be relieved of the responsibility of caring for the old men. In Virginia, convicts transported from England were rounded up and enrolled along with the unemployed. The American Regiment was a mixed bag of farmers, tradesmen, craftsmen, laborers, debtors, militiamen, ex-convicts, the destitute, and the unemployed, each with his own reason for joining. For some it was an opportunity for adventure and potential glory, while others wanted to escape from the burdens of their lives. Whatever their reasons for enlisting, the quota was met, and for the first time in the history of the colonies, an American army was about to go overseas to fight in a British war: a war of choice, against an enemy that posed no serious threat to the colonies in America. By October 1740, this odd band of would-be warriors was assembled at various locations along the coast. They were loaded onto ships that rendezvoused off the Virginia Capes and then proceeded to Jamaica, where the rest of the land army would join them.

In England, the six regiments of marines were gathered on the Isle of Wight during the late summer and drilled under the watchful eye of General Wentworth. While the majority of the men were new to the service, about a third, including the sergeants, corporals, drummers, and sentinels, had been drawn from existing regiments of foot soldiers and brought their experience with them. Only half of the officers had army experience. However, Lord Cathcart was pleased with the progress Wentworth made in turning the inexperienced men into soldiers, and as the American Regiment was getting under way in the colonies, the marine regiments were crammed onto eighty transport ships and the two army regiments were distributed among the thirty-one warships that would escort the troop transports and then be added to Vernon's fleet in the West Indies. This armada of more than one hundred ships under the command of Admiral Sir Chaloner Ogle sailed on October 26, with a long and arduous voyage before them. Six days into the transatlantic passage, they encountered a fierce gale, which damaged ships and terrified the seasick soldiers crowded belowdecks. An eyewitness describing the ordeal wrote that upon arriving on deck, he "found the prospect all together dismal. Of all the fleet, seven sail only were to be seen, and of these, two had lost their masts, while others scudded under reefed mainsails; the billows [waves] were incredibly vast and tremendous: there was nothing to be seen on board, but tumult, uproar, and dismay; the ship pitched with such violence, that the masts quivered like slender twigs; a cask of water broke from its lashings on deck, and maimed sixteen men before it could be stayed; the mainsail was split into a thousand tatters, and the yard being manned to bend on another in its room, one of the braces gave way with such a shock, as threw four men overboard, two of whom were lost, while the knee of a fifth was crushed in a terrible manner between the beryl and the mast." After two days, the horrendous storm moderated and forty of the original fleet gathered to continue on their way, with other stragglers joining them from time to time. A month into the voyage, the fleet was becalmed in the doldrums, and "the weather growing sultry and calm . . . began to produce ardent fevers among the men, and in a few days the fleet became very sickly." On December 19, this flotilla dropped anchor at the rendezvous location of Prince Ruperts Bay in Dominica, the southernmost of the Leeward Islands that separate the Atlantic from the Caribbean. Other ships of the fleet had been arriving since December 12, and it became apparent that most of the fleet had survived the crossing. However, sickness in the form of "the flux," or dysentery, had spread within the unsanitary ships, and many had died. The historian and novelist Tobias Smollett, who served as a surgeon's mate on HMS *Chichester* during the campaign, documented the great loss to the campaign when its universally respected commander, Lord Cathcart, died on the day the fleet arrived in Dominica. Smollett expressed the foreboding felt by many at the death of Lord Cathcart, because "he was succeeded in command by Brigadier-General Wentworth, an officer who had neither knowledge, weight, nor self-confidence, sufficient to conduct an enterprise of such importance." The complexion of the land campaign had suddenly changed for the worse, but the British had a massive force assembling and it was felt that little could stand up to this brute power. After a week in Dominica, the fleet moved on, picking up a number of other ships in a secondary rendezvous, and it became clear that virtually the entire fleet was intact. During this last stretch of their long voyage, Smollett documents another extraordinary event: a battle between British ships of the fleet and French ships, with whom they were not at war. He wrote that upon sighting five large ships, the admiral sent an equal number of British warships in pursuit. When the commodore of the British detachment demanded that the commander of the opposing force report to him, the Frenchman refused and a naval battle began. As Smollett wrote, "The two squadrons, being equally matched, fought all night with equal courage; and in the morning, the English commodore seeing French colours displayed, hailed his antagonist, and pretended he had mistaken them for Spaniards: the battle was forthwith suspended, mutual compliments passed, and, having treated each other with marks of politeness, they parted with the loss of about a hundred men killed on each side . . ." It is astonishing to observe the niceties of eighteenth-century warfare and to realize that a battle costing two hundred lives did not create an international incident and result in a declaration of war, but rather ended with courtesies exchanged.

The 113 vessels of the main fleet arrived in Jamaica on January 9, 1741, and it was clear that the seventy-five-day voyage had taken a heavy toll. When the first muster of British troops was taken on Jamaica, the dead numbered 483 in addition to Lord Cathcart, and an additional 1,288 were sick. The great army was significantly weakened before it faced any enemy other than disease.

The American Regiment, consisting of thirty-five companies of one hundred men each, was divided into three battalions, each commanded by a British major. Their voyage to Jamaica was shorter and less stressful than that of the British, and the regiment arrived in Port Royal, Jamaica, in early December, well in advance of the British contingent. The Americans immediately became aware of their second-class status. The military authorities in Jamaica informed Colonel Blakeney that they were not authorized to provide any food or support for this motley American mob, which, because only one in six wore any semblance of a uniform, did not look like soldiers. The officials further argued that the Americans couldn't be provided for as part of Lord Cathcart's army, since Cathcart had not yet arrived. Disgusted and discouraged, the Americans debarked from their ships, which had carried only enough supplies for the voyage south, and set up camp on the island. As the British historian John W. Fortescue described the situation, "The Americans were in a very bad state. Their ranks had been filled without difficulty, but with bad material: they were guiltless of drill or discipline, and on arrival in Jamaica had at once become disorderly and mutinous. There was good excuse for their discontent, for the English Government, though it had made arrangements for the payment and victualling of the British troops, had made none whatever for the Americans, who were thus compelled to fall back on such meager resources Jamaica could provide. Moreover, the Americans were even more sickly than the British, and had buried scores of men since their disembarkation." As conditions deteriorated, the Americans suffered from hunger and were deprived of what scant money they had by exploitive shop and tavern owners. Weakened by the voyage and hunger, they began to fall ill with tropical disease, which quickly took many lives and left 10 percent of the force ill. The situation reached crisis proportions when some Americans grew mutinous. The governor of Jamaica, Edward Trelawney, finally accepted responsibility and ordered that the Americans be provisioned, offering a temporary remedy for the Americans' problems.

But then the British army arrived, and instantly there was friction between the two forces. The British officers looked with derision on the scruffy, disillusioned, ill-disciplined American force that was paraded for inspection by Wentworth and other British officers. Wentworth expressed his grave concern that the American Regiment was composed significantly of "Irish papists" who could not be relied upon in a fight with the Catholic Spanish. Captain Charles Knowles, a brilliant naval engineer and captain of HMS *Weymouth*, was vituperative in his remarks about the Americans. In his *An Account of the Expedition Against Cartagena*, which would be published in London in 1743, he voiced contempt for the American soldiers and their officers, saying, "As for the American Troops, they were in general many degrees worse [than the raw British troops], but the officers in particular, who were composed of Blacksmiths, Taylors, Barbers, Shoemakers and all the Bandity them Colonies affords: in as much that the other part of the Army held them at Scorn." Despite this discomfiting beginning, the Americans prepared to do their part in the glorious expedition that the call for recruits had described. However, the delay in the arrival of the British force had cost the campaign a month and brought the effort closer to the start of the rainy season, which could debilitate troops and increase the chance of yellow fever.

There was debate and further delay in determining the first objective of the expedition, but the decision was ultimately made to bypass Havana, which was reported to have a significant Spanish squadron present, and attack Cartagena. This heavily fortified Spanish city lay on the mainland of South America on the coast of what is today Colombia, across from Panama. Vernon had reconnoitered the port soon after his victory at Porto Bello and determined that despite its fortifications it could easily be taken, thereby adding to his glory. Admiral Vernon was well aware that the French had successfully taken the city in 1697 but perhaps was not aware that during the intervening thirty years, under the direction of Juan de Herrara y Sotomayor, the defenses of the city had been substantially improved. The overconfidence of the British allowed the open discussions of Cartagena as the target to be heard by the Spanish intelligence agents, who sent word ahead to the city and placed them on alert. The defense of the city was the responsibility of two strong-willed, intelligent military veterans: Viceroy Sebastien d'Eslava and the grizzled admiral Don Blas de Lezo. Both men were in their early fifties and experienced in combat and the planning of military and naval actions. D'Eslava had seen action in earlier wars and was recognized as an astute military strategist. Don Blas had achieved numerous successes, and by the time he was sent to Cartagena he was an acknowledged hero in Spain. As would happen to Britain's Lord Nelson fifty years later, Don Blas lost an eye in one engagement and his right arm in another. Unlike Nelson, he had also lost his left leg and was known by the nickname "El Almirante Patapalo," Admiral Peg-leg. Having these two military heroes at Cartagena added further strength to the city, but the two strong personalities would chafe against each other during the attack that lay ahead. Anticipating the arrival of the British, d'Eslava engaged Don Carlos Desnaux, a skilled engineer, to design a network of defensive trenches outside the fortress and to build additional gun emplacements, known as fascine batteries, which were constructed from bundles of sticks lashed together. Don Blas positioned his ships strategically to impede the British ships. Their preparations were completed, and they waited for the British to appear.

As the British force of well over 150 ships prepared to depart Jamaica during a ten-day period in late January 1741, there was already rivalry within the command. Admiral Vernon had anticipated sharing equal command with Lord Cathcart, for whom he had great respect, but when confronted with the inexperienced Wentworth, Vernon asserted himself as the senior officer. The Americans were among the first to experience Vernon's power as their regiment was broken up, with the companies taken on board Vernon's undermanned ships. They had come to fight as soldiers, but because of their perceived inexperience, they were to be employed as laborers, essentially impressed into shipboard service. Admiral Vernon and other overconfident British officers found it hard to imagine needing these Americans in battle.

Once at sea, the three British squadrons rendezvoused but did not head immediately for Cartagena. The entire fleet went to investigate the rumored presence of a French squadron in Port Louis on the island of Hispaniola. While England and France were technically at peace, there had already been a bloody confrontation between French ships and some of those now included in Admiral Vernon's fleet, and if war was declared, a French squadron could play havoc with Vernon's plans. The British fleet anchored at the Isle of Vache, near Port Louis, and while investigations were made to discover the whereabouts of the French squadron (which had, in fact, sailed for Europe), the Americans were put to work. As Smollett witnessed and recorded, "During the seven days we were thus employed, detachments from the American regiment and the negroes were daily sent ashore to cut fascines and pickets" needed for the attack on Cartagena's harbor defenses. This was not the role the Americans had anticipated in this glorious expedition, and they resented the British officers' perception of them as the equivalent of the enslaved blacks, who had been gathered and volunteered by their masters for the expedition by Jamaica's governor.

When it was confirmed that the French had departed the area, Vernon's armada, which exceeded the size of the famous Spanish Armada that had been sent against England during Queen Elizabeth's reign, sailed for Cartagena. The battle that lay ahead would be anything but a fair fight. The enormous British force was vastly superior to the Spanish force defending Cartagena: The British had 186 ships, including 29 ships of the line, manned by 26,400 sailors and soldiers who were set on overwhelming the paltry 6 ships of the line and 4,000 sailors and soldiers that Don Blas and d'Eslava had under their command. With the massive force under his command, the hero of Porto Bello was in a position to wrest the Caribbean from Spanish control and enormously strengthen Great Britain through military and mercantile dominance in the New World. Cartagena was the first critical step on the path of conquest.

CHAPTER 13

Cartagena!

THE CITY OF CARTAGENA and its fortresses were perched on the shore of the Atlantic, at the head of a bay that stretched seven miles to the south, the only entrance to which was through a narrow channel, known as Boca Chica, the Little Mouth. The Spanish, well aware of the strategic importance of the site, had no fewer than four forts guarding the entrance and had added several fascine batteries as well as a barrier across the harbor channel entrance in anticipation of the English assault. The primary fort guarding the entrance was known as Boca Chica Castle, which was square and boasted twenty large, thirty-two-pound cannons on each of the four sides. The most formidable of the impediments was a boom that stretched across the entrance from Boca Chica Castle to Fort St. Joseph on the opposite bank. The boom consisted of three strong iron chains, three large cables, and a great number of masts all bound together. As if the boom itself were not sufficient, the Spanish had positioned within the boom four large men-of-war, each with at least sixty cannons, moored broadside to the channel so they could fire point-blank at any British ship attempting to break through, which would be unable to maneuver in the narrow channel and fire on the Spanish ships. At the same time, the British would have to fight both sides of their ships, firing at the forts and batteries that lined the channel.

Stalled by the boom, they would be cut to pieces by the crossfire from the nearly 150 cannons that bristled on both shores. The Spanish had erected an extremely formidable defense of the harbor mouth, and the penetration of this harbor entrance became the essential first objective of the British assault.

On March 13, 1741, the first three scouting vessels from Vernon's fleet appeared off Cartagena, but this raised little alarm in the city that had endured eight days of bombardment from a larger squadron under Vernon's command some months earlier. That time Vernon was simply testing the city's defenses; now he was determined to conquer the rich Spanish city. On the following day, March 14, the people of Cartagena were confronted by an awesome and intimidating sight: the arrival of Vernon's massive force consisting of nearly two hundred ships, carrying 2,070 guns. For Vernon, it was clear that the fleet could not risk attempting to force their way through the narrow harbor entrance, and therefore the forts guarding the channel had to be taken.

In the opening engagement, three British ships from Admiral Sir Chaloner Ogle's squadron anchored and battered the two small forts, St. Jago and St. Philip, that were the outermost defenses of the harbor entrance. The brief action was described by an observer, who

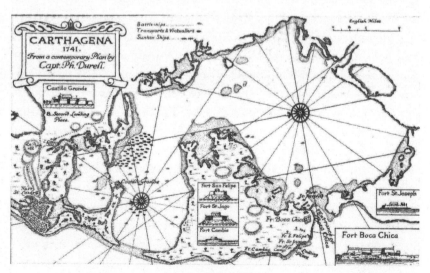

Map of Cartagena

said, "At Noon the *Norfolk*, *Russell* and *Shrewsbury* began to cannonade the Forts, and in about 3 hours time drove the Enemy from their Guns, and they ran out of the forts." However, this first success was costly since one of the three attacking British ships, the *Shrewsbury*, had her anchor cable shot through and drifted into the range of the powerful thirty-two-pound cannons of Boca Chica Castle and the fascine battery on the opposite shore. The *Shrewsbury* was badly mauled, "being greatly shattered in her Hull, Masts, Yards and Rigging, and a considerable number of Men [60] Killed and Wounded."

With the Royal Navy having cleared the way, Wentworth landed a force to attack Boca Chica Castle, which was under the command of a skilled military engineer, Don Carlos Desnaux. As the troops attempted to build their fascine batteries to use against the castle, they took fire from the Baradera battery across the channel. Now, a small number of Americans would have an opportunity to prove themselves in action. Lawrence Washington and his company had been among those assigned to serve on Admiral Vernon's flagship, the *Princess Caroline*, and Washington had caught the attention of the admiral. Washington's English schooling and genteel manner won Vernon's confidence. With the Baradera's cannon fire pinning down Wentworth's men, Vernon gave Washington a chance to demonstrate what the Americans could do. Vernon sent five hundred men ashore, including three hundred sailors led by navy lieutenant Arthur Forrest and two hundred soldiers including the Americans under the command of Captain Washington. It was a difficult mission, as the troops landed directly in front of a hidden battery of five cannons, which opened fire directly on them. Despite the point-blank fusillade, the sailors, marines, and Americans were able to rush the emplacement and overwhelm it. They then captured the Baradera, drove spikes into the touchholes of the cannons to disable them, burned the gun carriages, and set the rest of the battery ablaze to make sure that both their compatriots on the far side of the channel and the defenders of Boca Chica Castle knew that the Baradera was out of action.

The Americans had proven themselves under fire, but this did little to change the attitude of the British officers. When the attention returned to the attack on the castle, other American troops were sent ashore, not to fight but as labor to clear the ground for the British camp, from which the attack on the castle would be made. The attackers worked for a week to construct their battery and their camp. Unfortunately, the inexperienced Wentworth chose a disastrous location for the camp, which lay behind the British battery, in a direct line with the guns of Boca Chica Castle. When Wentworth opened fire on the castle, some of the return fire carried over his battery and tore through the camp, killing or wounding over one hundred men on the first day of the battle. To save Wentworth's land forces, the British ships hovering offshore poured cannon fire on the castle, suppressing the Spanish guns. The friction between Vernon and Wentworth grew, as the admiral urged an immediate assault and the hesitant general delayed. There was, however, friction on the Spanish side as well. Admiral Don Blas de Lezo felt that Boca Chica Castle (or Fort San Luis, as it was also known) could not be defended against the overwhelming British force arrayed before them and that it was more prudent to withdraw the four hundred Spanish troops so they could strengthen the defenses closer to the city. The castle commander, Desnaux, as an engineer, had great faith in the fort and felt that it had the best chance to stop the British. Desnaux protested against his superior's plans, and for the moment, Desnaux's dedication carried the day. The Spanish troops in Boca Chica Castle prepared for a siege.

After taking eleven days to erect his land battery of "four-and-twenty great guns, and forty small mortars and cohorns," General Wentworth began to pummel the wall of Boca Chica Castle, attempting to create a breach. As Smollett observed, "Next day, Commodore Lestock . . . went in to cannonade the forts of Boca Chica, St. Joseph, the Spanish men-of-war, and the [rebuilt] Baradera battery . . . This squadron having run in as near the forts as possible, each clapped a spring on her cable, and a terrible cannonading ensued . . . In the evening, they were called off, after having sustained considerable loss." Among the British casualties was the commanding officer of HMS *Prince Frederick*, Lord Aubrey Beauclerc, who had both legs shot off and died on the surgeon's table. The navy had bought the army the time to create a small breach in the wall, although at a high cost: The *Boyne* and the *Hampton Court* were badly damaged, and the *Prince Frederick* was completely disabled in the battle.

However, throughout the time from the landing of the troops to the making of the breach, testy messages flew back and forth between Vernon and Wentworth, with the admiral urging greater speed and a full-blown assault and the general hesitant to attack until there was a clear entry into the fort. Finally, on March 25, sixteen days after the first troops landed, the British soldiers stormed the castle. As Vernon had predicted, the Spanish did not stand and fight, but as the first British grenadiers mounted the breach, they fled and were able to reach the city to reinforce the defenders there. Only 2 of Wentworth's men were wounded in the assault. While army combat casualties amounted to 130 at this point, the other enemy, disease—against which the British were defenseless—had claimed the lives of 250 soldiers, and an additional 600 were sick. The navy had suffered many more casualties in their cannon duels with the Spanish, and disease was also adding to the list of dead and dying sailors.

After Boca Chica Castle fell to the British, the small Fort St. Joseph was abandoned and occupied by a British naval force. With both forts in British hands, Don Blas could do nothing to defend the channel with his four ships. The Spanish sank their *Africa* and *San Carlos* and set fire to the *San Philip*, which when the fire reached the powder magazine "blew up with a vast explosion." The only remaining Spanish ship still afloat at the barricade was Don Blas's flagship, the *Galicia*. When sailors under the command of Captain Knowles, who would play a key role in the entire campaign, boarded the flagship, they found not the peg-legged admiral, who had been wounded in the thigh and the hand the previous day, but the ship's captain, Juan Jordan, another officer, and about sixty sailors who had not had time to destroy the ship and escape. They also found a special prize, the admiral's flag belonging to Don Blas, which was presented to Admiral Vernon as a trophy of the battle.

The boom of chains, cables, and masts blocking the entrance was cleared, and the triumphant fleet worked its way into the bay and prepared to move toward the city and its fortifications to the north. The confidence that British might could overcome the best Spanish defenses had been confirmed. Having seen the Spaniards flee from Boca Chica and with his huge fleet pouring into Cartagena harbor, Admiral Vernon was confident that in a short time the remaining

Admiral Don Blas de Lezo

defenses of the city would be overwhelmed and Cartagena would be in British hands. To spread the great news, Vernon sent HMS *Spence* to England with Admiral Don Blas de Lezo's flag as evidence of another great victory. Vernon wrote to his wife, sharing the news of the triumph, saying, "After the glorious success it has pleased Almighty God so wonderfully to favour us with ... I ... acquaint you of the joyful news." He went on to briefly describe the success at Boca Chica and added his intention "to push this beginning with all possible vigour, to humble the proud Spaniards, and bring them to repentance for all the injuries and long-practised depredations on us." Vernon saw the initial success as the "beginning" and expressed his confidence of complete success, but others, eager for victory, interpreted the news as proclaiming complete triumph.

When the news reached London, the same euphoria that had greeted Vernon's victory at Porto Bello erupted again, with celebrations

throughout the city and around the country. The success was celebrated in ballads with verses such as the following:

> *We did so cannonade, and such breaches we made,*
> *And so many of their houses set in a flame,*
> *They did submit to fate and the town surrender*
> *To Admiral Vernon, the scourge of Spain.*

Of course, no houses had been set aflame and the town had not
surrendered, but nothing could quell the enthusiasm the British people felt for their hero. To further commemorate the triumph, medals
were struck depicting the vanquished Don Blas kneeling before the
victorious Vernon with various inscriptions that included "The Pride
of Spain Humbled by Admiral Vernon," "The Spanish Pride Pulld
down by Admiral Vernon," and "True British Heroes Took Carthagena."

In American cities, the response was much like that in England.
They too celebrated with great pride in their soldiers and loyalty to the
Crown. In Philadelphia they celebrated "So glorious an event, to which
even we may boast in some measure, to have contributed, inflamed
every loyal and honest heart here, with a warmth, unfelt before in this
infant country." The celebration continued with a parade through the
city, the firing of great guns, volleys of musket fire, barrels of beer, the
illumination of houses in the evening, all culminating with a bonfire at
which they "distributed a pipe of Spanish Prize Wine among the populace." Similar celebrations took place all along the coast. In Newport,

Medal commemorating British triumph

Rhode Island, "having the joyful News of Admiral Vernon's Fleet destroying the Forts and Castles of Carthagena, we had great Rejoycings
here, by firing of Guns, ringing of Bells, and a great Bonfire . . ." And in
Charleston, South Carolina, "the Garrison were making loud Hazza's"
because "Admiral Vernon has taken Carthagena." Throughout the
colonies they were celebrating the fall of Cartagena and the first victory of the glorious expedition.

Buoyant with the early victory, Vernon was impatient to attack the
city, but it took a full week for the army to reembark for the move up
the bay after the capture of Boca Chica, fueling Vernon's resentment.
He knew that the entire expedition started far later than it should
have and that the debilitating rainy season, which would bring an increase in dysentery and yellow fever, was fast approaching. The
sailors and troops were also coping with food that was marginal at
best. In addition to the filth and crowded conditions on the ships,
Smollett recounted the dismal state of the food: "Our provisions consisted of putrid salt beef, to which the sailors gave the name of Irish
horse; salt pork of New England which though neither fish nor flesh
savoured of both; bread of the same country, every biscuit of which
like a piece of clockwork moved by its own internal impulse, occasioned by the myriads of insects that dwelt within it, and butter
served out by the gill, that tasted like train oil thickened with salt."
Despite the difficulties of disease and bad food, the approach to the
city brought encouragement. Don Blas attempted to block the entrance to the inner harbor from which the guns of Vernon's warships
could pound the city into submission. The Spanish admiral scuttled
their last remaining warships, the *Dragon* and the *Conquistador*, to
block the entrance. However, the British found the stern of the *Conquistador* still afloat, and Vernon's flagship from his Porto Bello campaign, HMS *Burford*, managed to pull the ship aside and open a
channel. Realizing the way was open for Vernon's ships to enter the
inner harbor, the Spanish burned a French warship that was moored
deep in the harbor to keep it from falling into British hands. The
Spanish realized that it was futile to try to defend the inner harbor
with two small forts, so they abandoned them. Conditions looked
grim for the people of Cartagena. There was now only one fortress
between the British and the city: Fort St. Lazar.

On April 16, out of range of the Spanish guns, the British warships fired broadsides to clear the landing beaches of opposition, and Wentworth's men made their second amphibious landing. Their objectives: Fort St. Lazar and the city that lay beyond. Although General Wentworth insisted on five thousand men for the attack, Vernon ridiculed this request and ordered the general to make do with only fourteen hundred British soldiers and about two hundred Americans. While the troops made their way along a narrow path, with the water on their left and a thick wood on the right, they encountered a Spanish force of seven hundred, and a battle ensued. The British moved forward, while the Americans were ordered into the woods to flank the enemy. Before the Americans could encircle them, the Spanish once again fled. Had Wentworth's troops surged ahead and carried the fight forward, they might have been able to take Fort St. Lazar, but the hesitant general, wary of a possible ambush, halted his troops. Additional Americans were landed, along with more blacks from the slave regiment, and again given the task of clearing an area for the British encampment. Unfortunately, no tents were landed and the troops had to sleep exposed to the elements for several days as the rains came.

Vernon and Wentworth exchanged barbed messages concerning the assault on St. Lazar. Wentworth wanted more men, for Vernon's ships to bombard the fort, and he also wanted time to erect an artillery battery to breach the walls as they had done at Boca Chica Castle. Vernon reluctantly allowed additional troops to be landed, including all the Americans "that can be trusted," but he refused to risk his ships by moving them close enough to bombard the fort. With regard to the delay to build a battery, "the admiral treated the design of a battery with great contempt, alleging that cannon were not at all necessary for the taking of such a paltry fort, which would certainly be abandoned as soon as the English should appear in earnest to give the assault." As the days of delay continued, the rains increased, one eyewitness saying it rained ten days in succession, and yellow fever began to rage through the onshore force.

The keen observer Smollett set down his scathing indictment of the men in command of this deteriorating situation. He described the ridiculous and pernicious jealousy between the officers of the army and navy and how they argued and sought to protect themselves from criticism and possible court-martial while risking the success of the expedition and the lives of thousands of soldiers and sailors. Smollett summarized by saying, "In a word, the admiral was a man of weak understanding, strong prejudices, boundless arrogance, and over-boiling passions; and the general, though he had some parts, was wholly defective in points of experience, confidence, and resolution."

Under this deplorable shambles of leadership, the attack moved forward. Wentworth left hundreds of men in camp writhing in the grip of fever and organized his force for the assault on the fort. The force included 450 grenadiers, one of the veteran regiments, and Americans, who rather than carrying weapons brought defensive "woolpacks" and the ladders needed to scale the walls. In the hours of darkness before dawn on the morning of April 20, Wentworth's force moved forward against the Spanish, anticipating they would once again flee when confronted by the ranks of red-coated British soldiers. Don Blas and d'Eslava had thoroughly prepared for this assault on St. Lazar, however, and the fort was well situated, perched atop a seventy-foot hill. Wentworth had employed two Spanish "deserters" as guides, and one of them cleverly led Colonel John Wynyard's column of grenadiers not to a gentle road up to the fort, but to the base of the hill, which was so steep that the troops had to ascend on their hands and knees. They scrabbled their way up the hill in the darkness until nearly at the crest, thirty yards in front of them, the night exploded in a torrent of point-blank musket and cannon fire. The Spanish troops were protected in trenches before the walls, and cannons loaded with grapeshot from the fortress above shredded the disciplined oncoming British soldiers. A Colonel Grant's column, which approached from the other direction, encountered the same fierce resistance, and Grant was killed early in the fighting. An officer in the Massachusetts troops who was on the scene reported that the enemy "poured partridge shot in abundance upon us. However, our men nothing discouraged, march'd as brave as every any Romans could and drove our enemies out of their brest-works and fascine batteries, with great slaughter to them, and being prepared with scaling ladders, advanced to the walls of the fort and reared their ladders. But alas, they were eight or nine feet too short..." At this point, the disillusioned Americans dropped the useless ladders, and while some took cover, according to Smollett, "many of them took up the fire-locks [muskets] which they found on the field, and, mixing among the troops, behaved very bravely." As dawn eased into full daylight, the Spanish on the parapets took careful aim and picked off the British officers, adding to the confusion and discouragement of the attackers. Don Blas then launched a counteroffensive and sent a col-umn of troops out of the gates of Cartagena to cut off the British from their ships. Realizing all was lost, Wentworth ordered a retreat, which the officer of the Massachusetts troops said "was rather a direct Flight than a Retreat." The same American officer vented his disgust and put the blame for this defeat on Admiral Vernon, writing that af-ter the battle, "he never came with any of his Ships within two Can-non Shot of the City, altho' it is plain he might within two Cables Length . . . and I am confident, that Ten Sail of our Ships, with our Men to Land, would have beat the City all to Pieces, and not have lost half the men we did." After the assault, Vernon had made the token effort of sending the captured Spanish flagship, the *Galicia*, fitted with only fourteen guns, into the inner harbor to bombard the city. Vernon claimed that since the *Galicia* ultimately had to be aban-doned, that would have been the fate of his ships if he had risked them. However, it proved to many, as the Massachusetts officer stated, that he could have changed the outcome had his ships of the line en-tered the harbor and bludgeoned the city. For the British, whose force had already been reduced by sickness and combat casualties to 6,600 before this attack, the entire event was a slaughter. Two hundred British and American troops were killed in the three-hour battle and 400 wounded, few of whom would survive amid the disease and un-sanitary conditions. As disease raged, four days later, only 3,200 were men still capable of fighting.

Wentworth and Vernon argued and sent jibes back and forth for two weeks, while the sick and wounded continued to suffer and the plight of the men worsened. Smollett, writing as a medical man, gave his eye-witness account of the misery: "As for the sick and wounded, they were next day sent on board the transports and vessels called hospital ships, where they languished in want of every necessary comfort and accom-modation. They were destitute of surgeons, nurses, cooks, and proper provision; they were pent up between decks in small vessels, where they had not room to sit upright; they wallowed in filth, myriads of maggots were hatched in the putrefaction of their sores, which had no other dressing than that of being washed by themselves with their own allowance of brandy; and nothing was heard but groans, lamentations, and language of despair, invoking death to deliver them from their miseries." So many officers were ill that discipline broke down on the transports and those who were able simply threw the bodies of the dead overboard. The harbor, where little current flowed, was soon a ghastly scene, "for there they beheld the naked bodies of their fellow-soldiers and comrades floating up and down the harbour, affording prey to the carrion crows and sharks, which tore them in pieces without interruption, and contributing by their stench to the mortality that prevailed." The horror of the image added misery for those already suffering more than could be imagined. The dreams of a glorious expedition and riches from Spanish booty had evaporated, and the nightmare of disease and death took their place.

Finally, on May 5, Wentworth and Vernon concluded that the cause was lost and the Cartagena campaign had to be given up. Two days later, the despondent fleet departed Cartagena in defeat and headed for Jamaica to regroup and assess their options. The medals prematurely struck to celebrate Vernon's victory over Don Blas would become permanent grim reminders of the vice admiral's overconfidence and Wentworth's indecisiveness. As the fleet with its slow transports made its way to Jamaica, yellow fever took an increasing toll on the crowded, fetid ships. Within two weeks, by May 21, most of the transports were back in Port Royal, and a muster of the forces revealed the calamitous cost. Wentworth had only 1,909 of the original force of 8,000 British soldiers, and the Americans had only 1,086 of their 3,600-man regiment. By mid-June, disease was killing men at the rate of 100 per week. With Vernon's impressment of men to serve his ships, the land army was reduced to a mere 2,142. The West Indies campaign was in shambles.

In an attempt to salvage something out of the quagmire of the expedition, Vernon and Wentworth searched for a less ambitious target and an easy conquest. The two flag officers had been sending conflicting reports critical of each other back to England but were united in a request for reinforcements. As they awaited the response of the government, they determined that they could capture Cuba's second-largest city, Santiago, which was on the southern coast, 475 miles east of Havana. Wentworth assumed that Vernon and his unscathed warships would assault the city, but he discovered that Vernon intended to land Wentworth's depleted force in Guantánamo Bay for an overland, sixty-five-mile march and attack on Santiago. Vernon had manipulated the intelligence he had gathered from several Englishmen and an American who had been captive on Cuba. He made it sound as if there were a wide road from Guantánamo to Santiago, but when Wentworth reconnoitered, this was not the case. Despite his reluctance to release Americans for duty ashore and reduce the manpower on his ships, Vernon did send hundreds of Americans to assist. Wentworth was still skeptical of the loyalty of the Americans, suspecting that the Irishmen might desert. However, in an early scouting party consisting of ten sailors, two hundred Americans, and one hundred blacks, the force fought and dispersed a large Spanish patrol. In another instance, Lawrence Washington, still assigned to Vernon's flagship, led his men in another successful patrol. The Americans' accomplishments were not enough to motivate Wentworth to fight his way over the rough terrain to Santiago, and a permanent base, called Georgestadt in honor of King George II, was established with the thought that from a British base, Guantánamo, they could easily protect their shipping in the Windward Passage nearby. At this point, however, the expedition took on a bizarre twist.

Two American officers who were well respected back in the colonies were sent on a mission to recruit additional colonists to join in the fiasco of the West Indies expedition. It seemed incredible that there would be further enlistments, since the news of the debacle at Cartagena and the ravages of disease had been reported. The *Boston Weekly News-Letter* of July 2, 1741, reported the deaths of eight thousand men and added solemnly that "the officers and soldiers from North America behaved themselves with much bravery but many of them were dead." Nevertheless, in August, Vernon sent HMS *Sea Horse* northward with the American recruiting officers John Winslow of Massachusetts and William Hopkins of Rhode Island, to raise more troops from the colonies. They had an unusual sales pitch, as they described the splendors of the area around Guantánamo Bay and assured their countrymen that they would own the land they captured there and could grow wealthy living the plantation lifestyle. How the officers could perform this task in good conscience after the mismanagement, interservice arguments, and rampant tropical disease they had witnessed is hard to imagine. They did, however, manage to recruit about five hundred additional Americans for the expedition.

The enticement of Cuban land had evaporated by the time the recruits reached Port Royal, since after months ashore and a recurrence of yellow fever, the Cuban campaign was given up, Georgestadt was abandoned in early December, and the even more debilitated force withdrew to Jamaica. By this time, Wentworth's force consisted of 1,184 British soldiers and 279 Americans, with other Americans serving in Vernon's fleet. Finally, the terrible conditions under which the Americans had been serving began to receive official notice. While still in Cuba, General Wentworth wrote to the Duke of Newcastle and attempted to minimize the issue. In his letter of November 2, 1741, he ridiculed the American troops and their officers, writing, "In my letter of Feb. 23rd . . . I mentioned my reasons for ordering the Americans on board the King's ships . . . viz. great numbers of them being Irish or English convicts, the want of Camp necessarys, etc. . . . besides their being absolute strangers to discipline . . . I am very sensible, My Lord, that complaints have been made amongst the American soldiers; some were dissatisfy'd at the treatment they met with on board ye fleet (and perhaps with reason) but most of them would have been no less so on shore. I believe indeed the great source of their uneasiness was from their own Officers (of which some did not seem much qualify'd for that station) but that I hope to have remedied."

This cavalier attitude toward the Americans and their suffering was countered several months later, when on February 3, 1742, the field officers of the American Regiment wrote to General Wentworth, officially stating with specific examples their complaints of the American soldiers ordered into service afloat. They began with a general complaint that as the Americans were assigned to the British ships, their officers who had recruited them in their home districts were assigned to different ships and the soldiers were left without advocates.

The complaint continued with a list of abuses and specific horrors, saying, "Capt. Park Pepper of the First Battalion . . . on board the Rippon . . . had frequent Complaints made by his men of all the treatment they received on board but was never able to relieve them, tho frequently represented to the Officers of the Ship, particularly the cruel usage Sam Wilson . . . received from one Slaughter, a midshipman . . . by beating and kicking said Wilson in so barbarous a manner 'twas supposed he would have died." After this assault, Wilson, suffering from internal injuries, did indeed die. In another instance, "John Rutler . . . had his thigh broken . . . by a Boatswains Mate pushing him into the hold and . . . he believes it to be willfully done because the said Boatswains Mate before he pushed him gave him a blow with his Cane." Christopher Brackett of Captain Pepper's company was kept laboring on the chain pumps for hours on end when others were regularly relieved and "was so unmercifully beaten by Lieut. Huge of said ship with a Little Jack whilst naked at his work that he was cutt into the side, the mark whereof is very visible." The complaint continued, "In some Ships, the men have neither Hammocks or Sufficient berths aloud them, being miserably reduced to lye up and down the Decks, wherever they conveniently could, by which means their health has been vastly impaired and their clothing picked up by Sailors and thrown overboard, for which they had no redress . . ." Other complaints included "severe and cruel usage" for refusing to do personal work for naval officers, a general plea from the Americans aboard the *Jersey* for relief from their "misery and sorrow" having "undergone great and severe Crueltys as if they were the greatest Criminals" and having to "work like Slaves, therefore they had rather die than undergo such usage any longer." These were desperate men who were continuously abused with no means of redress or escape. The Americans were assigned the worst tasks on board and were "removed from Ship to Ship to pump and put to the hardest Labour." The Americans who survived the combat, disease, abuse, and mental torture of their servitude in the West Indies campaign would carry the physical and psychological scars of this experi ence at the hands of the brutish officers and men of the Royal Navy for the rest of their lives.

The Americans' formal complaint to General Wentworth fell on

deaf ears, and incredibly, despite the fiascoes at Cartagena and in
Cuba, the rival commanders attempted hapless adventures against
Panama and the island of Roatán off the Honduras coast, but there
was nothing to show for any of the efforts. In late September 1742,
Wentworth and Vernon were called home and the dregs of the expedition were sent home or assigned to the forces in Jamaica. The two
commanders would trade accusations of blame for years to come,
with Wentworth giving his side of the story in *A Journal of the Expedition to Cartagena*, published in London in 1744, and Vernon offering his version in the *Original Papers Relating to the Expedition to
Carthagena*, published later that same year. Captain Charles Knowles
authored the *Expedition of Carthagena in the Year 1741*, which supported Vernon. Tobias Smollett produced his interpretation, *Account
of the Expedition Against Carthagena*, in 1746. While the British population chafed under the indignity of the disastrous expedition, and a
continued debate over the blame took place in the *Gentleman's Magazine*, there were families all over the kingdom that felt the pain
more acutely. Of the 10,000 British soldiers who had been sent to participate in the expedition, only 2,400 were alive to return home.

In America, young men, some single, some with wives and children, had answered the call of the mother country to leave their
homes and fight across the sea under the command of British officers.
Their officers, in the complaint to General Wentworth, described
"the lamentable State of poor men who were led from their homes
upon an opinion of being Serviceable to their King and Country."
From the beginning they experienced ridicule, abuse, mistrust, and
misuse. Despite the fact that on a number of occasions they proved
themselves in battle, they were exploited and used as common labor
ashore and aboard Vernon's ships. Captain Lawrence Washington was
the exception, since he grew to greatly respect Admiral Vernon and
ultimately named his home Mount Vernon in honor of the admiral.
The Americans had paid a heavy price, and most blamed the commanders of the expedition, although the greatest killer had been disease. It can be argued that the British officers could not control that
enemy, but each of the delays and bad decisions they made cost lives.
Throughout the colonies, there was stunned disbelief that the "glorious expedition" could go so wrong. The Americans had been lured

into a British war of choice because Admiral Vernon "fixed" the intelligence to suit his concept. The general of the land forces had inadequate troops, and his superior kept insisting he should be able to manage with the men he had. The death toll of the colonies was proportionately similar to the British losses. Of the 4,183 Americans who had gone to fight, only 1,463 survived to return home in the fall of 1742, a 65 percent mortality rate. However, some colonies suffered even deeper anguish. For Rhode Island, the impact was still being felt four years later when a representative wrote to King George II in relation to participation in another war, saying, "The Colony had been drained of Men not long since by enlisting and sending 250 men in the Expedition against Cartagena of whom Scarce twenty returned." Tiny Rhode Island had experienced an astonishing mortality rate of 92 percent, and the agony was felt throughout the colony. For Massachusetts, which sent five hundred men on the ill-fated and grossly mismanaged expedition, only fifty survived to return home, a 90 percent loss. Those deaths represented a higher percentage of the Massachusetts population than the losses the state suffered in World War II.

CHAPTER 14

Promise Fulfilled

LOUIS XV POURED A FORTUNE into the creation of Louisbourg over a period of twenty-five years and is reputed to have said that with all the money spent on the distant fortress, he expected to be able to see its spires from France. After decades of investment and hard work, the active peacetime entrepôt and fishing center was about to fulfill its promise as a daunting fortress and naval base in time of war. The region had experienced thirty-one years of nominal peace, but on March 4, 1744, the French declared war on Great Britain. That news reached Louisbourg on April 22, and only three weeks later, 139 French officers and men, with 212 sailors, left Louisbourg and made their way southwest along the coast in a small fleet consisting of two armed privateers, fourteen fishing vessels adapted as troop carriers, and a supply ship. The soldiers and sailors aboard these ships were about to initiate the first military action in North America of the new war between Great Britain and France.

In the sleepy, neglected, and dilapidated fishing community of Canso, seventy-five miles southwest of Louisbourg, the inhabitants and their garrison, unaware that they were at war, faced the morning of May 13 with the casual attitude that had suited thousands of mornings during recent decades. The fishermen prepared to venture out for their day on the water, the shore workers spread out the earlier catch of cod onto the fish-drying flakes to cure in the sun, and the men of the garrison prepared to plod through another uneventful day. The garrison's eighty-seven men were ill equipped, poorly trained, and in marginal health, and it was doubtful that fifty of these men, commanded by Captain Patrick Heron, would be able to respond to a call to arms. It was of some reassurance that the settlement of Canso, situated on Grassy Island at the southern entrance to the strait that separated Nova Scotia from Cape Breton Island, had the protection of the small Royal Navy guard sloop commanded by Lieutenant George Ryall. The sloop had been left to winter over in Canso when the frigate HMS *Kinsale*, which was on station there during the summer months, departed the previous fall. On that mid-May morning, no one expected anything but a normal day. Their day would be anything but normal, however, and Canso would become the epicenter of a new phase of war in North America, which had begun with Jenkins's ear and was now spreading around the globe.

While Great Britain had waged a contained war against Spain in the West Indies in the early 1740s, and the British and Americans endured the humiliation of the failed military campaign against Cartagena with its miserable aftermath, there was constant concern that the French would enter the war on the side of the Spanish, because those two nations were already allied in a European conflict. The French saw it in their interest to ally with their Catholic neighbor and challenge Great Britain before she could regain strength and the initiative after the hapless West Indies debacle. During the time that the Spanish and British were fighting in the West Indies, there arose another issue of succession that absorbed the attention of the European countries. Just as the crisis of accession to the Spanish throne had drawn all of Europe into war in 1703, the crisis of accession to the Habsburg/Austrian throne erupted in 1740, when Maria Theresa inherited the throne after the death of her father, Charles VI, the Holy Roman Emperor. When the rulers of Bavaria and Prussia immediately sought to conquer the principalities ruled by Maria Theresa, a young woman they perceived as weak, all the major powers of Europe fell into alliances on the two sides of the issue. France, Spain, and Saxony joined with Prussia and Bavaria against Maria Theresa, while Great Britain and the Netherlands supported the twenty-three-year-old archduchess and queen. During the first years, Britain and France managed to avoid direct conflict, but by 1744, the French saw that it was inevitable and declared war.

The British did not reciprocate until three weeks later, on March 30, which enabled the French minister of the Marine Department, the Comte de Maurepas, who oversaw the French colonies, to alert his governors in New France and Louisbourg that a state of war existed and urge them to take action before the New Englanders had time to prepare. Jean-Baptiste-Louis le Prévost DuQuesnel, a cantankerous, heavy-drinking naval officer who was posted to Louisbourg in 1740, was in charge of the fortress at this time, as commandant rather than governor. DuQuesnel quickly became disillusioned with his new post. When it appeared that he would not be shifted to another assignment as requested, he set about to remedy some of the deficiencies he perceived in the fortifications at Louisbourg and with the troops that garrisoned the city. He was quickly at odds with many of his officers who had developed a system of enhancing their income at the expense of the soldiers. The soldiers' wages were paid to the officers, who set up canteens to sell food, alcohol, equipment, and other items to the soldiers at inflated prices. With no money in their pockets, the soldiers had no choice but to patronize the canteen for their needs and wants, and many soldiers went into debt to their officers. The primary purchases were "principally Drinks, for which [the officers] gain considerably." The result of the drunkenness was "the soldiers neglect their duties. They work without having anyone to emulate and they give themselves to excesses and disorders." The system eroded the effectiveness of the garrison, and DuQuesnel reined in the rampant process by limiting the officers' access to the soldiers' pay and restricting what they could sell to the exploited soldiers. Louisbourg was struggling with the strain of these poor relations between the officers and the enlisted men when news of war reached the city.

Stumping around on a peg that replaced his left leg, lost in the Battle of Málaga in 1704, DuQuesnel shifted easily from administrator to military commander. As he planned a two-pronged offensive, he was well aware that supplies had been so scarce in Louisbourg during the winter and spring that there was broad unrest among the citizens, who demanded that food be distributed from the government reserves that were to provide for the troops and officials. Food was urgently needed, and with the outbreak of war, two sources of supply would be cut off. The seasonal Basque fishing fleet, which usually brought food and supplies to the resident fishermen, would not venture to the area for fear of being captured by the English, and the flow of supplies from the steady trade with New England would stop as soon as the British colonies learned that they were at war. DuQuesnel reasoned that his best chance of resupply was from the sympathetic Acadians, from whom he could obtain cattle, sheep, and produce from their rich farms. However, Acadia had been British territory since the Treaty of Utrecht, and the Royal Navy frigate and sloop that guarded the New England fishing settlement of Canso during the summer could play havoc with any ships from Louisbourg that attempted to trade with the Acadians. In order to open the trade route, and also secure the bountiful regional fishery for the French, it was essential for DuQuesnel to capture Canso.

Command of the attack on Canso was given to François Du Pont Duvivier, who had grown up in Louisbourg and enlisted in the military in 1716 at the age of eleven, after the death of his father, also a military officer. Because Duvivier's service had been during a period of peace, DuQuesnel recruited a more experienced military veteran, Antoine Le Poupet de la Boularderie, to accompany the expedition and advise the commander if circumstances required. On the day Duvivier set off for Canso, the people of Boston received their first news of war from a merchant ship that had arrived from Glasgow, but that news could not reach Canso in time to prepare for an attack.

Duvivier was well aware that Canso had a blockhouse fortification manned by troops of Colonel Richard Phillips's Regiment of Foot, but he was uncertain of the resistance he would encounter. In fact, Canso was a dumping ground for old and infirm soldiers, who expected an uneventful life at the outpost. The fortifications themselves were in pathetic condition, having deteriorated over many years. The wild card was the Royal Navy guard sloop.

At dawn on May 13, the French fleet appeared off Canso's Grassy Island, the site of the blockhouse and primary settlement, and the two French privateers opened fire, sending cannonballs ripping through the rotten walls of the fortification and dumbfounding the residents of Canso. Captain Heron knew that his ill-equipped men and his dilapidated fortifications would be no match for the guns of these ships and the soldiers the fleet carried. He quickly ran up a white flag, in hopes of saving lives and negotiating generous terms of surrender. Although the guard sloop momentarily returned fire, it was quickly damaged by French gunfire. One man was killed and several wounded before Lieutenant Ryall struck his colors in the face of the superior force. With this brief attack, Captain Duvivier successfully executed the first action in King George's War, as the North American component of the War of the Austrian Succession would be known.

Duvivier and his men efficiently went about the work of securing their victory. The officers and men of Canso were taken to Louisbourg, where they were to remain as prisoners for a year. The women and children from Canso were transported to Boston. The French troops scoured the settlement for booty and appropriated significant amounts of cod to ease the food shortage in Louisbourg. They set fire to the structures at Canso, demolished the minimal fortifications, and triumphantly set sail for Louisbourg, with their ships and several others captured at Canso crowded with prisoners, refugees, cod, and plunder.

There was great satisfaction, both in Louisbourg and in France, that the planning, effort, and expense that had gone into the creation of the fortress were paying immediate dividends. Louisbourg had already become the entrepôt they had envisioned. With the conquest of Canso, it controlled the valuable fishery and was positioned to protect access to the St. Lawrence and become the base for the second aspect of DuQuesnel's two-pronged attack, the privateers that would take the war to sea.

After participating in the Canso offensive, one privateer, Captain Joannis-Galand d'Olabaratz, prepared to set off in pursuit of New England or British merchant ships and fishing vessels which, out at sea, were still unaware of the state of war. His eighty-ton schooner, *Cantabre*, carried a crew of ninety-four men and was armed with eight carriage guns on deck. At the age of fifty-eight, the most famous of the French privateers from Queen Anne's War a generation earlier, Pierre Morpain, set aside his responsibilities as Louisbourg's port captain to return to his old profession. His ship *Succes* had also been part of the Canso fleet. Adventuresome entrepreneurs in Louisbourg scrounged cannons and equipment to outfit several more privateers, including Captain

Pierre Detcheverry's *Marie Joseph* and Captain François Bauchet de Saint-Martin's *Signe*. By late May, the four Louisbourg privateers were at sea, and the unsuspecting New England and British ships fell as easy prey. In one instance, Detcheverry simply sailed up to a British ship, feigned hunger, and requested bread. When he and some of his crew were invited aboard, they took not only the food that was offered, but the ship itself.

In early June, Captain Saint-Martin captured seven New England fishing vessels in nine days. As these prizes arrived back in Louisbourg with their crews under guard of Saint-Martin's sailors, the people were buoyed by the success and were the beneficiaries of the food and cargoes. The vessels were sold, with the proceeds going to the sponsors, captains, and crews of the privateers. Those first weeks of the war were heady times for the officials, soldiers, sailors, and residents of Louisbourg.

When the news of war reached New England, there had been no way of warning the vessels at sea that the French privateers would be an active threat against them, but there was an immediate move to counter the threat. The governor of Massachusetts sent a message to the colony's primary guard ship, the *Prince of Orange*, which was on the Maine coast under the command of the experienced Captain Edward Tyng. The ship was ordered to race to Annapolis Royal on Nova Scotia to alert them to the declaration of war and the probability of attack. Tyng carried out this task and returned promptly to Boston, carrying twenty-six women and children who chose to leave the threatened outpost. In Boston, frantic preparations were under way to outfit privateers, which were given letters of marque permitting them to take French vessels. In the other New England colonies, similar preparations were being made. With reports that there were six French privateers off New England, Captain Daniel Fones took the *Tartar*, Rhode Island's guard vessel, to sea in search of the enemy. At the age of thirty-five, Captain Fones, whose grandfather had fought in the colonial wars of the seventeenth century, had been a captain for four years and had made numerous voyages, including at least one transatlantic crossing. His crew was motivated by the promise that the value of the prizes they captured would be divided among them: one eighth to the captain, two eighths divided among the other officers, and the majority, the remaining five eighths, split equally among the rest of the crew or their next of kin should they be killed. With their homes to defend and money to be made, the New England guard ships and privateers were highly motivated in their risky task.

Captain Tyng of the *Prince of Orange* was the son of Colonel Edward Tyng, who had fought against the French in earlier wars and had died in a French prison. At sixty-one, Tyng, who had been active against the Spanish, was given his chance to avenge his father's death. His wife, Ann, and his three children had experienced his long absences at sea, but now the sea was alive with enemy ships and his family had reason to worry. He got under way from Boston on June 17, 1744, to hunt down the predators who had ravaged the coast for a month. Less than a week later, on Saturday, June 23, the *Prince of Orange* was slatting around in a near calm about fifty miles off Cape Cod when a distant sail was spotted. The newcomer had enough breeze to work down toward the *Prince of Orange*, and a deadly game of cat and mouse began. Captain Tyng initially thought the distant ship was that of his friend Captain William Fletcher in the other Massachusetts guard ship, the sloop *Orphan*, but he was suspicious. Tyng used the strategy of disguise to lure in the other ship. He took down his flags, the British colors, hauled in his guns, closed the gun ports, and concealed his large crew behind the bulwarks in order to look as much like a becalmed merchantman as possible.

As the distance dropped between the two ships, Tyng could see that the approaching vessel flew British colors, but his suspicions remained high. On board the other vessel, Captain d'Olabaratz, fresh from the victory at Canso, prepared for another easy conquest. The crew on his ship, *Cantabre*, waited for the moment when d'Olabaratz would strike the false British colors, run up his true French colors, and fire on the New England merchantman to force its surrender. When that moment came, the gun ports of the *Prince of Orange* sprang open, her cannons were run out as her British colors were run up, and a full broadside attack from Tyng's ship raked the *Cantabre*. The astonished d'Olabaratz fired two cannons in a haphazard response and ran out his oars to attempt an escape in the light air.

Tyng responded with his oars and the chase was on, an exhausting ordeal that tested the endurance and commitment of both crews. The pursuit under oar power lasted over twelve hours. Tyng's men, encouraged by periodic rations of rum, labored at their long sweeps, which propelled the 180-ton *Prince of Orange* after the fleeing *Cantabre*. Whenever Tyng felt he was within range, his gunner fired the "bow chaser," a cannon mounted on the bow of the ship, facing forward. Nine times the cannonballs struck the French ship, killing several sailors, who were dropped over the side. It was the middle of the night when the New Englanders finally neared the *Cantabre*. Tyng realized that the courageous Frenchmen, in a final desperate move, were going to attempt to close with the *Prince of Orange* and board and capture her. Tyng's guns were instantly manned, and d'Olabaratz's crew scrambled belowdecks for protection from the devastating barrage from cannons and swivel guns that followed. The French captain surrendered his damaged ship, which was left with no mast or rigging, and the *Prince of Orange* took her in tow.

Within two months, the French privateer threat was neutralized. The New England guard ships and privateers patrolled the coast, continuing their quest for French prizes, and by August, there were twenty-four American privateers at sea: one from New Hampshire, four from Philadelphia, five from Boston, six from New York, and eight from tiny but tenacious Rhode Island. When Captain Tyng arrived in Boston towing the disabled *Cantabre*, there was public celebration, and the *Boston Evening Post* praised the captain's bravery and good conduct. Several merchants in Boston made a more tangible presentation to Captain Tyng in the form of a handsomely engraved silver urn weighing one hundred ounces. His prisoner, Captain d'Olabaratz, was kept under arrest in Boston for several months, but it was a casual form of constraint because d'Olabaratz was something of a celebrity. He had the freedom not only to move around the city, but also to travel around the colonies. Making his way to Newport, Rhode Island, and as far south as Philadelphia, he was a keen observer and gathered as much intelligence as he could. There is speculation that William Shirley, the governor of Massachusetts, used d'Olabaratz as a pawn in a disinformation campaign, planting the idea that the British government was planning an attack on Louisbourg the following spring, hoping that the French would be forced into the defense of their fortress rather than making offensive attacks against Annapolis Royal, Boston, or other New England ports.

Silver urn given to Captain Tyng

While d'Olabaratz was at liberty and traveling the eastern seaboard, another keen military observer was enjoying his liberty in Louisbourg. Captured at the fall of Canso, Lieutenant John Bradstreet must have felt that he was returning home when he arrived at Louisbourg. Bradstreet was born in Annapolis Royal in 1714, his father English and his mother a Frenchwoman from the prominent Acadian La Tour family. He had visited his La Tour relatives in Louisbourg often during the years of peace and had made friends among the upper tier of society in the French city. Quite naturally, he was given special treatment and was able to move about the city, observing conditions and talking with the inhabitants. After considering the drain on scarce resources of caring for the prisoners from the Canso victory and the crews from the ships captured by the privateers, DuQuesnel sent Bradstreet to negotiate a prisoner exchange with Governor Shirley. An agreement was reached in which the hundred prisoners held by each side would be exchanged in September. In addition, the New Englanders were forced to agree that they would not bear arms against the French for one year.

With his rich supply of intelligence, d'Olabaratz returned to Louisbourg. His perspective was that the New Englanders were interested primarily in making money from the conflict, and he perceptively cited the recent debacle under British command in the West Indies as a reason for New England reticence to fight. In his report he said: "I have talked to many people. I believe on the whole that the townspeople, except the bourgeois and the superior artisans, are privateering, and that the country people will not engage without large promises and rewards. It is true that there was very easily found plenty of men to engage in the expedition to Cartagena and elsewhere in the Spanish Indies, but beyond the fact that they were disgusted with the ill success of this enterprise, they were attracted to it by the hope of the gold and silver of that country, and they are persuaded that there are more blows to suffer than gold pieces to capture in an expedition against Isle Royale [Cape Breton], and they are free men." D'Olabaratz also said that Boston was a rich city, and with the reticence to fight, the city would pay a handsome ransom to avoid a destructive attack.

In addition to his opinion that the New Englanders had no will to fight, he reported the disinformation concerning the planning of an attack on Louisbourg from England that had been cryptically alluded to in Boston newspapers in August. As winter approached and the "season" for military operations in the northern reaches of New England closed, all this information was sent to France so the ministers could address the issues and the needs of their colonies the following year.

CHAPTER 15

Audacious Plan

Just as d'Olabaratz had returned to Louisbourg bursting with intelligence to share, so, too, did John Bradstreet on his return to Boston. He immediately delivered a report to Governor Shirley that described the conditions within the French fortress: The previous winter had been very difficult, the city was not well supplied, there was stress within the garrison troops and strain between Commandant DuQuesnel and his officers, and some of the fortifications were in poor condition. Bradstreet later admitted that he had "fixed" the intelligence, writing, "I did represent the strength of the place and every other circumstance relating thereto in a worse condition than they really were, by reason I found the people in general were greatly against undertaking any expeditions, from the bad success they always had of them . . ."

Clearly Bradstreet thought there was an opportunity for the conquest of Louisbourg, and he sensed the reluctance of the Massachusetts population to become involved in another perhaps inglorious expedition like Cartagena. As the governor considered his options, he and others were bothered by a gnawing concern that would haunt Lieutenant Bradstreet for years into the future: These reports came from a man born in Nova Scotia, of a French mother, with Louisbourg relatives and a thorough knowledge of the French fortress. The concern was whether Bradstreet was a French sympathizer or even a spy.

Could his intelligence be relied upon? With these doubts, Governor Shirley simply wrote to the Duke of Newcastle, urgently requesting ships of the Royal Navy to patrol the New England and Nova Scotia coasts the following year to prevent any French attack. In the fall of 1744, Shirley was thinking defensively.

There was, however, one man in New England who had the audacity to challenge that defensive attitude and ultimately change the history of America. That man was William Vaughn, a rash and impetuous entrepreneur, who since 1726, four years after his graduation from Harvard College, had been living on the eastern frontier of Maine. His enterprises included a fishing and trading post on Matinicus Isle off Penobscot Bay and lumber mills on Damariscotta Pond at the head of the Damariscotta River, near Pemaquid Point. In both of these projects, he encouraged settlers to move there and work in his industries, and he built garrison houses to protect them from Indian attacks and future hostilities with the French. Disturbed by the successful French attack against Canso, and particularly stirred by DuQuesnel and Duvivier's later attempt to take Annapolis Royal, which even though it failed was threatening to colonial interests, Vaughn was highly motivated to do his duty for his country. His father had been among the New England soldiers who captured Annapolis Royal in 1710 and was later lieutenant governor of New Hampshire. The Vaughns had been a leading family in the region since 1643. Determined to act, he left his vulnerable holdings in Damariscotta and traveled to Boston, where he began to foment a dramatic military action. He met with Bradstreet and heard his account of the situation at Louisbourg and then made exhausting trips on horseback to various locations to speak with other former Louisbourg prisoners, like John Tufton Mason in Portsmouth, New Hampshire, to verify the information. He also secured the assurance of Governor Benning Wentworth of New Hampshire that he would support an effort against the French fortress.

By early December, Vaughn was prepared to make the case for an attack on Louisbourg. He was not alone in advocating the conquest of the fortress city. Lieutenant Governor George Clarke of New York, Christopher Kilby, the Massachusetts agent in London, and Robert Auchmuty, the judge of Boston's Vice-Admiralty Court, envisioned an attack led by the British military, with full involvement of the Royal

Navy and only supplemental support from America soldiers. This was Governor Shirley's position as well in December 1744, when he met with the firebrand Vaughn, whose plan was similar to that advocated by Bradstreet and called for a surprise attack on the French stronghold by an American force before the winter passed. In Vaughn's overly ambitious scheme, a force of fifteen hundred New Englanders would use scaling ladders or steal over Louisbourg's wall on snowdrifts. Shirley, a British civil servant, could not imagine the task being as simple as Vaughn outlined, but he knew that Vaughn could back up his assertions about the conditions at Louisbourg and the willingness of the men of Maine and New Hampshire to respond.

With some reluctance, Shirley called for a special session of the Massachusetts General Court, to be held on January 9, 1745. As the session convened, the legislators were shocked when the governor insisted that they all swear to complete secrecy concerning the matter he was about to discuss: his recommendation that troops be raised and an American expedition against Louisbourg be financed without either the endorsement or the military support of the British govern-

Governor William Shirley

ment. A committee appointed to study the proposal and make a recommendation acted with surprising speed and opposed the governor's
proposal. It was, after all, an outlandish notion that a band of raw
American militiamen, few of whom had any combat experience,
could launch an attack without the aid of British soldiers on the most
heavily fortified city in North America and expect to conquer Louisbourg. It was a strong rejection, but perhaps a great relief to Shirley.
He had taken a risk in even making the outrageous suggestion, and if
the venture had been undertaken, his reputation and career would
have been in peril. Within a day of receiving the court's response,
Shirley accepted the decision and wrote to the Duke of Newcastle,
conveying and endorsing the general court's request that Great Britain
initiate a campaign to conquer Louisbourg.

The court's rejection might have been acceptable to the politician
William Shirley, but it was totally unacceptable to the energetic and
ambitious William Vaughn, who set out to rouse support and demonstrate to the Massachusetts government that not only could the project be managed, but that it was also the desire of the people. The
ambitious Vaughn wrote a letter to Governor Shirley on January 14,
urging an attack on Louisbourg and offering to raise one thousand
men and, immodestly, offering himself as leader. But he went on to
say, "If your Excellency thinks it proper to give the same to another . . .
I am ready with the same Diligence by Night and Day at my own Expence to encourage Men to act in the Affair with the utmost Vigour &
then to retire to my own private business." Despite swearing the legislators to secrecy, the news had leaked out, and word of the concept
raced through Boston and the surrounding towns and soon was carried to other colonies. Vaughn once again took to his horse and began
to muster popular support for a reconsideration of the proposal. In
the maritime center of Marblehead, where scores of fishing boats lay
idle because of the threat from Louisbourg's privateers, Vaughn generated a petition signed by more than one hundred fishing captains.
The fishermen guaranteed the legislature that on two weeks' notice
they could provide enough vessels to carry a force of thirty-five hundred men to Cape Breton. It was clear that the encouragement and
commitment of the prominent and influential merchants was also
required to sway the fretful legislators. In soliciting the merchants'

support, Vaughn enlisted the aid of James Gibson, a former officer in the British army, a respected Boston merchant, and a friend of the governor, who had sought his advice on the Louisbourg issue. In a short time, Gibson and Vaughn produced a petition in which two hundred of the city's "principal gentlemen" endorsed Vaughn's brash scheme.

Armed with these powerful popular endorsements, Vaughn took the case back to the wavering Shirley, and, convinced by Vaughn and his documents, the governor called for the general court to meet again. A new committee was appointed to consider the issue, chaired by a popular and well-respected merchant, William Pepperrell, who could speak convincingly on the issue as a Portsmouth, New Hampshire–based entrepreneur who had carried on trade with Louisbourg since the 1720s. He knew well the pros and cons of the French entrepôt and fortress and became a champion of the cause. The governor affirmed that the assistance of the other northern colonies would be requested and would, no doubt, be forthcoming. Six days after the committee was formed, it issued its endorsement of the plan and called for a vote of the general court. There were still many among the legislators who doubted the ability of their colony to lead this endeavor successfully, and the outcome of the vote was in real question. Whether it was through political manipulation, physical coercion, or simple happenstance, the vote was held at a time when several opponents were not in attendance, and one opponent conveniently broke his leg on the way to the vote. With this "odd" circumstance, the proposal passed by the slimmest of margins: one vote.

The people of Massachusetts were galvanized into action. If they could have had the benefit of more timely information on the situation in Louisbourg, the New Englanders would have been even more confident of their chances for success. In late September 1744, soon after Bradstreet and the other British and American prisoners left Louisbourg, Commandant DuQuesnel died. Since it would take many months for a successor to be selected and make his way to the French outpost, a temporary appointment was made. The acting governor was Louis Du Pont Duchambon, who had spent his entire career on Cape Breton and the Île St. Jean, the island to the north of Cape

Breton known today as Prince Edward Island. In April 1744, Duchambon was appointed king's lieutenant for Île Royale (Cape Breton),
which made him the highest-ranking military officer at Louisbourg
and a member of the ruling Conseil Supérieur. It was from this position
that he stepped into the commandant's role to replace DuQuesnel. At
age sixty-four, he bore a pessimistic attitude and immediately wrestled
with the burden of his new responsibilities. Influenced by d'Olabaratz,
he sent plaintive messages to the ministers in France, warning that it
was doubtful that the fortress, ill equipped and undermanned, could be
defended in a concerted attack.

Duchambon's fragile grip on conditions at Louisbourg was threatened when at dawn on December 27, the mercenary Swiss Karrer
Regiment formed up on the parade ground of the Louisbourg citadel
to protest their conditions. The Swiss, however, were perturbed that
the French soldiers had not joined them as promised. Quickly, one
of their officers, Ensign Jean-François Rasser, gave them assurances
that their complaint would be remedied, and the situation seemed to
be defused. The Swiss returned to their quarters in the Château St.
Louis, but instead of going about their routine, they went into the
French soldiers' area, berated them for reneging on their promise to
join in the demonstration, and began to foment a full-blown mutiny.
The mutineers sent the garrison drummer, protected by sixteen soldiers with muskets and fixed bayonets, on a march through the town
to announce the revolt. Officers with swords in hand tumbled from
their comfortable homes and raced to the citadel to suppress the
mutiny. The armed guards, posted by the soldiers, threatened the
lives of the officers and prevented most from entering. A few, including Major De La Parelle, managed to get in and got the recalcitrant
soldiers to form into ranks while the flustered Duchambon asked the
reason for the revolt. The soldiers' complaints were relatively inconsequential but reflected the control the officers had over the essentials
the soldiers required: firewood for warmth, proper food rations, and
appropriate clothing for recruits who had arrived three years earlier
and were still not issued what they deserved. The mutiny was resolved in a matter of hours, when Duchambon and Commissaire-
Ordonnateur François Bigot agreed to the soldiers' demands in

principle and promised to work with a committee of soldiers to resolve the details. With this commitment, a semblance of order returned and all seemed to be normal, but the soldiers had experienced
the success of flexing their collective muscle, and they bragged
around the community that they were their own masters. One consequence of the brief uprising was that soldiers intimidated merchants
and coerced them into selling items at prices determined by the soldiers themselves. Some disgruntled merchants felt that their city was
out of control and voiced their desire to leave Louisbourg the following fall. The more serious consequence of the mutiny was the doubt it
planted in the minds of Duchambon and others as to whether the
French and Swiss soldiers of the garrison would stand and fight if
Louisbourg came under attack. Virtually all the enlisted soldiers,
with the exception of a few noncommissioned officers and a thirty-
man company of newly arrived French artillery experts, had joined
in the uprising, and there was no assurance that they would remain
loyal if put to the test.

Had William Vaughn been aware of this mutiny when he was
generating support for the New England campaign against Cape
Breton, his job would have been easier, and the vote in the general
court would undoubtedly have been stronger in favor of the expedition. Yet without knowledge of this dire situation in Louisbourg, the
approval had been given and the decision was met with instant popular support. Speed was of the essence, and the vigorous Vaughn
sprang into action to raise as many troops as possible. His first stop
was New Hampshire, his native colony where his family had been
prominent for more than a century. He met with Governor Benning
Wentworth, a pompous, self-absorbed man with greater ambition
than ability. The great challenge for both Massachusetts and New
Hampshire was their deplorable financial condition. King George II
had forbidden Wentworth to issue any more paper currency, and the
governor fretted as to how New Hampshire could pay for its portion
of the cost. Vaughn carried a message from Governor Shirley, which
outlined a solution. Massachusetts was prepared to stretch its credit
by issuing £50,000 in "bills of credit," and he suggested the same
process to Wentworth. To Vaughn's frustration, the New Hampshire
Legislature authorized only 250 men, half the number anticipated.

Demonstrating his extraordinary commitment to the expedition, Vaughn offered to mortgage his New Hampshire property, valued at £4,000, to cover the immediate costs of an additional 250 men. Ultimately, New Hampshire produced 456 soldiers, with 150 of them paid for and sustained by Massachusetts.

Governor Shirley faced the particular challenge of selecting a commanding officer for the expedition, who would have an enormous influence on the success of future recruitment and loyalty of the soldiers. There were several eager volunteers for the top job, each with boundless ambition. John Bradstreet was only a lieutenant, but he envisioned himself an experienced professional soldier and felt that he was the appropriate person for the job because of his knowledge of Louisbourg, the intelligence he had gathered, and the advice he had offered Shirley. In a later letter Bradstreet wrote, "The Command agree'd upon with Mr. Shiorley [was] to be given to me, but he finding it would be difficult to raise a Sufficient Number of Men Unless under the command of one of their own country Men, appointed [another]." Bradstreet's Nova Scotian birth to a French mother continued to impede his professional progress, and when he learned of his rejection, he was determined to have no part in the endeavor.

The second eager applicant for the leadership role was William Vaughn, clearly a restless man of action who sought glory, stature, and a future government appointment. Shirley realized that Vaughn was a man of too much action, rash and reckless in his decisions, headstrong and impetuous. Vaughn had been invaluable in developing the scheme, gaining support, and rallying volunteers, but his leadership style would expose the expedition to great danger. Vaughn determined to continue to assist with recruitment, but like Bradstreet, he planned to let the expedition head off without his further involvement.

A third aspirant was Samuel Waldo, Captain Edward Tyng's brother-in-law. He had experienced serious financial misfortunes but was a close friend of the governor. His only military experience was in the militia, where he was the colonel of a regiment in eastern Maine, but Waldo hoped that through the successful leadership of the Louisbourg campaign he could achieve distinction and find a path to fiscal stability. Shirley wisely sensed that the appointment of his friend

Waldo would be broadly perceived as cronyism and would undermine the integrity of the expedition.

New Hampshire's governor Wentworth was the fourth person who openly expressed his enthusiasm for and expectation of being appointed commander in chief. Shirley was sufficiently perceptive to realize that placing the campaign in the control of the bombastic Wentworth would result in certain failure. To placate Wentworth, Shirley said he had excluded him because of his gout. The New Hampshire governor protested, but by then, Shirley had made his decision.

Convinced that the most important qualities required for the leadership of the expedition were sound common sense, broad respect, and great popularity, Shirley made a counterintuitive decision. He called upon a man who had great business acumen, with a track record of excellent business decision making and supreme respect in the region: William Pepperrell, the merchant from Kittery, Maine. As chairman of the legislative committee that had influenced the vote to approve the expedition, Pepperrell had already demonstrated his persuasive power and his ability to work diplomatically with various factions. His lack of military experience was a deficiency for the task ahead. Like most men in New England, he had been part of the militia and, because of his stature and popularity, was the senior colonel of the militia in Maine, but he had faced little action, and nothing on the scale of what would be encountered in an assault on Louisbourg.

Unlike the other ambitious aspirants, Pepperrell did not seek the position, and when initially approached, he turned down the request of the governor, indicating that his business affairs needed his attention, and more important, his wife's health prohibited his acceptance of the assignment. Twenty-two years earlier, William Pepperrell had won the affection of Mary Hirst, a fine young lady who was the daughter of a prominent Boston merchant. While Mary may have been in temporary ill health at the time of Shirley's request, there were other influences on Pepperrell, who was at the pinnacle of his career and had nothing to gain and much to lose in the risky adventure. Pepperrell was wealthy and successful. His daughter, Elizabeth, had married an ambitious, well-connected young merchant, Nathaniel

William Pepperrell

Sparhawk, in 1742, and Pepperrell's son, Andrew, had just graduated from Harvard and joined the family business as a partner. With his son and son-in-law to tutor in the business, and the potential for great opportunities in time of war, it was natural for Pepperrell to want to remain at home with his wife and family.

If Pepperrell accepted the governor's offer of command, a victory would bring him praise but could add little to the high position he already held in colonial society. A defeat, which was a very real possibility for the raw troops and inexperienced commanders, could bring ridicule and ruin on the Pepperrell family. Although Pepperrell had declined the honor of command, Shirley was persistent, confident in his choice, and ultimately, with his wife Mary's approval, William Pepperrell accepted his summons to greatness or humiliation.

The announcement of the decision was received enthusiastically in Massachusetts, Maine, and New Hampshire, and recruiting problems melted away. The goal for Massachusetts and its northern territory of

Maine was three thousand soldiers, the majority of those needed for the mission. The legislature had determined that the recruits would be given a blanket and one month's advance pay, but of greatest importance to the volunteers was their entitlement to all the plunder that their conquest of the rich French mercantile center would produce. This was high motivation that not only would encourage enlistment, but would sustain the American troops through the innumerable miseries that lay ahead. Massachusetts could not be expected to manage the campaign on its own, and while Vaughn rallied support from New Hampshire, Shirley contacted the governors of the other northern colonies to win their support.

Connecticut responded well and raised five hundred men for the campaign, once its requirement that its lieutenant governor, Roger Wolcott, be appointed second in command of the expedition was met. Rhode Island, frequently at odds with Massachusetts, received the proposal positively until it learned that this audacious scheme was going to be undertaken without the approval of the British government and without British military or financial support. At that point Rhode Island's zeal cooled, but it did commit its guard vessel, the *Tartar*, and her 130-man crew to the campaign, with Captain Daniel Fones in command.

Beyond New England, where Louisbourg posed little threat to home and hearth, the response was tepid. New York provided no troops or ships but loaned the expedition ten eighteen-pound cannons with their associated equipment. New Jersey turned down the appeal flatly. Pennsylvania debated the appeal but ultimately refused to participate on the basis that Louisbourg had nothing to do with it. The unusually skeptical Benjamin Franklin, in writing to his brother John, a Massachusetts volunteer, had some sage advice. He said, "Fortified towns are hard nuts to crack; and your teeth have not been accustomed to it. Taking strong places is a particular trade which you have taken up without serving an apprenticeship to it. Armies and veterans need skillful engineers to direct them in their attack. Have you any? But some seem to think forts are as easy taken as snuff." Government officials and military professionals in England shared Franklin's doubts when word ultimately reached them that the Americans, who were held in such low regard after the disastrous West Indies campaign, were going to attempt the impossible. Indeed, by this time the English military officers used "American" as a derogatory term.

In the West Indies, the officers of the Royal Navy squadron demonstrated the lack of confidence in the Americans when their commodore, Peter Warren, called them to a meeting. While soliciting the assistance of the other colonies, Shirley had also asked for the help of Warren's squadron. The commodore's wife, Susannah DeLancey, was American, and he had extensive American business dealings and investments. With this background, Warren was inclined to assist, but his captains had serious reservations, particularly because the British government had not sanctioned the Americans' scheme. The squadron had no orders to assist, and there was concern about leaving the West Indies vulnerable to attack by the French. The captains, including Charles Knowles, who had expressed his contempt for the American officers and men in the Cartagena campaign, could only imagine an American rabble failing in its attempt to conquer the famed fortress. Taking the counsel of his captains, Commodore Warren sent the message to Shirley that he would not be able to assist.

This disturbing news arrived only shortly before the expedition was due to sail and was a serious blow to Shirley and a potential threat to the entire endeavor. The governor shared the discouraging information with only Pepperrell and a few other trusted officers, for fear that the lack of British naval support would discourage the troops and the legislatures would derail the effort. They had made great progress. Sufficient troops had been recruited within New England, and the campaign had such momentum that Shirley and Pepperrell believed there was no reason for a delay. All the components of the campaign had come together, and Pepperrell had shown his supreme skill in managing people by bringing three of the four aspiring commanders back into the fold. Fortunately, Governor Wentworth would stay behind, but Bradstreet would serve as a military adviser to Pepperrell, Vaughn would go with the rank of colonel, but with no specific command, and Samuel Waldo would serve as brigadier general.

The spirit of the New Englanders was not dampened by the reticence of the other colonies to join their crusade. Indeed, the assault against the papist stronghold to the north was considered by many to be a religious crusade. Ministers throughout New England preached on the evils of the Catholic Church and the righteousness of the expedition's cause. The Great Awakening had heightened the religious fervor of many New Englanders, and symbolically, the tough seventy-year-old senior chaplain of the expedition, Reverend Samuel Moody, took an ax on the campaign to "hew down the altars of the Antichrist and demolish his idols." To obtain the proper religious imprimatur for the expedition, Lieutenant General William Pepperrell sought and received the blessing of his friend, the famous English evangelist Reverend George Whitefield. Whitefield also provided the motto for the expedition, which would emblazon its flag. With Whitefield's words *Nil desperandum Christo duce*—Despair of nothing with Christ as leader—the crusade would advance under a Protestant Christian banner.

As the force of over four thousand New Englanders began to assemble, the final element, transportation, was addressed. The ship owners from Marblehead, who had months before encouraged the effort, now were called on to fulfill their commitment. The fishing and small cargo ships of the coast had been kept in port by an embargo imposed to ensure that the French did not capture a New England vessel and learn of the preparations. Having lost valuable time at sea, the ship owners were eager to obtain contracts to transport the troops, and the armada began to assemble.

In forty-nine days from the approval in the Massachusetts Legislature, the remarkable feat had been accomplished. Troops were raised, the incredible amount of arms and innumerable supplies were gathered, officers were appointed, detailed plans were made, and the expedition was about to be set in motion. For the first time in history, an American army, serving under American officers, transported in American vessels, protected by American warships, and financed by American colonies, was about to attempt what many believed was an impossible mission.

CHAPTER 16

Voyage to War

MAJOR SETH POMEROY SET OFF from Northampton, Massa-chusetts, on Thursday, March 14, 1745, to join the forces in Boston assembling there for the campaign against Louis-bourg. Pomeroy was a typical provincial officer, experienced in frontier defense, dedicated to his country, literate but with little schooling. He was a fourth-generation American, his great-grandfather Eltweed Pomeroy having arrived in Boston with the first wave of the Great Migration in 1630. Eltweed's son, Medad Pomeroy, a blacksmith, gunsmith, and armorer, was recruited by the residents of Northampton to move to their frontier village in 1660. Not only was Medad's skill as a gunsmith put to the test in the conflicts on the frontier, but so also was his courage. He participated in numerous skirmishes as well as the Falls Fight on May 17, 1676, the last significant battle of King Philip's War. Medad's son Major Ebenezer Pomeroy followed his father in his trade, and his son, Seth, was welcomed into the world on May 20, 1706. Seth's birth came two years after three Pomeroys were captured in the Deerfield raid and marched off to Canada. It was in this tense atmosphere of a community on the edge of the wilderness that Seth Pomeroy matured and developed his skills as a blacksmith and noted gunsmith. He was active in the militia and gained military experience as captain of a company of snowshoe men, raised in 1743 for defense of the frontier as war with France grew more likely.

With his departure for the campaign against Cape Breton, Seth left behind his wife of thirteen years, Mary, and seven children, the youngest of whom, Sarah, was less than a year old. Many of those recruited for the campaign were attracted by the promise of booty and economic gain, but like many American officers, Pomeroy was an established, financially secure member of the community, and there was little for him to gain and much to lose. His response to the call for volunteers was one of patriotism and the all-important defense of his home, threatened once again by the French. As a young man, at a time when distant travel was difficult and dangerous, Pomeroy had ventured beyond the Hudson River. His wife, Mary, demonstrating her adventuresome spirit, accompanied Seth on a two-week journey south to the coast of Connecticut, but the adventure that lay ahead for Seth was unlike anything the rugged frontiersman had ever experienced.

After a two-and-a-half-day trip from Northampton, Pomeroy ar-

Seth Pomeroy's rifle

rived in Boston and discovered a city in a frenzy of preparation. Over three thousand soldiers were converging on the city from all directions, along with armaments, foodstuffs for the troops, barrels of gunpowder, kegs of rum, and all manner of materials needed to support the army in the field. Soldiers arrived in their civilian clothes with no expectation of being issued uniforms. The lucky ones carried a change of clothes in sacks or chests, but many were going to war with only the clothes they were wearing. These men were carpenters, hatters, masons, shoemakers, laborers, indentured servants, coopers, Native Americans, farmers, slaves, and representatives of virtually all the colonial occupations, who were leaving their families and their everyday tasks in response to the call for volunteers. Most brought their personal weapons, but those without muskets were sent to the commissary general, Mr. Wheelwright, to be issued the necessary gun and associated equipment. All the arriving men received the blanket they had been promised upon enlistment. On the day of Pomeroy's arrival, Saturday, March 16, the campaign began, as several of the colonial warships set sail to establish a blockade of Louisbourg. Leading this group was the new twenty-two-gun frigate *Massachusetts*, which had been financed by the colony and personally selected and fitted out by Edward Tyng, commodore of the colonial fleet and the senior officer. Sailing with Tyng was the twenty-four-gun *Molineux*, under the command of Captain Jonathan Snelling, and the fourteen-gun snow-type brig *Caesar*. The guns these ships carried were mounted on carriages that could be maneuvered on deck, but most of the colonial warships were also equipped with an equal number of smaller cannons, known as swivel guns, that were pivoted in brackets on the ship's rail and could fire small cannonballs or grapeshot into an enemy. The commodore rendezvoused with three other colonial warships, the twenty-two-gun *Fame*, his old ship the fourteen-gun *Prince of Orange*, and the twelve-gun *Boston Packet*, to complete his blockading squadron. None of these vessels would be a match for a large French frigate carrying more than thirty heavier cannons or for a dreaded French ship of the line of sixty guns or more, but it was hoped that together they could successfully blockade the French fortress and overwhelm any French merchant ships attempting to get supplies to the city. Without the assistance of Commodore Warren's

Royal Navy ships, this first American "navy" would have its mettle truly tested if it encountered a large French warship.

During the week he stayed in Boston, Major Pomeroy attended to the business of the Fourth Massachusetts Regiment, of which he was third in command, behind Colonel Samuel Willard and Lieutenant Colonel Thomas Chandler. The regiment consisted of ten companies and totaled 458 men. Amid the beehive of activity, soldiers from Pomeroy's regiment and the others gathering in Boston were assigned to transport ships. When these were filled, they would move down the harbor to the assembly point at Nantasket Roads. Each day, a dozen or so ships would make this short voyage to the anchorage, while the ships already there periodically disembarked their soldiers for drill and practice on one of the harbor islands. A week after his arrival in Boston, Pomeroy boarded his own transport, the *Hannah and Mary*, commanded by Captain David Cannida, and joined the fleet. All that was now required was the arrival of the commanding general, William Pepperrell, on board the twenty-four-gun snow *Shirley*. Named in honor of the governor, the *Shirley* was under command of the experienced privateer John Rous, who would act as commodore of the fleet of transports, supply ships, and warships about to sail toward Cape Breton.

Pepperrell arrived the following day, Sunday, March 24, with the thought that the Sabbath would be a propitious day to begin their religious crusade. After time for morning religious services and blessings on the undertaking, preparations were made to get under way, and in midafternoon, the ships carrying twenty-eight hundred troops, the main body of the army, hoisted their anchors and with a fair wind from the southwest sailed into the broad Massachusetts Bay for which the colony was named. Commodore Rous had over fifty ships in his convoy and herded his charges toward the northeast and their destination, Canso. Several days before, twelve transports carrying the New Hampshire Regiment, under the protection of that colony's guard sloop, the ten-gun *Abigail*, sailed from Newcastle. Additional small fleets would sail from Boston and New London, Connecticut, in the days following, bringing additional troops to Canso. In all, the American fleet would consist of over ninety transports carrying over four thousand troops, protected by a colonial navy of fourteen small warships. It was an astonishing achievement to assemble this army and fleet in forty-nine days.

Despite the fact that the troops were crammed into the small fishing sloops and schooners redolent with the residue of their normal occupation, spirits were high aboard the transports. With the blessing of Reverend George Whitefield, all were certain that their expedition also had the blessing of their God, a belief that was immediately challenged as the fleet sailed into the darkness. As the winds veered to the east, a severe storm developed. Like most of the soldiers huddled in the stinking hold of the transport and tossed about by large waves, Major Pomeroy was struck by seasickness as the fleet was scattered while beating into a gale. On Tuesday evening, March 26, the miserable Pomeroy's ship sought refuge on the Maine coast at the mouth of the Sheepscot River, where they found the *Shirley* and several dozen transports also seeking shelter from the storm. The fleet lay in this harbor of refuge for several days while the storm blew itself out.

With a fair wind from the northwest and the troops somewhat recuperated, on Friday, March 29, Pepperrell gave orders to continue the voyage to Canso. If the hand of providence was guiding this expedition, however, it could not be found in the Gulf of Maine. In the words of Seth Pomeroy, they sailed with "a Fair wind Till ye next Day about noon & then Came up a Tarible North East Storm all ye Day and night Till about Braak of Day a Sabath Day morning & then a Calm all ye Day which was 31 we Lay Rowling in ye Seas with our Sails Furl,d with Prodigious wave Monday another Turible Storm which was ye I : Day of april this Days Storm Scattered our Fleet ye Storm Towards night abated & then we were left alone." He goes on to recount that from Friday until Tuesday, "Sick Day and night So bad that I have not words To Set it Forth, nor Can I give any Body an Idea of it that hath not Felt ye Same or Some thinge like it & So Shall Say no more here." The full extent of the misery experienced by those suffering in their close quarters belowdecks is hard to comprehend. The nor'easter they endured was accompanied by wind and snow, with mountainous seas. On one of the transports, the captain and the mate sought courage from their supply of rum, and the terrified soldiers were saved only by the sailing ability of a fisherman from among their ranks. Most of the troops were landsmen, and riveting fear that the little ships would founder on the high seas or grind themselves to pieces on the rocky coast compounded their seasickness.

One of the chroniclers of the ordeal, Benjamin Stearns, wrote of this nor'easter, "The weather was Exceedeing Bad for us their arose a greate storm and the sea run mountainous high and it did rain very heard and the wind Did Blow very hard so that Wee was fain to let Down our sailes and lett Drive wheir the seas would carry us and a terriable storm we had so bad that I thought that Every minet would Be the Last . . ." Finally he reports that "the seays left hurricagning." When Seth Pomeroy later wrote to his wife of his thirteen-day ordeal of seasickness, he said, "If any Body Ever Dyed with Sea Sickness I Believe I Should If it had Continued a Little while Longer."

The fleet was scattered across a vast expanse of ocean as they fought for their lives. On April 1, the wind moderated and the battered vessels made their way toward their goal, where on Thursday, April 4, after a day of thick snow, the *Shirley*, with General Pepperrell aboard, sailed into Canso harbor to see what was left of the great fleet. Pepperrell found only twenty transports, and it appeared as if the terrible storm had taken a heavy toll, but on the following day, other transports, including the *Hannah and Mary* with Seth Pomeroy, began to glide in. Within a few days there were sixty-eight vessels at anchor, and others continued to straggle in. Ultimately, every vessel that had set out from Boston on March 24 arrived safely, a tribute to the colonial shipbuilders and also an affirmation of the skills and fortitude of the colonial sailors.

With his army intact and only the critical five hundred men of the Connecticut Regiment yet to arrive, Pepperrell began to assess his situation and prepare his troops for the battle ahead. They had received news that Gabarus Bay, where their landing would be made a few miles west of Louisbourg, was clogged with impenetrable drift ice. While this meant that they would have to remain in Canso until the ice cleared, it also provided the opportunity to recover from the voyage, organize the army into four divisions, study the plan for the surprise attack that Governor Shirley had laid out in excruciating detail, and assess the strength of the force. Shirley's plan called for an exceedingly dangerous night landing and surprise attack by the entire army. The first of the four divisions would storm and take the Royal Battery. The second would take the Dauphin Gate, the main portal to the city. The third would struggle through the swamp and storm the thirty-foot-high walls on the landward side of the city, and the fourth would be held in reserve to assist where needed. It was a daring plan that would require complete secrecy, precise timing, utmost discipline among the troops, and superb coordination and leadership from the officers. The plan would have been the consummate challenge for the most professional soldiers and officers in Europe and was far beyond the capabilities of the band of dedicated, enthusiastic amateurs who were assembling in Canso. Pepperrell nevertheless continued to prepare for the attack using Governor Shirley's plan, which also included an alternative approach if surprise were not possible. Fortunately, at the end of Shirley's detailed instructions was the declaration, "Sir, Upon the whole, notwithstanding the instructions you have received from me; I must leave it to you to act upon unforeseen emergencies, according to your best discretion." With these words, the general had the latitude he and his war council, which included Brigadier General Samuel Waldo, Colonel John Bradstreet, and Colonel William Vaughn, needed to make the necessary changes and adjustments demanded by circumstances on the field of battle.

One great concern was the lack of heavy cannons that would be required in the event the surprise was unsuccessful and a siege ensued. The artillery available to the troops consisted of only thirty-four cannons, with the largest able to fire only twenty-two-pound cannonballs, and several mortars, which could hurl explosive shells high into the air over the city walls to explode in or above the buildings of Louisbourg. The mortars could do serious damage to both structures and morale, but it would be difficult if not impossible to batter a breach in the city's defenses with the small cannons. In describing the situation at Louisbourg, Bradstreet had reported that the Royal Battery was armed with cannons using massive forty-two-pound balls, and in anticipation of capturing this impressive, stand-alone fortress, Pepperrell's army was well supplied with shot for these forty-two-pounders that could indeed demolish the city walls if the French guns could be captured and turned against the fortress.

While Pepperrell refined his plans and some of the troops drilled and exercised with their weapons, others erected a new fortress blockhouse, prefabricated in New England to replace the structure burned by Duvivier in the opening attack of the war a year before. Reverend Moody and numerous other chaplains who accompanied the troops looked after the religious needs of the army. On Sundays, morning and afternoon sermons were preached in open-air services that lasted for hours. Life at Canso settled into a routine, punctuated periodically by the arrival of ships bringing news of events beyond the confines of the harbor.

Of particular interest was the success the colonial warships had in capturing prizes. The *Boston Packet* captured a sloop from Martinique attempting to reach Louisbourg with its cargo of rum, wine, brandy, and valuable indigo. The indigo would fetch a good price in Boston, but the rum, wine, and brandy would be retained for the use of the army. The *Molineux* captured a vessel carrying £25,000 worth of rum, molasses, coffee, sugar, chocolate, and syrup, also from Martinique. Other ships succeeded in gathering intelligence. Flying French colors, Captain David Donahue's ten-gun Massachusetts sloop *Resolution* lured several Indians aboard and learned that the French were planning a new attack on Port Royal to win back Nova Scotia, making it clear that the attack on Louisbourg was essential to put the French on the defensive.

Flushed with their successes against the small merchant ships attempting to reach Louisbourg, the American blockaders rose to the occasion when faced with a far more formidable challenge. In February, the *Renommee*, a new French frigate with thirty-two eight-pound cannons on her decks, left France carrying dispatches to the government in Louisbourg. The frigate was spotted off Canso on April 18, and the Americans knew that if this Frenchman reached Louisbourg, their element of surprise would be lost. Captain Rous in the twenty-four-gun *Shirley*, along with the little sloop *Massachusetts* and the *Abigail*, each with ten guns, immediately set off in pursuit, but in the fog and darkness the French warship slipped away. The following day, as the *Renommee* attempted to approach Louisbourg, she encountered the pride of the colonial force, Commodore Tyng's new twenty-two-gun frigate, *Massachusetts*, and her two consorts, the *Fame* and the *Caesar*, with thirty-four guns between them. Captain Guy-François de Coëtnempren de Kersaint of the *Renommee* soon discovered he had stumbled into a hornets' nest, and the battle was instantly under way. The other New England warships, which had been hunting for the French frigate, were drawn by the sound of the gunfire, and as many as nine participated in the wild melee. The daring little *Caesar*, *Prince of Orange*, and *Boston Packet* maneuvered into range and exchanged broadsides with the far superior Frenchman, which with thirty-two guns outmatched any of the American ships, but the colonial vessels swarmed around, attempting to overwhelm their enemy.

Kersaint recognized his predicament. The *Shirley* fired 115 cannons at the *Renommee*, which continued to exchange gunfire as she sailed downwind, hoping to escape and fight another day. The chase lasted for hours, but with her superior speed, as darkness came on, the French frigate effected her escape. The Americans were frustrated that they had not taken what would have been a spectacular prize, but they were satisfied that they had prevented the *Renommee* from reaching Louisbourg with the news of the American armada in Canso. The Americans had also demonstrated their courage in engaging an enemy of superior force. Commodore Tyng and the blockading ships returned to their positions off Louisbourg to prevent any further attempts by the French frigate to reach the city. The *Shirley* and other cruisers watched for the *Renommee* to reappear near Canso, in the event the French ship attempted to attack the fleet of transports at anchor there.

For several days, watchful eyes scanned the horizon off Canso for any sign of the French intruder. Then, on April 22, four days after the battle with the *Renommee*, the topgallants of a large warship were spotted, with the ship itself hull down over the horizon. Anxious moments passed as the New Englanders prepared for another encounter with the unwelcome visitor, but then trepidation turned to celebration as the Yankee sailors recognized the familiar characteristics of the forty-gun Royal Navy ship HMS *Eltham*, under the command of Captain Philip Durell. This was a welcome sight since now there would be a ship on the colonials' side that could exchange broadside for broadside with the *Renommee* with almost assured victory. General Pepperrell and the few senior officers who knew that Commodore Warren had refused to help in the campaign were particularly encouraged and gratified by the arrival of the *Eltham*. Durell and his ship had been on the New England coast for some time, preparing to escort a convoy of "mast ships" scheduled to depart for England with their holds crammed with great lengths of American timber to be converted into masts for His Majesty's Navy. It appeared as if Warren had relented and allowed HMS *Eltham* and Durell, an experienced veteran of Vernon's West Indies campaign, to join the American venture as a token, but much appreciated, Royal Naval presence.

Durell came to anchor off Canso and reported to General Pepperrell that he was not the lone Royal Navy participant in the campaign, but the vanguard of a Royal Navy squadron under command of Commodore Peter Warren himself, due to arrive at any time. At the time Governor Shirley had written to Commodore Warren requesting his assistance, he also wrote to the Duke of Newcastle in London, informing the ministry of the Americans' audacious plan to attack Louisbourg and requesting support from the Royal Navy. Shirley candidly admitted that it was possible that the raw colonial troops would be unable to take the fortress, but he was confident that they could make a sufficiently strong attack to destroy the structures outside the fortress walls, thoroughly disrupt the French fishery, and put the French on the defensive so they could not consider an attack on Annapolis Royal and the reconquest of Nova Scotia. Certainly Newcastle and the experienced professional military men in England knew that the undisciplined American rabble would be no match for the French fortress and its professional garrison augmented by the militia. However, with war being waged in the colonies, he sent a message to Warren in Antigua, giving the commodore the latitude he needed to join the fray.

Warren received Newcastle's message only three days after sending off his reluctant refusal to Shirley. Once again he called his captains together to discuss the somewhat ambiguous orders, which directed Warren and several of his ships to proceed to Boston but did not specifically order them to join in the attack on Louisbourg. He was encouraged to, "as occasion shall offer, attack and distress the enemy in their settlements, and annoy their fisheries and commerce."

Despite his captains' continued reluctance, Warren was anxious to participate. The irascible captain Charles Knowles, who had been so critical of the Americans during the Cartagena campaign, was left behind in command of the remaining ships in the West Indies, as Warren commandeered Knowles's ship, the powerful sixty-gun HMS *Superbe*, as his flagship, much to Knowles's consternation.

When news reached New York that Commodore Warren and his squadron were bound for Boston, Warren's wife, Susannah, immediately left their New York home and headed north in hopes of seeing her husband in Boston. While making its way north, on April 10, Warren's squadron came upon a schooner out of Marblehead, and Warren learned from its captain that the army had departed Boston for Canso seventeen days earlier. Putting duty before personal pleasure, Warren asked the schooner to take the information to Boston that he would be sailing directly for Canso. Mrs. Warren would have to wait some time to see her husband.

Only one day after the arrival of HMS *Eltham*, Warren's flagship, the sixty-gun HMS *Superbe*, with HMS *Launceston* and HMS *Mermaid*, each carrying forty guns, arrived off Canso. The addition of this powerful squadron added 1,165 men and 180 cannons to the expedition, which was now officially a joint American and British adventure. Eager to immediately apply his force to the blockading of Louisbourg, Commodore Warren did not bring his squadron into Canso harbor but hove to off the harbor entrance and welcomed General Pepperrell on board the *Superbe* to discuss the situation and the sensitive issue of command. In his initial January 29 letter to Warren requesting the commodore's involvement in the expedition, Governor Shirley sought to entice him with a bold offer, suggesting, "If the service in which you are engaged would permit you to come yourself and take upon you the command of the Expedition, it would, I doubt not, be a most happy event for His Majesty's service and your own honor." Desperate to lure the naval officer into the campaign, Shirley gave little thought to the resentment and ill will that lingered among the New Englanders after the abuse they had experienced at the hands of the British officers in the Cartagena debacle.

As the old acquaintances Warren and Pepperrell met on board *Superbe*, overall command was there for Warren to assume and Pepperrell to forfeit, but Warren did not assert his claim. Instead, a joint command was established, in which Pepperrell remained in command of the land forces and Warren asserted his command over all the forces afloat, which included, in addition to his Royal Navy squadron, all of the colonial warships, transports, and supply ships. While this appeared to be a logical and equitable distribution of authority, it also had the potential for the debilitating acrimony that had developed between Vice Admiral Vernon and General Wentworth in the West Indies. It also had another critical dimension for Commodore Warren, who was favorably disposed toward the colonies and their success because of his involvement and investments. The success of the colonies meant success for him. However, Warren was a realist, with a keen eye for military and commercial risk. In this hastily put together expedition against the formidable French fortress, the British military minds saw virtually no chance for success and every opportunity for dismal failure. If he assumed overall command, Warren's reputation and fortunes would rise or most probably fall on the success or failure of taking Louisbourg. With the carefully structured shared command, Warren had a win/win situation. As commander of the naval forces, he would be seen as valiantly protecting the land forces and demonstrating Great Britain's support for her dauntless colonies. When, as was likely, the undisciplined New England soldiers botched and bungled their way to defeat, no blame would fall on Warren. It was likely that he could emerge as a hero for having protected the transports and providing a way for the fleeing troops to reembark, escape destruction, and return battered and defeated to New England. On the minuscule chance that the Americans achieved the impossible and conquered the city, Warren was perfectly positioned to swoop in for a good share of the glory as the man who kept the army safe.

He also stood to profit from his situation. Within the navy and among the privateers, it was the tradition that they would receive prize money equal to the value of the vessels captured as well as their contents. Warren had the opportunity to add further prizes to the six already taken by the colonial cruisers in the first weeks of the expedition, and as commodore, Warren was entitled to one eighth of any prizes taken by his squadron. To make things equitable, he ordered that any prize taken by any ship in the squadron would be

Commodore Peter Warren

shared by all ships in the squadron, after the commodore's eighth had been subtracted, of course. After these details were worked out, Peter Warren and his squadron departed Canso and headed for Louisbourg sixty miles to the east, to add their considerable force to the blockade. The arrival of the powerful ships of the Royal Navy was of great encouragement to all involved and immediately put minds at ease with regard to the threatening presence of the *Renommee* in the region. The French frigate's thirty-two guns were no match for any of the new arrivals, and certainly Captain Kersaint would not have the temerity to attempt to run their formidable blockade to reach Louisbourg. In fact, the *Renommee* was cruising far to the west and was no threat to either the army in Canso or the ships off Louisbourg. General Pepperrell now awaited the arrival of the long overdue five-hundred-man Connecticut Regiment, which would bring his army to the size calculated as necessary to carry out a successful campaign, once the ice cleared from the landing beaches near Louisbourg.

During the first week of April, the *Tartar* from Rhode Island sailed into the harbor of New London, Connecticut, to assist Connecticut's twelve-gun guard sloop *Defence* in protecting the Connecticut Regiment on its voyage to Canso. A week later, on Sunday, April 14, the Connecticut fleet of seven transports, escorted by the two warships, got under way. They had chosen the Sabbath day to commence their crusade, just as the Massachusetts troops had three weeks earlier. Major General Roger Walcott knew his contingent was behind schedule, and the sailors worked hard to get past Nantucket and her dangerous shoals before heading toward the northeast, which they did on April 19. Fortunately, the Connecticut force had fair winds and did not have to endure the miseries experienced by the Massachusetts contingent. By April 21, they were off Cape Sable on the southwest tip of Nova Scotia.

The realities of the life-and-death struggle of war intruded on their pleasant voyage when, early on the morning of April 23, the *Renommee* was sighted bearing down on the vulnerable fleet. The situation was grim since the bigger ship could easily bully her way past the guard sloops and into the midst of the defenseless transports. With powerful broadsides erupting from both sides of the French frigate, the destruction of the Connecticut Regiment was a near certainty. Quickly assessing the dire situation, Captain Daniel Fones boldly took the *Tartar* to challenge the Frenchman, leaving the Connecticut contingent in the protection of Captain John Prentice in the *Defence*. It was pure folly for a fourteen-gun brig to sail into single-ship combat with the far superior French frigate, the same ship that had fought off nine colonial cruisers and escaped through swift sailing only days before. Yet that was Fones's self-sacrificing decision, and he initiated the combat, firing his bow chasers at the oncoming frigate, which veered and answered with a broadside. The first fusillade did no damage, and as the *Tartar* maneuvered to get a favorable position to windward of the *Renommee*, the French unleashed three more broadsides. Over sixty cannons were fired at the *Tartar*, but the only damage the brig suffered was the loss of a jib halyard shot away by the torrent of cannonballs.

Fones's reckless action distracted Captain Kersaint from his potentially destructive assault on the vulnerable transports, and, following the customs of chivalry in the eighteenth century, Kersaint was unable to refuse the challenge Fones presented. The chase was on, and as the pursuer, Kersaint had to follow the dictates of Captain Fones. Positioned to windward of the *Renommee*, Fones chose to claw his way farther upwind, which would lead the French frigate farther and farther away from the transports. The chase went on all day as the *Tartar* tried to demonstrate that she was a match on the wind for the Frenchman, but clearly it was a losing race for Fones. In a final desperate attempt to improve the sailing ability of his brig, Fones directed the crew to take axes to the vessel and "cut down the waist," deliberately weakening his ship but adding a slight bit of speed. As darkness came on, the *Renommee* still loomed behind them, leaving Fones with only the consolation that he had led the frigate away from the transports and the five hundred men of the Connecticut Regiment might be saved even if the *Tartar* were lost.

The day after the *Tartar*'s sacrifice, the *Defence* successfully escorted the seven Connecticut transports into Canso, and word of the *Tartar*'s inevitable fate spread among the ships and troops. Finally, and miraculously, General Pepperrell had his entire army intact and now needed only the ice to clear to begin the assault. That news arrived the following morning when Captain John Griffith sailed the *Caesar* into Canso at dawn to alert the general. There was an instant increase in activity as word spread that the ice had cleared and preparations began for reembarkation and the attack. If the New England army needed one more sign that the hand of providence was guiding their destiny, it appeared at one o'clock in the afternoon as the battered *Tartar* fired a five-gun salute and sailed into the harbor to a hero's welcome.

It had taken Fones a day and a half to reach the rest of the fleet after slipping away from his pursuer during the night. Demonstrating their character and commitment, the crew of the *Tartar* made hasty repairs to their ship and, less than twenty-four hours after their arrival, headed back out to sea with the *Shirley* in search of the *Renommee*. Apparently, Captain Kersaint had had enough of the inhospitable waters off Nova Scotia, however. He abandoned his mission and sailed for France. He had not delivered his dispatches to Louisbourg and had not warned them of the large number of ships he had seen in

Canso, the additional transports sailing in that direction, or the multitude of colonial warships cruising in the territory. That information could have been of enormous help to those in command of the French fortress and given them time to prepare for an attack they did not expect. It seems incredible that with all the communications and preparations in New England and the presence of colonial cruisers in sight offshore, those in Louisbourg remained unconvinced that an attack was imminent. Duchambon thought the blockade was simply an attempt to keep Louisbourg from receiving supplies and was still certain that if there was to be an attack, it would be mounted from England. He was confident that the French spies would detect that activity in England and the French could get ships and reinforcements under way for Cape Breton in ample time.

For Duchambon and his city there was no time, however. As the *Shirley* and the *Tartar* scoured the sea for any sign of the *Renommee*, General Pepperrell's army was striking its encampment at Canso and reboarding their transports, awaiting only a favorable breeze to carry them on the short final passage on their voyage to war.

CHAPTER 17

The Landing

THE AMERICAN SOLDIERS CROWDED into the transport ships once again and began the tense wait for the command to set sail for Louisbourg. Most of the force had spent nearly a month in the desolate harbor preparing for this moment. The troops had drilled and practiced with their weapons on many cold days, enduring rain and snow, and had developed a strong sense of confidence. On a foggy Sunday, April 28, Major Seth Pomeroy and others went ashore on Burying Island in Canso harbor, where Reverend Crocker preached in the morning and Reverend Newman in the afternoon. Since the departure from Boston on a Sabbath day had seemed propitious, there was hope that similar benefits would follow the fleet if it could sail on this Sunday, so Pomeroy hurried back to his ship to await that possibility. At sunset there was a favorable breeze, and the order was given to sail, but before many ships had hoisted their anchors, the wind died away and the order was canceled. Amid their anxiety, the disappointed soldiers struggled to find comfortable spots to sleep in the improvised troop ships.

The surprise attack Governor Shirley had prescribed was still envisioned as a possibility. The officials and citizens of Louisbourg were aware of the presence of the colonial cruisers off their coast, but the Americans hoped that the French interpreted this as a harassing blockade rather than the prelude to a full-scale assault. When the morning of April 29 dawned with a favorable light breeze from the northwest, Pepperrell seized the moment and before six A.M. gave the order for the fleet to sail. Over ninety transports set off under the escort of three of the colonial warships, the sixteen-gun *Boston Packet*, the ten-gun sloop *Massachusetts*, and the six-gun *Lord Montague*. On a broad reach, they headed directly east to clear the treacherous ledges projecting out from the land and then settled on an east-northeast course, which would carry them to Gabarus Bay, the site of their proposed landing beaches. Pepperrell calculated that the fleet would arrive in Gabarus Bay at about nine that night, after dark. To sustain the element of surprise, the ships would show no lights that night, requiring exquisite seamanship by the captains in maneuvering the large fleet.

Nature foiled Shirley's meticulous plan. Within hours of their departure, the fleet was becalmed, and all morning the ships wallowed in the swells of the Atlantic. It was a warm and pleasant day, which allowed the soldiers to emerge from their confines and savor the blessing of the weather. One soldier expressed his mixed emotions, writing, "After wee have tarried 27 Days In this Harbour wee Are now Set Sail for Cape Breton, We did Rejoice. But Considering what Our Design was, Might'nt it Justly be with trembling." Clearly, these raw American troops were enduring the same anxieties and doubts that would haunt American soldiers on the eve of battles in centuries to come. A favorable breeze developed midday, and the fleet was able once again to make progress toward their objective, but too much time had been lost to achieve the surprise landing that night. The officers debated the decision of whether to delay their arrival by a day to maintain the benefit of surprise or sail through the night and make a landing the following morning in plain sight of the French. Their decision was influenced late that afternoon when they encountered Commodore Warren's blockading fleet about twenty miles southwest of Gabarus Bay and learned that the fortress was on a heightened alert.

The *Saint-Dominique* from Saint-Jean-de-Luz in the Basque country had approached Louisbourg on the night of Wednesday, April 24, and was confronted by Captain Edward Tyng's formidable frigate *Massachusetts*. The French Basque captain Samson Dufour was somehow able to bully his way past the blockade, despite his ship being mauled by the American frigate. Two members of the Frenchman's crew were killed, and the mainmast was shot through by a cannonball. By jury-rigging a temporary mast, the merchantman had managed to flee from the frigate in the darkness. At seven A.M. on April 25, the lookouts at Louisbourg spied the battered French ship making for the harbor entrance on a favorable wind from the northeast, and by ten that morning, the *Saint-Dominique* was safely in the harbor.

Dufour's report added to the concern within Louisbourg. Governor Duchambon continued to assume that they were contending merely with a blockade and not with an impending invasion, but he did take steps to inconvenience the blockaders. Since colonial ships had occasionally been seen entering Gabarus Bay to gather firewood and fresh water, Duchambon sent a patrol of twenty-five soldiers to guard the shore of the bay. He also sent Michel Daccarrette, a ship owner and merchant, in his armed privateer to interdict any New England vessels entering the bay. Upon seeing the French ship in the bay, two of the colonial cruisers immediately went after Daccarrette, and the Frenchman was forced to land his crew and scuttle his ship to prevent its capture. Taking further precautions, Duchambon ordered the foot patrol to stay out by the bay for at least a week. On Sunday, April 28, he called in the men from several outlying communities to augment the militia within the city. He wanted the added strength of these men but not the added burden of their wives and children, so they were advised to take to the woods and makeshift shelters to fend for themselves against whatever might come.

During the day of April 29, the French saw a number of the blockading ships sailing to the west. Because they were leaving only a few ships behind, it appeared as if the blockaders were leaving. That evening, Duchambon sent a small ship, *La Societe*, to make her way through the remaining blockade and carry a message to Comte de Maurepas, the minister of the Marine Department in France, that Louisbourg was under a blockade. Nevertheless, Duchambon had reason to feel confident on that evening. The blockade seemed to be weakening, and within the walls of the fortress and manning the outlying batteries was a substantial force of 560 French and Swiss soldiers, 30 artillery specialists, and a militia force of over 1,300 men. Commissaire-Ordonnateur François Bigot had imposed rationing on provisions soon after the first appearance of the blockading ships, so that Duchambon was convinced they could hold out until help arrived from France. The fortifications of the city, the Grand or Royal Battery and the Island Battery, all with ample gunpowder and shot to defend against any squadron of warships that attempted to force its way into the harbor, provided the greatest sense of security. In the late fall of 1744, Duchambon and Bigot had requested that six French warships be sent for their protection in early 1745, and they expected them any day. On the chilly but pleasant evening of April 29, it appeared that adequate precautions had been taken, and the citizens of Louisbourg would simply have to ride out the inconvenience of the blockade until the French navy arrived.

As Duchambon and his advisers enjoyed a feeling of security, Pepperrell decided to abandon Shirley's plan and land early the following morning, Tuesday, April 30. The American soldiers spent their last night aboard the cramped transports contemplating the unknowns of the next day. While some had combat experience on the frontier of New England, none had made an amphibious landing, and now they knew that their landing would be made in broad daylight, most probably against a determined enemy firing from protected positions ashore.

In Louisbourg, a city now on alert, the civil and military leaders forgave the fashionable dinners and gatherings that were part of their social life and continued to ruminate on what lay ahead. On the parapets of the city, soldiers stood guard throughout the chilly night. In the early morning hours of April 30, the weary lookouts at Louisbourg strained their eyes through the diminishing darkness. It promised to be another fair, warm spring day, but it would be a day like none other in the history of the city. As they stared out to the east, from which any naval attack would come, they could see no unusual activity. But then, looking to the south, across the marsh and out toward the entrance to Gabarus Bay, they saw the morning sun glinting off the sails of several ships. As they stood riveted at the sight, they saw more ships emerge from the morning mist, a dozen, then more, a score, and more and more. The alarm was raised in the city; bells were rung and cannons fired to alert the settlers outside the walls. For those who scampered up on the parapets for a better view, it was a staggering, awesome sight. The southern horizon was completely filled with the billowing white canvas of over one hundred ships. It was like nothing anyone there had ever seen.

The news raced through the city, and Duchambon's comfort of the evening before evaporated as he and his advisers realized that the approaching ships carried an invading army. It was a moment for quick decisions and instant action, but Duchambon was mired in confusion. Although the acting governor had two respected military veterans to advise him, he hesitated as they urged a decisive response to the impending threat. The legendary port captain Pierre Morpain, a daring privateer in Queen Anne's War, was now fifty-nine years old but was still feared among the New Englanders. He and Poupet de la Boularderie, the forty-year-old retired captain from the Duc de Richelieu's regiment, felt that it was imperative that a force be sent from the city to repel the invaders before they could establish a beachhead. Duchambon was haunted by the nightmare of the December mutiny, however. If he sent out garrison troops, weakening his force within the city, would they immediately surrender to the oncoming enemy? Duchambon wasted precious time by assembling the garrison and urging them to forget the past and join with their officers and the militia in confronting the invaders and fighting for their families, friends, the fortress, and France. Once again, the soldiers took advantage of their power. With the enemy in sight, they insisted that they would stand and fight only if promised that they would not be punished for having taken part in the mutiny. Duchambon and Bigot had no alternative but to make the agreement, but clearly the soldiers' reaction added doubt to the troubled mind of Duchambon. The "negotiations" with the garrison made it even more difficult for the acting governor to respond to the urgent pleas of Morpain and Boularderie.

As Duchambon floundered in his inability to assume leadership and struggled to come to grips with the conflicting demands of the troops and his advisers, the powerful British warships of Commodore Warren's squadron came into view. Until that morning, it was thought that the blockading ships were merely the small vessels of the New England colonies, which would be no problem for the French warships expected anytime. However, the forty- and sixty-gun ships of the Royal Navy would offer a fierce and hostile reception to the French ships as they approached Louisbourg. As tensions mounted in the fortress, the fishermen and their families who lived along the harbor shore responded to the alarm and streamed into the city or took refuge in the Grand Battery.

As the invading fleet approached, all was going in accordance with the new plan to make the landing against whatever force opposed them. The fleet came to anchor at about nine A.M. on what Seth Pomeroy described as "a Fair Pleasent morning," and the three escorting colonial warships prepared to support the landing with continuous fire from their cannons. As the sailors raced to prepare the whaleboats that would be the landing craft, a force of French fighters was seen making their way from the city toward the landing beach. Rather than leading the powerful force they had urged, Morpain led twenty-four handpicked soldiers and fifty militiamen. Assisted by Boularderie and Duchambon's son, Mesillac, they joined the twenty-five soldiers sent out four days previously. The brave French force of one hundred men faced the impossible task of turning back thousands of invaders from one hundred ships.

The elite troops of Colonel John Gorham's Rangers loaded into boats for the first wave of the assault. Made up mostly of Mohawk Indians and men of mixed race, Gorham's initial special company of fifty men had proven itself during its defense of Annapolis Royal in 1744 and the offensive attacks that followed. They were well disciplined and fierce, and their ruthless tactics made them feared by the French. Gorham had been induced to raise additional men and join the Louisbourg campaign as a lieutenant colonel in the Seventh Massachusetts Regiment, commanded by his father, Colonel Shubael Gorham, and both Gorhams were part of General Pepperrell's select war council.

The younger Gorham was charged with organizing the landing of the troops in this critical amphibious assault, and he and his men would set the example for the raw New England recruits. As the force headed for the landing site in Flat Point Cove, the French defenders raced to take up defensive positions along that shore. The colonial warships *Boston Packet*, *Massachusetts*, and *Lord Montague* bombarded the terrain behind the landing beach. The vulnerable Ameri-

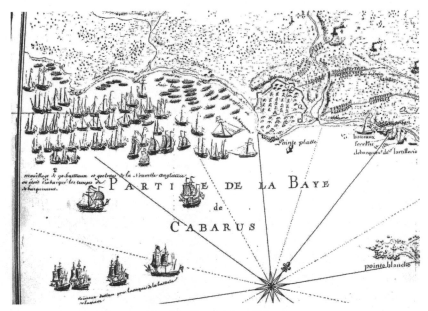

The landing at Louisbourg

can troops neared the beach and the French defenders opened fire, but their muskets had little accuracy at the long range and none of the men in the boats were injured. On a signal from General Pepperrell, the landing force surprised the French when they turned and began to retreat. For Morpain and Boularderie, the validity of their argument was confirmed; even a small force was able to turn back the invaders, who obviously had little stomach for a real fight.

The French triumph was very short-lived. The attack on Flat Point Cove had been a well-executed feint, intended to draw the French defenders away from the actual landing site. As the retreating landing craft neared their ships, they suddenly made another turn, this time heading west, and were joined by numerous other boats loaded with more troops that had been hidden behind the ships. The race was on as the warships continued to pour cannon fire on the French, who, aware of their mistake, pulled out of their original positions. An argument developed between Morpain and Boularderie. Acknowledging the magnitude of the invading force, Boularderie argued for an orderly retreat back to the fortress, but the daring Morpain ignored his second in command, ordering his troops to move as quickly as possible along the coast toward the bluff behind the sandy beaches of Kennington Cove, a mile and a half to the west. Their progress was slow because the men moved in single file, fifteen paces apart so the cannon fire could not strike more than one man at a time. The Yankee sailors strained at the oars of the loaded whaleboats and pulled ahead of the French force struggling through thick woods. There was high surf running in the bay as the American soldiers tumbled out of the boats into frigid, waist-deep water. Gorham's Rangers formed into ranks and prepared to advance on the enemy coming through the woods, as additional scouts fanned out to determine if a larger French force was waiting to spring a trap on the Americans.

As the exhausted French neared the edge of the woods, Boularderie continued to argue vehemently for an honorable and disciplined military retreat. Morpain would hear nothing of it. The French were met by a fusillade of musket fire from Gorham's Rangers when they emerged from the woods. Morpain, seeing hundreds of additional Americans gaining the beaches, then realized that theirs was a lost cause and the best course of action was to retreat to the fortress, where they could fight another day. Slightly wounded, Morpain ordered the retreat, with every man for himself. This was more than Boularderie, steeped in tradition and honor bound, could take. Morpain and most of the men fled into the woods, but Boularderie and twelve French troops stood their ground until the Frenchmen began to fall, dead and wounded. After a short skirmish the fight was over, and Boularderie, twice wounded, surrendered his sword to the American army. Six of the French lay dead, and Boularderie and the others were taken prisoner. The rest of the scattered French soldiers attempted to make their way back to the city as best they could. It took two days for the wounded Morpain, aided by two of his black slaves, to regain the security of the fortress. Only two Americans were slightly wounded in the action, and the first important victory went to Pepperrell.

With the two veteran fighters out of the city and possibly lost, Duchambon wrestled with his awesome challenges. From the reports of the returning soldiers, it was clear that the effort to repulse the landing had failed. It was determined to deprive the Americans of as much of what lay outside the fortress walls as possible. As thousands of Americans fought their way through the surf to the solid ground of Cape Breton, Duchambon sent out parties of men to burn the structures in the area between the city and the Barachois, a salt pond fifteen hundred feet west of the city's Dauphin Gate. He did not want any of these buildings to provide shelter for the invaders. He also did not want the Americans to capture the French vessels at anchor within the harbor, so crews were sent to scuttle the ships and boats that were vulnerable. A number of small craft moored near the fortress where they could be defended were kept for future use. By late afternoon, most of the refugees were either in the city or the Grand Battery, as the gates of both these fortresses were closed and Louisbourg prepared for an attack.

The crisp discipline exhibited by Gorham's Rangers contrasted with the disorganization of the rest of the force of two thousand who landed on that first day. Pepperrell did not establish an immediate central command and remained aboard his flagship, the *Shirley*, with his senior officers. Some of the troops began to establish the encampment, while others made their way up small hills closer to the city to get a better look at the fabled fortress. Scouting parties that had gone out on their own initiative discovered no significant enemy forces outside the fortress but tracked down half a dozen stragglers from Morpain's force, and by nightfall, seventeen French soldiers had been killed or captured.

The scouts had additional success beyond the capture of prisoners and returned to the American camp with wine, brandy, and cider, which they had liberated from surrounding farms, as well as five cows, three of which became the main course for the victory feast that night. In anticipation of a night assault, all the parapets of the fortress were manned with troops. No attack came, however. Instead, the defenders of the fortress, along with the bewildered inhabitants and refugees, had to listen to the boisterous celebration of the Americans, who were emboldened by their first taste of success. The weather was fair, and they had managed their difficult landing without any loss of life or serious injury. After the ordeal of the voyage to Canso and the weeks of cold, damp discomfort there, they were triumphantly ensconced on Cape Breton with roasted beef and ample libations to wash it down. Many were still wet from wading ashore and had no change of clothes, but this did not dampen their spirits on the first night ashore. They slept in the open, since no tents had yet been landed, and as one chronicler recorded the details of the night, "Wee Lay this Night in the open air—But wee Cut A few boughs to keep Us from the ground. Vastly the most Comfortable Nights Lodging This! Since I left Boston. There was Singing and Great Rejoicing. And there was Indeed great Cause But wee Should be Carefull to Rejoice in the Lord which has Done all for Us. It was a Very pleasant Evening it was the first time I've heard any frogs Peep or Birds Sing for there was none at Canso." The true test of these untrained soldiers was about to unfold, however, a siege of the most formidable fortress in North America. As Ben Franklin had pointed out, this was a task for which none of them had been trained.

If there was confidence and optimism in the American camp on the night of April 30, the opposite was the case within the city. Thousands of troops were now encamped on Cape Breton within a short distance of Louisbourg. They might attempt a full-scale assault at any time or begin the long process of a siege. It was questionable that help coming from France could get past the Royal Navy offshore, and Duchambon and his advisers huddled together throughout the night, debating their options.

As the sun rose on Wednesday, May 1, Commodore Peter Warren's flagship, *Superbe*, logged that there were "fresh gales and clear" weather. This would present a challenge for Pepperrell and the two thousand American troops who still needed to make their way ashore. All through the day, boats traversed back and forth between the landing beach and the transports, ferrying men and equipment ashore. Gabarus Bay is exposed to the Atlantic swells, and with a stiff breeze, a dangerous surf developed. The men were often up to their chests in the surf, with their weapons held high above their heads. The American cannons were relatively small, the largest firing only a twenty-two-pound cannonball, but they were heavy and unwieldy objects to unload from transports and move through the surf to the beach, each weighing over 4,500 pounds. Richard Gridley, the lieutenant colonel of the Train of Artillery, was in charge of the soldiers who wrestled the cannons ashore, and the task was accomplished without loss of life or serious injury. At thirty-five, Gridley was a skilled and respected military engineer and a member of General Pepperrell's war council. He acquired his training in military engineering from John Henry Bastide, a British military engineer who had been sent to Boston to plan fortifications for that city and other colonial locations. Gridley's expertise was a rare commodity among the American officers. Having accomplished his first critical task of getting the armament ashore, Gridley set about organizing the next phase of the assault, the erection of the siege batteries.

General Pepperrell came ashore, established his headquarters, and began to take control of the forces on land, which had been haphazardly managing their own affairs. As one soldier recorded, "We had no Particular Orders,—But Everyone Did what was Right in his own Eyes." This disorder was not to last, and the first two offensive operations were ordered. Pepperrell assigned the leadership of the first expedition to Colonel William Vaughn, apparently in recognition of his exhaustive efforts to bring about the Louisbourg campaign. Vaughn's task was to lead a force of five hundred Americans in a night raid on the settlement at the northeastern extreme of Louisbourg harbor, "to seize upon all Vessels, Men or Cattle that could be found beyond the Grand Battery." The charismatic Vaughn had no trouble gathering a force, since they were in high spirits and there was confidence among the men and a thirst for adventure.

Pepperrell assigned the much more strategically important task of capturing the Grand Battery to Vaughn's rival Colonel John Bradstreet, who had a full understanding of the significance of the Grand Battery as well as its weaknesses. Positioned about a mile north of Louisbourg across the harbor, the Grand Battery was an impressive and intimidating sight, with tall crenellated towers at each end and an array of gun emplacements atop the fort's walls that ran between the towers. Behind these walls was the large barracks for the troops, which also housed the supplies and equipment for the two hundred men who manned this installation. It was the formidable cannons that gave the battery its true power. It contained twenty-eight of the largest cannons in the region, each of which could hurl destructive forty-two-pound cannonballs well over a mile. Secure behind their fortifications, the gunners in the Grand Battery could safely pummel any warships that penetrated the harbor. If Commodore Warren's ships were going to play any significant role in support of the assault on Louisbourg, the threat of the Grand Battery had to be eliminated. Bradstreet knew from his time as a prisoner in Louisbourg ten months earlier that there were two breaches in the landward defenses of the Grand Battery. He speculated that because they were part of the repairs begun under the earlier governor, DuQuesnel, it was probable that they had not been completed. He was so confident that the Grand Battery could be taken that it was he who convinced Pepperrell that the army should bring a supply of forty-two-pound cannonballs with them as ammunition to use against Louisbourg when the battery was captured. On the evening of May 1, the two men who had most urgently advocated the campaign against Louisbourg prepared for the first organized attacks. Vaughn would conduct his raid that night, and Bradstreet would move against the Grand Battery the following night if conditions seemed appropriate.

Vaughn's force moved out on schedule. Staying well to the west, they skirted the Grand Battery and moved on to the settlement across the harbor from the fortress, where Vaughn found a deserted community. Inexperienced in command, the colonel allowed his men to loot and destroy the settlement. By the early hours of the morning of May 2, Vaughn's marauders were back in camp, loudly celebrating their adventure and showing off their loot, unconcerned over other valuable material they had destroyed when they torched the settlement.

Always independent, Vaughn did not return to camp with the majority of the troops nominally under his command. Instead, he stayed to reconnoiter the upper bay, where by dawn he and a dozen men had worked their way to the top of a "cliff" within a quarter of a mile of the Grand Battery. In the early light of the morning, Vaughn noticed an unusual stillness around the fortress. There was no smoke rising from the chimneys, no sense of activity, and, most conspicuously, no

John Bradstreet

flag flying. Apprehensive that this might be a French trick, Vaughn sent an Indian scout to penetrate the battery. When the scout signaled to Vaughn that he and his men were safe to advance, they found that the Grand Battery had been abandoned. The man who had most enthusiastically encouraged the Louisbourg expedition now claimed its most highly sought prize.

Having no flag with them, one of Vaughn's men, William Tufts, stripped off his red coat, which was run up the flagstaff to serve as a temporary banner. From within the Grand Battery, Vaughn then wrote a triumphant message to General Pepperrell, saying: "May it please your Honour, to be informed that with ye grace of God and ye courage of about thirteen men I entered this place about nine a clock and am waiting here for a reinforcement and flag." When Vaughn's message reached Pepperrell, it brought astonishment and a feeling of great satisfaction that God was favoring the Americans' campaign. Deprived of the honor of conquering the Grand Battery, Colonel Bradstreet was ordered to gather his men to relieve Vaughn, who with only a dozen soldiers had a tenuous hold on the prize.

When they saw the red banner flying over the Grand Battery, the French realized that their precipitous evacuation could now cause serious difficulties. This predicament had begun on the first night of the attack. As the two thousand Americans were celebrating their successful landing, Duchambon had received an urgent message from the commanding officer of the Grand Battery, Chassin de Thierry, who, acutely aware of the weaknesses in the landward side of his defenses, deemed his position untenable. He had only two hundred soldiers and the civilians who had taken refuge there, and the commander was certain that he could not hold out against the full assault that was sure to come. He recommended that the cannons of the fortress be disabled by steel spikes driven down their touchholes, that the soldiers and civilians be evacuated and the fortress blown up.

Duchambon was in a state of near panic as he considered the message from the Grand Battery, since it presented both a quandary and an opportunity. Etienne Verrier, the resident engineer at Louisbourg, was concerned that the masterpiece of military engineering not be demolished, and it was he who offered the disastrous compromise that the battery be abandoned after spiking the guns. His proposal was accepted, and Duchambon sent the order: "Mr. Thierry of the Royal Battery, is ordered to abandon the said Battery after having spiked the cannon and after having removed as much food and military supplies as possible to Louisbourg."

When de Thierry received the order, his troops responded with an unwarranted sense of fear and panic and hurriedly carried out only the assignment of spiking the cannons. They did nothing to destroy the carriages supporting the huge guns and failed to permanently disable them by knocking off the trunnions on which the gun barrels pivoted while being aimed. Disregarding the rest of the order, they gathered only a small quantity of the food and no military supplies before they fled to the security of the city. Responsibility for moving what was left behind was delegated to the civilians, but they, too, moved quickly to Louisbourg. Realizing that much valuable material remained, numerous fishing shallops ferried back and forth the following day, attempting to complete the task abandoned by the fleeing troops. While the Americans were preoccupied with landing the rest of their soldiers on May 1, the majority of the supplies from the Grand Battery were successfully removed. What remained were the most difficult items, the numerous forty-two-pound cannonballs, a number of eighteen-pound cannonballs, and an assortment of other munitions that the French planned to go after early on May 2.

As the French troops who were assigned to finish the evacuation prepared to set off by boat, the red flag was spotted flying over the Grand Battery. Without knowing the size of the force occupying the fortification, the French crowded into seven shallops and headed for a beach southwest of the battery. Vaughn had just sent his message to Pepperrell when the oncoming French force required his decisive action. He legitimately could abandon his prize in the face of this far superior force, or he could defend the battery in hopes that reinforcements would arrive before he and his few men were annihilated. With his usual bravado, Vaughn chose the latter course. Leaving four of his men to defend the fort, Vaughn led the other eight along the shore to meet the French invaders. As they raced to the spot, they were joined by four American soldiers who were out wandering on their own, and when the group, now numbering thirteen men, arrived at the landing, they began a steady fire at the approaching boats.

As the American defenders took up positions on the far shore near the Grand Battery, the cannons of Fortress Louisbourg opened fire, as did the men in the boats. During this hot exchange, Vaughn and his men stood their ground as cannonballs whizzed overhead or pounded into the turf nearby. In the face of Vaughn's stand, the French troops turned and headed back to the city, forfeiting the opportunity to dump the munitions into the sea and further disable the cannons.

Vaughn and his men were exhilarated by their valiant and successful battle. As they made their way back toward the fort, they examined several fishermen's homes along the shore and found two British flags, undoubtedly used by the fishing vessels to "fly false colors" when convenient. The flags were appropriated, and once back in the battery, William Tufts's red coat was retrieved and a proper flag hoisted in its place. Later in the day, Bradstreet and his troops arrived to occupy the Grand Battery, while Vaughn and his band of followers headed back to the encampment and the adulation of their compatriots. Their

"capture" of the battery was clearly by happenstance, but the timeli-
ness of it and the courageous stand against daunting odds had prevented the French from regaining access to the fort and doing
irreparable damage to it.

With the Grand Battery in American hands, it became Major Seth
Pomeroy's task to determine if any of the forty-two-pound cannons
were salvageable, in hopes that they could be turned against the city
and used to control the harbor. The Americans had experienced nothing but success in the first three days of the attack. Now it was time to
apply themselves to their primary mission, the conquest of the impenetrable Fortress Louisbourg.

CHAPTER 18

Advice and Dissent

WHEN COLONEL JOHN BRADSTREET arrived to relieve Vaughn and assess the condition of the Grand or Royal Battery, he sent an optimistic message to General Pepperrell, saying, "We can soon repair it as well as ever. I beg you'l send the smiths and armerores as soon as possible to drill open the vents of the cannon." Gunsmith Seth Pomeroy arrived, and by ten the following morning, "ye Tutcholes of one of our guns at Royal Battry Dril'd out & Fired at ye Towne," crowning the first three days of the assault and confirming that everything seemed to be going like clockwork. The following day, Friday, May 3, Pomeroy wrote that three guns were ready and had fired twenty shots at the city, and on May 4 they fired ninety-four shots. Pomeroy was making progress, but it was a huge task, and those in command sought to speed up the process. On Sunday, May 5, clearly not a day of rest, Pomeroy wrote, "This day I was ordred & had a Commission From ye General to over See Twenty odd Smith[s] in Clearing ye Cannon Tutch holes that ye Franch had Stopt up." Clearing the rest of the guns took six days, but by Thursday, May 9, all the forty-two-pounders of the Grand Battery, except one that had split while being fired, were functional. The American army had the powerful guns it needed to lay siege to the city.

As Pomeroy drilled out the cannons, General Pepperrell began to organize his force. His first challenge was to establish order within his command and get control of the independent-minded soldiers ranging throughout the region, destroying and looting. The general was hesitant to crack down heavily on his volunteers, and it took days before the American force was at work on their mission rather than stalking around the countryside doing as they wished. Supplies were landed, and the Americans set up their camp on either side of a brook that emptied into the bay at Flat Point Cove. The first shelters were crude, but eventually an orderly array of tents housed the soldiers and the brook provided an abundance of fresh water. From his head-quarters within the encampment near the shore of Gabarus Bay, General Pepperrell wrestled with the next steps to be taken. His wish was to immediately send an envoy to Duchambon demanding that Louisbourg surrender. It seemed logical that with an army of four thousand men surrounding Louisbourg and a powerful fleet blockad-ing the city, Duchambon would avail himself of the chance to avoid misery and loss of life, particularly when he had abandoned the Grand Battery and those guns were now being turned against the city. Pepperrell made the recommendation to his war council, but General Waldo and Colonel Bradstreet recommended that no mes-sage be sent until additional batteries were in place and the city was experiencing the steady pounding of the American assault. Taking the advice of his council, Pepperrell ordered that additional batteries be established.

Pepperrell then turned to his next concern, an attack on the Island Battery that dominated the harbor entrance and kept Commodore Warren and his ships out of the battle. The shared command of Pep-perrell and Warren, which they had structured so carefully, was imme-diately tested when Commodore Warren could not resist giving his advice and urging action. Seeming to admit the weakness of his own blockade, Warren had written to Pepperrell on May 2, urging the cap-ture of the Island Battery and saying, "If wee cou'd once get possession, of the Island Battery, nothing from Sea, of the Enemy's, cou'd gett in, and they must Starve in the town . . ." That suggestion was innocuous enough in itself, but two days later, Pepperrell received a document that directly challenged his authority and command of the land forces. With the receipt of "A Plan of Operation, for the Speedy Reduction of the Town, and Garrison of Lewisbourg, Propos'd by Peter Warren

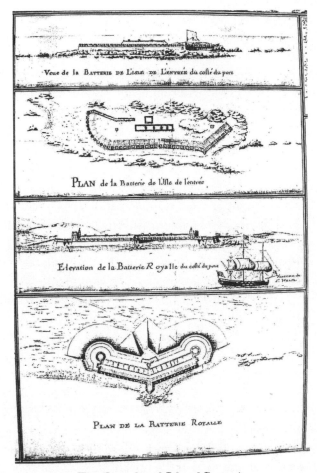

The Grand and Island Batteries

Esq.," dated May 4, the naval officer injected himself into the land campaign. Commodore Warren, who was frustrated by Pepperrell's lack of initiative and considered himself the most experienced military man on the scene, was violating his agreement with Pepperrell by taking the initiative and laying out his own plan of attack. Expressing his concerns, Warren wrote, "The Season of the year advancing a pace, that the Enemy, may expect Provisions, and Succours, from France, makes it highly necessary, that wee shou'd take some Vigorous measures, for the Sudden Reduction of Lewesbourg..." Warren's detailed plan included the storming and capture of the Island Battery, the entry of the warships and transports into the harbor, and a frontal attack on the city. While it was clear that Warren wanted quick action, he tempered his boldness by saying he would, of course, support some alternate plan. The fact that Warren with his powerful fleet was worried that "the Enemy, may expect Provisions, and Succours, from France" again reflects the commodore's apparent lack of faith in his naval forces or his desire to have the land army take terrible risks so the naval forces wouldn't be required to face French ships bringing supplies to the city. The American officers resented being told what to do by the British commodore and sought to avoid the inevitable carnage that would result from a frontal assault on the fortress. After considering the plan for several hours, the American officers closed their war council meeting with the statement deferring a decision on the commodore's plan to another opportunity. Warren's attempt to take control and instigate bold and immediate action failed, and an atmosphere of distrust and dissent quickly developed.

By Monday, May 6, two mortars were positioned on the high ground called the Rabasse near the Barachois, the tidal pond five hundred yards from the west gate of the city. From this location, they could easily lob their shells into all parts of Louisbourg. The Americans determined to strengthen this gun emplacement with cannons that could fire directly at the west gate in order to make a breach in the fortress walls. As the French well knew, however, it was impossible to transport even the smaller American cannons the arduous three miles from their landing spot, first across rough, rock-strewn terrain and then through the sodden marsh. Instead, Colonel Gridley planned to shift two of the restored forty-two-pound cannons and two eighteen-pounders from the Grand Battery. The massive size of these cannons, particularly the forty-twos, which weighed three and a half tons each, made this a challenging task, but with enough manpower it was accomplished. Once out of the battery, the cannons were man-hauled along the road for two miles to their new location opposite the west gate, from where they began to batter the city.

Some of Pepperrell's advisers still argued that the fortress should endure a longer bombardment before surrender terms were offered, but Pepperrell was eager to present a proposal to Duchambon. On

May 6, he argued his point to the war council, and it was agreed that a "summons to surrender" would be sent. If the terms were refused, an assault on the city would take place as soon as possible. At eleven in the morning the following day, the American batteries ceased firing, and one of Warren's Royal Marine officers, Captain Agnue, moved forward under a flag of truce, accompanied by a sergeant and a drummer who loudly announced their presence. As they awaited the response from Duchambon, the American force was mustered and formed into ranks in the hope of celebrating victory. Duchambon's reply was quick and firm: "Wee Cannot hearken to any Such Proposals till after the Most Vigorous Attack." He went on to echo the famous reply that Count Frontenac gave when Sir William Phips demanded the surrender of Quebec in 1690, saying, "Nor have wee any Other answer to this Demand but by the Mouth's of Our Cannon." He also refused the American offer for the women and children to leave the city and be protected away from the danger of battle. Upon hearing Duchambon's response, the American troops gave a cheer and resumed the attack, making it very clear that they had come to Cape Breton to conquer Louisbourg.

The time had come for action. The Americans were charged with enthusiasm, and it was decided that they would attack the Island Battery that same night. There was no shortage of volunteers for the dangerous mission since the Americans were spoiling for a fight, and Colonel John Gorham was chosen to lead the difficult undertaking. The force set out in whaleboats to row and paddle the perilous four miles through the open sea, past Louisbourg to the Island Battery. However, they got such a late start that they could not reach the target before sunrise, and Gorham prudently canceled the attack. The enthusiastic troops, who had waited late into the night for the attack to begin, were annoyed and disillusioned. Another attack was scheduled for the next night, but after waiting all night, the volunteers were dismissed, disgruntled and frustrated that they were denied their second opportunity for glory.

The following day, Pepperrell succumbed to Warren's continued pressure that the American force should mount a full attack and scaling of the walls of the city that night. Unfortunately, by this time the canceled attacks on the Island Battery had created a sense of doubt among the troops, and their confidence in the officers was waning. An hour before sunset, the army was gathered before Commodore Warren, who surveyed the troops that were to conduct the vigorous attack. What he sensed was anything but vigor. Instead, the troops reflected their concern and uneasiness. If these had been professional British regulars, their officers and sergeants might have harassed and coerced them into the attack, but the men arrayed before Warren were of a different sort. They were the farmers, clerks, and craftsmen who had voluntarily left their homes to join this campaign, and they were hesitant to risk their lives in an effort that seemed premature and suicidal. The troops knew that the bombardment of the city had been under way for less than a week, that most of the American guns were not yet in place, and that no breach had been made in the city walls. The process of making their way across the rough and swampy land, over the glacis embankment, and then across the wide ditch surrounding the fortress would subject them to deadly crossfire from the walls of the city and the cannons mounted in the bastions. If they survived that fusillade, the nearly vertical thirty-foot walls of the fortress would still loom above them. It was a prospect that few of the Americans wanted to face.

Warren was aware of the reticence of the troops, and after conferring with General Pepperrell, the company captains were told to report to the war council and speak their minds. The result was that "there wasn't So Much as one Vote in favour of it." This was an army unlike any military force Warren had ever dealt with, imbued with the right of self-determination. The minutes of the war council reflected the outcome of the vote, saying, "Advized, that inasmuch as there appears a great dissatisfaction in many of the officers & soldiers at the design'd attack of the town by storm this night, and as it may be attended with very ill consequences if it should not be executed with the utmost vigour whenever attempted, the said attack of the town be deferr'd for the present." In this extraordinary manner, the common soldiers of the American regiments demonstrated that they were full participants in the undertaking, including the decision making, and would exert their influence when necessary.

While the American soldiers were wise to avoid the slaughter that would have resulted from storming the city, their reluctance to blindly follow the order to attack did not reflect any reluctance to prosecute the siege. They perceived that the key to success lay in the establishment of more batteries from which the city could be beaten into submission with relatively little risk to the besiegers. This meant getting as many of their cannons as possible into position to effectively erode the French defenses and morale. Once again, the impediment was the terrain, with its combination of protruding rocks and frigid quagmires. Attempts to move the heavy cannons over this ground proved to be impossible, as gun carriages were shattered or the guns sank into the mire. If they had been schooled in the fine art of military siege, the Americans might have resigned themselves to the impossibility of the terrain. However, the Yankee ingenuity that would later be recognized around the world was already alive and well in these men. The New Hampshire Regiment, commanded by Colonel Samuel Moore, had a particularly talented second in command, Lieutenant Colonel Nathaniel Merserve, who in civilian life worked to procure the timber for ships' masts. In working with the enormous trees destined for His Majesty's Navy, Merserve was used to transporting unwieldy and heavy objects over rough ground, and he designed sledges upon which the cannons could be hauled overland to the desired location. Sixteen feet in length, five feet wide, and a foot thick, the massive sledges added significant weight to the burden but made it possible, if not easy, to move the cannons.

Under the cover of darkness to protect them against cannon fire from the fortress, the American soldiers pitted themselves against the terrain to deliver the heavy guns to the newly sited batteries. Hundreds of men were harnessed to each sledge, and they struggled through the cold, damp nights. The feat was graphically described by one of the chroniclers of the expedition, who wrote, "Got some of the Great Artillery on Shoar—and began to transport them—which was attended with incredible Difficulty there being no possibility of drawing them with Horses or oxen if we had had never so many—and the Distance near—over rocky Hills—or thro low marshy Grounds where the Cannon were oftentimes almost buried and the Men that hawl'd them, up to their knees in Mire and all to be done in the Nights, which were exceding cold foggy and rainy.—The Enemy did not seem to apprehend the possibility of our transporting Battering Cannon over those Grounds but our men seem'd resolvd to surmount all Difficulties—and tho no dry Cloaths nor worm Shelter to sleep in after their Fatigue there were no signs of Discouragement or Discontent—and in five days time, besides the great variety of other necessary Services they got 8–22lb Cannon and some smaller ones to the Battery where the Mortars were placed and mounted them in a fascene Battery there." The Americans accomplished the impossible mission and denied Louisbourg another of her significant defenses.

Once the newly positioned cannons were in action, the exchange of fire between the fortress and the besiegers increased. One of the witnesses recorded, "The Cannon Bums Cohorns [small mortars] etc. Continually Roaring on Boath Sides Women and Children heard to Screach and Cry out in the Citty when our Bums Came amongst them." Life for those within the city became increasingly dangerous and stressful. Most of the women and children were sheltered in dark, airless, underground casemates in the citadel's walls, while the soldiers of the garrison and the militia continuously manned the ramparts and worked the cannons. The ordeal of being under bombardment was physically and emotionally exhausting, but the inhabitants of Louisbourg were still adequately supplied with provisions and munitions and anticipated the arrival of the French navy. It was also hoped that a relief force from elsewhere in Canada would arrive soon, as Duchambon had sent a messenger in search of Paul Marin de la Malgue on May 15, asking him to immediately bring his force of six hundred French soldiers and Micmac and Malecite Indians to Louisbourg to attack the Americans from the rear.

The destruction within the city increased, but the French gunners also took their toll. A French cannonball tore through the troops at the Green Hill Battery, and three men were seriously wounded. One had both legs cut off, another lost part of his leg, and the third lost an arm. An American soldier recorded, "Another man had 6 inches of the main Bone of his Leg Carry'd away. The man who lost both legs died and the doctor was fearful that others of the wounded wouldn't survive." The cannon duel proved more detrimental to the French, as their fortress was a large enough target for most American shots to hit something and cause damage. With the Americans spread out and firing from positions protected by earthworks and fascine sticks, it took extreme accuracy or great luck for the French to score a direct hit on a cannon or its crew. As the days progressed, both sides began to feel the losses of battle, but the damage was greatest in the city.

With the refusal of the American troops to participate in the assault advocated by Commodore Warren, it was critical for General Pepperrell to reassert his authority and regain the confidence of the land army. While Pepperrell and Warren were outwardly cordial and respectful, it is clear that there was a struggle for command, since Pepperrell would later report, "It is true Mr. Warren did tell me he was the chief officer here. I told him, Not on shoar." This frank exchange may have clarified their relationship, but it damaged the rapport between the two men.

As he asserted his independence from Warren's influence, Pepperrell reverted to his own priorities, which were the capture of the Island Battery and the further development of gun batteries to batter the walls. After the unsuccessful attempts to attack the Island Battery from the long and exposed route across the open ocean from Gabarus Bay, Pepperrell realized that a different tactic was needed. Inspired by the backbreaking labor of moving the cannons across the morass, he reasoned that the heavy whaleboats that had served as landing craft could be transported over the same forbidding ground and brought to the harbor, and an attack could be made on the Island Battery in those calm, protected waters. While hundreds of men still labored with the cannons, others set to work dragging the boats for miles, and on May 10 they were gathered near the Grand Battery, where they would enable the raiding party to row or paddle to the Island Battery in less than an hour.

Late that afternoon, the Americans received the demoralizing news of a significant loss of their men. On a raid into the interior of Cape Breton, a French doctor lured twenty-one men of the Third Massachusetts Regiment into a trap. Attacked by over one hundred French and Indians, the outnumbered Americans quickly surrendered, with two of their number killed. Encouraged by the French, the Indians set upon the Americans and literally slaughtered them. Only two of the Americans survived the attack and escaped. When they reached their compatriots and told their grim tale, a pall fell over the troops as they buried the mutilated bodies of seventeen of their fellow soldiers.

After this grim episode, the decision was made to attack the Island Battery that night. Commodore Warren volunteered two hundred of his men, and the combined force gathered on the shore below the Grand Battery. When Colonel John Bradstreet canceled the attack, the question arose of his sympathies with the French and close ties to Louisbourg. Rumors of betrayal spread among the demoralized soldiers. Acting quickly to defuse this volatile situation, Pepperrell brought the issue to the war council at a hearing on the afternoon of May 11, at which he informed them that "some persons in the army had entertain'd and spread a report of Colonel Bradstreet that they were apprehensive that he was not hearty in the success of the expedition." Pepperrell demanded that any evidence of Bradstreet's disloyalty be brought forward. None was offered, and Lieutenant Colonel Thomas Chandler, the source of the rumors, was reprimanded for his slander of Bradstreet and ordered to ask his pardon. With this done, the immediate crisis was over, but the delay angered and frustrated Commodore Warren, who abruptly withdrew the two hundred men he had placed ashore for the Island Battery assault. In fact, the presence of those men had caused more harm than good, as the friction between the American soldiers and the British sailors increased. The sailors had been notoriously drunk and disorderly (on rum sold to them by the Americans), and in retribution for their crude behavior, the Americans had helped themselves to the sailors' muskets. After returning to their ships without their weapons, the sailors were reprimanded by their officers. The dislike of the British for the Americans was palpable, and the feeling was mutual.

Further increasing the tension between the besieging and blockading forces, the day Commodore Warren withdrew his sailors, his powerful ships failed in their blockade of Louisbourg. On the morning of May 13, an armed merchant ship from Bordeaux rounded Lighthouse Point opposite the Island Battery and sailed unscathed into the harbor. The clever French captain had evaded Warren's blockade and hugged the coast to the east of Louisbourg until he reached the harbor entrance. Then, while the guns of the Island Battery and the city's batteries sent a barrage of cannon fire at the Americans, the French snow slipped into the harbor and ran for the protection of the city. The ship was small enough to be sailed into the shallow water near the city's

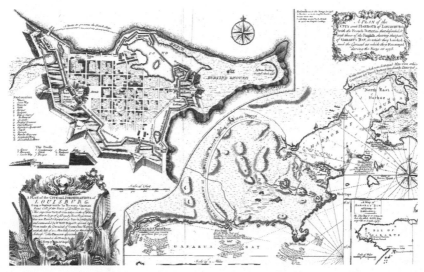

Richard Gridley's plan of Louisbourg

harbor gate, and frantic efforts were made to unload her cargo and add her cannons to those mounted on the city walls. It was astonishing and discouraging to the Americans that the Royal Navy had been unable to sustain the blockade and that supplies had gotten into the city. It was too late to stop this resupply, but William Vaughn sought a way to destroy the French ship and succeed where the Royal Navy had failed. On the night of May 13, Vaughn commandeered two small fishing shallops, which he loaded with combustible materials, set ablaze, and aimed for the French merchantman. The journal from the sloop *Union* documented, "Thay went and Got Shallop and Set on fire and set out for to set the Snow on fire and thay Cut the Cable and the wind Drove the Snow out of the harbour and the Grand battery Sunk it."

Warren's frustration continued, and in a letter dated May 16, 1745, he once again offered a plan for a frontal attack. Indicating that he expected many of the Americans to shrink from the task and desert in the face of enemy fire, he urged Pepperrell to have a force of two hundred men behind the assaulting force to cover a retreat if necessary and to prevent any men from turning back. Warren went on to say that any man turning from the battle or advocating an unauthorized retreat should be put to death. Further demonstrating his contempt for the American troops, he suggested that they would participate only because of their greed, and therefore only those who took part in the assault would be entitled to the rich plunder that a successful conquest of the city would produce. With these aspersions cast upon the American troops, the friction between the commanders only increased. Pepperrell and his council shoved aside Warren's thinly veiled insult and deferred action on it. Content to build up his land batteries, Pepperrell favored pounding the city into submission rather than risk the devastation that Warren's scheme would produce.

As May neared its end, the Americans established a new gun emplacement only 440 yards from the west gate and planned another one even closer. Because of the proximity to the city walls, the soldiers manning these batteries were subject to musket fire as well as fire from the French cannons. Supplying these forward batteries was dangerous, as the soldiers had to traverse open ground laden with their burdens of gunpowder and shot. Eager to advance the effort, Vaughn developed a plan to dig a network of trenches that would connect the batteries and allow the men to move between them in relative safety. Directing his large force of diggers for four days and nights, Vaughn not only completed the trench system sufficient to cover a thousand men, but also personally staked out the ground for the advanced battery. By May 29, that battery with two forty-two-pounders, under the command of Captain Joseph Sherburne, was in place only 220 yards from the west gate. The following day, another fascine battery was established along the trench, twenty yards to the east of the advanced battery. This new battery was equipped with one eighteen-pounder and two nine-pounders and so well positioned that it dominated the French guns of the King's Bastion and drove the gunners from them.

Once the trench system was complete, Vaughn turned his enthusiasm to the bombardment itself. While Captain Sherburne was briefly absent, Vaughn directed the soldiers to charge one of the cannons with more than the normal fourteen pounds of powder in order to make a bold statement. The result produced a disaster that not only cost American lives, but also cost the energetic and dedicated Vaughn much of his reputation. The cannon exploded, instantly killing two men and wounding two others. Two nearby barrels of gunpowder also exploded, seriously damaging one of the eighteen-pounders. This sad fiasco confirmed that Vaughn's reputation for rash action was well deserved, and despite all his efforts and triumphs, Vaughn was never again given significant responsibility. The damage at the battery was repaired, and they began to pulverize the west gate and batter a breach in the fortress wall. The French had now been under siege for almost a month, and the arrival of the relief forces became critical to their survival.

In fact, Duchambon had no idea that the squadron of ships he requested had been refused and Minister Maurepas had sent support in a piecemeal fashion. The first of the relief ships was the *Renommee*, which had returned to France without making contact with Louisbourg. Before the *Renommee* reached France, a second and more powerful French warship, the sixty-four-gun *Vigilant*, sailed for Louisbourg. Crewed by over five hundred men, in addition to her guns, she carried thirty new cannons for the fortress as well as urgently needed provisions and hundreds of barrels of gunpowder for the city's defense. Her commander, Alexandre de la Maisonfort du Boisdecourt, had been instructed to "succour Louisbourg without uselessly exposing his vessel," which was undoubtedly the same instruction given to Captain Kersaint of the *Renommee*. Maisonfort was an experienced and highly respected naval officer who had become a midshipman in 1699 and had distinguished himself over almost fifty years in service. To be given command of a new sixty-four-gun ship and be sent on a transatlantic mission was an honor for Maisonfort.

On his voyage to Cape Breton, he had captured two British prizes, and nearing land, his crew spotted another potential victim, HMS *Mermaid* of Warren's squadron, which was on patrol. Commodore Warren had received reports that French warships were in the area and had put his ships on alert. When the forty-gun HMS *Mermaid* spied the superior French warship, her captain, James Douglas, did not sail into battle but turned northward into the mist and fled. The French, confident from their capture of the earlier prizes, began the pursuit. As the *Vigilant* plied its bow chasers, the *Mermaid*'s stern guns answered, and Captain Douglas deftly led the French ship directly to the blockading fleet. At two in the afternoon, Maisonfort discovered his mistake as the masts of the British warships appeared through the fog, and he realized he was indeed about to uselessly expose his vessel.

The pursuer became the pursued as Maisonfort set his course to the southwest and set all possible sail in his effort to escape to the open sea. Fog rolled in and hours passed as the *Vigilant* struggled to gain her freedom, now pursued not only by the *Mermaid*, but also by the *Eltham, Launceston*, the commodore's flagship, *Superbe*, and the colonial cruisers *Massachusetts* and *Shirley*. The first of the pursuing ships came within range around six in the evening, and Captain Rous of the *Shirley* disregarded the far greater firepower of the French ship and harassed the *Vigilant* with his bow chaser cannons for two hours, slowing the *Vigilant* and enabling the British ships to reach the scene. An intense naval battle ensued. Maisonfort and his French crew, though their ship was more heavily armed than any of their opponents, were doomed in their fight against the four British ships and the two colonials. Surrounded, the *Vigilant* fought valiantly for more than an hour, exchanging hot, powerful broadsides with her adversaries. All of the ships were damaged, but the *Vigilant* was battered into submission, and Maisonfort, with sixty of his crew dead or wounded, was forced to strike his colors. The French ship was completely disabled and was towed into Gabarus Bay.

The capture of the *Vigilant* was a brilliant triumph that raised the morale of the besiegers and shattered that of the defenders. It was not only a rich prize for Warren and his blockading squadron, but also redemption after letting the French merchantman slip through a week earlier. The capture of the *Vigilant* deprived Louisbourg of the much needed cannons and gunpowder, as the city's supply was beginning to run low after a month of exchanging fire with the Americans. The loss of the powder to the French meant an enhanced supply for the blockading ships and the American land forces. While this victory is often cited as the Royal Navy's great contribution to the campaign, it is doubtful that the *Vigilant*, her crew, and her supplies would ever have reached the beleaguered fortress. Maisonfort had been expressly instructed not to uselessly expose his proud new ship. Had there been no squadron of British warships, the *Vigilant* would have encountered the swarm of blockading colonial cruisers and observed the city under siege. If he had succeeded in running the blockade, the inner harbor would have been a hellish place for the big French warship. Drawing eighteen feet two and a half inches, she could not have gotten in close to the city's walls as the French snow had, and sailing into the harbor, the *Vigilant* would have faced the full firepower of the Grand Battery forty-two-pounders as well as the other batteries in American hands. Colonel John Bradstreet said, "It would be difficult, if not impracticable, for any ships to Enter the Harbour, but if any should be so hardy to attempt getting in and succeed with provisions and Ammunition (which was much to be doubted when Seeing the British Flag flying at the Grand Battery and several other places) it would be impossible for the people of the Town to avail themselves of it, as no Boats could pass and repass from the Shore to the Ship." No matter how hard they fought to get into the harbor, Maisonfort's ship would have been a helpless target once at anchor, and it is highly doubtful that the French naval officer would have sacrificed his ship and his men in the potentially futile attempt to resupply the city. Had the Royal Navy not been present, the *Vigilant* would probably have savaged some of the smaller colonial cruisers before prudently sailing away as the *Renommee* had.

A supply convoy arrived from Boston two days after the *Vigilant*'s capture, adding to the gunpowder supply. Encouraged, Pepperrell pressed on with the construction of new batteries, and a powerful installation on the north side of the Barachois was completed on May 20. Commanded by Major Moses Titcomb of the Fifth Massachusetts Regiment, this battery turned two forty-two-pounders directly at the Dauphin Battery eight hundred yards distant and began pounding away. Four American batteries were now within one thousand yards of the main gate of the fortress, and the steady pummeling took its toll. The Americans' mortars continued to lob their explosive bombs over the walls. An eyewitness, the French diarist Gilles Lacroix-Girard, recorded this grim scene within the city at this time of the siege: "The bombs fell into the houses: one in Mr. Fauroux's, which crushed it, two in Mr Carerot's as well as a few cannonballs from the Grand Battery, hitting Mr. Fisel's house, one in Mr. Gilbert's, one in Mr. Prevost's house, which completely destroyed it and in many other houses. They did not kill anyone apart from a Basque who was running in the street and a pregnant woman who was cut in half." This description gives a sense of the continual destruction rained down upon the city and also the tragic realities, where the violent loss of two lives is preceded by, "They did not kill anyone . . ."

Pepperrell once again turned his attention to the Island Battery. Three days after the capture of the *Vigilant*, a new attack was prepared under the direction of Brigadier General Waldo and Colonel Shubael Gorham. Two attempts were called off, and once again the egalitarian spirit within the American force surfaced. The troops, disgusted with the leadership that had been imposed on them, determined to elect their own leader for the next attempt.

While the American army fumbled its way through the democratic process of selecting a leader, Commodore Warren again attempted to usurp control over the activities on land; this time, his proposed frontal attack on the fortress was to be led by his trusted Royal Marines captain, James MacDonald. Warren was brimming with confidence, not only because of the capture of the *Vigilant*, but also because his squadron had been strengthened by the arrival from England of the sixty-gun *Princess Mary* and the forty-gun *Hector*. Warren proposed that the squadron force its way past the Island Battery and into the harbor. He felt this was possible because of the addition of the two new arrivals and the repaired *Vigilant*, which he sought to man with American soldiers serving under British officers, again revealing the British lack of respect for the American leaders. The key element of the plan was the diverting of manpower from the Island Battery, making it ineffective. Once the frontal assault on the fortress began, it was Warren's speculation that troops from the Island Battery would be drawn to Louisbourg to reinforce the city, and the squadron could then sail into the harbor, uncontested, to add their firepower to the assault. Warren was willing to send the American troops into the slaughter of a frontal attack in order to protect his ships from the Island Battery's cannons. Pepperrell and his council continued to hold to their belief that the laborious siege had weakened and depleted the city. With conquest possible in the near future, they suspected that the British commodore was attempting to snatch the glory of victory, and the proposal from the eager opportunist Warren was yet again politely refused.

The troops selected a Captain Brooks to lead them against the Island Battery, and near midnight on the night of May 26, in the last minutes of the Sabbath, nearly four hundred Americans loaded into the whaleboats and began their voyage to the island, with the advanced battery firing regularly to serve as a diversion. This time the approach was successful, and over one hundred men silently landed from the first boats with their weapons and the ladders needed to scale the walls. As some of the men of the first wave erected twelve ladders and the rest of the boats approached, some overzealous soldiers let out a cheer. The commander of the Island Battery, Captain Charles-Joseph Dailleboust d'Argenteuil, who was walking within the fortification, immediately raised the alarm, and his two hundred troops sprang into action. The element of surprise was lost, and the assault turned into a pitched battle. Some of the Americans mounted the parapets, and one, possibly Captain Brooks himself, attempted to cut down the French flag but was cut down himself by a sharp French blade. Dailleboust's men manned their cannons and swivel guns, many of which were already loaded with langrell shot, which contained hundreds of pieces of irregularly shaped iron and was normally used to shred the sails and rigging of ships attempting to pass the battery. Now those guns were aimed at the Americans, and the murderous toll of the shrapnel was devastating as the men struggling on the shore were decimated. Whaleboats were shattered, sending wounded men into the icy water, and the few who had entered the fortress were overpowered.

The battle lasted two and a half hours. The Americans fought bravely, but as dawn came, they were stranded on the island, exposed in the daylight with no option but to surrender. After all the aborted Island Battery attacks, the one that finally managed to land troops on the island turned into a slaughter in which over 60 Americans were killed and 119, including some wounded, were taken captive. Those who managed to escape the debacle returned stunned to the Grand Battery or sought refuge across the harbor entrance at Lighthouse Point, where some of Gorham's troops were stationed. Lieutenant Daniel Giddings recorded the feelings that were widely felt by the Americans after this costly defeat: "I parted with Some of my frinds that was a Going to attack ye Iland Battery . . . About one of ye Clock this morning I heard ye Gons our people ware Ingagd in Battle & a heavy sorrowful Battle itt was to us a Great number of our Brave soldiers ware Kild taken & wounded ye Lord our God fround upon us."

The satisfaction and euphoria of success during the first month of the siege evaporated suddenly in the cold reality of the defeat. There had been so much to celebrate: Vaughn's capture of the Grand Battery, Pomeroy's drilling out of the forty-two-pounders, Gridley and Merserve's transportation of the cannons across daunting terrain, the erecting of gun batteries that were pounding the town, and the capture of the *Vigilant*, depriving the French of supplies and reinforcement. After so much success, this defeat was particularly bitter and discouraging. In addition, sickness had begun to spread through the American camp, disabling hundreds of soldiers. As the second month of the siege began, General Pepperrell faced the challenge of revitalizing the spirit of his army and continuing to prosecute the siege, while fending off Commodore Warren's attempts to usurp control of the land forces. Looming ominously at the harbor entrance still lay the Island Battery protecting Fortress Louisbourg, a bold symbol of French invulnerability and the obstruction that kept the British fleet and their firepower from joining the fight.

CHAPTER 19

Defeat or Victory in the Balance

I F THE AMERICANS WERE discouraged by their failed attack on the Island Battery, the French were jubilant at their success, the single bright spot in an otherwise grim and exhausting month. The 119 Americans herded into the fortress to begin their imprisonment gave the French leverage, as almost 1,000 French, including soldiers, settlers, and the crew of the *Vigilant*, were held as prisoners of the Americans. Duchambon and his advisers reasoned that if the Americans could not take the Island Battery, they would be no match for the defenses and defenders of the city. Clinging to the hope that Paul Marin and his French and Indian force would soon be attacking the rear of the American siege, Duchambon and Morpain redoubled their efforts to inspire their troops and mount a strong defense.

The rancor between the American general and the British commodore continued. On the day after the disastrous attack, Warren sent Pepperrell a sound rebuke, saying, "I have not been favour'd by your answer to the Plan of Operation I sent you, for God's sake let us do something, and not waste our time in Indolence." Knowing that over 180 of his men were lost, but with no idea how many of those had survived to be taken as prisoners or how they would be treated, the following day the indignant Pepperrell responded to Warren. He recounted the successes the American force had achieved and informed Warren of the losses the Americans had suffered attempting to capture the Island

Battery so the harbor could be opened to Warren's squadron. When he learned of the American sacrifice, Warren became more conciliatory but continued to express his frustration and urge action.

Conditions ashore added to Pepperrell's discouragement, as he had only fifteen hundred men available to sustain the siege. Over one thousand of the troops had been disabled by the bloody flux, dysentery. Six hundred soldiers had been dispatched to the interior to protect against attacks rumored to come from French and Indian bands, and other losses had further reduced the force. Gunpowder was again running low, as almost five thousand cannonballs and bombs had been fired against the city. Pepperrell borrowed some from the commodore but was warned not to expect any further supply. Fortunately, his needs were fulfilled on June 3, when a new mortar, along with a supply of shot and fifty barrels of gunpowder, arrived from Boston.

There was also a desperate need for a military engineer to assist Richard Gridley. Unexpectedly, his mentor, John Henry Bastide, came from Annapolis Royal, bringing several expert gunners with him. He also brought the unwelcome news that the French captain Paul Marin and his force of at least eight hundred French and Indians had received Duchambon's order to come to the aid of Louisbourg and were making their way toward the fortress. Steps were taken immediately to protect the troops and precious supplies: The American encampment was reconfigured into a compact twenty-acre site, fortified with defensive ditches, barricades, and several cannons. Additional patrols were sent out to scout the surrounding countryside to detect Marin's approach, so the Americans would be alerted to defend their positions. Three colonial cruisers, the *Tartar*, *Resolution*, and *Bonetta*, were sent through the Gut of Canso to patrol the waterway between Nova Scotia and Cape Breton and turn Marin back if he hadn't already crossed over. The Americans could only wait for Marin and his force to appear.

Steps were also taken to increase the pace of the attack on Louisbourg. A new plan evolved, in which Gridley was given the task of moving cannons by ship, from the harbor out into the ocean past Louisbourg, to be landed east of Lighthouse Point. The coast to the east was very rocky, with steep cliffs rising to impenetrable forests. The American troops were called on to again accomplish the impossible through the sheer force of their determination and muscle, and during the first days of June, ten eighteen-pound cannons were landed through the surf onto the rugged shore. The massive weights were hoisted up from the landing site to the top of the bluff. Using the sledges devised earlier, one by one the cannons were manhandled over "a mile and a quarter through an incredible bad way, which none but men, determined to surmount all difficultys wou'd ever attempt." Colonel Gorham's men who had been stationed at the point had prepared the fortification to accommodate the guns. The emplacement was configured so that six of the cannons pointed directly at the Island Battery and four were aimed out to sea, and because of the configuration of the Island Battery, only a few of its guns could be brought to bear on this new Lighthouse Battery, under the command of Richard Gridley.

The battle took a terrifying twist when the other American batteries, which continued to pound the west gate and lob mortar shells into the heart of the city, began the controversial use of heated shot. Heated to red hot, the cannonballs were carried quickly to the guns, already charged with powder that was protected by several layers of wet wadding to prevent the hot shot from prematurely igniting the powder. When sent on its destructive path, the cannonball would start a fire when it made contact with flammable material such as a building. Although the process was often used by shore batteries firing against wooden ships, and was viewed as an acceptable practice between military forces, at Louisbourg the Americans were firing into a city with women and children, and it was felt by some that Pepperrell was pressing the fight too hard. There seemed to be little compunction about firing explosive mortar bombs into the city, but the fearsome element of potential conflagration was viewed as uncivilized. Pepperrell, however, hoped that an escalation of the battle would encourage Duchambon to surrender.

On the day that the hot shots were first used, a French soldier deserted the fortress and made his way to the American lines, where he surrendered. He reported that there were 3,600 soldiers and militiamen within the fortress, ample ammunition, and adequate provisions to hold out until September or October. Countering this sobering information, he said that perhaps 800 of the military men were ready to surrender if they could do so safely. The most welcome information was that 116 of the Americans who had attacked the Island Battery had survived and were being held as prisoners within the city. The interrogators gave little credibility to the soldier's points concerning the French manpower and supplies, suspecting that the "deserter" might be part of a French "disinformation" campaign. If the French did have all those fighters, well armed and with provisions to endure a long siege, the Americans would have to carefully evaluate their ability to sustain the attack for the months ahead, which would soon bring the nasty, cold, damp autumn. While it served the French to inform the Americans of the number of prisoners they held, since they knew that the Americans held French prisoners and this would give each side some degree of parity, it is doubtful that the French realized that the Americans and English held almost a thousand. With the sense that this man's report was unreliable, the Americans put little stock in it.

When Commodore Warren heard the news of the American prisoners within the city, he raised the specter that they might be mistreated, if not brutalized, as those who surrendered to the French and Indian patrol in the countryside weeks earlier had been. He proposed that one of his officers carry a letter to Duchambon from the *Vigilant*'s captain Maisonfort, whose ship had been towed into and lay at anchor in Gabarus Bay only a short distance from the city. Maisonfort would attest to the fact that the French prisoners were being treated well. Warren's envoy, Captain James MacDonald, an arrogant Royal Marine, made his way toward the fortress on Saturday, June 8, under a flag of truce and was admitted and led to meet with Duchambon and several of his advisers. He delivered Maisonfort's letter, which read in part, "It is well that you should be informed that the captains and officers of this squadron treat us, not as their prisoners, but as their good friends, and take particular pains that my officers and crew should want for nothing; therefore it seems to me just to treat them in like manner, and to punish those who do otherwise and offer any insult to the prisoners who may fall into your hands." Captain MacDonald then presented Commodore Warren's real purpose in approaching Duchambon, revealing the selfish motivation and true intention behind Warren's bold move to engage the French authorities. Two French chroniclers of the siege documented the event. The first

anonymous diarist, known only as "the Habitant," described Mac-
Donald's remarks as follows: "The Admiral on his side was anxious to
secure the honor of reducing us . . . An officer [MacDonald] came to
propose, on the Admiral's part, that, if we must surrender, it would be
better to do so to him, because he would show us a consideration that,
perhaps, we should not find with the commander of the land force."
The French diarist Gilles Lacroix-Girard, a witness to the event, was
explicit in his documentation of MacDonald's presentation, writing,
"The deputy [MacDonald] said to Messieur Duchambon, and some
other officers that were with him, that if they had the intention of
surrendering that they should rather surrender to well ordered
troops, in other words, the English Crown, rather than the Bostonnois
[Pepperrell's troops], and that in surrendering to the latter, the town
would be pillaged and, conversely, there would be none of that if they
surrendered to the English Crown." The Americans had organized
and paid for the campaign, and their officers and soldiers had suffered all the hardships and deprivations of the voyage to Cape Breton
and the siege, and now Warren was making an underhanded attempt
to reap the glory of the conquest by having the French surrender to
him. The disrespect and contempt that the British military harbored
toward the Americans was again made painfully clear, as a resident of
Louisbourg described it, also writing of MacDonald's visit, "All this
shows very little co-operation between the two generals [Pepperrell
and Warren], and sufficiently confirms the remark which I have already made; in fact one could never have told that these troops be-
longed to the same nation and obeyed the same prince."

The French dismissed Captain MacDonald at around three A.M. As
the haughty officer passed through the American lines to report back
to the commodore, he made the discouraging comments that he had
seen large numbers of well-disciplined troops and that it would be
impossible to scale the walls, but the Americans resumed their siege
against the city despite the reports from the deserter and MacDonald
that Louisbourg was in good shape and prepared to resist for months.

Reality within the fortress was far from what had been conveyed to
the Americans, however. Many of the structures, including the chapel
within the Château St. Louis, lay in ruins, and every building but one
was damaged. Business was nonexistent. Rather than the adequate

supplies reported, there was a severe shortage of food and a drasti-
cally low supply of gunpowder. The dissatisfaction of the troops mentioned by the deserter did seem to be true, and on June 10, the day
after MacDonald's departure from the fortress, a French soldier was
arrested for treason. He had befriended one of the American prisoners, who induced him to write out the details of how the fortress was
manned and where its vulnerable spots were, in order to facilitate an
American attack. The French soldier was to desert, and his information was to be delivered to Pepperrell. When the plot was discovered,
the French soldier was hanged. There was also rivalry among the
leaders in Louisbourg. The hero of the Island Battery defense, Dailleboust, protested the increased responsibilities offered to Morpain, but
the soldiers sided with the popular Morpain and threatened to put
down their arms if command was taken from him. The soldiers recognized real leadership, but those in command once again failed to
acknowledge their own inadequacies and removed Morpain from
command.

Amid this atmosphere on June 9, two members of the Swiss Regiment of the garrison fled Louisbourg and deserted to the Americans.
They painted a grim and realistic picture of what was happening in
the city, recounting the hanging of the soldier and reporting that the
gunpowder supply was only 150 barrels, which would charge each
gun only nine times. They elaborated on the conditions the inhabitants were enduring, saying that many would be glad to deliver
themselves up. The tide appeared to be changing in favor of the
besiegers.

The officials within the fortress wrestled with their deteriorating
situation as Paul Marin and his force, now numbering twelve hundred, made their way toward Louisbourg. The patrol of colonial cruisers under the command of Daniel Fones in the *Tartar*, along with
Captain Donohue in the *Resolution* and Captain Moses Bennett in
the *Bonetta*, were in Northumberland Strait about eighty miles west
of the Strait of Canso on June 8, scouring the Nova Scotia coastline
for any sign of Marin. The Frenchman and his force could already
have crossed over the twenty-mile-long strait, but the colonial vessels
continued their vital patrol. In a light breeze at dawn on the morning

of June 15, smoke was seen near Tatamagouche harbor in Amet Sound, downwind from the three warships, and the *Tartar* and the *Bonetta* went to investigate.

The smoke proved to be a clever ruse that Marin employed to divide the force that opposed him. As soon as the two cruisers were out of sight of Captain Donohue's *Resolution*, the French appeared in force, in two schooners, two sloops, a shallop, and about fifty Indian canoes, all packed with French and Indian fighters. The *Resolution* fired her cannons and swivel guns to keep the approaching enemy at bay. Hearing the gunfire, Fones and Bennett turned their ships around and attempted to return to the scene of the battle. The wind had died, however, and in utter frustration they drifted helplessly. Donohue and his forty-man crew were in a fight for their lives as the enemy vessels swarmed around them, and every gun on the *Resolution* was in action as they fought both sides of the ship simultaneously. Describing the two-and-a-half-hour battle, Donohue wrote, "I fired two Hundred four-Pounders, double Round and Partridge [containing numerous projectiles], fifty three-pounders, my Swivel and Small Arms continuously playing on them. My Stern by Force of firing, is down to the Water Edge, Round House all to pieces, but bold hearted; had it not been so calm I should have done as I would, but not one Breath of Wind, and they rowing all around me both Head and Stern."

Finally the breeze came up and the *Tartar* and *Bonetta* were able to get to the fight. The *Resolution* was close to being overwhelmed, but the arrival of the two American ships turned the tide. Marin and his vessels were forced to retreat toward the shore, and his men fled into the safety of the forest. Donohue said, "This was the Army that besieged Annapolis, and was ordered to assist Louisbourg, but their Design is prevented." With that simple understatement, Donohue marks the event that sealed the fate of the great French fortress. Two weeks later, Donohue and several of his men went ashore, where they were surprised and attacked by a force of three hundred Indians. As the crews of Fones's *Tartar* and Donohue's *Resolution* looked on in horror, Donohue and his men were slain, butchered, and eaten. Despite this horrid conclusion to their mission, Fones, Donohue, Bennett, and their crews had turned back the force that was Louisbourg's best hope for relief.

On June 11, the Americans' new Lighthouse Battery opened fire on the Island Battery and began the process of knocking out its guns. A few days later, a large mortar added its terrifying blasts to the chorus of cannon fire. Of nineteen mortar shells fired, seventeen plummeted down into the island fort, exploding among the soldiers and penetrating the roof of the barracks building. Other cannons sent 194 eighteen-pound cannonballs streaking toward the twenty Island guns. When one of the mortar shells made a direct hit on the Island Battery's powder magazine, there was no place to seek shelter from the potential massive explosion, and some of the French soldiers leapt into the water for safety. The Island Battery had been neutralized, not by another frantic and costly amphibious attack, but by the methodical cannon and mortar assault that had been the hallmark of Pepperrell's plan of attack.

No response came from the French officials to Warren's secret proposal that they surrender to him and his disciplined troops, and once again he renewed his call for a full-bore attack, combining the penetration of the harbor by his squadron and a frontal assault and scaling of the walls by the Americans. With the recent arrival of two new sixty-gun ships, the *Sunderland* and the *Canterbury*, as well as the

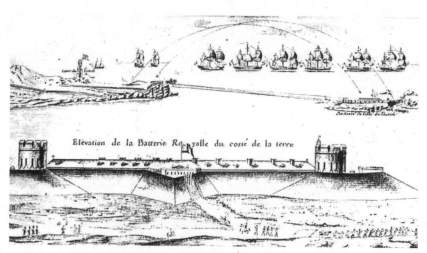

View of Grand and Island Batteries from Louisbourg

forty-gun *Lark*, the commodore had an impressive squadron of eleven large warships, and Warren and his captains could sail past the Island Battery, disabled by the Americans, to enter the battle, since there was now little risk to their ships and crews. Pepperrell also felt that the time had come for an all-out assault, despite the fact that it would cost many American lives. The general did not know if Marin was still on his way and felt they had to capture the city quickly to be ready for an attack from the rear. The forty-two-pounders from the advanced battery had bludgeoned two fifty-foot breaches in the wall near the demolished west gate. The cannons mounted in that area had been systematically disabled by American fire, and the other batteries within the fortress were in similar distress. Pepperrell's methodical approach of continuous bombardment to destroy and demoralize the fortress had succeeded, and it was time now for the combined naval and army forces to take the city. The American guns continued to exchange fire with those from the fortress, as the Yankee soldiers built ladders to scale the fortress walls and harvested large amounts of moss for the fleet, several boatloads of which were carried out to Warren's squadron. The moss was to be packed along the sides of the ships that would face the Island Battery, to absorb the langrell shot they feared could still be fired at them. The Americans went about their preparations with the sobering knowledge that they faced a deadly, exposed assault on the towering walls of the fortress, feeling certain that many American lives would be lost as the French fought to protect their battered city and the families sheltered in it.

Inside Louisbourg, nearly all the buildings were seriously damaged, gunpowder was in short supply, and there was widespread discontent. The lookouts had observed the heightened activity around the American gun emplacements, the gathering of ladders and other equipment, and it was apparent that the English squadron and the American army were about to launch an attack. Duchambon was too proud to surrender, but pressure to do so began to build from various factions within the fortress. On June 15, Duchambon was presented with a petition signed by many of the merchants and citizens of property. Although their once proud city was in ruins, much of their merchandise and personal property was intact. Believing that an American assault on the battered walls would probably be successful, they feared that all would be lost as the victors sacked the city. They stood to lose not only their property, but possibly their lives as well, and they appealed to Duchambon to surrender. With this petition from the citizens in hand, Duchambon could legitimately negotiate a settlement without the blame for defeat falling solely on his shoulders, and he ordered his engineer and artillery expert to make full assessments of the fortress and its armaments. The engineer, Verrier, reported that both the Dauphin Battery near the west gate and the north side of the King's Bastion had been completely destroyed and that by using their ladders, the Americans could easily enter the city through the two breaches in the walls. Verrier felt the situation was hopeless. The artillery captain, Allard St. Marie, confirmed that there remained fewer than fifty barrels of gunpowder, which would provide only four rounds per gun, and that they were also out of fuses for the cannons. He, too, saw the situation as untenable. François Bigot, the *commissaire-ordonnateur* of Louisbourg, summed up the grim reality: "The townspeople said that they did not want to be put to the sword, and were not strong enough to resist a general assault."

As these discussions were being held inside the fortress, six hundred Americans were sent to help man Warren's squadron, and on June 15, Commodore Warren came ashore to discuss the final details of the attack with Pepperrell and address the American troops assembled for an inspection by the general and himself. His speech was intended to rouse their enthusiasm and steel the troops for the bloody assault that lay ahead. The plan was set. When the winds were right, Warren would signal by hoisting the Dutch flag under his commodore's flag on the *Superbe*, and Pepperrell would respond by igniting large bonfires erected on three small hills outside the city. With that exchange of signals, the general attack would commence. The American force settled down for what would probably be their final night before the attack, and many contemplated whether it would be their final night on earth, but then, as recorded by Seth Pomeroy, "just Before Sun Set the French Sent out a Flag of Truce."

Duchambon and his advisers requested a cease-fire so they could hold a war council within the city to draft their terms of surrender. It appeared that the ominous and costly attack might be avoided.

Encouraged that the siege and blockade had been successful, the general and the commodore responded with the following: "We have yours of the date proposing a suspension of hostilities for such time as shall be necessary for you to determine upon the conditions of delivering up the garrison of Louisbourg, which arrived at a happy juncture to prevent the Effusion of Christian blood as we were together and had just determined upon a general attack. We shall comply with your desire until eight of the clock to-morrow, and if in the meantime you surrender yourselves prisoners of war, You may depend upon honour and generous treatment."

The following morning, before the appointed hour, a French officer, Captain Bonnaventure, emerged with Duchambon's conditions, a wish list that benefited the French far more than they had reason to expect under their dire circumstances. Incredibly, with only minor modifications, Pepperrell and Warren accepted Duchambon's proposed terms. The generous agreement began with a provision that would have a shocking effect on the American soldiers who had suffered so much during the two and a half months of the campaign, stating, "That all the subjects of the French King now in said city & territory shall be treated with utmost humanity & have their personal estates secured to them & have liberty to transport themselves & said effects to any part of the French King's dominions in Europe." With those words, the plunder that the Americans had been promised as part of their "pay package" evaporated. The soldiers had signed on for the campaign at the meager wage of less than one shilling per day because of lavish promises from Vaughn and others that the conquest of the city would produce a vast amount of plunder that would be distributed to the soldiers to properly compensate them for their time away from home and the risks and hardships they endured. The very people they had forced into surrender were going to be able to retain their property and take it with them to France, and they would be transported at British expense. One anonymous American soldier made the understated entry in his diary, "They came to Termes for us to Enter the Sitte to morrow and Poore Termes they Be Two."

There were also generous provisions for the French military, in which the commissioned officers as well as the civilians in the city were to be permitted to continue to reside in their battered homes with their families, practice their Catholic religion, and not be misused or molested while waiting to be transported to France. The noncommissioned officers and the soldiers of the garrison were to be held as prisoners on board the British warships until they, too, were transported to France, but they were to receive civil treatment. Proper care of the sick and wounded among the French was provided for as well. There were also two very strange provisions in the terms of surrender. In the first, Pepperrell and Warren agreed that the French could send two covered wagons from the city, which could be inspected by only one British officer to ensure that they contained no weapons. While it was not known what would be in the wagons, the logical conclusion was that they could contain sensitive government documents and the treasury and private money that would have been part of the plunder. The other very unusual provision allowed, "That if there are any persons in the town or garrison who shall desire not to be seen by the English they shall be permitted to go off mask'd." Presumably, this was to allow persons known to the Americans who might have been revealed as spies to leave undetected. It also might have permitted former business associates, who might have had outstanding debts with Americans, to escape without being held accountable for their indebtedness. Whatever the reasons, Pepperrell and Warren let the provisions stand.

The commodore and the general did impose several conditions in exchange for granting these exceptionally generous terms. They called for the surrender to be made promptly and for the Island Battery to be surrendered by six P.M. that same day. They also demanded that the ships of Warren's squadron be allowed to enter the harbor unopposed and the American prisoners be released immediately. One other provision prohibited the French soldiers from fighting against the British for the period of one year. The French had made a similar agreement when the prisoners from Canso had been released, but some of them, including Colonel John Bradstreet, had disregarded the agreement on the basis that it had been made under coercion. The French knew that Bradstreet was among those participating in the siege and witnessing their surrender, and it is likely that they would ignore this condition of their parole once they were safely back in France.

The revised terms were sent back to Duchambon, who made one final request, that the French soldiers be allowed to march out with "military honors," carrying their weapons and with their flags flying. In separate responses, from Pepperrell ashore and Warren afloat, the French were granted this final courtesy, and the terms of surrender were completed. On June 16, 1745, 142 days after the Massachusetts Legislature had approved the campaign by one vote, the army they had raised and the general they had selected were on the eve of accomplishing what few had thought possible. The Americans had demonstrated that they could not only raise and equip an army, but also support that force as it waged a prolonged siege almost one thousand miles from home. The American citizen soldiers had shown the world that their ingenuity and dogged determination could compensate for their lack of military experience and skill, and they could triumph against professional soldiers to conquer the most heavily fortified city in North America. There was certainly bitterness as word spread through the American camp that there was to be little or no plunder. Some, who were realistic about the situation, realized that giving up plunder in exchange for the surrender of the city may have saved their lives, which could have been lost in the proposed frontal assault. It is easy to wonder why such generous terms were awarded when the Americans had learned from the deserters that the gunpowder supply was so low. The reason is undoubtedly that the besieging force had no way of knowing that Daniel Fones, with the *Tartar*, *Resolution*, and *Bonetta*, had turned back Marin's relief force, and they feared the prospect of fighting a two-front battle.

As the evening of June 16 came, the Island Battery was surrendered, and despite their deep disappointment, the American troops began to relax and reflect on their extraordinary accomplishment. They had made New England's greatest conquest.

At this moment of triumph, the relationship between Great Britain and her American colonies rested in equilibrium, on the balance point of the shared victory at Louisbourg. Despite the frequent friction between the leaders of the American and British forces, they had managed to work together successfully to bring about the victory and had maintained an outwardly cordial and respectful relationship. The presence of the Royal Navy had contributed to the success, but they had been called on to do little other than blockade and had not fired a single shot at the fortress. Nevertheless, the two forces shared in the triumph. The Americans had earned respect as fighting men, and the old derision so often expressed by the professional British officers could now be set aside.

CHAPTER 20

Opportunity Squandered

THE OPPORTUNITY FOR FUTURE harmony between the British and the Americans after their shared victory at Louisbourg, however, never had a chance to develop. Commodore Warren's duplicitous behavior in sending Captain MacDonald to Duchambon to plead the case for the French to surrender to the British, rather than the undisciplined Americans, continued. When on the evening of June 16 Warren received Duchambon's final condition in the terms of surrender, which specified that his troops would be allowed the honors of war, the admiral responded directly to the French governor, without the courtesy of sharing his response with Pepperrell. In agreeing to offer the honors of war, Warren posed his own condition, attempting to usurp the surrender by saying "that the keys of the town be delivered to such officers and troops as I shall appoint to receive them, and that all the cannon, warlike and other King's stores in the town be also delivered up to said officer." Philip Durell, a French-speaking Royal Navy captain from the Isle of Jersey, carried this message to Duchambon and renewed the argument that it would be safer to surrender to the British than to the Americans. Warren's intention was to be the person to officially accept the surrender of Fortress Louisbourg.

Pepperrell and the members of his war council awoke on the morning of June 17 looking forward to the culmination of their victory. It was inconceivable to them that the surrender would go to anyone other than General Pepperrell. Early that morning, the general sent a letter to the French governor outlining his expectations for the turnover of the city and expressing his concern for the welfare of the inhabitants. He wrote, "I desire the favour that your officers and families, with the inhabitants and their families, may repair to their own homes as soon as possible where they may depend they shall not meet with the least bad treatment . . . I shall send Colonel Bradstreet with a detachment at four o'clock this afternoon to take possession of the town and fort, to whom I desire you will deliver them up with all warlike stores, and the keys." Pepperrell's message was a sound and simple plan for the surrender that reflected none of the rioting and pillaging that Warren had attempted to conjure up in the French imagination.

When Warren learned of Pepperrell's plan, he was incensed and immediately took steps to undermine the Americans by accompanying Captain MacDonald and his marines as they took possession of the city. Sailing into the harbor at Louisbourg on HMS *Eltham*, rather than his conspicuous flagship, the underhanded Warren snatched the surrender from the man who had the clear right to receive it. In a report sent to Thomas Corbett, the secretary to the Board of the Admiralty, Warren asserted, "The seventeenth, I landed with Captain James Macdonald. Sent him with twelve officers and 400 marines to take possession of Louisbourg and place proper guards. The governor having delivered me the keys of the town, magazines of powder and other warlike stores, which were immediately opened on that land side . . ." This action was confirmed by Captain Philip Durell's *Account of the Taking of Cape Breton* when he wrote, "They delivered the keys of the Town to Mr. Warren." In the war within the war, the underhanded Warren had won.

Unaware that the commodore had swooped in ahead of them, the Americans proceeded according to the plan sent to Duchambon, and in midafternoon a significant detachment of American troops headed for the fortress. Without the news that Fones and the colonial cruisers had turned back Marin and his reinforcements, some American troops continued to prudently man the defensive positions. Major Seth Pomeroy was one of those on guard at the American encampment, and Colonel

Richard Gridley continued to man the Lighthouse Battery. Gridley and Pomeroy were proud to watch their victorious compatriots march toward the city. This date, June 17, 1745, had additional significance for Pomeroy. It was the first birthday of his youngest child, Sarah, far away in Northampton, Massachusetts.

The honor of leading the American troops into Louisbourg was given to John Bradstreet. Pepperrell wanted to acknowledge his role in instigating the campaign, as well as demonstrate that the suspicion of treason that had plagued Bradstreet was not valid. An additional motivation was the offer of a mild insult to the French, who had held Bradstreet as a prisoner and paroled him. The troops marched in orderly fashion behind the colonel, with General Pepperrell and his senior officers following at the rear. They skirted the demolished west gate, passed the ruined west side of the King's Bastion, and entered the city through the still intact queen's gate on the south side of the fortress. Once in the city, the Americans formed into neat ranks on the main street, Rue D'Orléans, and marched smartly past the hospital. At the intersection of Rue D'Orléans and Rue Toulouse, they turned up the hill to the parade ground in front of the Château St. Louis, where the French garrison had assembled. Salutes were given by the vanquished to the victors. The fortress fired an eighteen-gun salute with six cannons. The ships of the squadron, which had entered the harbor as the Americans approached the fortress, responded with their salutes. At six P.M., the French flag that had flown over Louisbourg for a quarter of a century was lowered, the British flag was raised, and King George II became the sovereign of the powerful Fortress Louisbourg, once considered impregnable. Fifty-three French soldiers had been killed and another eighty wounded in the siege. The number of civilian casualties was unknown. One hundred and one Americans were killed in combat, another thirty succumbed to disease, and an additional fifty American sailors were lost when the *Prince of Orange* disappeared in a storm. Among Commodore Warren's Royal Naval vessels, no men were lost at sea, but a single sailor was killed while ashore.

As soon as the surrender took place and the American forces occupied the city, Pepperrell and Warren took steps to announce the victory to their respective governments, and on June 20, Pepperrell sent

Captain Moses Bennett's ship racing to Boston with the news. It took a full thirteen days for the vessel to beat against adverse winds and reach New England, where it arrived in the early morning hours of Wednesday, July 3. It was, in fact, at four A.M. that Colonel Wendell's company of militia, unable to restrain their joy at the news, had woken the town with three volleys from their muskets. The town's bells began pealing at five A.M., continuing to ring all day as people from the surrounding communities, including those who had gone to Cambridge for the Harvard commencement, flooded into Boston to participate in the joyous event. That night the city looked as if it were on fire, since almost every residence was illuminated with candles positioned in the windows. The streets were full of fireworks and there were several bonfires, the primary one on the Boston Common, where a tent had been set up and there was "plenty of good Liqour for all that would drink." The *New York Weekly Post-Boy* summed up the Boston celebration: "In a word, never before, upon any Occasion, was observed so universal and unaffected a Joy; nor was there ever seen so many Persons of both Sexes at one Time walking about, as appeared that Evening . . ." The *Boston Gazette* emphasized this as an American victory when it said, "Thus ended this Expedition, to the perpetual Honour of His Majesty's *American* arms." All along the east coast, in New York, Philadelphia, Annapolis, and other cities, the papers recounted the news and the populace celebrated this American victory.

For those in the legislature who had doubted the viability of the campaign against Louisbourg, the victory was clear evidence of their misplaced temerity. For those who had believed in the words of William Vaughn and John Bradstreet, the validity of their position had been affirmed. No one was more pleased than Governor Shirley, who, after his initial reluctance, had virtually risked his career as a British civil servant when, without the knowledge of the British government, he endorsed and oversaw the campaign. Shirley expressed his restrained enthusiasm for the conquest in a letter to General Pepperrell, saying, "I congratulate you and the other officers and the whole army under your command, who by their late bravery and unparallell'd services before Louisbourg have lay'd a most lasting foundation for the wealth, peace and prosperity of this country, and acquir'd an honour to themselves and glory to the New England arms which must make a shining part of the English history to the latest posterity." He also affirmed Pepperrell's use of the siege rather than Warren's plan for a frontal assault and pointed out that if that had been necessary, it "must in all human probability have cost the lives of 1,000 or 1,500 brave New England men, which I should have esteem'd an irreparable loss." Shirley was quick to recognize the extreme disappointment of the American troops in the terms of surrender, which deprived them of the plunder on which they had been recruited and felt they deserved. Demonstrating that he was certain that the grateful nation of Great Britain would make up the loss, he said, "Whereas the army's disappointment of the plunder of the town may be recompens'd to 'em by their King and country, for obtaining which . . . my best endeavours, they may depend upon it, shall be exerted."

Always looking for the opportunity to advance his position, Warren sought to curry favor with the powerful Earl of Sandwich by choosing the earl's brother, Captain Montague of HMS *Mermaid*, as his emissary to carry news of the victory to England. Montague was to leave the *Mermaid* in Warren's squadron to travel to England in the improbably named British vessel *Wheel of Fortune*. To ensure that the critical message got through, Warren had a duplicate dispatch prepared and entrusted to Captain Geary of HMS *Chester*, who was also to leave his ship in Louisbourg. The honor of transporting Captain Geary and the news to England was given to one of the New England ships, the *Shirley*, whose captain, John Rous, had distinguished himself in the battle with the *Vigilant* and earned the respect of Commodore Warren. Montague was affronted by the fact that the fast American frigate might beat him to England and steal his thunder, and he appealed to Warren to delay the *Shirley*'s departure by ten days. Warren agreed and held the *Shirley* until July 6, when she departed amid salutes from all the ships in the harbor at Louisbourg. Montague was first to reach London, arriving on Saturday, July 20, three days before the *Shirley*. The news was received with astonishment, since no one had taken the American attack seriously. The people of Great Britain made it an occasion for rejoicing and great celebration, particularly appreciated during a war that had produced no other British land victories. Here at last was a triumph. They celebrated in the streets, and bonfires were seen throughout the country as the news spread. The guns of the Tower of London were fired in salute, and poems and broadsides were published, heaping tributes on both Warren and the New England forces. There was a new respect for the Americans, since it was clearly understood, despite Commodore Warren's usurpation of the surrender and British chauvinistic exaggeration of Warren's role, that the Americans had originated the campaign and carried out the successful siege. The people of England recognized the raw determination of the rough-hewn Americans, contrasted with the vain, fashion-conscious British officers who had produced so few successes. One poem in England's *Gentleman's Magazine* honored the Americans and reflected this popular feeling:

> *Hail, heroes born for action, not for show!*
> *Who leave toupees and powder to the beau,*
> *To war's dull pedants tedious rules of art*
> *And know to conquer by a dauntless heart,*
> *Rough English virtue gives your deeds to fame.*
> *And o'er the Old exalts New England's name.*

In contrast with the joy seen among the people, the reaction within the government was mixed. A number of highly placed officials, including King George II, former secretary of state John Carteret, the first lord of the Admiralty, William Pitt, and the Earl of Sandwich, expressed their satisfaction with the accomplishment and the thought that this new territory should be retained and not considered as any part of a peace settlement. For others in the government, the victory brought consternation. With the war going badly, the government was hoping for a quick conclusion through a negotiated peace. They had given the Americans no chance of actually capturing the French fortress. Now they had a significant prize that was going to complicate the peace plan, which consisted simply of returning to the status quo ante bellum, with both sides acknowledging each other's territories as they existed before the war. With the enormous popular support for the conquest of Louisbourg, both in En-

gland and in her American colonies, it would be unthinkable to negotiate a peace that called for its return to France. The leader of the
government, Henry Pelham, first lord of the Treasury, saw the capture as a stumbling block to all negotiations for peace. For the first
time in history, the decisive actions of the British colonies in America
were influencing and even dictating British foreign policy.

Perhaps the most significant endorsement of the newly recognized
American military prowess came not from a fellow American or Englishman, but from the most professional military man in Louisbourg.
Captain Pierre Morpain said, as recorded in the journal of Stephen
Williams, a colonial chaplain, "that he thot the n[ew] England men
were Cowards—but now he thot that if they had a pick ax and
Spade—they would dig their way to Hell and Storm it which they
had done." High praise indeed for the Americans. In England, there
developed a broadly based respect for the people of New England. In
the August 1745 edition of the *Craftsman*, there was an article entitled "The Virtue of the New England People," which said in part:

"When I reflect on the Sagacity and Bravery of Mr. Pepperrell,
and of the *New English* Engineer who left his Shop-board, and the
Intrepidity of the rest of the *New Englishmen* in this Expedition,
when I consider the Coolness and Bravery with which they marched
to Action, and their Return from Victory to their several Occupations,
I take into my Mind the great image of the ancient *Romans* leaving
the Plow for the Field of Battle, and retiring after the conquest to the
Plow again.

"But while I contemplate the Virtues of the *New English*, I grieve
and blush at the Reproach of the *Old*, and I cannot conclude this
paper, without observing that if a neglect of the publick *Justice* pre-
vails much longer in this Land, we may possibly have reason to think
this Country no safe abode, and may find it necessary to seek a Refuge
in *New England*, where *Justice* and *Industry seem to have taken their
Residence*."

THE AMERICANS AT the captured fortress found the satisfaction of
watching their flag, the British flag, flying over the fortress short-
lived. The day after the surrender, the French flag was once again

waving in the wind above the citadel, hoisted aloft in the hope that
French ships approaching the city would not know that the fortress
had been conquered and would sail unsuspecting into the harbor. A
French merchant ship, the *Saint-François-Xavier*, loaded with wine,
brandy, clothes, shoes, bread, butter, pork, precious soap, and one
hundred thousand silver pieces of eight, was captured as it entered
the harbor on June 18. Warren's share of the proceeds of this prize
was a significant £5,740, and his sailors would benefit from their
shares as well, but the American soldiers who occupied Louisbourg
gained nothing and found themselves in a very disagreeable situation. Although the French merchants opened their damaged businesses to sell their goods to the French residents and American
soldiers, the soldiers felt that as the victors, all that was in the town
should have been theirs for the taking. Even more frustrating, many
of the Americans were assigned to guard the homes and property of
the French citizens. While the residents of Louisbourg packed their
belongings for the trip back to France, and the merchants added to
their cash supply, the soldiers, often barefoot or with worn shoes and
wearing their one set of tattered clothes, had to witness their plunder
being carted away. As one soldier recorded, "A great Noys and hub-
bub a mungst the Solders a bout the Plonder Som will go out and
Take it again Som one way som a Nother." For these rough men, the
niceties of the surrender were lost in the midst of their deep dissatisfaction. There were some complaints of looting in the days following,
but no egregious violations. The French chronicler the Habitant
sings the praises of the genteel and courteous commodore Warren,
while ridiculing and criticizing the American soldiers and General
Pepperrell, whom he mistakenly calls the son of a shoemaker from
Boston. Despite their bitter disappointment, the occupying Americans carried out their distasteful tasks, and the process of shipping the
French troops and civilians back to France moved relatively quickly.

Only a few French ships capable of making the transatlantic voyage to France remained at Louisbourg, and Warren decided that several British and New England ships would participate in the mass
deportation of the French. The largest of these was the Royal Navy's
forty-gun *Launceston*. The ship was old and so badly deteriorated
that it was of little use as a warship, so all but two of its guns were

removed and carpenters went aboard to build accommodations for twelve hundred passengers. As the procurement of ships and the loading of the French and their belongings proceeded, Warren responded to the French complaints about the conduct of the American troops. Writing to Pepperrell, Warren once again used a chastising tone: "For God's sake give strict orders to your troops to comply with the capitulation." He went on to express his fear that any perceived mistreatment of the French from Louisbourg could provide an excuse for the French to seize Warren's HMS *Launceston* when it entered a French port carrying the Louisbourg refugees. Warren had little concern for the deprived American soldiers, but great concern for his ships. As the evacuation continued, the two covered wagons left the city, undoubtedly carrying the city's treasury of over two hundred thousand French livres. Almost three thousand people had departed Louisbourg for France by mid-July, and the occupying troops scavenged for whatever scraps of plunder had been left behind.

With the departure of the French, the occupation of the city settled into a routine, and the government in England assessed the ramifications of the unanticipated victory. There had been no contingency plans to send a force of regular British soldiers for the occupation, because it had been considered inconceivable that the campaign would succeed. The government was now scrambling to determine which troops could be spared to go to Cape Breton to relieve the American citizen soldiers, who, having accomplished their task, were eager to return to their homes, families, and occupations. The king and his government also were considering the recognition and reward for those who had accomplished this victory. In this regard, Commodore Warren was calculating in his recommendations. While often at odds with Pepperrell, Warren could see that significant recognition of the general might be helpful in enabling him to rally thousands of American soldiers, for whom Warren had a new appreciation, if England should need them in the future. He wrote to the Duke of Newcastle, recommending Pepperrell be given the title of baronet and expressing the thought that the American officers, who now had combat experience, should be given preference to fill future positions in regiments raised in America. Captain MacDonald and Colonel John Bradstreet were singled out for their dedicated service and recommended for special recognition by the king. Warren was not shy in putting forth a request on his own behalf, describing how he would like to be made governor of New Jersey and expressing his desire that since his wife was from New York, he would like to have that governorship when Governor George Clinton retired from that position. It would take many weeks for Warren's recommendation to reach England, further time for the government to decide on the honors and recognition, and additional weeks for the news to travel back to America.

As the British government continued to wrestle with the issues surrounding their new possession in North America, the situation in Louisbourg was growing more restive. Warren's squadron swung at anchor in the capacious harbor, and the sailors were allowed to go ashore; there was little concern that they would desert because the barren wilderness held little appeal for them. The wonders of Fortress Louisbourg were an attraction, and when the sailors went ashore, they came into close contact with the ragtag American soldiers. The well-turned-out sailors bragged about their dominant role in the conquest of the city, claiming that it was their presence that had permitted the amateur American force to take the city and touting that the surrender had been to their commodore. Reflecting the general feeling among the self-aggrandizing officers of the squadron, Captain Durell wrote in his published account, "During the Time of our cruizing here, Mr. Warren disposed so well of his Ships, that we cut off all Communications by Sea; which distressed them so much, that they at last were left with but very little Ammunition; which obliged them to capitulate the 17th of June. They delivered the Keys of the Town to Mr. Warren, agreeable to the Articles specified in the Capitulation, saying, that if it had not been for the Ships, the Land Forces would never have been in Possession of the Place." The arrogant sailors and officers of the Royal Navy flaunted this attitude, without consideration that the colonial warships had maintained a tight blockade prior to the arrival of Warren's squadron and had beaten off the superior *Renommee*. They also knew that it was highly doubtful that Maisonfort would have placed his *Vigilant* directly under the devastating guns of the Grand Battery and other American batteries. The sixty-four-gun *Vigilant* could bring the guns of only one side of the ship to bear on the well-fortified batteries ashore, and that one side would consist only of twelve twenty-four-pounders, twelve twelve-pounders, and four six-pounders, since the bow chasers and stern chasers could not be used. These twenty-eight relatively light guns would have been no match for the massive forty-two-pounders being carefully aimed from solid fortification. The forty-two-pound cannonballs would have shattered the hull, and the ship would have been doomed. The Americans knew well that it had been they who had carried the burden of the campaign and suffered the loss of friends and compatriots, and their contact with the braggart mariners brought such animosity that any sense of mutual achievement was eradicated.

With this friction brewing, the first month of the occupation passed. Virtually all of the French had departed, and it was clear that Marin and his force posed no threat. The Americans began to grumble about the lack of news of a relief force that would garrison the fortress and allow those who had captured it to return home. The French flag still flew over the city in hopes of luring unsuspecting ships, but in the five weeks since the *Saint-François-Xavier* had wandered in, no significant prizes had been taken. That drought changed dramatically on July 23. The previous evening, a large French ship had been seen in the distance, and early that morning, the Connecticut sloop *Defence* accompanied the two sixty-gun warships, the *Princess Mary* and the *Canterbury*, out of the harbor, all flying French colors. They casually made their way toward the wary stranger, which took flight. Showing their true colors, the British and colonial ships pursued the French East Indiaman the *Charmante*, armed with twenty-eight guns. By afternoon, the British were close enough to fire a broadside, after which the outgunned French ship struck her colors. As the British relaxed and prepared to send a boat over to board the captured ship, the *Charmante* ran up her colors again and attempted to escape, but the French captain's dishonorable attempt was useless, and as the British ships once again closed in, he surrendered for the second and final time. The ship was making her way back to France from Bengal, carrying a rich cargo estimated to be worth £200,000, a fabulous sum equal to over £25 million today. Warren and his sailors had seized a truly significant prize.

Two days later, one of the last ships carrying the refugees to France sailed out of Louisbourg, escorted by the heroic Captain Fones in the

Tartar, which accompanied the French vessel for sixty miles out to sea to ensure that they had no opportunity to alert any Louisbourg-bound French ships that the city had fallen. Heading back to Louisbourg, Fones spied an unfamiliar large ship, and the *Tartar* broke out her French flag to decoy the newcomer toward the Cape Breton coast. On July 28, Warren sent the *Chester* and the *Mermaid* to assist the *Tartar*, and the French East Indiaman the *Heron*, also from Bengal, was forced to surrender. This prize was of equal value to the *Charmante*, and the sailors, who would divide the prize money, were truly getting rich.

The ruse of flying the French flag above the fortress, over the Grand Battery and Island Battery, and from the ships in the harbor and on patrol was working well. Three days after the arrival of the *Heron*, Captain Fletcher of the colonial cruiser *Boston Packet* spotted a ship's barge well to the east of Louisbourg and approached, flying the French flag. The barge was from the captured *Heron* and had been sent to secure a pilot to guide the *Heron* into Louisbourg but had discovered that the fort had fallen. Thinking the *Boston Packet* was French, the barge crew tried to warn them away from Louisbourg, but instead of encountering their French compatriots, the barge crew was captured and taken on board the *Boston Packet*. Captain Fletcher continued to cruise off Louisbourg, and the following morning, August 2, he sighted a large ship approaching, which the French officer from the barge indicated was the French forty-gun *Triton*. Realizing that this ship was too powerful for his sixteen-gun colonial cruiser, Fletcher fired three guns to signal Louisbourg that he had a ship in sight. He also sent a request for help ashore in the *Heron*'s speedy barge. Fletcher then hoisted the French flag and sailed back and forth, attempting to reassure the approaching stranger that his was a friendly vessel. There was insufficient wind in the harbor for large ships to sail out from Louisbourg, but the crews of the *Chester* and *Sunderland* manned their boats and, along with others, towed the two huge warships flying French colors out of the harbor, where they caught a breeze. Joining the *Boston Packet*, the three ships sailed toward the unidentified vessel. One cannon shot from the *Chester* was all it took to convince Captain Pierre Litan of the *Notre Dame de la Deliverance* of the mistake he had made. With only twenty-two guns, the French merchant ship had no choice but to surrender. When they arrived in Louisbourg harbor with the new prize, the cargo was examined carefully. At first assessment, the hold seemed loaded with South American cocoa, Peruvian wool, and "Jesuit bark," the source of quinine, but as the examination became more thorough, they discovered a true treasure of Peruvian gold and silver hidden beneath the cocoa: 972,000 pieces of eight, 13,278 gold double doubloons, 291.5 pounds of virgin silver, and 65.5 pounds in gold bars. This single ship had a value of between £300,000 and £400,000, far more than the cost of the entire Louisbourg campaign.

In less than a week, three ships had produced between £600,000 and by some estimates £1 million, potentially providing riches beyond imagination for the sailors of the squadron. When the sailors swaggered ashore, they no longer bragged about their role in the capture of the city, but boasted of their newfound wealth. This was a huge, agonizing blow to the American soldiers, who had been deprived of the modest plunder they should have obtained in the conquest and now stood by dumbstruck as they realized that through their bloodshed and conquest of the city, the rich French ships had sailed into a trap that the Royal Navy had only to snap shut, with no loss of life, to become rich. One of the American officers, William Waldron, expressed the universal, extreme frustration, writing, " 'Tis galling to little minds (who consider that the world is govern'd by an all wise God) that the army should both fight for & afterwards guard the city & yet they have none of the prizes which cost the men of war nothing more than go & meet them which we could do was the city afloat."

If there was any satisfaction for the soldiers, it was that with such a vast fortune at stake, arguments developed among the mariners as to who had the right to claim this treasure. At the crux of the argument was the arrangement that Commodore Warren had made when he first joined the expedition and took command of the sea forces, that they all would share any prize captured by any ship under his command. This policy was sworn to in a deposition taken from Captain Fones in the trial relating to the *Notre Dame de la Deliverance*, in which Fones described his taking of the French ship *Deux Amie*. He testified, "Commodore Warren sent to his Agent at Boston in New

England to be by him sold and disposed of in order that the money arising therefrom might pursuant to his order and Declaration . . . be distributed and Divided among all and every the Ships under his Command in the said Expedition . . ." If Warren's plan remained in place, the solution would be simple. The American sailors had shared all their prizes and would expect a share of the other prizes. Several issues arose, however. The Royal Navy ships that actually captured the *Notre Dame de la Deliverance* with the *Boston Packet* claimed that since they had joined the squadron late in the campaign, they had not been a party to the original agreement and that the wealth from the ship was theirs alone. The issue became more complicated by discussion over which ships were still under Warren's command after the fall of the city, as well as whether the sailors from some ships who labored to tow the two captors out of the harbor had a stronger claim than others.

It was a snarled, complex mess, which meant that the legal challenges as to who got what share would creep through the legal system for years; but there was one beneficiary who was not affected by those legalities. There was no doubt that the ships were under the overall command of Commodore Peter Warren and as commodore he was entitled to a one-eighth share of the value of the prize. Since there could be no challenge to his claim, Warren helped himself to his share of the silver and gold, estimated at between £70,000 and £80,000, before the ships and their treasure were turned over to the courts. This amounted to a vast fortune, equivalent to between £9 million and £11 million in the year 2000. The annual salary for the lieutenant governor of Newfoundland at that time was less than £200, so Warren's fortune from these prizes could pay that salary for 375 years. Warren's exorbitant payoff at the expense of the Americans brought further resentment and discontent, which grew and spread, not just among the soldiers at Louisbourg, but to the citizens and officials in the American colonies.

Attitudes hardened between the occupying soldiers and sailors, and resentment built against Warren in the Massachusetts Legislature. It was known that he had maneuvered to have Duchambon surrender the keys to the city to him and that Warren later turned over the keys to General Pepperrell, but an added insult was the fact that Warren's name came above Pepperrell's on the official ratification of the surrender. Legislators in Boston saw Warren's moves as another indication of the British military's arrogant attitude toward the Americans. While Warren had an appreciation for the American colonies, this may have been the result of the great economic opportunities they provided, of which he took full advantage. Perhaps the most vivid reflection of Warren's true attitude toward the American soldiers was revealed by his friend the Earl of Sandwich in a speech in the House of Lords some years after Warren's death. The earl said with regard to Warren's attitude toward the American troops: "[Peter Warren] told me very frankly they [the Americans] were the greatest set of cowards and poltoons he ever knew; they were all bluster, noise and were good for nothing . . . Soon after their landing, there was a battery, called the Island Battery, which commanded the entrance of the harbour. Sir Peter having ordered them to attack it, they engaged to perform it; but what was the consequences? They ran away on the first fire. And how did you manage? Did you employ them afterwords, or upbraid them with their cowardice, says I?— No, answers Sir Peter, neither would it have been prudent; I formed up the marines and part of the ship's crew into a body to act ashore; and instead of upbraiding them, I told them they had behaved like heroes; for, if I had acted otherwise, I should have never taken the town, as their presence and numbers were necessary to intimidate the besieged."

This statement may accurately represent Warren's attitude, since it corresponds with his actions to position himself as the conqueror of Louisbourg. He indicates that he was ordering the American troops, that he needed them as intimidating window dressing, and that *he* took the town. The statement gives no credit for the Americans' three-hour pitched battle on the Island Battery or the sixty men who gave their lives to silence the battery and allow the British ships to sail unmolested into the harbor. It also says nothing about the refusal of the British captains to risk their ships, their lives, and those of their men to force their way past the Island Battery. It was not until the Americans had put the battery out of action through their bombardment from the Lighthouse Battery that the Royal Navy was prepared to enter the harbor. The truth of Warren's attitude may lie somewhere between this scathing report and the amicable appearance he presented after the fall of the city, but his actions caused true resentment among the troops and many of the colonists.

As that summer wore on, the troops became more disillusioned and rebellious. The sick and wounded Americans and those with large families to care for at home or who had other "hardship" excuses were allowed to return to New England. With his wife, six children, and widowed mother-in-law dependent upon him, Seth Pomeroy was one of those released during the summer. He reached Boston on July 29 and, after conducting some business, set out for his home in Northampton a week later. He reached his home in the late afternoon of July 8, 117 days after saying good-bye to his family to head off on the campaign. Pomeroy's friend Lieutenant Colonel Richard Gridley remained in Louisbourg, since his skills as a military engineer were in high demand during the reconstruction of the shattered city. Joining Gridley and the rest of the American garrison were some fresh reinforcements, including, finally, the company pledged by Rhode Island. Despite the reinforcements, the majority of the original army was retained in Louisbourg. With the weeks passing, the friction between Warren and Pepperrell continued. On July 16, the commodore reprimanded the general, writing, "I beg leave to recommend to you, Sir, that greater care be taken ... in seeing that your men are duely and justly supply'd with the full allowance of provisions intended for them by the provinces, and I cannot help pitying them with regard to their cloathing, many of them being bare-footed." Warren was speaking as if Pepperrell had no concern for his men, when he had actually been pleading for supplies from Boston.

Amid this rancor among the leaders, the disgruntled troops disputed the interpretation of their enlistment that forced them to remain as a garrison force. The volunteers had signed on to capture Louisbourg and had done so. Now their tours of duty were being involuntarily extended, and the troops had little recourse. Rumors spread through the army that the relief force of British regulars, who were to come from Gibraltar, might not be able to get there before winter. The troops were disgusted, and once again the British government was failing them. For generations, they had heard British promises of support in defense of the colonies and experienced continuous disappointment. The men wanted to go home.

To calm the troops, Governor Shirley was asked to come to Louisbourg. On August 17, HMS *Hector* sailed into the harbor, carrying the governor and his wife, Susannah DeLancey Warren, the commodore's wife, two of the commodore's children, and other distinguished visitors. All signs of rivalry between Warren and Pepperrell were set aside, and the diplomatic and pragmatic Pepperrell later sent a letter explaining the friction and that all the past animosity was forgotten. He wrote to the governor, "I am sorry you should meet with any thing to damp yor joy relating to any dispute between Comodore Warren & myself, & considering that we are both quick in our tempers . . . It is true Mr. Warren did tell me he was the chief officer here. I told him, Not on shoar. I look upon it that these disputes are all over, as we both aim at ye good and security of this place."

With this veneer of cordiality between the senior officers, the governor and his party were received with lavish honors and salutes from the ships. The following morning, as the governor first set foot on the former French land, all the cannons of the fortress fired in a tumultuous salute. The soldiers were ordered to line the streets to honor the governor as he passed by on his way to the French governor's quarters, which Warren had appropriated for himself and now had to vacate. A week after Shirley's arrival, the troops were assembled and the governor spoke, but his words had only a modest effect on lifting the low morale. One witness recorded, "His Excellency Made an Excellent Speech Both to Officers and Soldiers But all Insufficient to make 'em Really Willing and Contented to tarry all Winter." This grim prospect for the Americans was compounded by disease taking a continual toll.

As the situation grew worse, the troops grew mutinous. There were plans for seven hundred of them to put down their arms and refuse to defend their prize. On September 18, after a meeting with his advisers to discuss the crisis, Governor Shirley attempted to quell the incipient rebellion by addressing the troops a second time. One soldier recorded, "His Excellency Made a Speech to the army which (I conclude) was

Occasioned by a Great Uneasiness in the army Especially those that Came first in the Expedition. because they were not Dismis'd (as they Suppose) according to Contract." The governor promised to dismiss all but two thousand of the troops, increase the pay of those who remained, provide better bedding and clothes, distribute captured French muskets, which the soldiers coveted, and return them all to New England in the spring when the relief troops arrived. Four hogsheads of rum were allocated to the troops so they could drink to the good health of the king, and the sullen soldiers were left to contemplate their future. The troops who were then dismissed to return to New England included the most vocal of the troublemakers who had been fomenting the mutiny. It seemed as if the governor had accomplished his task.

On September 23, five days after Shirley's speech, Captain Rous, who had sailed the *Shirley* back from England in only nineteen days, arrived with the news of how the victory had been received in England, as well as the recognition and honors that were awarded to the key participants and the troops. It became immediately clear that despite the valuable prize that had been won for the Crown, the government was restrained in its rewards. As Warren had suggested, Pepperrell was made a baronet, the first native-born American to receive that honor. He was also made a colonel in the British army and authorized to raise a regiment of soldiers in New England who would be paid by the British government. This status offered Pepperrell significant financial gain and prestige. Warren had not made any recommendation on behalf of Governor Shirley, but Newcastle realized the key role he had played, and Shirley was also made a colonel with the right to raise an American regiment. Warren was made a rear admiral in the Royal Navy. He did not receive the New Jersey or New York governorships he coveted but was appointed governor of Louisbourg, a position that he distinctly did not want. Beyond that, there was scant recognition or reward. John Bradstreet was made not lieutenant colonel of Pepperrell's regiment, but fifth captain, which he viewed as an insult. William Vaughn, who had done so much and had risked his own capital to finance troops for the expedition, received no recognition. Indeed, he had already gone to England to argue his own case. Captain John Rous was awarded a commission as a captain in the Royal Navy, and in a tribute to the New England shipbuilders, the *Shirley* was bought into the Royal Navy as HMS *Shirley*. There was no action by the king to compensate the rest of the soldiers for the lack of the reward of plunder. Warren's request that something be done for the widows of the Americans killed and for the troops maimed in action also fell on the cold, deaf ears of the British government. However, Warren and his wife each donated five hundred pieces of eight to be distributed among the widows and orphans of the American sailors lost on the *Prince of Orange*. This was generous but was a minuscule fraction of the prize money he had received. Beyond this lack of regard for the people involved, the British response created a serious crisis for the governments of the New England colonies. All, but particularly Massachusetts and New Hampshire, had dug deep into their treasuries or gone into serious debt to finance the victorious campaign and had anticipated that the British government would show its gratitude for the conquest by reimbursing the colonies. However, there was debate in England as to whether there was any obligation to cover the campaign expenses, since the expedition had been conceived and mounted by the New Englanders without prior approval from Britain. There was no immediate reimbursement or any assurance that compensation would ever come.

While there was pride in the elevation of Pepperrell, the rest of those involved felt bitterness at their mistreatment. The governor himself, William Shirley, was incensed over the adulation, wealth, and honors that fell on Warren. He wrote to Henry Pelham and critically pointed out Warren's reluctance to assist in the defense of Annapolis Royal the year before and his refusal to assist in the Cape Breton campaign when first requested. He went on to say, "When I compare my services in respect of Nova Scotia and this acquisition to his majesty's dominions with Mr. Warren's, who besides gaining near seventy thousand pounds sterling (the direct consequence of this expedition, wholly formed, set on foot and carried into execution, in New England, by myself and into which he was forced by his orders) is immediately distinguished with a flag, a government, and as I further hear the dignity of a baronet, & compare the fate of his services, with that of my own, which seem degraded below those of Mr. Warren and Sir William Pepperrell . . ." Despite this resentment, Shirley and Warren collaborated on their recommendation that the British government capitalize on this conquest and launch a future attack on New France to drive the French out of North America. In the chill of late September at Louisbourg, Warren and Pepperrell might have been content with their rewards, but they were perhaps the only ones who were.

CHAPTER 21

Disintegration

THE BRITISH TROOPS, WHO were sent from Gibraltar to relieve the Americans occupying Louisbourg, made it across the Atlantic before winter, but not to the fortress. They ensconced themselves in comfortable barracks in Virginia and New York to spend a milder winter, while the ill and exhausted American troops and the crews of two of Warren's ships prepared for a harsh winter in the inhospitable conditions of Cape Breton Island. Some repairs had been made to the shattered structures within the fortress, but as winter weather set in, they were still in poor condition. In addition, insufficient wood and coal had been gathered to provide heat for the long, frigid season ahead. When Governor Shirley left for Boston in November, Admiral Warren and Sir William Pepperrell were left to oversee the occupation of Louisbourg. Although Warren had been appointed governor, his commission had not been delivered, so the two men agreed to manage the city jointly. Pepperrell was responsible for the American troops, and Warren was in command of the one thousand sailors from the *Chester* and the *Vigilant*, which remained in the harbor. In a further reflection of Warren's lack of respect for the American soldiers, he wrote to Thomas Corbett that he had to keep the *Vigilant* there to prevent desertion in the troops as much as to strengthen the garrison.

It was hoped that the onset of winter would eliminate the

outbreak of disease, but there was little letup in the toll that illness was taking. Throughout the summer and into the fall, Reverend Stephen Williams, who as a boy had been captured in the 1704 Deerfield attack with his father, Reverend John Williams, and taken to Canada, ministered patiently to the sick and dying. He had not served as a chaplain during the siege but arrived in Louisbourg on July 6, 1745, two weeks after the surrender. His journal gives the most grim and graphic account of the first six months of the occupation, and his daily entries list the people who died each day. In the ruined city, conditions were deplorable. Williams's entry for September 26 describes praying with the dying during the day and then "evening I went to the Hospitall—but the smell was so Nauseous, that I could not tarry." Within a few days of that entry, the other remaining minister departed, leaving Williams as the only chaplain to bring succor to the desperate souls who were wrestling with their sickness. A month later, his entry for November 1 was typical and documented the deteriorating situation. In the single day, he visited and prayed with the sick in a dozen locations and recorded the deaths of eleven men.

His sad journal records his efforts to minister to the sick and dying and, in total, chronicles the deaths of over four hundred soldiers. By November 21, Reverend Williams was seriously ill himself but was able to commemorate the fortieth anniversary of his return to Boston after his capture at Deerfield. The next day, he documented the death of another fourteen men. Williams's health continued to decline, and he was carried on board the frigate *Massachusetts* on November 27, as it was about to depart to return Governor Shirley to Boston. Williams survived the voyage and on December 11 was placed in a cradle and carried to the home of a Boston friend, where over the next month he was nursed back to health. The Massachusetts General Court awarded him £28 for his exceptional service in Louisbourg. While Reverend Williams had survived, that was not the case for many others left behind in the city. On January 28, 1746, Pepperrell and Warren wrote to Governor Shirley that they had buried 561 and had 1,100 ill with dysentery. They expressed their hope that the worst was over, since they were burying only 4 or 5 a day, compared with 14 to 17 a day earlier in the winter. The bodies of these American heroes were buried in shallow unmarked graves on Pointe a Rochefort immediately beyond the city wall to the east. Today, the bleached white bones of those anonymous soldiers still emerge periodically from that shallow grave as vivid reminders of the American sacrifice over 260 years ago.

When Governor Shirley returned to Boston after several months in Louisbourg, he was confronted by another serious manifestation of the friction between the Royal Navy and the people of Boston. The issue of impressment was once again reaching crisis proportions. Four years earlier, as the devastating news of the Cartagena defeat was arriving in Boston, there had been riots over the heavy-handed tactics of Captain James Scot of HMS *Astrea*, who pressed men out of coasting and merchant ships to replace some fifty men, including two midshipmen and the master's mate, who had deserted his ship during the month of May 1741. When Scot refused to release the men, the Massachusetts Council determined to treat Captain Scot and his ship as Lieutenant Governor Povey had treated Captain Jackson and HMS *Swift* in 1702 and fire on the *Astrea* if she attempted to leave. Eventually, Governor Shirley managed to gain the release of the men, but the Boston sensitivities toward the feared press were heightened.

With the siege of Louisbourg completed, Shirley found that the press gangs in Boston were meeting with protests and resistance. When the governor's namesake, the former colonial cruiser *Shirley*, returned to Boston as a new vessel in the Royal Navy, most of her crew who had signed on as volunteer members of the Massachusetts ship did not want to remain as sailors in His Majesty's Navy. Consequently, Captain Rous had to resort to the press to fill ninety-two positions on HMS *Shirley*. During the process, both Rous and the Suffolk County sheriff were manhandled by angry mobs. However, when Governor Shirley returned to Boston that December, he confronted a far more serious issue. While Shirley had been in Louisbourg, HMS *Wager*, under the command of Captain Arthur Forrest, who had served alongside Lawrence Washington in the attack on Cartagena four years earlier, arrived in Boston. He had been ordered to refit his vessel there and proceed to sea, but he was undermanned. With the governor away, Forrest approached the lieutenant governor with his request for a warrant to press men into the service. There was resistance from both the lieutenant governor and the legislature, and when Forrest attempted to press seven men who had just been released from the colonial cruiser *Resolution*, which had been heroic in the Louisbourg campaign, Forrest was ordered by the lieutenant governor to release the men. Forrest did so but then resorted to paying an undersheriff £5 per man taken in a new press.

On the night of November 20, 1745, the undersheriff led Forrest's four-man press gang to a boardinghouse where several mariners were in residence. As the gang from the *Wager* barged up the stairs of the boardinghouse, one of the residents grabbed a musket, pointed it at the intruders, and pulled the trigger. When the gun failed to go off, the press gang forged ahead and a violent fight ensued. The lone candle in the room was knocked over and extinguished as the men fought. The *Boston Weekly News-Letter* of November 21, 1745, reported, "Last night two Men belonging to the Sloop Resolution, formerly Capt. Donohew's, were grievously wounded by a Gang that were impressing for one of the Ships of War in this Harbour, who with Cutlasses cut them in the Head and Belly, so that their Lives are in great Danger; one of them especially, whose Belly was laid open so that Part of his Inwards turn'd out." The following week (November 28, 1745), the paper reported that both men from the *Resolution* had died and that the *Wager*'s boatswain and a gunner's boy, who had been seen by witnesses to be wielding a cutlass and a wooden club, had been arrested on the charge of murder. Others in the press gang were being sought but were in hiding. The violence over impressments had taken lives, and the tension grew in the city. The level of resistance to the press in Boston and its premonition of what would develop in the future were revealed in a letter sent to the first lord of the Admiralty by the Earl of Sandwich and Admiral George Anson as they sought to bring the prisoners in Boston under the king's protection. They wrote complaining of "the violent Spirit that reigns in all his Majesty's Colonies in America to oppose and obstruct the officers of His Majesty's Ships" and went on to urge that actions be taken to suppress this American spirit.

Clearly, the crisis in Boston was recognized by all to be of great importance, since those at the highest levels of government in the colonies and in England were now focused on it. The frustration for the colonies grew when the murderers were tried and found guilty but then, because of a flaw in the indictment, were never sentenced and went free. One outcome was a change in the law the following year. The old law, known as the Sixth of Anne, enacted in 1708 after the earlier impressment crises during the reign of Queen Anne, gave protection to American sailors. That law exempted Americans from the impressments, but the British argued that the Sixth of Anne applied only during Queen Anne's War. The Americans contended that since the Sixth of Anne had not been repealed, its provisions were still in effect. In practice, the colonial authorities and navy captains followed the policy that allowed impressment with the authorization of the colonial governors. In 1746, with the Sixth of Anne still on the books, a new law was added that restricted the protection to the sugar colonies of the Caribbean. That meant that the American colonies from Maine to Georgia were open to the arbitrary abuses of the press gang, and this heightened awareness of the vulnerability of men being taken off the street or from ships and forced into involuntary service in the Royal Navy. The North American colonists resented the fact that the home government felt they were less important than the island colonies. The Americans were becoming keenly aware of the threat of impressment to individual rights.

During this period of stress over the *Wager*'s impressment in Boston, the soldiers in Louisbourg continued to fight for their lives against the ravages of illness, and Warren himself was fighting a different illness, the traditional plague of sailors, scurvy. The disease had developed the previous spring, and during the grim winter in Louisbourg it produced painful running sores on his legs. Although scurvy had long been recognized, it was not until 1747 that a Scottish naval surgeon, James Lind, began his studies and determined that diet was the cause and that citrus fruit and other sources of vitamin C would cure the condition. The diet in Louisbourg was monotonous for soldiers and officers alike. As the winter wore on, the food supply was insufficient and resupply impossible until the ice cleared from the harbor entrance.

In the midst of this misery, there were rumors that a large force of Canadians was on its way to retake the city. To prepare for that eventuality, the weakened troops dragged all the guns of the Grand Battery over two miles into the fortress. Pepperrell and Warren wanted to ensure that they would not be subjected to the same bombardment they had given the French. Guns were also shifted from Warren's warships, and the fortress bristled with cannons. The troops peered into the rain, fog, and snow of the fall and winter, searching for an enemy that never came.

The enemy within the city, dysentery, continued to take its toll as conditions deteriorated. The troops were crowded into their makeshift, damaged quarters, where in some instances they tore apart portions of the structure and burned the wood to keep warm. Orders had to be given forbidding the tearing down of the wooden piquet walls within the fortress. Sanitation was deplorable, with human waste accumulating in portions of the dwellings, since conditions were too bleak for the sick soldiers to venture outside. By late winter, over one thousand had perished. The losses were greatest among the Americans, whose living situation was worse than that of the sailors from Warren's ships who were quartered in the Grand Battery, which had not been damaged by bombardment. As the last of the winter weather faded and the first faint signs of spring appeared, the decimated force that occupied the fortress seethed with resentment that they who had signed on to capture the city had been left to die amid its ruins.

Relief arrived with the coming of spring. The British troops of the Twenty-ninth Foot Regiment, commanded by Lieutenant Colonel Peregrine Thomas Hopson, and the Fifty-sixth Foot Regiment, under Lieutenant Colonel John Horsman, appeared in Louisbourg on April 2. In addition, nearly 1,000 colonial soldiers, recruited for Shirley's and Pepperrell's new regiments, also arrived to augment the 1,219 British soldiers. There had been difficulty filling the new regiments because the deplorable hardships experienced by the occupying forces at Louisbourg were well-known throughout the colonies. It was said that it would be easier to raise 10,000 troops for an attack on Canada than 1,000 for garrison duty at Louisburg. Despite Admiral Warren's recommendation that priority for commissions in the new colonial regiments be given to the American officers who had distinguished themselves at Louisbourg, Shirley and Pepperrell discovered that preference continued to be given to officers from England. One disgruntled colleague wrote to Pepperrell, "Tis a most scandalous contempt of our brave officers that they should not be thought worthy, after they have behaved so well." The old, much resented pattern of abuse and insult was again at work. Pepperrell, not averse to some nepotistic patronage, intended to award valuable captain's commissions to two of his sons, one only sixteen, but the appointment of English officers initially prevented it. However, during their voyage to America, several of those British officers were lost at sea, and Pepperrell snatched the chance to make his own appointments from American stock. Although colonial men resisted serving under the British officers, the ranks of Shirley's and Pepperrell's regiments slowly filled, and they were nearly up to full force when they arrived in Louisbourg to relieve their beleaguered countrymen.

Before the weary Americans departed for home, Admiral Warren addressed the assembled troops, acknowledging their accomplishment, suffering, and loss. It was a fine speech, but in stark contrast with other comments from Warren and of little consolation to the Americans, who had witnessed the Royal Navy sailors getting rich on the prizes, while, as a measure of the meager plunder rounded up after the French departure, one American soldier's share amounted to nine small-toothed combs. After more than a year away, the Americans finally sailed for home. There were no bands and parades to celebrate the returning heroes, and the embittered, debilitated men straggled off toward their homes and families. While it was estimated that they had buried between fifteen hundred and two thousand soldiers and sailors that winter, the loss of Americans was certainly well over twelve hundred. This was a staggering number for the sparsely populated region. Virtually everyone in New England had lost a family member, friend, or acquaintance in the campaign and the occupation that followed.

A month after the Americans departed, Peter Warren's replacement arrived: his old rival Charles Knowles, the man from whom he took the *Superbe* as his flagship in the Louisbourg campaign and the man who had been so critical of the American Regiment in the Cartagena fiasco five years earlier. While Warren had been engaged at Louisbourg, Knowles had played a key role in the fortification of English Harbour on the island of Antigua and because of this was chosen to govern Louisbourg and oversee its reconstruction. Following the capture of the city, Warren had carried on a steady

Monument to American dead at Louisbourg

correspondence with British authorities about the merits and future potential of the conquered French fortress, arguing that in addition to its ideal location in the rich fishing region, Louisbourg could serve as a trading center. He recommended that it be promoted as a duty-free port to give it a competitive advantage to attract settlers and businessmen. He also advocated that the Admiralty take advantage of the fine harbor and turn Louisbourg into a major naval base, since the harbor could accommodate a vast number of ships but also offered an ideal spot where ships could be careened to have work done on their bottoms. The plentiful supply of timber in the region made the site ideal as a repair facility.

With Knowles's arrival in Louisbourg on May 23, Warren began the process of transferring responsibility for the government of the colony to him and the naval protection of the region to Vice Admiral Isaac Townsend, who had arrived with three warships two weeks earlier. Ten days later, Warren officially resigned. As he sailed from Louisbourg in the *Chester* with Pepperrell that day in June, Warren anticipated a summer of rest in Boston, where his wife and children awaited him. His scurvy had grown worse, and the strain of the winter demanded a period of recuperation. He and Governor Shirley would have ample time to discuss in detail their plans for an attack on Canada the following year.

Warren's ship had been homeward bound for Boston only a few hours when it encountered the sloop HMS *Hinchinbroke*, carrying the astonishing orders from England that the attack on Canada that

Commodore Charles Knowles

Shirley and Warren envisioned for the summer of 1747 was to be launched immediately. The plan called for a repeat of the classic strategy that had been attempted several times in the past. Warren was to command the naval force, which would sail up the St. Lawrence, escorting the transport ships that would carry five thousand British soldiers, under the command of Lieutenant General James St. Clair, and five thousand American troops to be raised from the New England colonies. Using Warren's naval guns, they were to attack and capture Quebec. Another contingent, composed of twenty-nine hundred Americans from New York and the colonies to the south, under command of William Gooch of Virginia, was to rendezvous at Albany. From there, they would move north and capture the French fort at Crown Point near the south end of Lake Champlain and then move on to conquer Montreal.

The *Chester* reversed her course and returned to Louisbourg to inform Knowles and Townsend so they could reallocate their assets, as some of the troops from the Louisbourg garrison would be required to carry out the plan of attack. Then, Warren and Pepperrell once again sailed for Boston, and Pepperrell, who had been given no leadership role in the new campaign, looked forward to completing his duties in Boston and returning to his home and wife in Kittery, Maine, to recover his health over the summer. Rather than a summer of rest, Warren's would be one of frantic preparation for an attack he thought was doomed to failure. The season for launching such an attack in the northern climes was already well advanced, and Warren could not imagine that the colonies could raise the troops expected in such a short time and on the heels of the terrible winter spent occupying the fortress.

According to the proposed schedule for the attack, the American troops were to rendezvous with the British force at Louisbourg in late May, but Warren didn't receive his orders until June 6. Already the effort looked like another debacle. Back in Boston by late June, Warren met with Shirley, who like the governors of the other colonies was shocked by their orders to levy troops in quick order for this attack. Despite the financial difficulties and time constraints, a conscientious effort was mounted throughout the colonies to raise the troops. Amazingly, enticed by enlistment bonuses and encouraged by the previous year's success against Louisbourg, a significant American force, larger than that raised for the Louisbourg campaign, was assembled by mid-August. The New England troops numbered over 5,000, with Massachusetts providing 3,500, Connecticut 1,000, New Hampshire 500, and Rhode Island 300. The colonies to the south were not as impacted by the French presence in Canada, but they responded to the call, with New York raising 1,600 troops, New Jersey 500, Pennsylvania 400, Maryland 300, and Virginia 100. Throughout the colonies, these soldiers waited for news of the arrival of General St. Clair and the British troops.

Warren and Shirley waited for their arrival in Boston, growing more and more anxious that the time had long passed when a viable attack could be launched without the hazards of the Canadian winter destroying the effort at a great cost in lives and ships. Amid this anxiety, word reached them that a massive French naval and military force was on its way to retake Louisbourg and attack other sites, including Boston. As the northern colonies braced themselves for attack, there was great resentment that they were left undefended by the Royal Navy and that the British blockade of the French coast had failed, allowing the huge French force to escape. The troops raised for the attack on Canada now prepared to defend Boston, augmented by militia troops who came into the city from the frontier.

The Americans had just cause for alarm. When the French learned that the American rabble had captured their most prestigious North American fortress, they immediately developed plans to recapture their prize. Jean-Baptiste-Louis-Frederic de Roye de la Rochefoucauld, Duc d'Enville, departed La Rochelle on June 20, 1746, in command of the French force of 3,150 soldiers, thirty-four transports, and thirty-one warships. His plan was to retake Louisbourg first and then ravage other British settlements, starting with Boston. From their first moments at sea, the French experienced one challenge after another. The Bay of Biscay off La Rochelle was a maelstrom, and a number of the ships were damaged. In midocean, they wallowed in heat and dead air and then were struck by a fierce squall, during which lightning hit several ships and killed at least sixteen. The scourge of the military in the eighteenth century, disease, broke out as they continued toward their rendezvous spot of Chedabucto Bay in

Nova Scotia, the future site of Halifax. As they groped their way through the fog toward the Nova Scotia coast in mid-September, they were hit by a hurricane that sank one of the transports with all on board, damaged many ships, and scattered the fleet. A week later, d'Enville's flagship, the *Northumberland*, a ship captured from the British, accompanied by only two other warships, made its way into Chedabucto Bay. They found only one of the transports and no sign of four heavy warships from the Caribbean that were scheduled to meet them there. The ships were riddled with sickness, and the admiral was certain that other ships that might have survived from his once magnificent fleet would be plagued by the same illness. They had left a trail of bodies along their path through the ocean, and the admiral saw his expedition in ruins. Depressed by this reality, in the early hours of the morning of September 27, d'Enville died, possibly of a stroke but rumored to be from poison.

Later that day, the fleet's second in command, Vice Admiral d'Estournel, arrived in the bay with a number of ships in equally bad condition. During the long, arduous passage, provisions had been consumed and the men were near starvation, making them all the more susceptible to the pestilence racing through the ships. Having inherited the bleak command, d'Estournel called together the captains of the ships and recommended that the campaign be abandoned, that the battered fleet replenish their supplies from the Acadian settlers and return to France. A heated discussion followed, in which the captains went against their new commander and decided to continue the effort. When the meeting ended, d'Estournel returned to his cabin, locked his door, and literally and deliberately fell on his sword. The appalled officers rushed to the mortally wounded admiral, and the ship's surgeon withdrew the blade. D'Estournel lived long enough to name his successor, the newly appointed governor of New France, Jacques-Pierre de Taffanel de la Jonquière, who finally brought some leadership to the disastrous situation. While they gathered supplies from the settlers in the region over the next month, disease continued unabated. The French buried two admirals and 1,135 men on the shores of Chedabucto Bay before their departure. An equal number had perished before reaching Nova Scotia.

Courageously, the depleted French force was determined to attempt an attack on Annapolis Royal to salvage something from the ill-fated campaign. As the fleet made its way around Cape Sable on the southwestern tip of Nova Scotia, they were hit by another storm, which once again scattered the ships. When two of the French warships managed to approach Annapolis Royal, they found it well defended by HMS *Chester* and HMS *Shirley*, and the fate of the French expedition was sealed. With nothing to claim as success, they headed for France, encountering another bad storm on November 4. The fleet straggled home, some ships dropping three or four bodies into the sea each day. In early December, the remnants of the French expedition reached Port Louis on the southern coast of Brittany. They were desperate, diseased, and defeated, and France had suffered a second humiliation. When the New Englanders heard of the grim fate of the French, they once again saw the hand of God in their salvation. The Royal Navy had done nothing to intercept this powerful threat, but *providence* had rescued them.

As had happened twice before, the Americans, who had been preparing for the attack on Canada since June, did not learn until early October that the English troops and Royal Navy ships were not coming. They had been initially delayed by adverse winds and then sent on a failed mission to attack L'Orient on the Brittany coast. The colonies had rallied to the cause once again and borne the expense of raising and sustaining troops for many months, before discovering that the military leadership in Great Britain had on August 23 turned their back on the Canadian campaign and their American colonies. The 1746 campaign against Canada was canceled. With the Duc d'Enville's French fleet retreating for home, Admiral Warren decided to sail for England himself. He relocated his family from Boston to his wife's home city of New York and set off, arriving in Spithead on Christmas Eve 1746.

Warren's intention was to personally lobby for a new Canadian campaign in 1747. He also sought to attempt to obtain the further reward of a colonial governorship in America and to push for reimbursement of the personal funds that he and General Pepperrell had expended during the campaign and occupation of Louisbourg. The recognition, reward, and reimbursement for the leaders of the Louisbourg effort had been meager and slow. Shortly after the surrender of Louisbourg, while Warren and Pepperrell were coping with the mutinous American volunteers, William Vaughn, the moving force behind the victorious campaign, traveled to England to personally seek the recognition he felt he deserved.

After three futile attempts to speak directly to the Duke of Newcastle in London, on October 31, 1745, Vaughn reluctantly submitted a lengthy memorial to make his case in writing. The document, addressed "To the King's Most Excellent Majesty" from "William Vaughn of Damariscotta," explained in detail the efforts he had made to initiate the campaign and his various exploits during the siege. He also pointed out his family's long service in New Hampshire, particularly his father's active role in capturing Nova Scotia in 1710. Vaughn backed up his claims with a sworn written statement from Governor Shirley, who attested that Vaughn "had been very instrumental in setting on Foot the present Expedition" and vouched for his achievements in the field of battle. A similar statement from Governor Wentworth of New Hampshire recounted how Vaughn "had been very industrious in promotg. & encourgaging the enlistmt. of Voluntiers . . ." From General Pepperrell came the statement that Vaughn "did as a Voluntier without Pay, embark with me for the sd. Expedition, & has attended his Majesty's Service in the Field, & behaved with Loyalty, Zeal & Industry . . ." For the next eight months, Vaughn was shunted from office to office as he attempted to make his case. He sent further appeals to the Duke of Newcastle in February 1746 and again in May, when he itemized his family's unreimbursed expenses, amounting to £10,000.

Even with the support of friends of the Vaughn family in London, the solicitations seemed to fall on deaf ears. A letter from one such friend indicates that politics and personal pride had worked against Vaughn, stating, "Were I to be the judge and rewarder of his merit, I should think him worthy of the utmost notice, profit and honor. And yet I am afraid of the upshot of his time, fatigue, bravery and expense. You may depend that . . . I will do him all the good service I honorably can, for I have a great value for his virtue in general and for his solid, firm, intrepid, persevering temper, but I suspect [Governor Shirley] has cut the grass under his feet, and set him in a languid light here, lest he should otherwise eclipse his own luster." Despite his exhaustive efforts to gain compensation and reward, and apparently with his case undermined by Shirley, Vaughn's effort produced no response from the British government. During the summer and fall of 1746, Vaughn continued his discouraging task without success. In December, a few weeks before Admiral Warren arrived at Spithead, William Vaughn died of smallpox. Because of his contagious disease, this true American hero of Louisbourg was buried in England in an unknown grave.

It is not known whether Admiral Warren learned of Vaughn's death before he undertook his own frustrating quest. Before leaving Massachusetts in October, Warren had worked with Shirley on the plan for a 1747 Canadian attack. This included eighteen ships of the line, numerous frigates and transports, eight thousand British troops, and twenty-two thousand soldiers to be raised in the colonies. This massive and hugely expensive undertaking was received with little enthusiasm by the British government, which was growing weary of the costly and unproductive war. Warren was unaware that the strong case he had made for the importance of Louisbourg as a future British naval base and entrepôt had been methodically dismantled by his successor as governor of Louisbourg, Charles Knowles. From his first days in office, Knowles sent messages to the Duke of Newcastle and others citing the weaknesses and deficiencies of Cape Breton and minimizing the importance of New France. Against this backdrop, Warren found it impossible to advance the plan for a summer attack that year.

Turning his attention to his personal matters, he was equally unsuccessful in obtaining a governor's post. The governor of New Jersey had been recently appointed, and Warren's attempt to use his prize money from Louisbourg to purchase the governorship of New York from its incumbent, George Clinton, was also unsuccessful. As the spring of 1747 approached, the admiral focused on getting reimbursement for his expenses and those of Sir William Pepperrell. Before resigning as governor of Louisbourg, Warren had totaled up their joint expenditures. With no money flowing from the Crown during their occupation, the admiral and the general had spent £8,649 on clothing for the troops, fuel for the winter, gunpowder for the cannons and muskets, and other miscellaneous items. In addition, they had spent nearly twice that amount, £16,318, on the reconstruction of the fortress and the buildings within the city. Their expenses totaled £25,000, and there was a natural desire for the two men, despite being wealthy individuals, to want their personal investments reimbursed. Just as the late William Vaughn had discovered, the government was in no hurry to pay their Louisbourg debts. It would take years for Warren and Pepperrell to receive their compensation.

The needs of the colonial governments for reimbursement of their costs were critical, since several colonies were nearly bankrupt as a result of carrying the cost of the Louisbourg campaign. Governor Shirley's son-in-law, William Bollan, and Christopher Kilby were sent to London to act as agents of the New England colonies, but they, too, found that the wheels of the British government turned very slowly. There would be years of negotiations over the actual costs, the comparative value of the colonial currencies against the pound sterling, and innumerable other details. The desperate colonies had to string out their fragile credit for years, hoping for reimbursement. This poor treatment and the resulting financial hardship generated even more frustration and disgust among the people of New England.

Within a few months, this frustration erupted in open insurrection in yet another impressment crisis. In November 1747, Commodore Charles Knowles, who had been replaced as governor of Louisbourg, arrived with his squadron in Nantasket, in the outer reaches of Boston harbor. Immediately, he ordered a press to fill out the shortages of crew members in his squadron, and on the night of November 16, a number of boats from Knowles's squadron fanned out through the harbor, snatching entire crews from coasting vessels, apprehending anyone out on the water in small boats, and sweeping the wharves and docks for any men they could find. Word of the indiscriminant press raced through the town and incensed many who were still bitter from the murder the previous year of two veterans of the Louisbourg campaign by the press gang of HMS *Wager*. By early the following morning, a mob of over three hundred men surged through the streets seeking retribution, grabbing three Royal Navy officers and a person referred to as Knowles's menial servant. They also beat the county sheriff and took one of his deputies hostage. By late morning, the mob had forced their way into the courtyard in front of Governor Shirley's residence, demanding the release of the men taken in Knowles's press. The governor had called out the militia, but with sympathy for the crowd, they did not appear. Shirley addressed the crowd and succeeded in getting the three officers and Knowles's servant safely into his house, where there were a number of armed men loyal to him. The door was shut in the face of the crowd, and after making several token attempts to force open the door, the mob moved off with their one remaining hostage, the deputy sheriff, whom they beat and locked in the stocks.

During the afternoon, Governor Shirley made his way to the council chambers in the Town House, where he prepared a proclamation condemning the uprising and offering a reward for the ringleaders. While he was in the Town House, the mob returned, swelled to several thousand people. Not just an unruly band of seamen, the rioters included a broad representation of the male population of Boston. The throng hurled rocks and bricks and broke most of the windows in the lower floor of the building. The few militia officers who had responded to Shirley's call were forced to retreat up the stairs to the council chambers. The governor once again addressed the crowd, this time from the Town House balcony, but Shirley had little success in defusing the situation, and the angry crowd demanded that one of Knowles's officers be turned over to them. Still incensed over the 1746 HMS *Wager* impressment incident, they asked why the convicted murderers in that case had not been hanged. Shirley refused to turn over the officer and insisted that the murderers were under the king's protection at that time, but he did agree to present their demands to Knowles and do his utmost to obtain the release of all the Americans taken by the commodore. Only partially appeased, the frustrated demonstrators set off to burn a Royal Navy ship being built in Boston. They were diverted when they spied a barge that they thought was from one of Knowles's ships, which they captured and carried through the street to the governor's house. The governor had returned home, along with a number of men, including Sir William Pepperrell. His house was under siege, and Governor Shirley ordered armed men to the windows and another group of ten out to confront the rioters. He had given orders to open fire on the mob, which would have surely enraged the crowd and inflamed the situation beyond control, but Pepperrell "instantly call'd out to the officers to hold, 'till such, who might only be spectators could be warned to seperate from among the Mob." Pepperrell's timely intercession averted a disaster and enabled the crowd to head off to the Common, where they burned the barge in rage.

During the night, Shirley managed to get some of the Royal Navy officers out of town unseen, and they reached their squadron. The governor himself fled the city for the safety of the fort on Castle Island, from where he wrote to Knowles, requesting the release of some of the impressed men. Knowles refused on the basis that one of his captains and several petty officers, who had been in the hospital ashore, were now under the control of the mob.

Knowles was a man with much disdain for the Americans, and on learning the details of the insurrection, he threatened to move his squadron up to the city and bombard it to quell the "arrant rebellion." Knowles knew that one of the major irritants that angered the New Englanders was their belief that they should be exempted from impressment by acts passed by Parliament. Knowles wrote, "The Act [of 1746] against pressing in the Sugar Islands, filled the Minds of the Common People ashore as well as Sailors in all the Northern (but more especially in new England) colonies with not only a hatred for the King's Service but [also] a Spirit of Rebellion each Claiming a Right to the same Indulgence as the Sugar Colonies and declaring they *will* maintain themselves in it." With Knowles's threat to bombard the town, the city was in crisis, with the potential for one impetuous action to ignite a firestorm.

The first step in defusing the volatile situation came on the third day of the stalemate, when the Massachusetts Council, not the officers of the Crown, took action. They passed a resolution condemning the uprising, commanding the militia to disperse the mob, and pledging their cooperation in suppressing future mob actions. However, recognizing the legitimacy of the cause of the rioters, both houses of the legislature resolved that they would do everything possible to redress the grievances of the people. Rather than responding to edicts from the king's representatives, but with this assurance from their elected representatives, the rebellion began to dissolve. The following day, a town meeting confirmed the resolutions of the legislature, and a sense of order was restored. The governor returned to his residence, and the crowd's hostages were released. Reluctantly, Commodore Knowles released the Americans he had pressed, and his squadron sailed from the city.

The immediate crisis was over, but once again, the people of Boston had demonstrated their willingness to stand up and defend the rights of their fellow citizens against arbitrary forced service on England's warships. In the two years since the victory at Louisbourg, the potential for an improved relationship between Great Britain and her New England colonies had disintegrated, and the Knowles riots would herald a new era of political thought and expression.

CHAPTER 22

Betrayal

I N THE WAKE OF THE KNOWLES RIOTS, it became clear that the people needed a new forum to communicate their frustrations with their government and its leader, William Shirley. The governor had become a continual advocate of offensive actions against the French in North America, and the colonists had responded to several of his calls to arms, only to have the expensive mobilizations result in nothing but frustration and more debt for the colonies. The war that had begun with the victory at Louisbourg was now unpopular, as was its proponent, Shirley. The official reports on the Knowles crisis referred to it as "a tumultuous riotous assembling of armed Seamen, Servants, Negroes and others," but the rioters included thousands of Bostonians, a cross section of the population incensed by the press gangs' attacks on the town's citizens and their liberty. A number of young men felt the need to champion the cause against Governor Shirley and the government. At the center of this group was twenty-five-year-old Samuel Adams Jr., who had recently received his master's degree from Harvard College, with his thesis titled *Whether it be lawful to resist the Supreme Magistrate, if the Commonwealth cannot be otherwise preserved*, to which he made an affirmative argument. He was brimming with thoughts of the natural rights of man espoused by the English philosopher John Locke, who in his *Second Treatise on Government*, published in the year of the Glorious Revolution, 1689, made the case that a government could govern legitimately only if it had the consent of the governed. Within the framework of a social contract established when the people agreed to be governed, the government took on the responsibility to protect the citizens' natural rights to life, liberty, and the property they earned through their labor. If the government failed to protect these rights or systematically violated them, the citizens had not only the right, but also the obligation to rebel against the government. Adams and his fellow activists chose to protest against Knowles's abuses and others that they perceived were being inflicted upon the Americans.

In the days following the riot, they formed a secret club where they could freely discuss politics, and within two months, they had launched a newspaper. At that time, most newspapers reported the latest news from European capitals, published official notices, advertised a broad range of items and services, and only cursorily reported local news. For example, in October 1711, the *Boston Weekly News-Letter* informed its readers about activities in cities around the world, including Frankfurt, Hamburg, Cologne, London, and Danzig. Only a single paragraph on the second page was devoted to the news that a massive fire had roared through Boston, consuming numerous structures on both sides of prestigious Cornhill Street, upper King Street, and Queens Street, where it destroyed the famous Town House and killed and burned a number of people. The fire was stopped only when a number of houses were blown up to create a firebreak. That news of this kind of massive disaster was relegated to page two clearly demonstrates the priority given to old news from the Old World. In addition, newspaper reporting seldom ventured opinions on the issues, but the young men of Boston were about to change that.

With young Sam Adams as editor and published by Gamaliel Rogers and Daniel Fowle, the first issue of the *Independent Advertiser* appeared on the streets of Boston on January 4, 1748. In a statement to the readers, the paper's publishers promised "that we shall take the utmost Care to procure the freshest and best Intelligence, and publish it in such Order as that every Reader may have the clearest and most perfect understanding of it." They went on to say that "for our selves we declare we are of no Party, neither shall we promote the narrow and private Designs of any such— We are our selves free, and our

Paper shall be free,—free as the Constitution we enjoy—free to Truth, good Manners, and good Sense, and at the same time free from all licentious Reflections, Insolence and Abuse . . . to state and defend the Rights and Liberties of Mankind . . ." Adams, Rogers, and Fowle had made their commitment and lived up to it. They did occasionally print contributed pieces in support of the government or individuals such as Commodore Knowles, but the vast majority of the opinion pieces argued against the government in England and Shirley's administration in Massachusetts. These writings came from the mem-

Samuel Adams

bers of the secret club, particularly Sam Adams, who had agreed to anonymously submit articles for the paper. They lashed out against the government, and as a result their secret club obtained the nickname "the Whipping Post Club."

Daniel Fowle was a thirty-three-year-old printer who had gone into business with Gamaliel Rogers in 1742. They had experienced the enthusiasm in Boston for the campaign against Louisbourg and all the disappointments that had followed. Together they provided the printing presses and skills to put the words of Adams and the others onto paper. Fowle's dedication to the cause of liberty and free speech cannot be doubted, since it led to his arrest and imprisonment in 1755 and an eloquent defense of freedom of the press when he published his *A Total Eclipse of Liberty*. In 1748, however, Fowle and Rogers provided the medium for voicing the discontent that was growing in New England.

The first issue of the *Independent Advertiser* was devoted entirely to the Knowles riots, and throughout the short, two-year life of the paper, it constantly returned to the impressment issue and the Knowles riots as examples of British abuse and Shirley's complicity. The specific motivation for starting the paper was most probably the controversy ignited by a bold pamphlet that was published on November 30, 1747, just after the riot. The pamphlet was entitled *An Address to the Inhabitants of the Province of Massachusetts-Bay in New England, More Especially, To the Inhabitants of Boston, Occasioned by the late Illegal and unwarrantable Attack Upon their Liberties, And the Unhappy Confusion and Disorders consequent theron*. The author, almost certainly Samuel Adams, used the pseudonym Amicus Patriae, referring to himself as a lover of his country. Reflecting the principles of John Locke, the pamphlet dissected the incident and allocated blame, and Shirley is implicated as an abettor because of his failure to resist Knowles's actions. Feeling his reputation impugned by the pamphlet, Shirley wrote to the Lords of Trade on December 1, recounting the events in a manner that reflected well upon his actions and describing Boston as a town of "about Twenty thousand Inhabitants, consisting among others of so many working Artificers, Seafaring Men, and low sort of people, that a factious and Mobbish Spirit is Cherished." This and another of Shirley's letters were published in the *Boston Weekly News-Letter* two weeks later, and the citizens of Boston were incensed. When within a week the first issue of the *Independent Advertiser* appeared on the streets of Boston, the public debate was under way. In asserting that the riots were justified as self-defense in response to Knowles's press gangs, the new newspaper advocated the citizens' right to respond violently if their government did not protect them, their lives, and their liberties from Knowles's assault.

Adams and his colleagues accused Shirley of making huge personal profits during the raising of the regiment awarded to him after the success at Louisbourg. The further case was made that the war in America was being prolonged by Shirley's supporters in the Massachusetts House of Representatives, who had been seduced through commissions granted by Shirley, since those commissions enabled them to wring illegal profits from the supplying and payment of their troops. Another accusation was made that the representatives were supporting the continuation of the war not only for their own benefit, but also as a ploy to get Great Britain to compensate New England for the expenses of the Louisbourg campaign and occupation. The integrity of the House of Representatives was compromised, and Adams and his compatriots felt justified in fueling the discontent among the population. While the primary focus of the *Independent Advertiser* was the removal of Governor Shirley, numerous articles hotly debated the issue of recompense and how the funds should be used if they were ever received.

Another loud and controversial voice joined this debate in the spring of 1748. Dr. William Douglass, a Scotsman with European medical training, had created controversy from the time he first began medical practice in Boston in 1718. The outspoken doctor loudly resisted the use of inoculation against smallpox in 1721 when the disease broke out in Boston. While he and other medical men in the city argued against inoculation, the minister Cotton Mather advocated it, and almost three hundred were inoculated. The minimal death rate for those inoculated proved the viability of the process. Despite having that error in judgment so publicly visible, Douglass remained an active and vocal member of the community. In 1748, he began to publish his opus, *A Summary, Historical and Political of the First Planting, Progressive Improvements, and Present State of the British*

Settlements in North America, which first appeared in serial form from the printers Rogers and Fowle.

Instantly, the pamphlets stirred discussion and controversy since they heavily reflected the personal opinions and bias of the author. He began with the early history, moved on to the recent, and then focused on current events. When he reached the sacrosanct topic of Louisbourg, he ignited a firestorm. While a large part of the population was exhausted and disgusted by the prolonged and seemingly futile war, they still clung to their moment of glory, the taking of Louisbourg. Douglass in his version strongly criticizes Governor Shirley but then goes on to pick apart numerous other aspects of the campaign. He attributes the success to pure luck and casts aspersions on the leaders of the colonial troops. He voiced withering criticism of the conditions during the occupation. These strong comments prompted public rebuttals, including one that consumed no fewer than four full, double-columned pages of the *Boston Weekly News-Letter* on June 10, 1748. The author of this response felt compelled to defend the heroic performance of the troops on their overseas mission. However, Douglass was undeterred and continued his assault on Governor Shirley and Commodore Charles Knowles. Dr. Douglass was ruthless in his condemnation of impressment in general and Knowles's excesses the preceding fall. Not only did Douglass criticize the actions of Knowles and his press gang, but he also cast doubt on the commodore's courage, judgment, and character. As a result, Knowles sued Douglass for libel late that June. Shirley also sued Douglass, but in both instances the courts found in favor of Douglass in 1749.

The *Independent Advertiser* found itself in support of Douglass's scathing accounts in almost all instances. One point on which Sam Adams and Douglass differed was the issue of the mob. Douglass condemned riots and mob action as solutions for problems, but this was imbued in Adams from his studies of Locke. Another area of disagreement was how to use the compensation money if and when it finally was awarded by Parliament. Adams and the *Advertiser* advocated that it be deposited in a bank in England to act as security behind the paper money of the New England colonies. Douglass strongly argued that the money be used to retire the enormously inflated colonial currency and put Massachusetts on a silver-backed currency scheme. Beyond those differences of opinion, Douglass and the *Advertiser* worked in harmony, with their primary focus being the removal of Governor Shirley.

Thomas Hutchinson, Speaker of the Massachusetts House of Representatives, was also a staunch advocate of using the reimbursement to retire the paper currency and shift to a hard currency system. Shirley might have seen the long-term merit of that plan, but he was preoccupied with continuing the war and his call for another campaign against the French fort at Crown Point. To pay for this adventure, he needed more paper money, which caused more inflation. When the neighboring colonies failed to respond to Shirley's call, the Crown Point campaign was abandoned, and more fuel was added to the effort to remove Shirley from office. Men of significant stature, such as General Samuel Waldo, who had long supported Shirley, joined the chorus calling for his removal. This was an issue of great interest in the summer of 1748.

Another significant event began to draw the attention of the Americans. On March 17, negotiations commenced to end the War of the Austrian Succession, the global conflict of which the American component, King George's War, was a part. Diplomats from the numerous belligerents converged on the town of Aix-la-Chapelle. The primary participants were the French, represented by the able diplomat the Marquis de Saint-Severin, and the British, represented by the young and relatively inexperienced John Montague, Earl of Sandwich. The discussions were complicated by the complexity of the war, which had involved not only France and Great Britain, but also Austria, Spain, Italy, Prussia, and the Netherlands. Some of these nations were reluctant participants, and their delegates did not arrive for weeks or even months, leaving the focus on the major combatants. The experienced Saint-Severin quickly pushed forward a plan that favored the French and their main ally, Spain. By April 30, the basic structure of a peace agreement had been hammered out, and the thirty-one-year-old Earl of Sandwich signed it on behalf of Great Britain. This preliminary agreement returned the various conquests of the war to their original owners, proposing that France would give up the Netherlands and return her major conquest, the Indian trading city of Madras, to England. The British would return their sole significant conquest, the fortress city of Louisbourg and Cape Breton, to the French.

The British government was willing to risk the resentment of its citizens in America and England to obtain a peace treaty, and the Americans were stunned and incredulous that the great prize of Louisbourg, won by their sacrifice of lives and resources, could even be considered as part of the negotiations. Throughout the summer of 1748, newspapers published reports on the peace conference and the fate of Louisbourg. The ponderous weight of realization that they were mere pawns in this global conflict fell heavily on the Americans, who slowly began to realize that despite the value and importance of Louisbourg, there was nothing they could do.

While the New Englanders searched for a way to express their frustration and disgust, they were impeded by a major coercive factor. The British government procrastinated on the recompense of the expenses for the Louisbourg campaign and the occupation. The New England colonies teetered on the precipice of bankruptcy. Parliament had already voted for compensation in the following amounts: Massachusetts—£183,649; Connecticut—£28,863; New Hampshire—£16,355; and Rhode Island—£16,322. But the funds had not been delivered. Everyone knew that the hundreds of thousands of pounds sterling, which they had been counting on for over three years, would make the difference between the financial solvency of the colonies and economic disaster. Through the coercive leverage of these funds, the British were successful in stifling protest over the negotiated fate of Louisbourg. Protest by the Americans would have done nothing to alter the British decision concerning its return and would certainly undermine, if not destroy, any chances of getting the long overdue funds. Using the cudgel of financial security, the British government secured the acquiescence of the American colonists by delay. Mass public protest was quelled, but newspapers, particularly the *Independent Advertiser*, voiced the anguish and frustration of the people.

A lengthy article, almost assuredly written and certainly edited by Sam Adams, filled a page and a half of the *Independent Advertiser* on November 14, 1748.* It is the boldest, most passionate, and

---

* The entire article is reproduced in the appendix.

most comprehensive account of the grievances many Americans felt
with regard to their relationship with the British government. Adams
knew only that the preliminary peace agreement called for the return
of Cape Breton at the time the article was written, but the final treaty
had in fact been signed on October 18, a month before the *Advertiser*
article appeared. With the stroke of a pen, Britain had signed away the
American prize. The loss of Louisbourg was the catalyst for the article,
and the issues of disrespect, mistreatment, impressment, and the ultimate betrayal through the return of Louisbourg to France are dis-
cussed with great passion. It is also a clear statement of the seeds of
discontent that brought the Americans to the brink of revolution. The
author addresses the grievances of the colonists one after the other, in
a tone consistent with the writings of Sam Adams, the very hero who
continued to stoke the embers of discontent over the next three decades. Speaking in a patriotic voice, the author addresses his words to
"any man who truly loves his country," reflecting Adams's feeling that
America, not Great Britain, was his country, their country.

Early in the article, after demonstrating the importance of the
conquest, the author addresses the shoddy treatment the colonies
were receiving. He points out that despite the success at Louisbourg,
the colonial militias and their officers were not treated with respect
by the British military. In quoting an unnamed great man, he reveals
the British attitude to compensating the colonies for their expenses of
the Louisbourg campaign, saying, "That if any thing was allowed us
as a reimbursement of our expedition charges, it must be received as
a bounty, we having engaged in that undertaking without orders."

The next sore subject to be addressed was the inequity of the officers and men of the Royal Navy getting rich on prize money while
the army got nothing. He says, "We had very early the mortification
of hearing, that those rich East India and South-Seamen, the capture
of which was the immediate consequence of this conquest, and more
directly owing to the bravery of our men than any other cause, were
to be the sole property of those who never slung a shot against that
citadel."

The author then condemns the Royal Navy for leaving New England exposed to the intended attack of the Duc d'Enville and moves
on to the perpetual issue of impressment, along with the inequity of

exempting the sugar islands from the press while pursuing it vigorously and violently in the northern colonies. With passion, he states,
"The execution of this illegal and cruel measure has been conducted
with insolence and wantonness, which it will be as difficult to forget
as to attone for. Such scenes of merciless rapine, barbarity, and even
Murder, have been opened to us" and have gone unpunished.

The consummate insult, the return of Cape Breton, is then addressed beginning with, "But what consummates all our misfortunes
is the rendition of Louisbourg" with discontent over the inadequate
and delayed compensation and the recruiting abuses and scandals associated with the filling of Pepperrell's and Shirley's regiments. The
most painful aspect is remembered with the statement, "The loss of
those men who inlisted from this province into that service, added to
our former losses [at Cartagena] has been an unspeakable damage to
us . . ." He goes on to complain that the colonies have been informed
that the compensation is not, in fact, for their past expenses, but payment in advance for future loyalty and service.

Raising the specter that if Britain would trade Cape Breton for
peace, what would prevent them from trading Massachusetts or the
New England colonies to France for peace in a future war, the author
wrote: "Upon the whole, it is impossible for any man who truly loves
his country, to be unaffected with the present melancholly situation of
its affairs. To behold the fruits of all our labours, toils and hazards,
given up at once to our proud insulting enemies! And ourselves, after
all the brave attempts we have made, and the blessings of divine providence on our bravery, in a far worse condition than when the war commenced! To see our enemies (for enemies they are and will be in peace
and war) again in possession of that dreaded fortress, of which it cost so
much New-England blood and labour to dispossess them! Those hated
ensigns again display'd on those walls which once bore the triumphs of
our valour. It is neither possible, nor safe to look into futurity, and our
present load of affliction is so great, we need not increase it by raising
imaginary dangers. Yet the mind opprest with grief, anxious and fearful, cannot help raising to the most frightful prospects. Who can tell
what will be the consequence of this peace in times to come? Perhaps
this goodly land itself—even this our beloved country, may share the
same fate with this its conquest—may be the purchase of a future

peace—our posterity, for whose sakes, as well as our own, the glorious expedition was undertaken, may be the same and abject vassals of those, whose growing power gives us so much uneasiness—Our religion and liberties, which animated us with such mighty resolution, the very name of them lost, and the things swallowed up in blind obedience to the infallible church, and blind adoration of the grand monarch—the children of those brave men who fought so gloriously in this celebrated expedition, be the contented slaves of those whom their fathers conquered."

With true passion, the Adams rhetoric culminates with the suggestion that they are slaves to their British masters. Lamenting the loss of his country, he concludes with the suggestion, only thinly veiled, that his country may need to rise in revolution and possibly die in the attempt for freedom: "Far be it, that I should arraign the conduct of those, who are our lawful and undoubted rulers. It lies not in our breast to make peace or war, and we ought patiently to submit to that made by our superiors, who ought to know better than we, what is best for us. Yet since even to slaves it is permitted to rejoice and grieve at their own pleasure, and they who have their bodies in subjection, cannot pretend to control their affections, I hope it will not be criminal in us to grieve and mourn our country. Yes, O my much lov'd country, thee I will lament with the most tender, though unavailing grief! — Nor shall time, which lessens all other mourning, erase from my breast, while I live, the memory of thee!—ESTO PERPETUA [Let it be forever] would be my wish for thee, yet if fate has decreed otherwise, I can only wish thou mayst die in character, and not dishonour the great glory thou hast won; and as thy name will necessarily live to future times, it may be said of thee, THOU LIVED GLORIOUSLY, AND FELL BRAVELY."

The Adams article from the *Independent Advertiser* was read and picked up by other papers throughout the colonies. Benjamin Franklin took notice and devoted the entire front page and considerable interior space to reprinting the article verbatim in the December 20, 1748, edition of his *Pennsylvania Gazette*. Through the newspapers, the patriotic thoughts and fearful possibilities that Adams so clearly delineated were circulated around the country. Boston and its relationship with the king and his governor, William Shirley, became of great interest.

Confirmation of the signing of the peace treaty and the loss of Louisbourg reached Boston in early December 1748. The daring words in the *Advertiser* fomented a growing opposition to Shirley, and an increasing number of powerful, influential, and distinguished people worked openly for his ouster, including not only Shirley's longtime friend and political ally Samuel Waldo, who had served as a general at Louisbourg, but also Shirley's handpicked Louisbourg commander, Sir William Pepperrell. Shirley was seen as part of the British scheme that had betrayed the colonies. By midsummer, there was such opposition to Shirley that he determined it was necessary to leave Massachusetts and go to England to personally defend himself against the assaults of his critics. Lieutenant Governor Spencer Phips was to govern in his absence, and his faithful political friend Thomas Hutchinson would manage the politics of the colony as his "prime minister." Shirley departed for England in September 1749, followed soon after by his prime opponents, including Waldo and Pepperrell. At the time of Shirley's departure, the long awaited reimbursement funds were finally expected to arrive in New England, and to eliminate any protests, a bill had been passed by the legislature prohibiting riots and unlawful assemblies. The voice of the people was being suppressed, and even the *Independent Advertiser* was struggling for life. A bill to censure the paper had been introduced in the legislature but was defeated. The paper was declining in any case and publishing only irregularly during the fall of 1749. By December, it was to become a thing of the past.

Sullen crowds watched as the ship carrying Massachusetts's share of the reimbursement was unloaded at Long Wharf in late September 1749. Greeted with resentment, the money that would restore the colony's financial health was slowly transported up King Street to the treasury in twenty-seven huge carts. The trucks lumbered along under the weight of 217 chests of Spanish dollars and 100 barrels of copper coins, while the hostile public milled about, muttering their disgust about the "too little, too late" payment. To some it represented blood money, exchanged for Louisbourg and the lives lost there. The citizens found methods to express their frustrations despite the anti-riot legislation, and small groups roamed the streets, verbally abusing the legislators. When Thomas Hutchinson's house caught on fire, the town's firefighters simply ignored it and urged others to "let it burn!"

As America reached the midpoint of the eighteenth century, there was one last insult to close the unhappy chapter on the victory at Louisbourg and the fiasco that followed. Hope had long been given up that the vast fortune captured by Commodore Warren's ships when the unsuspecting French treasure ships approached Louisbourg would be shared with the soldiers who captured the fortress. There was never a realistic chance for the soldiers' cause, but there was a case to be made for the colonial cruisers to be included in the distribution. They had agreed to Warren's plan of sharing prizes with all in the squadron and had seen the prizes they captured sold and distributed in this manner. It seemed only fair that the riches from the three French prizes should be similarly shared. However, their case was methodically dismantled during the five years of legal battles that followed the capture of the *Notre Dame de la Deliverance* and the two French East India Company ships. Methodically, the Admiralty Court of Appeals eliminated almost all of the American vessels. A number of the cruisers that had shared their prizes had been released to return home and were determined to no longer be part of the squadron. Those ships still attached to the squadron but on missions away from Louisbourg at the time were deemed ineligible. In 1750, the Admiralty Court of Appeals ruled that Warren's agreement did not apply to the Royal Navy ships that arrived at the end of the siege, that only the ships directly involved in the capture could share in the wealth. This meant that the American sailors on the *Defence* shared in the distribution of prize money from the *Charmante*, and those on the *Tartar* shared in that of the *Heron*. In the case of the *Notre Dame de la Deliverance*, it meant that the sailors from the *Boston Packet* shared in the capture of the richest of the French prizes, but their shares were significantly diluted. Instead of simply dividing the treasure among the officers and men of the three ships that were directly involved in the capture, the court included the crews of the two ships that had helped tow the *Chester* and the *Sun-*

derland out of the harbor to effect the capture. Three of the American colonial cruisers received some prize money, but the other eleven cruisers experienced the same exasperation and disgust that the soldiers endured when deprived of the plunder they felt they had earned. With this last bitter chapter, the sad tale of the 1745 siege of Louisbourg ended.

Despite these events, which had caused so much turmoil and distress, by 1750, the English colonies were solidly established, with cosmopolitan cities and a growing sense of national identity. They had been drawn into three European wars, endured numerous attacks, been abused in several failed and mismanaged expeditions, and celebrated a few victories, the most glorious of which they saw evaporate with the Treaty of Aix-la-Chapelle. The appalling series of deep disappointments and resulting protests that followed created broad discontent in 1750.

Late in his life, Sam Adams's younger second cousin John Adams recalled the comments his father made with regard to the Louisbourg expedition. Adams, twelve or thirteen in the late 1740s, said he "received very grievous impressions of Great Britain." He also reflected on discussions at the home of Colonel James Putnam a few years later, which "gave me such an opinion and such a disgust of British government, that I heartily wished the two countries were separated forever." Clearly, by the time the last of the insults and abuses related to the Louisbourg campaign had played themselves out, seeds of discontent were firmly planted in New England.

Samuel Adams's grandson and biographer, William Wells, expressed the prevailing attitude of that day, writing in the 1820s, "The impressment riots indicated that the fire of discontent already existed, and needed only the proper occasion to be fanned into flame. The events of the war, and the government mismanagement . . . prepared the people for the struggle which was to rend the colonies from the mother country. The press commenced the discussion of popular rights, and no doubt many speculative minds calculated the probable fate of America at some future date as a separate sovereignty." The next quarter century would see that fire of discontent fanned into flame, as Sam Adams and the other young men of the Louisbourg era, carrying their impressions of that time, became the leaders of the new generation. As they experienced the increasingly heavy hand of British colonial rule suffered by their ancestors a century before, their resistance would lead to a much more decisive confrontation than that of 1689. Indeed, it would lead to revolution and the birth of a new nation.

Road to Revolution

THE PEACE THAT WAS PURCHASED at the cost of Louisbourg and the lives of over twelve hundred American men buried in unmarked graves on *Pointe a Rochefort* lasted only six years. As had happened after the Treaty of Utrecht almost forty years before, the northern frontier was saturated with tension because the hastily drawn Treaty of Aix-la-Chapelle failed to clearly define the territorial limits of the French and British holdings. Governor Shirley, after successfully defending himself against the criticism of Waldo and others from Boston, was sent to Paris in the spring of 1750 to act as one of the king's commissioners at a peace conference. Shirley hoped to be able to add to Britain's North American holdings by asserting claims to disputed territory and clearly defining borders. In this task he failed and was recalled to London in April 1752. At that point Shirley, who had complicated his life by marrying the young daughter of his Parisian landlord, hoped that he would be given the governorship of another colony, away from his political enemies in Boston. His wish was not granted, and in late May 1753 he sailed for Boston. Rather than have his young bride face a hostile reception in Boston from both the anti-French citizens and his seven children, most of whom were older than their new stepmother, Shirley left his young wife in England. It is thought that he never saw her again.

Once back in Boston, Shirley was welcomed by many who had set aside the ill feelings and controversy that had forced him away three years earlier. The governor had a reputation for dealing firmly with military issues and was expected to respond decisively to threats along the disputed border that were heating up, not only in the north, but also in the middle Atlantic colonies. Shirley began to plan for a military expedition into Maine. Far to the south, a group of Virginia expansionists, known as the Ohio Company, with the support of Virginia's lieutenant governor, Robert Dinwiddie, began to push west of the Allegheny Mountains into territory claimed by the French. In the spring of 1754, Dinwiddie sent a small force of thirty-three militiamen and some Indians, under the command of a young militia major, George Washington, to assert the Ohio Company's rights to the territory to the west of Virginia, Maryland, and Pennsylvania. Washington and his troops won a brief, brutal victory after surprising a French patrol, but within a month a larger French force surrounded Washington's small band, which had taken refuge in a dilapidated frontier fort called Necessity. Washington's spirited defense convinced the French to allow the Americans to go free if they surrendered. Washington took that option, but the defeat at Fort Necessity accelerated the hostilities.

The British government, in response to the increased skirmishes in America, determined to finally send two regiments of regular British troops to America and put General Edward Braddock in command of the British forces there. Braddock arrived in Virginia and quickly called a meeting of colonial governors in Alexandria in April 1755. Governor Shirley came to Braddock's conference with an enhanced military reputation as a result of his successful campaign securing the frontiers of Maine. Despite the fact that England and France were still nominally at peace, Braddock outlined his plan to lead his regiments, augmented by colonial militia, against the French at Fort Duquesne, located where the Allegheny and Monongahela rivers meet, west of Pennsylvania. He also outlined several other expeditions and designated William Shirley second in command of British forces in North America. As Shirley set off to plan the mission assigned to him—an attack on Fort Niagara—he left his eldest son, William Shirley Jr., with General Braddock to gain professional military experience.

While the presence of the two regiments of British troops might have been encouraging to the Americans, the heavy-handed way in which the troops were forced on their host communities caused instant resentment. The people were compelled to house the soldiers in their homes, and this order was forcefully carried out despite protests of the Americans over the brutish behavior of some of the troops. Despite difficulties in gathering the provisions, munitions, horses, and wagons necessary to support the expedition, Braddock set off for Fort Duquesne in late April. Marching west with his force, including Major Washington and young William Shirley, the overconfident and arrogant Braddock alienated those officers with local knowledge and refused the advice of his Indian guides. Braddock, with his advance contingent of 1,373 soldiers and 86 officers, had no warning on July 9, 1755, when they marched into a trap set by over 1,000 French and Indians. In the slaughter, 63 of Braddock's officers were killed along with a staggering 914 of his soldiers. The first major British-led expedition of this new war with France in North America had ended as another debacle and humiliating defeat.

Unaware of the Braddock fiasco, William Shirley, accompanied by Louisbourg instigator John Bradstreet, who would have a successful military career until his death in 1774, marched north with his force to attack Fort Niagara. While in a temporary headquarters on the way to Oswego, Shirley received the devastating news of the defeat of Braddock's force, which had cost the lives of so many, including General Braddock and William Shirley Jr. Carrying the burden of his personal grief along with the burden of now being commander in chief, Shirley led his troops forward, but they were defeated in their attack. In addition, William Johnson, the nephew of Admiral Peter Warren, leading a force against the French at Fort Ticonderoga, met defeat south of the fortress. To compound the problems, the able French general Louis-Joseph de Montcalm, the Marquis de Saint-Veran, arrived in New France with two regiments of fresh, well-trained troops, who quickly won victories at Fort Oswego on Lake Ontario and Fort William Henry on Lake George. In the early days, this new war in America was off to a miserable start for the British and American forces.

While the war between the French and the British and American troops escalated in North America, it still remained officially undeclared. Shirley's management as commander in chief brought widespread complaints in the form of highly critical letters from his political enemies to the Duke of Newcastle and other authorities in England. Throughout the remainder of 1755, Shirley's position deteriorated, and in January 1756, Newcastle made the decision to recall Shirley and replace him as both the military commander in America and governor of Massachusetts. After fifteen years as an efficient administrator and a formidable leader in tumultuous times for the colonies, Shirley was once again returning to England to defend his actions and attempt to salvage his career. He managed to be appointed governor of the Bahamas and served in that uneventful post for twelve years until 1770. He then returned to Boston as a private citizen and built a substantial home, where he died the following year.

Shirley's recall in 1756 had been only a minor part of a major restructuring within the British government, which brought the talented William Pitt into the War Ministry. After two years of undeclared conflict in North America, England finally acknowledged the reality and declared war on France in May 1756. France made their complimentary declaration the following month. The French and Indian War in North America initiated the European war that would come to be known as the Seven Years' War. For the first time, military action in the colonies leveraged a British declaration of war against another European power. The rise of Pitt also elevated the importance of Britain's colonies around the world since he was a strong advocate of the importance of empire and commerce. The direct result in America in 1757 was to finally recognize the potential of the American fighting force by promising colonial officers below the rank of colonel full equal ranks in the British army and by guaranteeing full reimbursement of colonial war expenses. This revitalized the American enthusiasm for the war that had gone so badly. Further encouragement came with the recall of Shirley's replacement as commander in chief, John Campbell, Earl of Loudon, in early 1758. Loudon's second in command, James Abercromby, replaced him, but Pitt also sent the dynamic, forty-one-year-old general Jeffrey Amherst and several other able officers, including Colonel James Wolfe, to America. These men reported directly to Pitt rather than their nominal commander, Abercromby.

These critical changes breathed life into the American campaign and immediately produced positive results. Tens of thousands of

British troops arrived, and additional tens of thousands of Americans responded to the call to arms. The first of Pitt's objectives carried the most bitter irony for the Americans. Pitt realized the significance and strategic importance of Louisbourg. Ten years before, Great Britain had turned a deaf ear to the arguments of the Americans on the value of Louisbourg and opted for the expedient of its return to the French. Over that decade of occupation, the French had rebuilt and reinforced the fortress and had added new fortifications to protect the logical landing beaches from an amphibious attack after a 1757 attack was aborted. Pitt ordered Amherst to recapture Louisbourg in the spring of 1758. It is not surprising that the New Englanders, for the most part, lacked enthusiasm for this undertaking. They had already faced the fearsome task of conquering that city and had no appetite for a second attempt. The prevailing New England attitude was, if the British now realized their mistake, let them pay for it. A small number of New Englanders, about five hundred, including Richard Gridley, who had been instrumental in the first siege, did participate. Gridley's knowledge and experience would be invaluable to Amherst.

The British force assembled to lay siege to Louisbourg in 1758 held little resemblance to the motley band that had set off from Boston thirteen years earlier. Instead of 4,000 raw American troops crowded into 100 fishing boats and guarded by 14 little colonial warships carrying a total of 200 small cannons, the British assault force consisted of over 13,000 soldiers who were transported in nearly 150 proper troop transports that were protected by no fewer than 39 warships manned by 14,000 sailors and armed with 1,842 cannons. The British government obviously had great respect for the French fortress and was providing General Amherst with a force sufficient to guarantee success. It is interesting that with all the professional British military expertise assembled for the attack, including Amherst, the bold and energetic Colonel James Wolfe, the naval commander, Admiral Edward Boscawen, and his third in command, Commodore Philip Durell, who had been one of Warren's captains in the earlier siege, the plan of attack was the same as had been used by the amateur American general William Pepperrell.

This time there was no surprise at Louisbourg when the massive fleet came to anchor in Gabarus Bay, since the French had been alerted by friendly Indians that the force had been assembling in Halifax, the British fortress and harbor that had been developed to counter Louisbourg. Although the fleet arrived on June 2, foul weather prevented the landing of troops for four days. On D-Day, ironically June 6, three divisions of invaders made their way toward three landing beaches: White Point nearest the fortress, Flat Point in the middle where Pepperrell had conducted his feint, and the wide beach at Kennington Cove where the Americans had landed successfully in 1745. The French had remembered their hard lesson and had troops and artillery entrenched at all three locations. The French did not waste their shots and waited until the attackers were within range. The fusillade from the beach seemed destined to turn back the assault until Colonel Wolfe spotted a location in Kennington Cove that was sheltered from the French fire. He led his troops ashore over menacing rocks and crashing surf and managed to flank the French defenders. The exhausted Frenchmen, who had been at their posts for four days and nights, saw the mass of Wolfe's men and fled for the fort. With the defense collapsing to their west, the French at Flat Point also made for the safety of the fortress, and only the French at White Point held out until it was clear the landing had been accomplished and then made an orderly retreat. Once again, an invading army had landed at Louisbourg and the city was under siege.

The British faced much the same challenge the Americans had confronted years before. To consolidate their forces, the French had destroyed their battery at Lighthouse Point and the Grand Battery, but the famous Island Battery continued to dominate the entrance to the harbor. However, there was one major difference from the earlier siege: Four large French ships of the line and several frigates were trapped in the harbor. While the warships and the fortress attempted to impede the progress of the siege with their cannons, Wolfe led a handpicked force around the harbor and rebuilt the Lighthouse Point battery. As it did for the Americans, this battery began to neutralize the Island Battery, while Wolfe developed other emplacements that enabled the British to shower shot and shell on the city and the French ships in the harbor.

The French, heavily outnumbered, put up a valiant resistance. The ships did their best to direct fire at the British forces, and determined French troops made a number of sallies from the fortress to meet the British in the field. Ultimately, the sheer power of superior numbers took its toll on the French. As the siege crept closer and closer to the city, a British shell tore into the French seventy-four-gun *L'Entreprenant*, which exploded and damaged other nearby ships. Cutting-out parties from Admiral Boscawen's fleet successfully destroyed the two remaining large French ships. Morale within the beleaguered city continued to fall as numerous shells exploded within the walls, indiscriminately taking lives. Finally, a red hot shot lodged in the King's Bastion, setting it ablaze. On July 26, three days after the destruction of this symbolic structure, the French and British met to discuss the French surrender. This time there would be no courtesy of "honours of war" for the French as Amherst exerted his dominance. The French troops became prisoners of war, and once again, a decade after Great Britain had relinquished the American prize, Louisbourg was under the British flag.

It was too late in the season to push on toward Quebec, but the following year an attack against Canada was launched. Colonel John Bradstreet had gained the ear of influential men in England and had presented a plan for a two-pronged attack on New France. Although Bradstreet did not receive credit for the plan, Pitt's orders to his generals in America duplicated Bradstreet's concept. Bradstreet's proposal was a simple variation on the attacks that had been attempted several times over the preceding half century. Amherst was to lead his forces up the Hudson River and into Canada, taking French forts and Montreal before moving on toward Quebec. James Wolfe, who through his boldness and initiative at Louisbourg had been promoted to the rank of general at age thirty-two, was charged with leading an amphibious force up the St. Lawrence. Quebec would face Amherst to the west and Wolfe to the east.

Amherst, however, found strong resistance, while Wolfe arrived on schedule. Perched atop sheer cliffs, Quebec bristled with guns overlooking the river, and a cannon duel between the city and the Royal Navy ensued. After almost three months of waiting for Amherst, Wolfe was faced with either retreating or seizing the initiative. He discovered that a trail to the west of the city led up the cliffs to a broad plain. Under cover of darkness, Wolfe managed to get a significant force, including an American artillery contingent under the command of Richard Gridley, onto the Plains of Abraham, as the stretch of land was called. Montcalm, in command of Quebec, was astonished to see the British force arrayed before the city and feared that since they had gotten two cannons up the cliff, more cannons might arrive and put the city under artillery siege. Montcalm made the decision to face the British in the field. It was a decision that would prove fatal to him and his cause. In the fierce battle, the French were defeated; Montcalm was taken back into the city, fatally wounded, and Wolfe, felled by a bullet in his chest, learned of his victory only moments before he died.

Richard Gridley's contributions at Louisbourg and Quebec were recognized when the British government granted him the Magdalen Islands, with a valuable proprietary seal and cod fishery, half pay as a British officer, and three thousand acres in New Hampshire. Such rewards were not unusual for well-connected British officers, but they were nearly unheard of for provincials. Small as it may have been, the American involvement at the conquest of Louisbourg and Quebec had been acknowledged.

The fall of Quebec in 1759 and the control of the St. Lawrence, cutting off French resupply, set the stage for the successful British attack on Montreal the following year. With the fall of Montreal, New France was no more and the British controlled a vast new territory. For generations, military and political leaders in America had pleaded for British support for the kind of concerted attack that had finally taken Canada from the French. Had it been accomplished earlier, the relationship of Great Britain and her American colonies might have been very different. But now, in 1760, it had been accomplished. In addition, General John Forbes had avenged Braddock's defeat when he captured Fort Duquesne and removed the French authority in the west.

The war in North America was essentially over, but the European struggle continued for two more years. In 1763, the Treaty of Paris brought an end to the Seven Years' War and an official end to the French and Indian War. Although there was much for the British and the Americans to celebrate, the success had come at a heavy cost both in lives and, particularly, in financial resources. Great Britain had amassed a staggering £146 million in debt in order to finance the empire and their military expeditions on the continent and in America. It would take years to retire that debt, and the British lawmakers reasoned that since their American colonies were the prime beneficiaries of the expulsion of the French from Canada, they should contribute significantly to the support of British troops needed to defend the newly won lands to the north and west. There was no doubt that the governance and security of the vast Canadian territory was going to be costly to Great Britain and no doubt that the military campaigns involving tens of thousands of British soldiers and sailors had been expensive, but the colonies in America had also suffered from lives lost and, owing to the end of wartime spending, were slipping into economic depression. The Americans felt they needed to apply their energies and resources toward their own economic recovery, which in turn would benefit the mother country. With these conflicting perspectives, Britain and America were on a collision course.

Sam Adams, after the demise of the *Independent Advertiser*, continued to voice the discontent he felt and saw around him. He met regularly for political discussions with the Caucus Club, which had been founded by his father, was a consistent agitator in town meetings, and continued to write well-reasoned protest articles under a number of pseudonyms. When his malt business failed in 1764, he was elected to the Massachusetts Legislature and entered politics full-time. This placed Adams in a key position to experience and resist the heavy hand of British colonial policy that was falling on the Americans. In order to offset some of the annual £350,000 expense of maintaining an army of ten thousand British soldiers in the colonies, Parliament began the imposition of new taxes and duties. The first, in 1764, was the Sugar Act, which imposed a series of new taxes and regulation on the importation of sugar and molasses used in the rum-distilling process. Since the colonies were already restricted from developing manufacturing industries that might compete with British manufacturers, the rum business was critical to the colonies. In addition to the new taxes, the Sugar Act called for a more efficient system of tax collection and strict enforcement of the Acts of Trade, which had been largely ignored during the era of salutary neglect. The American economy immediately felt the impact of this legislation, and the economic pain increased the following year when the Stamp Act was passed. This legislation imposed duties on a wide range of items, including legal and commercial documents, newspapers, almanacs, pamphlets, and even playing cards and dice. These duties restricted commerce and impinged upon the freedom of the press. Additional fees were extracted in 1765 with the passage of the Quartering Act, which required the colonies to pay for the accommodations and living expenses of the British troops in America. Virtually everyone in the colonies was touched by these acts, and public protests appeared in cities all along the coast.

In response to the protest, minor alterations were made in the provisions of the Sugar Act, and the Stamp Act was repealed in 1766. There was little time for the Americans to celebrate their relief, since in 1767 the Townshend Acts were passed. They established vice-admiralty courts to adjudicate customs cases, taking control out of local areas. In addition, they applied new duties on imports of such basics as glass, paints, paper, and tea. These duties were quickly recognized as new taxes, and protest erupted in 1768. In that same year, the issue of impressments continued to be an important source of consternation for the Americans. In Boston, four American sailors were apprehended for killing a British naval officer, Lieutenant Panton, when his press gang attempted to take them into Royal Navy service. Impressment had taken another life in Boston, and the people of the city were ready to fill the streets in support of the sailors' rights. The respected attorney John Adams, cousin of Sam, successfully won an acquittal for the sailors on the basis of self-defense. This was a bold victory, but had the decision gone in the other direction, the tinderbox of protest was ready to burst into flame. These protests and actions proved to be critical since they caused the British government to shift its troops from the defense of the northern and western frontiers to being stationed in the major cities on the eastern seaboard. The British army in America had been transformed from one of defense to an unwelcome army of occupation and tax enforcement.

The presence of these troops in American cities was a constant irritant. On the snowy Boston evening of March 5, 1770, some local youths began to harass the British sentry outside the customs office. As snowballs pelted the sentry, other soldiers came to his aid, and the resulting loud confrontation brought other Bostonians to the scene. The crisis escalated when the mob assaulted two of the British soldiers, whose compatriots responded with musket fire. The Boston Massacre left five citizens dead and others wounded. Stunned, Boston seethed with volatility until Acting Governor Thomas Hutchinson ordered the British troops out of their quarters in the heart of the city and into Castle William on Castle Island in the harbor. The soldiers who had fired into the crowd were taken to trial, and despite a vigorous defense by John Adams, whose conscience forced him to accept the unpopular task, two were convicted of manslaughter. This was salve on an open wound, but anxiety was also reduced by the repeal of some aspects of the Townshend duties and easing of other restrictions. A facade of apparent calm descended over the colonies for two years, but behind the scenes, activists were nurturing the seeds of discontent.

Sam Adams, instilled with democratic ideals, championed the cause of the common man while he worked to expose and undermine the privileged colonial aristocracy. He galvanized the working-class and middle-class Bostonians into a politically informed contingent that was ready to resist further British oppression. Many in the upper classes had experienced financial losses owing to the "taxation without representation" that had been imposed on them. A powerful coalition was taking shape. To establish a communications network throughout Massachusetts, Adams convinced the town meeting of Boston to establish a committee of correspondence, which was to contact other communities and develop a list of grievances. The concept caught on, and soon there was a steady flow of information among the numerous committees. The first test of the effectiveness of this communication came in 1773, when the British government blundered into a very sensitive issue. In an attempt to revive the fiscal health of the revered British East India Company, the government awarded them a monopoly on the importation of tea in America. With tea having become a staple of American life, this action wreaked havoc throughout the colonies and among tea trading firms in England and on the continent. In major American cities, protests forced East India Company ships to turn away without unloading their cargoes, and in other towns, tea was impounded. None of these actions resulted in the loss or destruction of the tea, but in

Boston the situation was different. Sam Adams had the ability to communicate and bring into union the farmers, urban workers, and merchants. With Adams as its instigator, a group of men disguised as Indians raided three vessels at anchor in the harbor and dumped their cargoes of tea overboard.

This famous event was a watershed moment, as Great Britain's authority was directly challenged and cargo valued at approximately £15,000 had been destroyed. This set in motion a series of crucial events. Since the perpetrators of this "crime" were not identified, it was impossible for British authorities in Boston to arrest anyone. The offense, however, was too grievous to be left unpunished since that would signal to all in America and abroad that British authority could be challenged with impunity. The British decided to impose a series of acts to punish Massachusetts and bring the radicals to heel.

Known by the colonists as "the Intolerable Acts," five acts of Parliament raised the resistance to another level. The first act, the Boston Port Act, closed the port to all commerce until the value of the tea was repaid. The second, the Administration of Justice Act, exempted British agents from prosecution for false arrest of suspected rioters or scofflaws. The Massachusetts Government Act wrested control of the provincial government from the general assembly, curbed town meetings, and placed control firmly in the hands of those supporting the British position. The Quartering Act brought the army back into the center of Boston and housed the troops either in barracks or in taverns and commandeered buildings at citizen expense. The fifth act was only tangentially connected with Boston, since it dealt with Quebec. It extended the province of Quebec into the territory to the west of Massachusetts and Connecticut, depriving those colonies of the ability to expand westward. Since it also gave the Quebecois the right to retain their Catholic faith, it was viewed as repudiation of the Puritan city's long abhorrence of Catholicism and raised fears that the Church of England with its popish trappings would be forced on Massachusetts. The oppression of Massachusetts by the British government was accentuated when General Thomas Gage, who commanded the troops occupying Boston, was designated governor of Massachusetts. The restive colony had been stripped of its self-rule, and Boston was essentially under martial law.

All eyes in the American colonies were on Boston. It was clearly understood that if Great Britain could suppress protest and rule Massachusetts with an iron fist, she could do likewise throughout the colonies. Boston was the focus, but the threat was felt throughout the emerging nation. The initial response was the calling of the First Continental Congress in 1774. With Sam Adams representing Massachusetts, the Congress issued a Declaration of Rights, which rang with Locke's clarion call for protection of the rights of life, liberty, and property. The declaration also rejected the long claimed right of Parliament over the colonies, but it stopped short of defying the king's authority. Ultimately more important than the statement of rights was the establishment of a Continental Association, a cooperative agreement by which the colonies would work together to impose sanctions against Great Britain in retaliation for the Intolerable Acts. This union instituted an escalating series of protest actions that were to be imposed during the year ahead if Britain didn't withdraw her coercive acts. In December 1774, the colonies would stop importing specified British goods. If no change occurred, the colonies would give up tea, beginning on March 1, 1775, and if that failed to exert sufficient pressure, the colonies would cut off exports to Britain on September 10. It was hoped that this colonial countercoercion would induce Britain to rethink her position.

While the other colonies were exhibiting solidarity with their Massachusetts compatriots, that colony was quietly mobilizing its militia and gathering arms and munitions with which to resist the occupation of Boston by General Gage and his ten thousand troops. Richard Gridley, with his long experience as a military engineer and artillery expert, and obviously not seduced by the rewards from the British government, held the rank of general. Seth Pomeroy, who had continued to lead militia forces during the French and Indian War, also carried that rank. Throughout the province, men were preparing for the fatal confrontation, which seemed inevitable. Gage was well-informed of the actions of the militia and aware of the most flagrant incendiaries, Sam Adams and John Hancock. These two men were conspicuously absent from a roster of those offered amnesty by General Gage. The British general had orders to arrest these two men and send them to England for trial and probable execution. On April 18, Gage sent a force of one thousand soldiers out from Boston with the mission of capturing Adams and Hancock, who were thought to be in Lexington, and destroying the rebels' arms cache in Concord. Forewarned, Adams and Hancock disappeared, as did most of the weapons and munitions in Concord. What Gage's men encountered were the now famous minutemen, who attacked them in Lexington, fought them in Concord, and then harassed Gage's force, reinforced by fifteen hundred additional British soldiers, all the way back to Boston. British casualties were three times those of the Americans. Adams and Hancock made their escape and worked their way back to the Second Continental Congress, which was in session in Philadelphia, where the two Boston patriots were welcomed as heroes.

There was no need for colonial sanctions anymore, war had broken out. Colonies immediately took actions to assert themselves and depose the British authorities. The Second Continental Congress declared war in May and, using the network of committees of correspondence, established the Continental Army in June. George Washington was put in command of the army, and when the Congress issued its list of ten brigadier generals, Seth Pomeroy was at the top as the most senior. The force with which Pomeroy was serving, the Massachusetts militia, was now part of the Continental Army. They had placed Boston under siege after the confrontations at Lexington and Concord and had General Gage and his force bottled up in the city.

It was determined that Breed's Hill in Charlestown would give the Americans a strategic location from which they could rain shells down upon the British troops in Boston and their ships in the harbor, while being above the range of the British cannons. On the evening of June 16, the Americans occupied the heights, and General Gridley, aided by his two sons, laid out the gun emplacements and supervised the digging of defensive trenches on the heights. As dawn came, General Gage and his fellow generals realized their vulnerability and acted decisively. A British force was assembled for an attack on the American position. Gridley, from his vantage point at the crest of the hill, could see the gathering British force, but then he looked in the other direction. There, striding up the hill, having ridden all night, was Gridley's Louisbourg brother-in-arms, Seth Pomeroy, carrying the same musket he had used at Louisbourg. The two friends, who on June 17, 1745, had witnessed and celebrated the victory at Louisbourg, stood side by side thirty years later on June 17, 1775, facing their new enemy in the Battle of Bunker Hill, the first major battle on the path to another victory.

The seeds of discontent that had been accumulated and sown over more than a century had been nourished by abuse, exploitation, mismanagement, and disrespect and had blossomed into revolution.

Appendix

From the *Boston Independent Advertiser*, Number 46,
November 14, 1748

(This newspaper was published by Gamaliel Rogers and
Daniel Fowle for two years, 1748 and 1749, and was edited by
twenty-six-year-old Samuel Adams, who is the probable author of this editorial. Sam Adams had recently obtained his
master's degree from Harvard, where he was influenced by
the writing of John Locke. The piece is transcribed with the
period spelling and punctuation. The comments within
brackets are those of the author of this book.)

"A Late paper contained some political reflections on the conduct of
the Military during the war, wherein it was observed how the nation
in general will probably be affected, if what is transmitted to us as the
preliminaries of Aix-la-Chapelle should be the basis of the approaching peace—what related particularly to this province, was the Zeal
and Importance of our services—the treatment we have received, and
our present Situation, was left to an after consideration. [Despite
heroic performance, the colony is receiving ill treatment.] And although we are not quite arrived at that point of time which will coun-
tenance our treating this subject with unlimited freedom I shall yet
observe that honest plainness which becomes an Englishman, and is
not yet dangerous in an English country.

It is beyond my present purpose to look further back than the Year

1744, when the flame of war which was first enkindled in the east spread itself to the western parts of the world—our frontiers being now exposed to the depredations of a savage and merciless enemy, and our coasts infested by our Cape-Breton neighbors, Canceau, a place of importance to our fishery was soon taken and destroyed, and their successes prompted them to attempt even the gaining of Annapolis, which were it not for the generous assistance afforded them from this province [reinforcements sent from Massachusetts raised the siege], must infallibly have fallen into their hands ... These daring actions were sufficient to alarm New-England, and raise very gloomy apprehensions of increasing mischief.—But by the return of many of our seamen who were carried into Louisbourg [prisoners taken at Canso], we learned how much that fortress had been weakened by supplying and manning a large fleet of East-India ships, and some men of war which sailed from thence for Old France late in the fall—that they were short of necessaries, and their garrison not a little mutinous—as also that their grand supplies were not expected till late in the spring. We then very naturally concluded, it was the important crisis, when an attempt upon that fortress might be any way practicable.—These advices affording a little prospect of success, raised such a spirit in New Englandmen to this undertaking, as no appearance of difficulty and hazard could damp;—New-England men— whose breasts always burn with brave and loyal sentiments, and who catch at all opportunities of displaying their regard for their mothercountry, and the affection they have for their own.

I believe it will not soon be forgot, with what a mighty ardour this undertaking was pushed forward by all orders and degrees amoung us,—as we were all united in the same common interest, we seemed in this inspired with the same common wish.—Although the number of males in this province was but about thirty seven thousand, yet near one sixth part of this number readily inlisted into this service— they boldly committed themselves to the tempestuous sea—an element untried and unknown to the greater part of them. The trading part of the province cheerfully submitted to a long embargo, which the neighbouring governments excused themselves from, and so had an opportunity of supplying foreign markets, to our very great loss.— Our fishery and husbandry were almost entirely neglected—and every man's private concerns seemed to be swallowed up in this grand concern of the public. The levies were soon made, and every thing necessary for the siege got ready in so short a time as can scarce be thought credible, and on the 17th of March the fleet sailed, followed by the wishes and prayers of all they left behind, as upon their success—not their own interest, but the fate of their country, seemed to depend. Through the remarkable assistance of divine providence this most hazardous and surprising attempt succeeded!

But the particulars relating to this siege, which gained the attention of all Europe, I hope will be faithfully transmitted to posterity more at large than can be expected from this paper.

The importance of our conquest was so considerable, that our own fishery was not only wholly secured, but the enemies entirely ruined—our navigation in these seas were now freed from danger, and our seaports no longer dreaded their depredations—they were now deprived of the only convenient port they had for their East and West-India ships to recruit and take convoy at—and by gaining the entire command of St. Lawrence river, those supplies might have been cut off which enabled Quebec to furnish our Indian enemies with the means of our distress, and a glorious opportunity was presented to our Military, of making an easy conquest of all Canada. And had not those regiments, which by the order of his Majesty, were raised, been kept for long in a state of inactivity, and those brave men which reduced Cape-Breton been detained there,—we might in all probability have surprised the nation with that conquest also—and to have put all North America—the most valuable branches of trade, and the finest nursery for seamen, into their possession [discontent that there was no follow-up against Canada]—France has now very plainly discovered the sense she has of the importance of keeping this island in her own possession;—we see her ready to give up her five years triumphs in the Netherlands, purchased with the blood of Myriads of her people, and the expense of millions of her money, if she may but again obtain it.

Thus important have our services been to the nation, but what returns have we received, and what advantages has my country derived? Has she gained the favour of the British Military by her glorious achievements? Or does not the Treatment she has received from them speak the contrary? A certain great man's reply to one of our Agents, to be sure seems to intimate it, when he observed, "That if any thing was allowed us as a reimbursement of our expedition charges, it must be received as a bounty, we having engaged in that undertaking without orders," and several other thing, to the same purpose, tis said, were dropped, too disagreeable for him to mention. [Discontent at the lack of respect for victory—a holdover from earlier disrespectful treatment.]

We had very early the mortification of hearing, that those rich East India and South-Seamen, the capture of which was the immediate consequence of this conquest, and more directly owing to the bravery of our men than any other cause, were to be the sole property of those who never slung a shot against that citadel. [Discontent over gain of Royal Navy sailors and officers with nothing for American troops.]

The Year following an admiral of France failed with a most powerful fleet, to retrieve this fatal loss, and spread desolation and ruin throughout all our seacoasts. Elate they came with the prospect of success, and the hopes of revenge—they came unnoticed, unwatched—let not futurity say avoided by a squadron of English men of war; they came possest with the means of our destruction, with the strongest hopes of finding us unprotected by a superior force, on what just reasons grounded, let the world judge. Deserted and defenceless, we were cast upon the care of that kind providence, who had before crowned us with a success, at least adequate, to our largest wishes [discontent at the lack of protection provided by the Crown]: By a train of remarkable events, the dreaded evil was warded off from us, not by human might or wisdom, without the friendship, without the interposition of fleets, who lay unactive at home, for puzzled were the Military to know where to send them at that critical juncture. [Discontent at British military incompetence and indecision.]

Great as our real services have been, though mightily exhausted by the loss of multitudes of our valuable brethren in the service of the crown, we have not appeared respectable enough to obtain any relaxation from impresses for the King's ships, although the West-India islands were thought of importance enough to deserve a total exemption. [Vehement discontent over the ongoing volatile issue of impressments.] On the contrary, the King's ships (not without leave) have made this province their only resort for men, and not only supplied their own necessity, but very neighbourly, as we have reason to think, carried off more than their compliment for other ships. [Discontent at the suspicion of exploitation through "over-impressments."] The execution of this illegal and cruel measure has been conducted with insolence and wantonness, which it will be as difficult to forget as to attone for. Such scenes of merciless rapine, barbarity, and even Murder, have been opened to us, as in any other country would have called down the distinguishing rigour of justice upon the guilty actors, if possible to be found: Yet some of those worthless men survive to upbraid the negligence of those who sacrifice the strength and security of the bed laws to a criminal love, or inglorious fear, of a scoundrel Captain or Commodore. [Discontent referring to the Commodore Knowles Riots of 1747.]

But what consummates all our misfortunes is the rendition of Louisbourg—a place of equal importance to the nation with Gibraltar—Louisbourg gained at the expence of New England blood, and with the ruin of half the estates of the province, is again to return to its former masters, as an equivalent for the Netherlands, which is to our nation no equivalent at all, and this without any consideration to the brave captors for the cannon, stores, or the town itself—without any consideration to the province ! It is true, that our parliament have voted the reimbursement of the charge of taking it, which we would dutifully acknowledge, but our consequent damages have prodigiously exceeded that sum [discontent over inadequate and delayed compensation and the sense of coercion since Massachusetts was in dire financial condition and protest would cancel any urgently needed compensation]: And it must also be confessed, that the two gentlemen who were principally concerned in conducting the expedition were rewarded with the command of two regiments, which were ordered to be raised among us; but how much abused was my country by the base insinuation of some, who as it is said suggested to the Military, that those officers who had served so gloriously, were unwilling to accept of any military posts, but that those whom they commanded were extremely desirous of being taken into his Majesty's service for life: However this be, the loss of those men who inlisted from this province into that service, added to our former losses [discontent referring to

the massive 90% death rate for Massachusetts troops in the West
Indies/Cartagena debacle of the early 1740s], has been an unspeakable
damage to us: Publick justice has detected and punished some of those
worthless men, who by the most base and villainous artifices have enticed and abused the unwary into the service of the Government with
barbarities hitherto unknown, and as yet abhored in a free country:
some of these villainous scenes are come to light, some of the actors
discovered, and the curtain half drawn away from the others. [Discon-
tent over recruiting scandals.] The men who were posted to defend
our frontiers, alured into other services, and fresh and useful members
of the community pressed in their stead—nay, to the supply of these
Regiments, tis said, the commissions of the Peace have been made
subservient, and J——s genteelly required to find a man for the service of the King, and the convenience of the Colonel. The solicitations
of our reimbursement we have been taught did not depend upon the
merits of our past services, but upon new compliances, new expences,
and new expeditions. [Discontent over payments made in demand of
future loyalty and not compensation for past victory.] We have been
cajolled and intimidated, as the circumstances of things, and the necessity of the proposal required—I could here enumerate many other
things of this nature—but the subject is ungrateful, it sufficiently appears, that the compliment paid to the province by the very few
favours granted them for this affair, are no ways comparable to many
apparent inconveniences which have risen out of it.

But now—Cape-breton is lost; our fishery in the most imminent
danger—our debt heavy—the ballance of trade against us—valuable
lands given away to other colonies—unprotected and unredressed under the most cruel impositions—our remaining commerce labouring
under great inconveniences—sunk by our most laudable
achievements—whilst every other province gains the advantage of our
zeal, and their own indolence [discontent over the peril into which the
return of Louisbourg puts N.E.]—

Upon the whole, it is impossible for any man who truly loves his
country, to be unaffected with the present melancholly situation of its
affairs. To behold the fruits of all our labours, toils and hazards, given
up at once to our proud insulting enemies! And ourselves, after all the

brave attempts we have made, and the blessings of divine providence on our bravery, in a far worse condition than when the war commenced! To see our enemies (for enemies they are and will be in peace and war) again in possession of that dreaded fortress, of which it cost so much New-England blood and labour to dispossess them! Those hated ensigns again display'd on those walls which once bore the triumphs of our valour. It is neither possible, nor safe to look into futurity, and our present load of affliction is so great, we need not increase it by raising imaginary dangers. [Here the author imagines the British colonies in America being traded away as the price for peace in a future time—a powerful image.] Yet the mind opprest with grief, anxious and fearful, cannot help raising to the most frightful prospects. Who can tell what will be the consequence of this peace in times to come? Perhaps this goodly land itself—even this our beloved country, may share the same fate with this its conquest— may be the purchase of a future peace—our posterity, for whose sakes, as well as our own, the glorious expeditions was undertaken, may be the same and abject vassals of those, whose growing power gives us so much uneasiness—Our religion and liberties, which animated us with such mighty resolution, the very name of them lost, and the things swallowed up in blind obedience to the infallible church, and blind adoration of the grand monarch—the children of those brave men who fought so gloriously in this celebrated expedition, be the contented slaves of those whom their fathers conquered. But whether, alas! Do my thoughts hurry me?

Far be it, that I should arraign the conduct of those, who are our lawful and undoubted rulers. It lies not in our breast to make peace or war, and we ought patiently to submit to that made by our superiors, who ought to know better than we, what is best for us. Yet since even to slaves it is permitted to rejoice and grieve at their own pleasure, and they who have their bodies in subjection, cannot pretend to control their affections, I hope it will not be criminal in us to grieve and mourn our country. Yes, O my much lov'd country, thee I will lament with the most tender, though unavailing grief!—Nor shall time, which lessens all other mourning, erase from my breast, while I live, the memory of thee!—Esto perpetua would be my wish for thee, yet if fate has decreed otherwise, I can only wish thou mayst die in character, and not dishonour the great glory thou hast won; and as thy name will necessarily live to future times, it may be said of thee, thou lived gloriously and fell bravely." [A veiled call for revolution. His country, America, may have to fight to stay alive.]

Notes

ABBREVIATIONS

DAB: Dictionary of American Biography
DCB: Dictionary of Canadian Biography Online
DNB: Dictionary of National Biography
NA/PRO: National Archives/Public Records Office, Kew, Richmond, UK
All sources are cited in full in the bibliography.

A NOTE ON DATES: During most of the period covered by this book, two different calendars were in use, so that the events of a certain day would have two different dates if mentioned, for example, in French and English sources. In 1582, Pope Gregory XIII issued a papal bull to correct a deficiency in the Julian calendar that was then in use. Most Catholic countries and the Dutch Protestants adopted the calendar soon after the bull, but other countries such as England and her colonies retained the Julian calendar. This meant an eleven-day difference in the date of the same day in English and French sources cited in this book. Great Britain finally adopted the Gregorian calendar in 1752. The world continues to use the Gregorian calendar today.

PROLOGUE

2   *In 1815, John Adams, when reflecting* John Adams, *Letterbook*, p. 45.
    August 24, 1815.

1: LIBERTIES AND BENIGN NEGLECT

4 *The earliest of these adventurous groups* Taylor, p. 119.
4 *White wrote, "Of the same chests three"* John White *The firſt voyage of M. John White into the West Indies and parts of America called Virginia, in the yeere 1590.*
5 *The next attempt at colonization* Nettles, p. 154.
5 *The aristocracy accelerated a program* McDougall, pp. 19–21.
6 *He wrote: "Now all of us att James Towne* George Percy, *A Trewe Relacyon of the Pcedeinges and Ocurrentes of Momente wch have hapned in Virginia from the Tyme Sr Thomas GATES was shipp-wrackte uppon the BERMUDES ano 1609 untill my depture outt of the Country wch was in ano Dñi 1612.*
6 *After enduring fifteen years of hardship* Taylor, p. 130.
7 *The monarch was the head of the church* Ibid., p. 160.
7 *Favorable winds and currents—which would* McDougall, p. 53.
7 *Describing that cruel period* Bradford, p. 134.
9 *The note read, "By a late grant"* Cecil Calvert, Lord Baltimore, *RENT DEED AGREEMENT FROM LORD CECIL BALTIMORE TO WINDSOR CASTLE, 1633.*
9 *Few English Catholics took* Taylor, p. 137.
11 *In 1643, the New England Confederation was* "The Articles of Confederation," Thorpe, p. 77.
12 *This unique early cooperative venture* Osgood, *Seventeenth Century*, vol. I, p. 399; and Nettles, pp. 214–217.
12 *Parliament passed the Declaratory Act in 1650* McDougall, p. 69.

2: SEEDS OF REBELLION

15 **In that same year, the king** Taylor, p. 263.
16 *Robert Beverley, in his* **The History and Present State of Virginia** Beverley, p. 67.
16 *When Berkeley refused, the settlers* Ibid., p. 69.
16 *Stepping into the role of leader* Ibid.
16 *"He was young [29 years old]* Ibid.
16 *In the document he said* Bacon, p. 1.
18 *In the* **Complaint** *the author makes* Anonymous, *Complaint from Heaven*, p. 138.
18 *One of Governor Berkeley's complaints* Hening, vol. II, p. 516.
19 *He told the king of his conversation* Toppan, vol. II, pp. 216–217.

19 *Voicing the colonies' position in March* Nowell.

19 *Mather said, "As the Question"* Hall, part 2, pp. 307–308.

20 *Charles and the French king Louis XIV* Arnold-Baker, p. 275, item 13.

21 *This megacolony was first led* Nettles, p. 298.

21 *Governor Andros, backed by English soldiers* Warden, pp. 3–8.

21 *With no colonial assemblies to interfere* McDougall, p. 95.

22 *When the Reverend John Wise led a* Taylor, p. 277.

22 *Wise was put in prison, fined* The £50 would be the equivalent of just under $140,000 in the year 2000. The calculation was made with the use of McCusker's *How Much Is That in Real Money?*

23 *The response to the governor's request* Sewall, vol. I, p. 162. The original King's Chapel on the corner of Tremont and School streets was built over a portion of Boston's first burying ground, because no one would sell land for construction of an Anglican chapel.

23 *On receiving the rejection* Lovejoy, p. 193.

23 *Service was compulsory for nearly all* Leach, p. 14.

24 *The leaders of the colony expressed* Andrews, ed., pp. 175–182.

3: REVOLUTION!

26 The description of the Town House is drawn from the illustration, plate 4, in Bridenbaugh's *Cities in the Wilderness*, 1938, which is reconstructed from the original specifications of Thomas Joy and Bartholomew Bernard.

27 *Once there, Mather published* Increase Mather p. 1.

27 *As Mather sailed for England, tantalizing* Warden, p. 7.

27 *As Samuel Mather recorded the mood* Samuel Mather, in Whitmore, vol. III, p. 145.

28 *As the day began, it was Governor Andros* Warden, p. 6.

28 *As Nathanael Byfield wrote in his eyewitness* Byfield in Hall et al., eds., pp. 46–47.

28 *The group from the north end* Charnock, vol. II, p. 98; and Hall et al., eds., p. 38.

28 *The inflamed colonists seized the Dominion's* Byfield in Hall et al., eds., p. 47.

29 *The declaration related the New Englanders'* Andrews, ed., pp. 175–182.

29 *The letter read, in part* Ibid.

30 *While an early part of the statement* Warden, p. 10.

30 *A tense confrontation ensued* Prince in Andrews, ed., pp. 186–190.

31 *Andros was haughty and belligerent* Byfield in Hall et al., eds., p. 46.

32 *As Samuel Prince related the situation, "The frigate"* Prince in Hall et al., eds., p. 41.

32 *However, Prince reports that the self-concerned* Ibid.

33 *Nathanael Byfield confirmed the prudence* Byfield in Hall et al., eds., p. 47.

33 *Making his way back, he arrived* Ibid.

The details of the revolution in Boston are drawn from two eyewitness accounts: Samuel Prince's letter to Thomas Hinckley, April 22, 1689, reproduced in Hall et al., eds., pp. 40–42, and Nathanael Byfield's *An Account of the Late Revolution in New England . . .* reproduced in Hall et al., eds., pp. 46–48.

4: THE REVOLUTION SPREADS

35 *Word of the revolution spread quickly* McDougall, p. 96.

35 *Nicholson called together the three* "Minutes of the Councell att New Yorke," *New-York Historical Society Collections* 1:1868, 241–242.

36 *On May 3, the freeholders of the county* O'Callaghan, vol. III, p. 577.

36 *Lieutenant Governor Nicholson wrote in mid-May* Ibid., pp. 259–261.

36 *In utter frustration, on May 30, Nicholson* Hall et al., eds., p. 100.

37 *These complaints along with supporting evidence* "Letter from the Privy Council," in Browne, vol. V, pp. 300–301.

38 *First Joseph urged the assembly* "William Joseph's Address," in Browne, vol. XIII, pp. 148–153.

39 *This heavy-handed treatment did not produce* "The Grievances of the Lower House," in Browne, vol. XIII, pp. 171–173.

39 *A colorful character, John Coode* Hall et al., eds., p. 145.

39 *Arriving on July 27, Coode's men "marched"* McAnear in Hall et al., eds., p. 184.

40 *From the statehouse, the center* "The Declaration of the Protestant Association," in Browne, vol. VIII, pp. 101–107.

40 Pennsylvania briefly became a royal colony, but the pacifist Quaker Assembly proved so difficult that its original charter was reinstated.

42 *Bearing testament to the colonial attitude* Toppan, vol. VII, pp. 373–385.

42 *In New York, the impact of the rebellion* Jacob Leisler was swept up in an atmosphere of ethnic exuberance as the Dutch in New York took great pride in their Prince of Orange, William, being on the English throne and there was resistance to the English forces occupying New York (New Amsterdam).

42   *The future for Leisler was bleak* DNB, vol. 5, p. 482.

42   *He was named president of the court* Lovejoy, pp. 354–358.

5: Proof of Loyalty

46   *By early 1690, he had a plan in place* In Canada, the French had a
     population that was only a small fraction of that of the English
     colonies to the south. They therefore depended on allying them-
     selves with native tribes and adapting the Indian tactic of hit-and-
     run raids to create a new form of state-sponsored terrorism. The
     English colonists, frustrated by the inability to respond quickly and
     effectively to specific French and Indian attacks, struck out in bru-
     tal retaliatory raids but also employed a more conventional strategy
     to oust the French from North America. This consisted of initial at-
     tacks on the outer defenses of Nova Scotia or sites protecting the ap-
     proaches to the St. Lawrence, followed by two-pronged land and sea
     attacks on Quebec, the heart of French Canada.

46   *Captured by the Iroquois at the age of nineteen* DCB, entry for
     "Hertel de la Fresniere."

46   *By the time of King William's War* Haefeli and Sweeney, p. 48.

46   *At dawn on February 9, 1690, they overwhelmed* Peckham, pp. 29–31.

46   *An eyewitness, Robert Livingston, recorded* Livingston.

47   *When news of the attack reached* Greene, p. 121.

47   *William Vaughn and Richard Martyn made* Baxter, vol. V, pp. 57–59.

48   *Phips, originally from a Maine outpost near* DAB, vol. XIV, p. 551;
     and DNB, vol. 44, p. 188.

48   *James II awarded him a knighthood* DCB, entry for Phips.

49   *When they arrived at Port Royal on May 9* Leach, p. 91.

49   *The "journal" of the Phips expedition reported* DCB, entry for Phips.

50   *Representatives of Connecticut, Massachusetts, New York* Leach, pp.
     96–99.

51   *His arrival and the perspective on his appointment* Felt, p. 304.

52   *Impressment, which had been in existence since* J. R. Hutchinson, p. 5.
     While it was felt by the citizenry in both England and the colonies
     that such drastic recruitment and forced service was against the basic
     rights of Englishmen, legal opinions from the Crown's advisers sanc-
     tioned the process. In 1215, King John had been forced into signing
     the Magna Carta, which asserted the rule of law and restricted the
     power of the king. As a charter of English liberties, it protected the
     rights and liberties of citizens. However, within a year, King John

issued warrants that made it clear that the Magna Carta did not protect the liberties of sailors. Mariners, at the time of King John and for
centuries to follow, were generally viewed as a low sort and definitely
second-class citizens. They had a reputation for violence, drunkenness, and loose living. The image of the swaggering Jack Tar, reeling
around the waterfront from one sordid establishment to another,
stayed with sailors into the twentieth century. Because of this reputation, they were given little standing in the community and little
regard when it came to individual rights. From the time of the
Magna Carta, the press was employed for over five hundred years,
with the concerns of the mariners being given little consideration. In
the early eighteenth century, it was determined that, as with
conscription practiced to this present day, a government could legally
press or draft men into service for the common good.

52   *Life on the ships of the Royal Navy* Rodger, pp. 37–75.

52   *The press was a feared but accepted evil* J. R. Hutchinson, p. 311.

53   *Twice in the middle of the night* NA/PRO CO 571/15; CO 5/751/9.
The details of the Captain Short/HMS. *Swift* case are contained in
the above cited Colonial Office files at the National Archive/Public
Records Office, and information on Captain Short is found in
Charnock's *Biographia Navalis*.

54   *On arrival in England on January 1, 1695* Lounsberry, pp. 303–305.

55   *Hannah Dustin, a woman of about forty* Taylor, p. 290.

55   *Cotton Mather recorded the events* Mather, vol. 2, pp. 634–636.

56   *Fifty pounds was the annual salary for a village leader* Parkman,
vol. I, p. 41. Tragically, with this significant incentive, a few heinous
individuals slaughtered friendly Indians just for the scalp reward.

6: WAR RETURNS

58   *Late in the spring of 1702, the English* NA/PRO CO 5/862/121-i-1.

58   *The European powers initially seemed content* Leach, p. 117.

59   *However, by 1701, France and Spain were working* Sweeney, p. 35;
and Leach, p. 121.

59   **Swift** *was a small ship* Lyon, p 31.

60   *As Lambert and Fair described* NA/PRO CO 5/862/121-iii.

60   *The only person aboard was the cook* NA/PRO CO 5/862/121-iv.

60   *When another sailor, William Best* NA/PRO CO 5/862/121-v.

60   *With continued threats and profanity* NA/PRO CO 5/862/121-vi.

61   *Within moments of his arrival there* NA/PRO CO 5/862/121-ii-2.

61   *According to Holmes's description* NA/PRO CO 5/862/121-xii-1.

62   *The sloop was clearly getting under way* Ibid.

62   *Holmes warned again, and more* NA/PRO CO 5/862/121-xix-2.

62   *When the captain reappeared on deck* Ibid.

64   *As the* Swift *passed south of Ireland* Hepper, listing for the date August 18, 1702.

64   *It seemed certain that Jackson would* The subsequent information on Robert Jackson comes from Charnock, vol. 3, pp. 335 and 336, Pitcairn Jones—listing under "Jackson, Robert (1)."

64   *To establish his authority, Povey had quoted* NA/PRO CO 5/862 folio 121/II-1-2. The instructions from Queen Anne read, "That upon the complaints that had been made to Her Majesty of the irregular proceedings of ye Captains of some of Her ships of war in the impressing of seamen in several of the Plantations, Her Majesty had thought it fit to order and had given directions to her Lord High Admiral accordingly, that when any Captain or Commander of any of Her Majesty's Ships of War in any of Her Majesty's said Plantations should have occasion for seamen to serve on board Her Majesty's ships under their command, they do make their application to the Governors and Commanders in Chief of Her Majesty's Plantations respectively, to whom as Vice Admirals Her Majesty had been pleased to commit the sole power of impressing Seamen in any of Her Plantations in America, or in sight of any of them. Upon such application made to him by any of ye Commanders of Her Ships of War within her province of Massachusetts Bay to take care that Her Ships of War be furnished with the number of seamen that may be necessary for Her service on board them from time to time."

66   *The new governor was Joseph Dudley, the man* DAB, vol. 5, p. 482.

66   *In the fall of 1702, South Carolina's governor, James Moore* Leach, pp. 123–127.

67   *The governor of New France, Louis-Hector de Callière* Haefeli and Sweeney, pp. 38–41.

68   *Dudley was making progress with his peace* Ibid., pp. 88–92.

68   *Dudley opened the conference by* Penhallow, pp. 3–5.

7: Terror

70   *The community consisted of nearly* Bourne, pp. 234–249.

71   *One woman who was not involved* Parkman, vol. I, pp. 42–46.

71   *The morning exploded in violence* Ibid.

73   *As Penhallow records, "At first he"* Penhallow, p. 7.

73   *Just when it seemed likely* Ibid., p. 8.

73   *As a preview of the brutality that lay ahead* Ibid., p. 10.

74   *In an attack on Berwick* Ibid.

74   *In this instance another heroine emerged* Penhallow, p. 11.

74   *Motivated by the need for revenge* Retaliatory raids were led by Colonel John March, Captain Edward Tyng, and Caleb Lyman. These raids are recorded in Parkman, p. 50, and Penhallow, pp. 10 and 20–22.

75   *This time, command was given to Lieutenant Jean-Baptiste Hertel de Rouville* DCB, entry for "Hertel de Rouville, Jean-Baptiste."

75   *Springfield had been established in 1636* Haefeli and Sweeney, p. 14.

76   *Unlike the village of Wells, which was strewn* Ibid., pp. 16–22.

77   *Since the mid-1680s, Deerfield had benefited* Ibid., pp. 31–32.

77   *Queen Anne's War brought danger to the colonies* Ibid., pp. 96–97.

78   *The native contingent at Chambly consisted of* Ibid., p. 102–105.

79   *The fortification itself was old and weakened* Parkman, vol. I, p. 59.

80   *One of the larger homes, that of Reverend Williams* Ibid., pp. 62–65.

80   *In Williams's published account* Williams, pp. 10–12.

81   *The slain Hannah Sheldon was spared* Parkman, vol. I, p. 64.

82   *Despite numerous assaults by the raiders* Haefeli and Sweeney, pp. 117–121.

83   *The French and Indians had lost ten* Ibid., p. 123.

83   *Some of the Indians, recognizing* Williams, p. 14.

83   *The next morning, after one New Englander* Parkman, vol. I, p. 71.

84   *On March 7, a week* Williams, p. 20.

85   *The historian Francis Parkman observed* Parkman, vol. I, p. 73.

85   *Of the 111 who began the trek* Haefeli and Sweeney, p. 125.

8: RETRIBUTION

86   *To provide additional security for these settlements* Leach, p. 132.

87   *On May 15, ten weeks after the Deerfield attack* Penhallow, pp. 16–17; and McDougall, p. 92.

87   *They proceeded to a rendezvous* Ibid.

87   *Numerous other small settlements along the shores* Hutchinson, vol. 2, p. 108.

87   *In a lengthy report to Governor Dudley, Church* Church, p. 268.

88 *The feelings of revenge secured by the destruction* Peckham, p. 64.

88 *Over the several years that the captives remained* Haefeli and Sweeney, pp. 154–155.

88 *Ultimately, twenty-two of the Deerfield captives converted* Ibid., appendix F, p. 290.

89 *Dudley initially sent two Deerfield men* Ibid., pp. 165–167.

90 *The man chosen to command the voyage to Quebec* Parkman, vol. I, p. 103.

90 *These accusations broadened to include suspicions* Haefeli and Sweeney, pp. 172–175.

92 *In 1706, as captains in the Royal Navy continued* O'Callaghan, ed., vol. IV, pp. 1183–1184 (Lord Cornbury to Lords of Trade, October 3, 1706).

92 *The angry governor wrote* Ibid.

93 *As a result of the enmity that* O'Callaghan, ed., vol. V, p. 60 (Lord Cornbury to Lords of Trade, December 14, 1706).

93 *Unexpectedly, and to the great consternation* Clark, pp. 206–207.

93 *Among the provisions of the Sixth of Anne Lords Journals*, vol. XVIII, pp. 550–566.

94 *Massachusetts raised two regiments, the Red and the Blue* Peckham, p. 87.

94 *Lieutenant Colonel Samuel Appelton landed 350 men from the Red* Parkman, vol. I, p. 127.

95 *With the odds four to one against* Penhallow, pp. 42–43.

95 *The one professional English officer* Parkman, vol. I, pp. 128–129.

96 *Morpain, his ship, and his sailors* DCB, entry for "Morpain, Pierre," p. 1.

96 *There was better success in defense along the war's* Parkman, vol. I, pp. 96–97.

97 *The following year, de Rouville had his last opportunity* Haefeli and Sweeney, pp. 200–201.

9: The British Are Coming?

98 *In 1709, with Queen Anne's War in a stalemate* DCB, entry for "Vetch, Samuel."

98 *In July 1708, "Col. Vetch"* Penhallow, p. 49.

99 *They carried "her Majesty's"* Ibid., pp. 49–50.

100 *With the assurance of significant* Ibid., p. 50.

101   *In June, after Nicholson sent an advance party* Leach, p. 141.

101   *Vetch wrote to Lord Sunderland, warning that* Parkman, vol. I, p. 144, quoting Vetch to Lord Sunderland, letter of August 2, 1709; and Vetch to Lord Sunderland, letter of August 12, 1709.

101   *Word from Great Britain that the expedition had been "laid aside"* Peckham, p. 70.

102   *Samuel Penhallow expressed the discouragement* Penhallow, p. 50.

102   *The discontent with Britain's high-handed disregard* Leach, p. 142.

102   *Representatives from Massachusetts, Connecticut, Rhode Island* Peckham, p. 70.

102   *Their reticence seemed well-founded, until* Penhallow, pp. 51–52; and Parkman, vol. I, pp. 149–155.

103   *That night a British bomb ketch* Penhallow, p. 53.

104   *Nicholson sent one of his own officers with a response* Parkman, vol. I, p. 152.

104   *Nicholson's force then entered the fort* Leach, p. 143.

105   *Buoyed by this success, General Nicholson returned to England* Peckham, p. 71; and Leach, pp. 143–144.

105   *The commander in chief of the expedition was Sir Hovenden Walker* DCB, entry for "Walker, Sir Hovenden."

105   *Nevertheless, the colonials realized* Penhallow, p. 63.

106   *Admiral Walker accused the people of Boston* Leach, p. 147.

106   *The ill will that developed fueled long-lasting antipathy* To make this point, Parkman in vol. I, pp. 166–167, quotes from a letter of July 25, 1711, from a British officer, Colonel King of the artillery, to Secretary of State St. John, which said, "You'll find in my Journal what Difficultyes we mett with through the Misfortune that the Coloneys were not inform'd of our Coming two Months sooner, and through the Interestedness, ill Nature, and Sowerness of these People, whose Government, Doctrine, and Manners, whose Hypocracy and canting, are unsupportable; and no man living but one of Gen'l Hill's good Sense and good Nature could have managed them. But if such a Man mett with nothing he could depend on, altho' vested with the Queen's Royal Power and Authority, and Supported be a Number of Troops sufficient to reduce by force all the Coloneys, 't'is easy to determine the Respect and Obedience her Majesty may reasonably expect from them."

106   *The army commander, General Hill, owed his* Leach, p. 144.

107   *He was also traumatized by the* Ibid., pp. 150–152; and Walker, *Journal* introduction.

108 *Ironically, after the admiral's departure from his flagship* DCB, entry for "Walker, Sir Hovenden," p. 3; and Penhallow, p. 67.

108 **Samuel Penhallow once again gave voice** Penhallow, p. 66.

108 *The man who was most furious over the disaster* Leach, p. 153.

10: PEACE AND PREPARATION IN FRENCH CANADA

110 *Ironically, the last significant Indian attack* Penhallow, pp. 73–74.

110 *During the months of negotiations* Parkman, vol. I, pp. 185–186.

111 *The Treaty of Utrecht, signed on April 11, 1713* Peckham, p. 73.

112 *The French government would not allow* McLennan, pp. 10–15.

113 *Representatives of Massachusetts and New* Penhallow, pp. 74–80.

113 *In the agreement, the Indians agreed* Ibid., p. 78.

113 *In order to ensure a Protestant succession* Williams, pp. 10–13.

113 *In the New World, the French governor Vaudreuil* DCB, entry for "Rigaud de Vaudreuil, Philippe de, Marquis de Vaudreuil," p. 5.

114 *One, from Quebec, carried the hero* McLennan, pp. 11–13.

115 *Under Saint-Ovide's command, the two* Declaration of French Officers, quoted in ibid., pp. 11–12.

117 *As Port St. Louis, it carried the name* Johnston, *Control and Order*, pp. 10 and 11.

117 *Just over a year later, on September 1, 1715* McLennan, p. 41.

118 *The legendary young privateer Pierre Morpain* DCB, entry for "Morpain, Pierre," p. 1.

118 *By the time their new king, Louis XV* Julian Gwyn and Christopher Moore, in introduction to Lacroix-Girard, p. 17.

118 *The French minister of marine, Count Pontchartrain* McLennan, p. 22.

119 *Two hillocks, about one thousand feet inland from* Johnston, *Control and Order*, Map fig. XXVIII.

120 *A similar situation existed on Cape Breton* Ibid., p. 17.

121 *Within the citadel would be found the crowning glory of Louisbourg* Way.

122 *The first mercenaries, fifty soldiers from what* McLennan, pp. 49, 87, 91; and Johnston, *Control and Order*, p. 47.

123 *The fortress plan called for the orderly development* Johnston, *Control and Order*, pp. 97–100.

123 *At the head of the social order were the governor and* McLennan, pp. 44–46; Johnston, *Control and Order*, pp. 19–34; and *A Louisbourg Primer*.

125 *By 1730, the hospital of the Brothers of Charity* Johnston, *Control and Order*, pp. 23–24.

125 *Farther to the west, enterprising New Englanders saw* Donald F. Chard, "The Price and Profits of Accommodation: Massachusetts/Louisbourg Trade, 1713–1744," in Allis, ed., pp. 131–151.

11: FRAGILE PEACE AND SALUTARY NEGLECT

128 *Her new Germanic king, George I, went through* McDougall, p. 117; and Williams, p. 185.

128 *Walpole followed his favorite principle* Williams, pp. 192–193.

128 *This policy worked for twenty-five years* Burke, vol. I, p. 186.

129 *Highlanders, Lowland Scots, and even the Ulster Scots* Taylor, p. 317.

129 *Another source of fresh energy* German immigrants also had the encouragement of having a Hanoverian German on the English throne.

130 *When the issue threatened to cut off the flow* Taylor, p. 303.

130 *At the time in England there were 160 offenses* Ibid., p. 314.

131 *The preponderance of Africans who made the Middle Passage* Ibid., p. 324.

131 *James Oglethorpe proposed a new colony* McDougall, pp. 129–130; and Moore, pp. 3–9.

131 *In 1739, he wrote, "If we allow Slaves"* Taylor, pp. 242–243.

132 *With diplomatic courtesies, the two* Lanning, pp. 44–45.

132 *Neither country wanted or could afford* DCB, entry for "Rale (Rale, Rasle, Rasles), Sebastien," pp. 1–2.

134 *From correspondence between Vaudreuil* Parkman, vol. I, pp. 235–236.

135 *The attack was accomplished with complete surprise* Penhallow, p. 105.

135 *When the French governor denied the charge* Parkman, vol. I, p. 251.

136 *Once again, the New Englanders were* Peckham, p. 85; and Parkman, vol. 1, pp. 261–267.

137 *With the growth of the population* McDougall, p. 123.

137 *New England was still the most densely populated* Purvis, p. 128.

138 *Distillers throughout the colonies used molasses* McDougall, p. 117.

138 *The first settlers and soldiers reached Louisbourg in 1713* Chard, in Allis, ed., p. 134.

138 *Those ships that did make the return voyage carried* NA/PRO CO6/794 folio 85, Massachusetts House of Representatives to Governor Shute, November 1720.

139   *Ships were sent on triangular voyages* Chard, in Allis, ed., pp. 139–146.

140   *In correspondence with Governor Saint-Ovide, Faneuil* Ibid., p. 148.

141   *The practitioners of this trade were evangelical ministers* McDougall, pp. 127–135.

12: Captain Jenkins's Ear

144   *The Spanish dealt violently with English mariners* Pares, p. 17.

144   *Conveniently, he had preserved his severed ear* Lanning, pp. 130–131.

145   *Walpole, however, continued to work for peace* Williams, pp. 208–210.

145   *In mid-May 1739, the* **asiento** Lanning, p. 133.

145   *The colonial governors granted "commissions of marque"* Ibid., p. 142.

146   *The keel for this 115-ton brig* Chapin, *Tartar,* pp. 2–4.

146   *Captain Edward Vernon was tapped to make good* DNB, vol. LVIII, pp. 268–269.

147   *His audacity and force made* Leach, pp. 210 and 211.

147   *News of this first great victory* Williams, p. 234.

148   *His plan called for his force to attack* Leach, pp. 214–215.

150   *In an astute political move* Harding, p. 75.

151   *When his mother died* Cooper, "Lawrence Washington," p. 516.

151   *To oversee the sensitive recruitment process* Harkness, pp. 62–63.

152   *The American Regiment was a mixed bag* Harding, p. 74.

153   *While the majority of the men* Ibid., p. 69.

153   *An eyewitness describing the ordeal* Smollett, "An Account...," pp. 429–430.

153   *A month into the voyage* Ibid., p. 431.

154   *The historian and novelist Tobias* Ibid., pp. 431–432.

154   *During this last stretch of their* Ibid., pp. 432–433.

155   *Disgusted and discouraged, the Americans debarked* Harkness, p. 72.

155   *As the British historian John W. Fortescue* Fortescue, p. 62.

156   *In his* **An Account of the Expedition Against Cartagena** Knowles, p. 28 (CO 5/41, p. 295).

157   *The defense of the city was* Fernandez, pp. 8–10.

158   *As Smollett witnessed and recorded* Smollett, "An Account...," p. 435.

13: Cartagena!

159   *The Spanish, well aware of the strategic* Daily Post, London, June 4, 1741.

160   *The brief action was described* Knowles, p. 3 (CO 5/41, p. 282).

161   *The Shrewsbury was badly mauled* Ibid., footnote "B," p. 3 (CO 5/41, p. 282).

161   *Vernon sent five hundred men ashore* Lanning, p. 193; Harkness, p. 76; and Smollett, "An Account . . . ," p. 438.

162   *Unfortunately, the inexperienced Wentworth chose* Harding, p. 194.

162   *There was, however, friction on the Spanish* Fernandez, p. 18.

162   *As Smollett observed, "Next day"* Smollett, "An Account . . . ," p. 439.

163   *As Vernon had predicted, the Spanish did not stand* Fortescue, p. 68.

163   *Having seen the Spaniards flee from* Lanning, p. 194.

164   *Vernon wrote to his wife* Moorhouse, Vernon letter of March 31, 1741.

165   *The success was celebrated in ballads* DNB, vol. LVIII, p. 270.

165   *To further commemorate the triumph* Storer, in *Massachusetts Historical Society Proceedings* LII, p. 209.

165   *In Philadelphia they celebrated* New England Weekly Journal, May 26, 1741, p. 1.

165   *In Newport, Rhode Island, "having"* Ibid., p. 2.

166   *And in Charleston, South Carolina* New England Weekly Journal, June 9, 1741, p. 1.

166   *In addition to the filth and crowded conditions* Smollett, *Roderick Random*, pp. 185–186.

167   *The keen observer Smollett set down* Smollett, "An Account . . . ," p. 448.

168   *The force included 450 grenadiers* Ibid., p. 451.

168   *An officer in the Massachusetts troops* New England Weekly Journal, June 30, 1741.

168   *At this point, the disillusioned Americans* Smollett, "An Account . . . ," p. 452.

169   *Smollett, writing as a medical man* Ibid., p. 453.

170   *Wentworth had only 1,909 of the original* Harding, pp. 123–124.

172   *In his letter of November 2, 1741* General Wentworth to the Duke of Newcastle, NA/PRO CO5/42, November 2, 1741, pp. 96–98.

172   *They began with a general complaint* Field officers of Colonel Cooch's regiment to General Wentworth, NA/PRO CO 5/42, February 3, 1742, pp. 116–119.

173   *The Americans' formal complaint* Harding, pp. 123–144.

175   *Their officers, in the complaint* Field officers of Colonel Cooch's regiment to General Wentworth, NA/PRO CO 5/42, February 3, 1742, p. 119.

175   *For Rhode Island, the impact was* Letter from Richard Partridge to King George II, April 15, 1746, Rhode Island Historical Society.

175   *Those deaths represented a higher percentage* This is based on 9,750 Massachusetts World War II deaths when the 1940 Massachusetts population was 4,316,721, compared with 450 deaths when the 1740 Massachusetts population was 151,613. Also, the loss of .297 percent of the population of 6,349,097 in 2000.

14: Promise Fulfilled

178   *He was quickly at odds with* Johnston, *Control and Order*, pp. 183–184.

178   *The primary purchases were, "principally"* Letter from Maurepas, May 26, 1739, Archives Nationales, France, Archives des Colonies, B., vol. 68, F, pp. 347–348.

178   *Stumping around on a peg that replaced his left leg* DCB Online, entry for "Le Prévost DuQuesnel, Jean-Baptiste-Louis," p. 1.

179   *On the day Duvivier set off for Canso, the people of Boston* Johnston, *Summer*, p. 28.

181   *In one instance, Detcheverry* Ibid., p. 31.

181   *With reports that there were six French* Chapin, *Privateering*, p. 74, and *Tartar*, p. 16.

182   *Less than a week later, on Saturday, June 23* Chapin, *Privateering*, pp. 74–76.

183   *The French captain surrendered his* Boston *Weekly News-Letter*, June 29, 1744.

183   *The New England guard ships and privateers patrolled* Rawlyk, p. 21.

183   *When Captain Tyng arrived in Boston towing* Chapin, *Privateering*, pp. 76–77. Note: The silver urn awarded to Captain Tyng survives and is in the collection of the Boston Museum of Fine Arts.

183   *His prisoner, Captain d'Olabaratz, was kept under arrest* McLennan, pp. 121–122.

183   *There is speculation that William Shirley* DCB, entry for "Olabaratz (De Laubara, Dolobarats), Joannis-Galand D'," p. 1.

184   *Bradstreet was born in Annapolis Royal* DCB, entry for "Bradstreet, John (baptized Jean-Baptiste)," p. 1.

184   *In addition, the New Englanders were forced to agree* As the privateers waged their war at sea and the number of prisoners on each

side grew during the summer of 1744, another land campaign was launched by the French. With the easy victory at Canso, DuQuesnel logically turned his attention to Annapolis Royal, which had been in British hands since the New England conquest in 1710. If he could recapture Annapolis Royal, DuQuesnel could reclaim all of Acadia for France. It would be a significant prize and an instant morale boost. The first attack on Annapolis Royal was made not by French troops, but by a group of Micmac Indians led, in the tradition of Father Rale, by a missionary, Jean-Louis Le Loutre. The Indians surprised and killed two British soldiers who were unarmed and outside the palisade and then tested the resolve of those inside the little fort. The British, under the able command of Paul Mascarene, fired cannons and muskets at the attackers, and the Indians retired to a safe location to await two ships carrying reinforcements from Louisbourg. They had to wait only four days before they saw two ships entering the harbor of Annapolis Royal, but one of the ships was Captain Tyng's *Prince of Orange* and the other was a troop transport. They were reinforcements, but for the British, not for Le Loutre and his Micmacs. Mascarene and his men were overjoyed by the providential arrival of Tyng and the new men and were further relieved when the priest and his band gave up their attack and returned to Minas, almost one hundred miles to the east.

However, Annapolis Royal was too important a target, and DuQuesnel planned a more serious military and naval operation. To lead the land campaign, DuQuesnel chose the officer who had performed so well at Canso, François Duvivier. In order not to weaken the defenses of Louisbourg, Duvivier departed for Annapolis Royal with a small force of only thirty soldiers and picked up an additional twenty on the Île St. Jean. They were taken by sea to the Nova Scotia mainland and from there began an overland march toward Annapolis Royal. DuQuesnel anticipated that as Duvivier made his way through Acadia, the formerly French residents who had been subjected to British rule for thirty-four years would leap at the chance to overthrow their oppressors and rally to Duvivier's call. To the consternation of the French force, the great majority of the Acadians preferred to remain neutral. Life had not been difficult under British governance, and they were fearful of the treatment and retribution they would experience if the French attempt at conquest failed. In early September, when Duvivier arrived before Annapolis Royal, the place of his birth, his force had grown to only 280, with the majority being Indians, both Malecite and Micmac. Knowing that his force could not hope to take the fort, which was defended by a nearly equal number of soldiers, Duvivier put on a grand display of force, marching his men around at some distance from the fort and giving the impression that he had more men than he actually did. The French commander was now dependent on the naval side of the campaign, the arrival of the new fifty-two-gun ship the *Caribou*, which had been built in Quebec and placed under the command of Pierre Morpain, and the *Ardent*, a sixty-four-gun French ship that was expected to arrive in Louisbourg in August. Having received confirmation that the ships should arrive at Annapolis Royal around September 8, Duvivier took a bold step. He informed Mascarene that these two powerful warships were soon to arrive and gave the British the opportunity to surrender. Mascarene called a meeting of his officers, who advised him to accept the offer, but Mascarene, to the delight of his troops, ignored the advice and refused the offer. Duvivier then began a series of night attacks, which harassed the British but did not reveal the small numbers on the French side. For two weeks the inconsequential skirmishes continued, while Duvivier constantly searched the harbor entrance for the *Caribou* and *Ardent*. On September 26, the sails of two ships were sighted, but just as with Father Le Loutre months earlier, these proved to be Captain John Gorham's Rangers, a select group of fifty men, mostly Mohawks and men of race who were the "special forces" of their day. They reversed the military balance at Annapolis Royal. With these formidable reinforcements joining Mascarene's men in the fort, Duvivier's potential for success was entirely dependent on the arrival of the *Caribou* and the *Ardent*. Despite this blow to his campaign, Duvivier and his force stayed in place until they received official word a week later that the French ships would not be coming. With no hope for success and orders to return to Louisbourg, Duvivier abandoned his quest and the impotent siege of Annapolis Royal was lifted. . . . Biography of John Gorham, John Gorham Papers, Clements Library, University of Michigan at Ann Arbor.

185   *In his report he said: "I have"* D'Olabaratz report quoted in McLennan, p. 129.

15. AUDACIOUS PLAN

186   *Bradstreet later admitted that he had "fixed" the intelligence* Bradstreet, in de Forest, *Louisbourg Journals*, p. 172.

187   *That man was William Vaughn, a rash and impetuous* Goold, pp. 295–296.

187   *He met with Bradstreet and heard his account* NA/PRO CO 5/753 folio 15.

187   *Lieutenant Governor George Clark of New York, Christopher Kilby* Rawlyk, pp. 30–34.

188   *As the session convened, the legislators were shocked* Parkman, vol. II, pp. 66–67.

189   *Within a day of receiving the court's response* Rawlyk, pp. 37–39.

189   *The ambitious Vaughn wrote a letter* Letter from Vaughn to Shirley, January 14, 1745, in McLennan, p. 360.

190   *The acting governor was Louis Du Pont Duchambon* DCB, entry for "Duchambon, Louis Du Pont," pp. 1–2.

191   *Duchambon's fragile grip on conditions at Louisbourg* McLennan, pp. 123–124.

191   *Quickly, one of their officers, Ensign* Johnston, *Control and Order*, pp. 208–209.

191   *A few, including Major De La Parelle* McLennan, pp. 123–124.

192   *Vaughn carried a message from Governor Shirley* Parkman, vol. II, p. 71.

193   *Governor Shirley faced the particular challenge of selecting* Rawlyk, pp. 41–43.

193   *In a later letter Bradstreet wrote* Bradstreet, in de Forest, *Louisbourg Journals*, p. 171.

196   *At that point Rhode Island's zeal cooled, but it did commit* Parkman, vol. II, pp. 71–72.

196   *He said, "Fortified towns are hard nuts to crack"* Labaree, *The Papers...*, vol. III, p. 26.

197   *While soliciting the assistance of the other colonies* Rawlyk, p. 55.

198   *The Great Awakening had heightened the religious fervor* Parkman, vol. II, p. 80.

198   *With Whitefield's words* **Nil desperandum Christo duce** Ibid., p. 77.

16: Voyage to War

199   *He was a fourth-generation American, his great-grandfather* de Forest, ed., *Pomeroy,* p. 1.

199   *Seth's birth came two years after three Pomeroys* Haefeli and Sweeney, appendix D, p. 285.

201   *Most brought their personal weapons* de Forest, ed., *Louisbourg Journals*, p. 2.

201   *Sailing with Tyng was the twenty-four-gun* **Molineux** Chapin, *N. E. Vessels*, p. 61.

202   *A week after his arrival in Boston, Pomeroy* de Forest, ed., *Pomeroy*, p. 16.

202   *Commodore Rous had over fifty ships* Chapin, *N. E. Vessels*, pp. 60–62.

203   *In the words of Seth Pomeroy* de Forest, ed., *Pomeroy*, pp. 15–16.

204   *One of the chroniclers of the ordeal, Benjamin Stearns* Stearns, "Louisbourg Diary," pp. 137–138.

204   *When Seth Pomeroy later wrote to his wife* de Forest, ed., *Pomeroy*, p. 56.

205   *Fortunately, at the end of Shirley's detailed instructions* Rawlyk, p. 61.

206   *The* **Boston Packet** *captured a sloop from Martinique* Chapin, *N. E. Vessels*, pp. 63–64.

206   *In February, the* **Renommee,** *a new French frigate* Balcom, *The Siege*, p. 10.

206   *The following day, as the* **Renommee** Chapin, *N. E. Vessels*, pp. 65–66.

208   *He was encouraged to, "as occasion shall offer"* NA/PRO CO 5/809.

209   *In his initial January 29 letter to Warren requesting* Quoted in McLennan, p. 140.

212   *During the first week of April, the* **Tartar** *from* Chapin, *Tartar*, p. 24.

212   *The situation was grim since the bigger ship* Notre Dame brief, *Massachusetts Historical Society Collections*, 1st ser., I (1792): 24; and NA/PRO HCA, 42/41 Box 2, deposition of Captain Fones of the *Tartar*.

212   *Yet that was Fones's self-sacrificing decision* Fones letter, Rhode Island State Archives, Letters, p. 139.

213   *In a final desperate attempt* Notre Dame brief, NA/ PRO HCA, 42/41 Box 2, deposition of Captain Fones of the *Tartar*.

213   *The day after the* **Tartar's** *sacrifice, the* **Defence** *successfully* Bidwell, "Journal," p. 153.

213   *That news arrived the following morning* Chapin, *N. E. Vessels*, p. 68.

213   *Demonstrating their character and commitment* Bidwell, "Journal," p. 153.

213   *Apparently, Captain Kersaint had had enough* Balcom, *La Renommee*, p. 10.

17: THE LANDING

215 *On a foggy Sunday, April 28, Major Seth* de Forest, ed., *Pomeroy,* p. 21.

216 *One soldier expressed his mixed emotions* de Forest, ed., *Louisbourg Journals,* 1st journal, p. 9.

216 *The* Saint-Dominique *from Saint-Jean-de-Luz* Lacroix-Girard, p. 66.

217 *Taking further precautions, Duchambon ordered* Ibid., pp. 67–68.

217 *The blockade seemed to be weakening* Wrong, *Habitant,* pp. 31–32.

219 *Duchambon wasted precious time by assembling* Greer, "Soldiers of Isle Royale," p. 49.

220 *The fleet came to anchor at about nine A.M. on what* de Forest, ed., *Pomeroy,* p. 21.

220 *The elite troops of Colonel John Gorham's Rangers* Rawlyk, pp. 84–87; and biography of John Gorham, Clements Library, University of Michigan at Ann Arbor.

222 *After a short skirmish the fight was over* McLennan, pp. 149–150.

223 *As thousands of Americans fought their way* Lacroix-Girard, pp. 70–71.

223 *Pepperrell did not establish an immediate central command* de Forest, ed., *Louisbourg Journals,* p. 10.

223 *The scouts had additional success* Rawlyk, p. 88.

224 *Many were still wet from wading ashore and* de Forest, ed., *Louisbourg Journals,* p. 10.

224 *If there was confidence and optimism in the* Wrong, *Habitant,* pp. 38–39.

225 *At thirty-five, Gridley was a skilled and respected* DAB, vol. VII, pp. 611–612.

225 *As one soldier recorded, "We had no"* de Forest, ed., *Louisbourg Journals,* p. 11.

225 *Pepperrell assigned the leadership of the first expedition* NA/PRO CO 5/753, p. 139.

226 *By the early hours of the morning* Letter, Waldo to Pepperrell, May 3, 1745, "The Pepperrell Papers," p. 143.

226 *In the early light of the morning, Vaughn* Rawlyk, pp. 94–95.

228 *This predicament had begun on the first night* Ibid., pp. 90–91.

228 *Etienne Verrier, the resident engineer at Louisbourg* DCB, entry for "Verrier, Etienne," p. 2.

228 *His proposal was accepted, and Duchambon* Letter, Duchambon to de Thierry, quoted in Rawlyk, p. 91.

229   *Leaving four of his men to defend the fort* NA/PRO CO 5/753,
      p. 140.

18: ADVICE AND DISSENT

231   *When Colonel John Bradstreet arrived to relieve* Bradstreet to Pep-
      perrell, May 2, 1745, *Massachusetts Historical Society Collections*,
      6th ser., X (1899): 138.

231   *Gunsmith Seth Pomeroy arrived, and by ten* de Forest, ed. *Pomeroy*,
      pp. 22–23.

232   *The first shelters were crude, but eventually* Rawlyk, p. 101; and de
      Forest, ed., *Louisbourg Journals*, p. 12.

232   *Seeming to admit the weakness of his own blockade* Warren to
      Pepperrell, May 2, 1745, in de Forest, ed., *Louisbourg Journals*, p.
      189.

233   *Expressing his concerns, Warren wrote,* Peter Warren's plan, in
      ibid., pp. 190–194.

235   *On May 6, he argued his point to the war council* Rawlyk,
      pp. 106–107.

235   *"Wee Cannot hearken to any Such Proposals"* de Forest, ed., *Louis-
      bourg Journals*, p. 14.

235   *The force set out in whaleboats* Rawlyk, pp. 109–111.

236   *Warren was aware of the reticence of the troops* de Forest, ed.,
      Louisbourg Journals, p. 15.

236   *The minutes of the war council reflected* Massachusetts Historical
      Society Collections, 6th ser., X (1899): 17.

237   *The feat was graphically described* de Forest, ed., *Louisbourg Jour-
      nals*, pp. 69–70.

238   *One of the witnesses recorded* Bradstreet, "Diary," p. 427.

238   *It was also hoped that a relief force* This force of French soldiers,
      along with Micmac and Malecite Indians, was led by Paul Marin
      de la Malgue, a fifty-three-year-old veteran who had spent twenty
      years on the Canadian western frontier among the Sioux, Fox, and
      Sauk tribes. He had the confidence of the governor of New France,
      who said Marin was always ready to risk his life for France. As King
      George's War broke out, Marin was in eastern Canada and put his
      Indian experience to work creating a respected force. In April 1745,
      confident that Louisbourg would not be attacked, Duchambon had
      urged that Marin and his band of men be sent against Annapolis
      Royal, but on May 5, with Louisbourg under siege, Duchambon

sent an urgent message to Marin asking him to head immediately for Louisbourg. Confident that the French naval and land forces would arrive in the near future, the people of Louisbourg, still adequately supplied with provisions and munitions, simply had to wait out the siege. Sources: "He had the confidence of the governor" DCB, entry for "Marin de la Malgue, Paul," p. 1; and "In April 1745, confident that Louisbourg" Parkman, vol. II, p. 294.

238 *A French cannonball tore through* This was recorded by an American soldier, thought to be Dudley Bradstreet. Bradstreet, "Diary," p. 428.

239 *While Pepperrell and Warren were outwardly cordial* Massachusetts Historical Society Collections, 6th ser., X (1899): 330.

239 *On a raid into the interior* de Forest, ed., Louisbourg Journals, p. 16 and p. 76.

239 *Encouraged by the French, the Indians* Bradstreet, "Diary," p. 428.

240 *Acting quickly to defuse this volatile* Massachusetts Historical Society Collections, 6th ser., X (1899): 19.

241 *The journal from the sloop* Journal of the Sloop UNION, p. 10.

242 *Supplying these forward batteries* Rawlyk, p. 123.

242 *Directing his large force of diggers* NA/PRO CO 5/753, pp. 139–140.

243 *This sad fiasco confirmed that Vaughn's* Rawlyk, p. 126.

243 *Her commander, Alexandre de la Maisonfort du Boisdecourt, had* McLennan, p. 156.

245 *Drawing eighteen feet two and a half inches, she could not have* Lyon, p. 197.

245 *Colonel John Bradstreet said, "It would be difficult"* de Forest, ed., Louisbourg Journals, p. 173.

245 *An eyewitness, the French diarist Gilles Lacroix-Girard* Lacroix-Girard, p. 79.

246 *Pepperrell once again turned his attention* Rawlyk, pp. 126–130.

247 *Lieutenant Daniel Giddings recorded the feelings* Giddings, p. 300.

19: DEFEAT OR VICTORY IN THE BALANCE

249 *On the day after the disastrous attack* Warren to Pepperrell, May 26, 1745, Massachusetts Historical Society Collections, 1st ser., I (1792): 32–34.

251 *Using the sledges devised earlier* Rawlyk, p. 138.

251 *The emplacement was configured so that* de Forest, ed., Louisbourg Journals, p. 89.

251   *The battle took a terrifying twist when* Rawlyk, p. 137.

251   *There seemed to be little compunction* Ibid.

251   *He reported that there were 3,600 soldiers* Pepperrell to Warren,
          Massachusetts Historical Society Collections, 6th ser., X (1899):
          262.

251   *Countering this sobering information* Bradstreet, "Diary," p. 43.

252   *He delivered Maisonfort's letter, which read in part* Parkman, vol.
          II, pp. 125–126.

253   *The first anonymous diarist, known only* Wrong, *Habitant*, p. 57.

253   *The French diarist Gilles Lacroix-Girard, a witness* Lacroix-
          Girard, pp. 93–94.

253   *The disrespect and contempt that the* Wrong, *Habitant*, pp. 57–58.

254   *Amid this atmosphere on June 9* Bradstreet, "Diary," p. 433.

254   *In a light breeze at dawn* Chapin, *Tartar*, pp. 37–42.

255   *Describing the two-and-a-half-hour battle, Donohue* Pote, foot-
          note, pp. 41–42.

256   *Of nineteen mortar shells fired, seventeen* de Forest, ed., *Louisbourg
          Journals*, p. 119.

257   *The forty-two-pounders from the advanced battery* Wrong, *Habi-
          tant*, p. 60.

258   *The artillery captain, Allard St. Marie, confirmed* Lacroix-Girard, p.
          42.

258   *François Bigot, the* **commissaire-ordonnateur** *of Louisbourg*
          Quoted in Parkman, *Atlantic Monthly*, p. 626.

258   *As these discussions were being held* Seth Pomeroy, who was in the
          formation with his troops, said, "Comodore Worren made a Fine
          Speech To ye army & marched through Together with ye General
          & Some other Gentlemen and agreed with the General & Pub-
          blickly with ye whole army that as soon as ye wind & weather
          Should Favour he with all his Ships Shou'd go into ye harber In-
          gage ye Island Battre & ye Citty: we upon ye Land with all our
          Forces at ye Same Time Shou'd Ingage them with all our artillery
          & Escaling Ladders." Source: de Forest, ed. *Pomeroy*, p. 35.

259   *Encouraged that the siege and blockade had been* McLennan, quote
          Warren and Pepperrell to Duchambon, p. 179.

259   *The generous agreement began with a provision* Massachusetts His-
          torical Society Collections, 6th ser., X (1899). 67–69.

259   *One anonymous American soldier* de Forest, ed., *Louisbourg Jour-
          nals*, p. 91.

260   *One other provision prohibited the French* McLennan, p. 165.

261   *They had made New England's* de Forest, ed., *Louisbourg Journals*, p. 27.

20: OPPORTUNITY SQUANDERED

263   *In agreeing to offer the honors of war* McLennan, pp. 179–180.

264   *He wrote, "I desire the favour"* Pepperrell to Duchambon, June 17, 1745, *Massachusetts Historical Society Collections*, 1st ser., I (1792): 46.

264   *In a report sent to Thomas Corbett* Gwyn, ed., *The Warren Papers*, p. 121.

265   *As soon as the surrender took place and the American* Pepperrell, *Journal*, p. 166.

266   *It was, in fact, at four* A.M. *Boston Gazette*, July 9, 1745.

266   *The* **New York Weekly Post-Boy** *summed up* Letter published in the *New York Weekly Post-Boy*, July 22, 1745.

266   *The* **Boston Gazette** *emphasized this as an American victory* *Boston Gazette*, July 16, 1745.

266   *Shirley expressed his restrained enthusiasm* Shirley to Pepperrell, July 7, 1745, *Massachusetts Historical Society Collections*, 6th ser., X (1899): 320–322.

267   *Montague was affronted by the fact that the fast* Montague to Warren, June 22, 1745, in Gwyn, ed., *The Warren Papers*, pp. 129–130.

268   *The guns of the Tower of London* Gwyn, *Admiral*, p. 105.

268   *One poem in England's* **Gentleman's Magazine** "A Poetical Essay on the Reduction of Cape Breton on June 17, 1745," *Gentleman's Magazine* XVI (1746).

268   *A number of highly placed officials, including* Gwyn, *Admiral*, p. 105.

269   *The leader of the government, Henry Pelham* Williams, quoting Coxe, p. 261.

269   *Captain Pierre Morpain said, as recorded* de Forest, ed., *Louisbourg Journals*, p. 130.

269   *In the August 1745 edition of the* **Craftsman** *Craftsman*, August 1745.

270   *A French merchant ship, the* **Saint-François-Xavier** de Forest, ed., *Louisbourg Journals*, p. 27; also Lacroix-Girard, footnote 53, p. 99.

270   *Warren's share of the proceeds of this prize* Gwyn, *Enterprising Admiral*, p. 19.

270   *As one soldier recorded, "A great Noys"* de Forest, ed., *Louisbourg Journals*, p. 92.

270 *The French chronicler the Habitant sings the praises* Wrong, *Habitant*, p. 65.

271 *Writing to Pepperrell, Warren once again used a chastising tone* Warren to Pepperrell, July 1, 1745, in Gwyn, ed., *The Warren Papers*, p. 131.

271 *He wrote to the Duke of Newcastle* Warren to Newcastle, June 18, 1745, Gwyn, ed., *The Warren Papers*, p. 125.

272 *Reflecting the general feeling among the* Durell, pp. 3 and 4.

273 *The previous evening, a large French ship* Chapin, *Vessels*, pp. 106–108.

275 *One of the American officers, William Waldron* Waldron to Waldron, quoted in Gwyn, *Admiral*, p. 103, and footnote 14, p. 189.

275 *This policy was sworn to in a deposition* Sworn deposition of Daniel Fones, NA/PRO HCA 42/41 Box 2.

276 *Since there could be no challenge to his claim* Grahame, pp. 1–8.

276 *The annual salary for the lieutenant governor* de Forest, ed., *Louisbourg Journals*, p. 178.

277 *The earl said with regard to the American troops* Quoted in McLennan, p. 172.

278 *He reached Boston on July 29 and, after* de Forest, ed. *Pomeroy*, pp. 46–48.

278 *On July 16, the commodore reprimanded* "The Pepperrell Papers," pp. 327–328.

278 *Warren was speaking as if* Ibid., pp. 333–334.

279 *He wrote to the governor* Ibid., p. 330.

279 *One soldier recorded, "His Excellency Made"* de Forest, ed., *Louisbourg Journals*, p. 43.

280 *It became immediately clear that despite* Ibid., pp. 45–46.

281 *However, Warren and his wife each donated* Boston Weekly News-Letter, December 19, 1745, p. 3.

281 *He wrote to Henry Pelham and critically pointed* Gwyn, ed., *The Warren Papers*, p. 165.

21: DISINTEGRATION

283 *In a further reflection of Warren's lack* Gwyn, ed., *The Warren Papers*, p. 187.

284 *His journal gives the most grim and graphic* de Forest, ed., *Louisbourg Journals*, pp. 121–169. The entry for November 1 read, "Morning citadel and after prayers visitd—Charles Colton in one

of the rooms in the Hospitall, who is amiss—and visited at capt. Isaac Coltons and prayd with them—J Pease is taken (ill) anew there. visitd and prayd with mr. metcalf visitd—dr. pearse—visitd at major Twings. And prayd—old mr puffer of Wrentham is dead in that house; visitd at the colonels—House—and prayd—in two Rooms—Sergt. Wait and one Kimberly are very bad, visited at Collonell Williams and prayd—with Smith who is yet alive—dined at home—afternoon visitd and prayd—at capt doolittles—and—in both rooms in the House, where capt. Baker livd—with Joseph Cooley, and with mr Raynolds—and with mr osborn—visitd—in the Evening at dr Taylors—Lt. Morgan of Cape Ann dyd—and a Lieuetenant of capt. Lights company, and another of N Hampshire men, one Durham, and mr Thos Sewell, of collonell Storers company, one of Lt Throops men, and one of capt. Fitchs men and 2 at Grand Battery and one of Capt. Frys-, and one of capt. Rhodes men."

284 *On January 28, 1746, Pepperrell and Warren* "The Pepperrell Papers," p. 442.

285 *Four years earlier, as the devastating news* Boston Weekly News-Letter, May 28, 1741.

285 *With the governor away, Forrest approached* Statements relevant to the *Wager* case, 1745, NA/PRO SP 42/30, pp. 107–134.

286 *They wrote complaining of "the violent Spirit"* Letter to the Earl of Granville from the Earl of Sandwich, A. Hamilton and G. Anson, February 11, 1746, NA/PRO SP 42/30, pp. 108–109.

286 *The frustration for the colonies grew* Lax and Pencak, p. 179.

288 *One disgruntled colleague wrote* Chauncy to Pepperrell, January 18, 1746, Belknap Papers, 1745–1746, vol. 33, Massachusetts Historical Society, Boston.

289 *Before the weary Americans departed* Undated copy of the speech, signed by Commodore Warren, in the Fogg Autograph Collection, Maine Historical Society, Portland.

289 *It was a fine speech, but in* Craft, *Journal*, p. 194.

292 *Warren was to command the naval force* Osgood, *Eighteenth Century*, vol. III, p. 535; and Gywn, *Admiral*, pp. 114–119.

293 *The New England troops numbered over* Parkman, vol. II, pp. 152–153.

293 *From their first moments at sea, the French* Ibid., pp. 157–168.

296 *Vaughn backed up his claims with* NA/PRO CO 5/753, pp. 136–167.

296 *A letter from one such friend indicates* Quoted in Goold, p. 308.

299 *Shirley refused to turn over the officer* Hutchinson, *History*, vol. II p. 331.

300 *However, recognizing the legitimacy of the cause* Boston Weekly *News-Letter*, December 17, 1747.

22: BETRAYAL

303 *For example, in October 1711, the* Boston Weekly News-Letter *Boston Weekly News-Letter*, October 1–8, 1711.

303 *In a statement to the readers, the paper's Independent Advertiser*, January 4, 1748.

305 *They lashed out against the government* Irvin, p. 35.

305 *The author, almost certainly Samuel Adams* Lax and Pencak, "Knowles," p. 204.

305 *Feeling his reputation impugned* Shirley to the Lords of Trade, December 1, 1747, Shirley, vol. I, pp. 412–419.

306 *The outspoken doctor loudly* Mather had learned of the "Circassian" or Turkish method of inoculation, which was risky but effective. This pre-dates Edward Jenner's work by seventy-five years.

308 *On March 17, negotiations commenced* Anderson, pp. 202–204.

309 *Throughout the summer of 1748* In August, the *London Evening Post* published a lengthy "Ode on the Restitution of Cape Breton," which began with the plaintive verse:

> At length the melancholy morn appears,
> When poor *Britannia* must, alas! Resign
> Yon favourite isle. Her sons, dissolv'd in tears,
> Reluctant quit, and each cries, "she was mine"
> The same ode ends with the sarcastic words:
> Ambitious *Gaul* will now record in story
> This is the period of *Great Britain*'s glory.

Verses like these, however, had no effect on the British government, which was willing to risk the resentment of its citizens if it could obtain a peace treaty. Source: *London Evening Post*, August 23, 1748, published in the *Boston Weekly Journal*, February 7, 1749.

309 *A lengthy article, almost assuredly written Independent Advertiser*, November 14, 1748.

313 *Shirley was seen as part of the British scheme* Schutz, p. 143.

313 *Greeted with resentment, the money that would* Parkman, *Atlantic Monthly*, p. 630.

314   *The citizens found methods to express their* Bridenbaugh, *Revolt*, p. 91.

315   *When Thomas Hutchinson's house caught* Warden, p. 140.

315   *Late in his life, Sam Adams's younger second cousin John Adams* Quoted in Pencak, *War, Politics*, pp. 124–125.

315   *Samuel Adams's grandson and biographer, William Wells* Wells, vol. I, p. 15.

EPILOGUE: ROAD TO REVOLUTION

317   *Governor Shirley, after successfully defending himself* Schutz, pp. 162–167.

318   *He also outlined several other expeditions* Ibid., pp. 195–196.

318   *While the presence of the two regiments* McDougall, pp. 186–188.

319   *Carrying the burden of his personal grief* Schutz, pp. 195–196.

321   *The British force assembled* McLennan, pp. 241–242.

322   *On D-Day, ironically June 6* Leach, pp. 424–425.

322   *He led his troops ashore over menacing rocks* McLennan, p. 252.

322   *The French, heavily outnumbered, put up a* Fowler, pp. 169–170.

323   *He discovered that a trail to the west of the* Leach, pp. 460–462.

324   *Richard Gridley's contributions at Louisbourg* DAB, vol. VII, p. 612.

324   *Great Britain had amassed a staggering £146 million* Anderson, p. 562.

325   *He met regularly for political discussions* Irvin, pp. 45–49.

326   *In Boston, four American sailors* Clark, p. 220.

327   *Stunned, Boston seethed with volatility until* McCullough, p. 66.

327   **To establish a communications network** Nettles, p. 640.

328   *Since the perpetrators of this "crime"* They were not identified at the time and never have been identified.

330   *Adams and Hancock made their escape* Irvin, p. 129.

330   *George Washington was put in command* DAB, vol. XV, p. 55.

330   *There, striding up the hill, having ridden* Boatner, pp. 875–876.

Bibliography

Primary Sources and Journals

Adams, John. *Letterbook, Letter of August 24, 1815, from John Adams to Thomas Jefferson.* Original manuscript. Massachusetts Historical Society.

Adams, Samuel (attribution writing as "Amicus Patria"). *Address to the Inhabitants of the Province of the Massachusetts-Bay in New England, More Especially, to the Inhabitants of Boston; Occassioned by the Late Illegal and Unwarrantable Attack upon Their Liberties* . . . Rogers & Fowle: Boston, 1747.

————. *The Writings of Samuel Adams.* Harry Alonzo Cushing, ed. Octagon Books: New York, 1968.

Anonymous. *Complaint from Heaven with a Huy and crye and a petition out of Virginia and Maryland.* Proceedings of the Council of Maryland, 1667–1687/8. *Archives of Maryland Online* 5 (2006): 135.

Anonymous. *The Journal of the Sloop UNION.* Privately printed for Paul C. Nicholson: Providence RI, 1929.

Auckmuty, Robert. *The Importance of Cape Breton to the British Nation.* W. Bickerton: London, 1745.

Bacon, Nathaniel. *The Declaration of the People, July 30, 1676:* http://www .constitution.org/bcp/baconpeo.htm

Baxter, James P., ed. *The Documentary History of the State of Maine.* Maine Historical Society: Portland, 1869–1916.

Beverley, Robert. *The History and Present State of Virginia.* R. Parker: London, 1705.

Bidwell, Adonijah. "Expedition to Cape Breton. Journal of the Rev. Adonijah Bidwell, Chaplain of the Fleet." *New England Historical and Genealogical Register* XXVII (April 1873): 153–160, 192–193.

Book of the General Lauues and Libertyes Concerning the Inhabitants of the Massachusets. General Court: Cambridge, MA, 1648.

Bradford, William. *History of Plymouth Plantation, 1606–1646.* Charles Scribner's Sons: New York, 1908.

Bradstreet, Dudley. "Diary." *Massachusetts Historical Society Proceedings,* 2nd ser., XI (1897): 417–446.

Browne, William H., ed. *Archives of Maryland.* Maryland Historical Society: Baltimore, 1883–1990.

Burke, Edmund. *The Works of the Right Hon. Edmund Burke.* C. C. Little & J. Brown: Boston, 1839.

Calvert, Cecil, Lord Baltimore. *Rent Deed Agreement From Lord Cecil Baltimore to Windsor Castle, 1633.* Maryland Historical Society, http://www.mcps.k12.md.us/curriculum/socialstd/ETF/cache92833.html.

Church, Benjamin. *The History of the Great Indian War of 1675 and 1676.* H. Dayton: New York, 1859.

Cleaves, Benjamin. "Journal of the Expedition to Louisbourg, 1745." *New England Historical and Genealogical Register* (Boston) LXVI (1912): 113–124.

Craft, Benjamin. "Journal of the Siege of Louisbourg." *Historical Collections of the Essex Institute* VI, no. 5 (October 1864): 181–194. Published by the institute.

Curwen, George. "Extracts from Letters Written by Capt. Geo. Curwen of Salem, Mass., to His Wife While on the Expedition Against Louisbourg." *Historical Collections of the Essex Institute* VI, no. 3 (October 1864): 186–188. Published by the institute.

de Forest, Louis Effingham, ed. *The Journals and Papers of Seth Pomeroy.* Society of Colonial Wars in the State of New York: New York, 1926.

———. *Louisbourg Journals.* Society of Colonial Wars in the State of New York: New York, 1932.

Durell, Philip. *A Paricular Account of the Taking of Cape Breton from the French, by Admiral Warren and Sir William Pepperrell, the 17th of June, 1745.* W. Bickerton: London, 1745.

Emerson, Joseph, Jr. "Diary of a Naval Chaplain in the Expedition against Louisbourg, 1745." *Massachusetts Historical Society Proceedings,* vol. 44 (October 1910): 65–84.

Gibson, James. *A Boston merchant of 1745, or, Incidents in the life of James Gibson, a gentleman volunteer at the expedition to Louisburg: With a journal of that siege, never before published in this country / by one of his descendants.* Redding & Co.: Boston, 1847.

Giddings, Daniel. "Journal Kept by Lieut. Daniel Giddings of Ipswich During the Expedition Against Cape Breton in 1744–45." *Historical Collections of the Essex Institute* XLVIII, no. 4 (October 1912): 293–304. Published by the institute.

Gorham, John. John Gorham Papers. Manuscript. William L. Clements Library, University of Michigan at Ann Arbor.

Hall, M. G., ed. "The Autobiography of Increase Mather." *American Antiquarian Society Proceedings* (Worcester, MA) 71 (1962).

Hening, William Waller. *The Statutes at Large: Being a Collection of All the Laws of Virginia, from the First Session of the Legislature, in the Year 1619*. Printed for the editor by R. & W. & G. Bartow: New York, 1823.

Holman, Richard B. *Index to marine insurance policies written in the office of Benjamin Pollard of Boston. 1743 Feb. 27–1745 Oct. 31*. Manuscript. Phillips Library, Peabody Essex Museum: Salem, MA.

Knowles, Charles. *Expedition to Cathagena in the year 1741*. NA/PRO CO5/41, pp. 230–296.

Lacroix-Girard, Gilles. *La chute de Louisbourg: Le journal du 1er siege de Louisbourg du 25 mars au 17 Juillet 1745 par Gilles Lacroix-Girard*. Éditions de l'Université d'Ottawa: Ottawa, 1978.

Livingston, Robert. *Journal, 1689/90*. Gilder Lehrman Document, GLC 3107, http://www.digitalhistory.uh.edu/documents/documents_p2.cfm?doc=238.

Mather, Cotton. *Magnalia Christi Americana; or The Ecclesiastical History of New-England*. Reproduced from the edition of 1852 by Russell & Russell, a division of Atheneum House: New York, 1967.

Mather, Increase. *A Narrative of the Miseries of New England, by Reason of an Arbitrary Government Erected There*. London, 1688.

Mather, Samuel. "Account of the Preliminary to Revolt, April 1689." In W. H. Whitmore, ed. *The Andros Tracts*. Prince Society Publication, vols. 5–7, published between 1868 and 1874. Reprinted by Burt Franklin: New York, 1967.

"Minutes of the Councell att New Yorke." *New-York Historical Society Collections* 1 (1868).

Moore, Francis. *A Voyage to Georgia, Begun in the Year 1735*. Robinson: London, 1744.

Niles, Samuel. *A Brief and Plain Essay on God's wonder working Providence for New England, in the Reduction of Louisbourg*. T. Green: New London, 1747.

Notre Dame de Deliverance: The Case of Three Respondents, to be heard before the Right Honorable the Lord Commissioners for Appeals in Prize Causes, at the Council-Chamber, at Whitehall, on Thursday the 3d Day of May, 1750, at six of the Clock in the Evening. Printed account, original in the New York Public Library. London, 1750.

Nowell, Samuel. "Letter to John Richards, March 28, 1683." *Massachusetts Historical Society Collections* (Boston), 5th ser., 1 (1871).

O'Callaghan, E. B., ed. *Documents Relative to the Colonial History of the State of New-York.* Weed, Parsons & Co., printers: Albany, 1853–1887.

Penhallow, Samuel. *The History of the Wars of New England, with the Eastern Indians.* A facsimile reprint of the first edition, printed in Boston in 1726. Corner House Publishers: Williamstown, MA, 1973.

Pepperrell, William. "The Journal of Sir William Pepperrell, Kept During the Expedition Against Louisbourg." *Proceedings of the American Antiquarian Society* 100 (October 1909): 134–176.

———. "The Pepperrell Papers." *Collections of the Massachusetts Historical Society*, 1st ser., 1792 I, and 6th ser., X (1899).

Percy, George. *A Trewe Relacyon of the Pcedeinges and Ocurrentes of Momente wch have hapned in Virginia from the Tyme Sr Thomas GATES was shippwrackte uppon the BERMUDES ano 1609 untill my depture outt of the Country wch was in ano Dñi 1612.*

Virtual Jamestown, University of Virginia at Charlottesville, 2000. http://etext.lib.virginia.edu/etcbin/jamestown-browse?id=j1063

Pote, William. *The Journal of Captain William Pote, Jr.* Garland Publishing: New York, 1976.

Records from the British National Archives (Kew, Richmond, UK) (files): ADM 1/38/7–14; ADM 96/512; CO 5/41/234–244; CO 5/41/280–296; CO 5/41/319–320; CO 5/42/96–98; CO 5/42/116–120; CO 5/45/49–60; CO 5/75/9; CO 5/75/15; CO 5/75/15–19; CO 5/753/136–168; CO 5/862/121-1–4; CO 5/862/121-I; CO 5/862/121-ii-1–4; CO 5/862/121-iii; CO 5/862/121-iv; CO 5/862/121-v; CO 5/862/121-vi; CO 5/862/121-vii; CO 5/862/121-viii-1–3; CO 5/862/121-ix; CO 5/862/121-x; CO 5/862/121-xi; CO 5/862/121-xii-1–3; CO 5/862/121-xiv; CO 5/862/121-xv; CO 5/862/121-xvi-1–2; CO 5/862/121-xviii; CO 5/862/121-xix-1–2; HCA 42/41/Box 1; HCA 42/41/Box 2; SP 42/30/11 Feb. 1745; SP 42/30/107–110; SP 44/67; SP 89/45/35–36; WO 4/46/99 and 105–106; WO 34/1/37; WO 26/14/44–48; WO 34/1; WO 34/27/583; WO 4/41/5–8.

Records of the Rhode Island Historical Society (Providence): Document 4.9.71. *Petition of Richard Partridge to George II, April 15, 1746.*

Sewall, Samuel. "Diary of Samuel Sewall." *Massachusetts Historical Society Collections* (Boston), 5th ser., 5 (1878).

Shirley, William. *Correspondence of William Shirley, Governor of Massachusetts and Military Commander in America, 1731–1760.* Edited under the auspices of the National Society of the Colonial Dames of America, by Charles Henry Lincoln. Macmillan Company: New York, 1912.

————. *A Letter from William Shirley, Esq.: Governor of Massachusetts Bay to His Grace the Duke of Newcastle: with A Journal of the Siege of Louisbourg, . . .* Rogers & Fowle for Joshua Blanchard: Boston, 1746.

Smollett, Tobias. "An Account of the Expedition Against Carthagena." In James P. Browne, ed. *The Works of Tobias Smollett, M.D.,* vol. VIII. Bickers & Son, H. Sotheran: London, 1872.

Stearns, Benjamin. "Louisbourg Diary." *Massachusetts Historical Society Proceedings,* 3rd ser., II (1909): 135–144.

Toppan, Robert N., and Alfred T. S. Goodrick, eds. *Edward Randolf; Including His letters and Official Papers.* Vols. 24–28 and 30–31. Prince Society Publications, published between 1898 and 1909. Reprinted by Burt Franklin: New York, 1967.

Vernon, Edward. *Authentic Papers Relating to the Expedititon Against Carthagena.* L. Raymond: London, 1744.

Walker, Hovenden. *A Journal, or, Full Account of the Late Expedition to Canada.* D. Browne: London, 1720.

White, John. *The firft voyage of M. John White into the West Indies and parts of America called Virginia, in the yeere 1590.* Virtual Jamestown, University of Virginia at Charlottesville, 2000. http://etext.lib.virginia.edu/etcbin/jamestown-browse?id=j1019.

Wigglesworth, Michael, and Edmund S. Morgan, eds. *The Diary of Michael Wigglesworth 1653–1657.* Peter Smith: Gloucester, MA, 1970.

Williams, John. *The Redeemed Captive Returning to Zion.* Hopkins, Bridgman & Co.: Northampton, MA, 1853.

Wolcott, Roger. "Journal of Roger Wolcott at the Siege of Louisbourg 1745." *Connecticut Historical Society Collections* (Hartford) I (1860): 131–161.

SECONDARY SOURCES

Allis, Frederick S, Jr., ed. *Seafaring in Colonial Massachusetts.* Colonial Society of Massachusetts: Boston, 1980.

Anderson, Fred. *Crucible of War: The Seven Years' War and the Fate of Empire in British North America, 1754–1766*. Faber & Faber: London, 2000.

Anderson, M. S. *The War of the Austrian Succession 1740–1748*. Longman: London, 1995.

Andrews, Charles M., ed. *Narratives of the Insurrections, 1675–1690*. C. Soribner's Sons: New York, 1915.

Arnold-Baker, Charles *The Companion to British History*. Routledge: London, 2001.

Bailyn, Bernard. *The Ideological Origins of the American Revolution*. Belknap Press of Harvard University Press: Cambridge, 1967.

Baker, William A. *Sloops & Shallops*. University of South Carolina Press: Columbia, 1966.

Barrow, Thomas C. *Trade and Empire: The British Customs Service in Colonial America, 1660–1775*. Harvard University Press: Cambridge, 1967.

Berkin, Carol. *First Generations: Women in Colonial America*. Hill & Wang: New York, 1996.

Black, Jeremy. *British Foreign Policy in the Age of Walpole*. John Donald Publishers: Edinburgh, 1985.

———. *Eighteenth-Century Britain 1688–1783*. Palgrave: Basingstoke, UK, 2001.

Boatner, Mark Mayo. *Encyclopedia of the American Revolution*. D. McKay Co.: New York, 1966.

Boorstin, Daniel J. *The Americans: The Colonial Experience*. Vintage Books: New York, 1958.

Bourne, Edward E. *The History of Wells and Kennebunk*. B. Thurston & Co.: Portland, 1875.

Bridenbaugh, Carl. Cities in Revolt: *Urban Life in America, 1743–1776*. Capricorn Books: New York, 1964.

———. *Cities in the Wilderness*. Ronald Press Company: New York, 1938.

Browning, Reed. *The War of Austrian Succession*. St. Martin's Press: New York, 1993.

Burrage, Henry S. *Maine at Louisbourg, in 1745*. Burleigh & Flynt: Augusta, ME, 1910.

Butler, Jon. *Becoming America: The Revolution Before 1776*. Harvard University Press: Cambridge, 2000.

Carse, Robert. *Ports of Call: The Great Colonial Seaports*. Charles Scribner's Sons: New York, 1967.

Chapin, Howard M. *Privateering in King George's War 1739–1748*: E. A. Johnson Co.: Providence, 1928.

————. *The TARTAR: The Armed Sloop of the Colony of Rhode Island in King George's War*. Society of Colonial Wars of Rhode Island and Providence Plantations: Providence, 1922.

Charnock, John. *Biographia Navalis, or Impartial Memoirs of the Lives and Characters of Officers of the Navy of Great Britain, from the Year 1660 to the Present Time*. R. Faulder: London, 1795.

Clowes, W. Laird. *The Royal Navy*. Sampson, Low, Marston & Co: London, 1898.

Colbert, David, ed. *Eyewitness to America*. Pantheon Books: New York, 1997.

Collins, James B. *The State in Early Modern France*. Cambridge University Press: Cambridge, 1995.

Commager, Henry Steele. *Documents of American History*. Appleton-Century-Crofts: New York, 1963.

Coward, Barry. *The Stuart Age: England, 1603–1714*, 2nd ed. Longman: London, 1994.

Cress, Lawrence Delbert. *Citizens in Arms: The Army and Militia in American Society to the War of 1812*. University of North Carolina Press: Chapel Hill, 1982.

Douglass, William. *A Summary, Historical and Political, of the first Planting, Progressive Improvements, and Present State of the British Settlements in North America*. Rogers & Fowle: Boston, 1749.

Downey, Fairfax. *Louisbourg: Key to a Continent*. Prentice-Hall: Englewood Cliffs, NJ 1965.

Drake, Samuel G. *A Particular History of the Five Years French and Indian War*. Joel Munsell: Albany, 1870.

Duncan, Roger F. *Coastal Maine: A Maritime History*, Countryman Press: Woodstock, VT, 1992.

Eccles, W. J. *Canada Under Louis XIV 1663–1701*. McClelland & Stewart: Toronto, 1964.

————. *The Canadian Frontier 1534–1760*. Holt, Rinehart & Winston: New York, 1969.

Fairchild, Byron. *Messrs. William Pepperrell: Merchants at Piscataqua*. American Historical Association, Cornell University Press: Ithaca, NY, 1954.

Faragher, John Mack. *A Great and Noble Scheme: The Tragic Story of the Expulsion of the French Acadians from Their American Homeland*. W. W. Norton & Co.: New York, 2005.

Felt, Joseph B. *The Annals of Salem: From Its First Settlement*. W. & S. B. Ives: Salem, MA, 1827.

Fernandez, Jose. *The Forgotten Battle: The Defense of Cartagena During the War of Jenkins' Ear.* Online at www.agonswim.com/Josef/cartagena.

Ford, Worthington Chauncey. *Broadsides, Ballads, Etc., Printed in Massachusetts 1639–1800.* Massachusetts Historical Society: Boston, 1922.

Fortescue, J. W. *A History of the British Army.* Macmillan & Co.: London, 1910.

Fowler, William M., Jr. *Empires at War: The French and Indian War and the Struggle for North America, 1754–1763.* Walker & Co.: New York, 2005.

———. *Samuel Adams: Radical Puritan.* Longman: New York, 1997.

Francis, Douglas R., Richard Jones, and Donald B. Smith. *Origins: Canadian History to Confederation.* Holt, Rinehart & Winston of Canada: Toronto, 1988.

Greene, Evarts B. *Provincial America, 1690–1740.* Harper & Brothers: New York, 1905.

Gwyn, Julian. *An Admiral for America: Sir Peter Warren, Vice Admiral of the Red, 1703–1752.* University Press of Florida: Gainesville, 2004.

———. *The Enterprising Admiral: The Personal Fortune of Admiral Sir Peter Warren.* McGill-Queen's University Press: Montreal, 1974.

———. *Frigates and Foremasts: The North American Squadron in Nova Scotia Waters, 1745–1815.* UBC Press: Vancouver, 2003.

———, ed. *The Royal Navy and North America: The Warren Papers, 1736–1752.* Navy Records Society: London, 1973.

Haefeli, Evan, and Kevin Sweeney. *Captors and Captives: The 1704 French and Indian Raid on Deerfield.* University of Massachusetts Press: Amherst, 2003.

Hall, Michael G., Lawrence H. Leder, and Michael G. Kammen, eds. *The Glorious Revolution in America: Documents on the Colonial Crisis of 1689.* W. W. Norton & Co.: New York, 1972.

Hamilton, Milton W. *Sir William Johnson: Colonial American, 1715–1763.* Kennikat Press: Port Washington, NY, 1976.

Harding, Richard. *Amphibious Warfare in the Eighteeenth Century: The British Expedition to the West Indies 1740–1742.* Royal Historical Society, Boydell Press: Woodbridge, Suffolk, UK, 1991.

Hardy, John. *A Chronological List of the Captains of His Majesty's Royal Navy.* T. Cadell: London, 1784.

Hawke, David F. *The Colonial Experience.* Bobbs-Merrill Company,: New York, 1966.

———. *Everyday Life in Early America.* Harper & Row: New York, 1988.

Hepper, David J. *British Warship Losses in the Age of Sail, 1650–1859.* Jean Boudroit Publications: Rotherfield, UK, 1994.

Higham, Robin. *A Guide to the Sources of U.S. Military History.* Archon Books: Hamden, CT, 1975.

Hohman, Elmo Paul. *Seamen Ashore: A Study of the United Seamen's Service and of Merchant Seamen in Port.* Yale University Press: New Haven, 1952.

Hosmer, James Kendall. *Samuel Adams.* AMS Press: New York, 1972.

Hutchinson, J. R. *The Press-gang Afloat and Ashore.* G. Bell & Sons: London, 1913.

Hutchinson, Thomas. *The History of the Colony and Province of Massachusetts-Bay.* Harvard University Press: Cambridge, 1936.

Irvin, Benjamin H. *Samuel Adams: Son of Liberty, Father of Revolution.* Oxford University Press: Oxford, 2002.

Jaenen, Cornelius, and Cecilia Morgan, eds. *Documents in Pre-Confederation History.* Addison-Wesley: Don Mills, Ontario, 1998.

Jennings, John. *Boston, Cradle of Liberty 1630–1776.* Doubleday & Co.: New York, 1947.

Johnson, Claudia Durst. *Daily Life in Colonial New England.* Greenwood Press: Westport, CT, 2002.

Johnson, Warren B. *The Content of American Colonial Newspapers Relative to International Affairs, 1704–1763.* University Microfilms, Inc.: Ann Arbor, 1962.

Johnston, A. J. B. *Control and Order in French Colonial Louisbourg, 1713–1758.* Michigan State University Press: East Lansing, 2001.

———. *Life and Religion at Louisbourg 1713–1758.* McGill-Queen's University Press: Montreal, 1996.

———. *The Summer of 1744: A Portrait of Life in 18th Century Louisbourg.* Parks Canada: Ottawa, 2002.

Jones, Colin. *The Great Nation: France from Louis XV to Napoleon 1715–99.* Columbia University Press: New York, 2002.

Ketchum, Richard M. *Divided Loyalties: How the American Revolution Came to New York.* Henry Holt & Co.: New York, 2002.

King, Dean, John B. Hattendorf, and J. Worth Estes. *A Sea of Words: A Lexicon and Companion for Patrick O'Brian's Seafaring Tales.* Henry Holt & Co.: New York, 1995.

Labaree, Benjamin W. *Colonial Massachusetts: A History.* KTO Press: Millwood, NY, 1979.

Labaree, Leonard Woods, ed. *The Papers of Benjamin Franklin.* Yale University Press: New Haven, 1959.

————, ed. *Royal Instructions to British Colonial Governors, 1670–1776*. D. Appleton-Century Company: New York, 1935.

Lacroix-Girard, Gilles. *La chute de Louisbourg: Le journal du 1er siege de Louisbourg du 25 mars au 17 juillet par Gilles Lacroix-Girard*. Éditions de l'Université d'Ottawa: Ottawa, 1978.

Lanning, John Tate. *The Diplomatic History of Georgia: A Study of the Epoch of Jenkins' Ear*. University of North Carolina Press: Chapel Hill, 1936.

Leach, Douglas Edward. *Arms for Empire: A Military History of the British Colonies in North America, 1607–1763*. Macmillan Company: New York, 1973.

Lengel, Edward G. *General George Washington: A Military Life*. Random House: New York, 2005.

Lincoln, Charles Henry. *Correspondence of William Shirley*. Macmillan Company: New York, 1912.

A Louisbourg Primer: An Introductory Manual for Staff at the Fortress Louisbourg National Site. Parks Canada, 1991. http://fortress.uccb.ns.ca/search/eprim.html

Lounsberry, Alice. *Sir William Phips: Treasure Fisherman and Governor of the Massachusetts Bay Colony*. Charles Scribner's Sons: New York, 1941.

Lovejoy, David S. *The Glorious Revolution in America*. Wesleyan University Press: Middletown, CT, 1987.

Lyon, David. *The Sailing Navy List: All the Ships of the Royal Navy, Built, Purchased and Captured, 1688–1860*. Conway Maritime Press: London, 1993.

MacLean, Terry. *Louisbourg Heritage: From Ruins to Reconstruction*. University College of Cape Breton Press: Sydney, NS, 1995.

Marshall, John. *Royal Naval Biography*. A bound typescript in the collection of the National Archives. Kew, London, undated.

McCullough, David. *John Adams*. Simon & Schuster: New York, 2001.

McCusker, John J. *How Much Is That In Real Money?: A Historical Commodity Price Index for Use as a Deflator of Money Values in the Economy of the United States*. American Antiquarian Society: Worcester, MA, 2001.

McDougall, Walter A. *Freedom Just Around the Corner: A New American History 1585–1828*. HarperCollins: New York, 2004.

McLennan, John S. *Louisbourg from Its Foundation to Its Fall, 1713–1758*. Fortress Press: Sydney, NS, 1969.

Miller, John C. *Sam Adams: Pioneer in Propaganda.* Little, Brown & Co.: Boston, 1936.

Moore, Christopher. *Louisbourg Portraits: Five Dramatic, True Tales of People who Lived in an Eighteenth-Century Garrison Town.* McClelland & Stewart: Toronto, 2000.

Moorhouse, Esther H. *Letters of English Seamen.* Chapman & Hall: London, 1910.

Morgan, Edmund S. *Inventing the People: The Rise of Popular Sovereignty in England and America.* W. W. Norton & Co.: New York, 1989.

―――. *The Genuine Article: A Historian Looks at Early America.* W. W. Norton & Co.: New York, 2004.

Morison, Samuel Eliot, et al. *Concise History of the American Republic.* Oxford University Press: New York, 1980.

Nettles, Curtis, P. *The Roots of American Civilization,* 2nd ed. Appleton-Century-Crofts: New York, 1963.

New England Historic Genealogical Society reports: *Massachusetts Officers and Soldiers in the Seventeenth-Century Conflict,* 1982; *Massachusetts Officers and Soldiers 1702–1722,* 1980; *Massachusetts Officers and Soldiers 1723–1743,* 1979; *Massachusetts Officers and Soldiers in the French and Indian Wars 1744–1755,* 1978; *Massachusetts Officers and Soldiers in the French and Indian Wars 1755–1756,* 1985; *Massachusetts Officers in the French and Indian Wars 1748–1763,* 1975; *Massachusetts Militia Companies and Officers in the Lexington Alarm,* 1976, New England Historic Genealogical Society: Boston.

Osgood, Herbert L. *The American Colonies in the Eighteenth Century.* Columbia University Press: New York, 1924.

―――. *The American Colonies in the Seventeenth Century.* Macmillan Company: New York, 1904.

Otis, James. *The Boys of 1745: At the Capture of Louisbourg.* Estes & Lauriat: Boston, 1897.

Palfrey, John Gorham. *History of New England, from the Revolution of the Seventeenth Century to the Revolution of the Eighteenth.* Little, Brown & Co.: Boston, 1890.

Pares, Richard. *War and Trade in the West Indies, 1739–1763.* Frank Cass & Co.: London, 1963.

Parkman, Francis. *A Half-Century of Conflict: France and England in North America.* Little, Brown & Co.: Boston, 1898.

Parsons, Usher. *The Life of Sir William Pepperrell, Bart.* Little, Brown & Co.: Boston, 1856.

Peckham, Howard H. *The Colonial Wars 1689–1762.* University of Chicago Press: Chicago, 1964.

Pencak, William. *War, Politics, & Revolution in Provincial Massachusetts.* Northeastern University Press: Boston, 1981.

Phillips, Leon. *The Fantastic Breed: Americans in King George's War.* Doubleday & Co.: Garden City, NY, 1968.

Pitcairn-Jones, Charles Gray. *The Commissioned Sea Officers of the Royal Navy, 1660–1815.* Typescript, in the National Archive/Public Records Office Library: Kew, London.

Polk, William R. *The Birth of America.* HarperCollins: New York, 2006.

Purvis, Thomas L. *Almanacs of American Life; Colonial America to 1763.* Facts on File: New York, 1999.

Randall, Willard S. *George Washington: A Life.* Henry Holt & Co.: New York, 1997.

Rawlyk, G. A. *Yankees at Louisbourg.* University of Maine Press: Orono, 1967.

Reid, William J. *Castle Island and Fort Independence.* Trustees of the Public Library of the City of Boston: Boston, 1995.

Richmond, Herbert W. *The Navy in the War of 1739–48.* Cambridge University Press: Cambridge, 1920.

Rodger, N. A. M. *The Wooden World: An Anatomy of the Georgian Navy.* Fontana Press: London, 1988.

Rogers, Alan. *Empire and Liberty: American Resistance to British Authority, 1755–1763.* University of California Press: Berkeley, 1974.

Rolde, Neil. *Sir William Pepperrell of Colonial New England.* Harpswell Press: Brunswick, ME, 1982.

Schutz, John A. *William Shirley: King's Governor of Massachusetts.* University of North Carolina Press: Chapel Hill, 1961.

Shy, John. *Toward Lexington: The Role of the British Army in the Coming of the American Revolution.* Princeton University Press: Princeton, NJ, 1965.

Smith, Philip Chadwick Foster, et al. *Seafaring in Colonial Massachusetts: A Conference Held by the Colonial Society of Massachusetts.* Colonial Society of Massachusetts: Boston, 1980.

Smollett, Tobias. *The Adventures of Roderick Random.* Oxford University Press: Oxford, 1999.

———. *The Works of Tobias Smollett, M.D.* Bickers & Son: London, 1872.

Stephenson, Nathaniel W., and Waldo H. Dunn. *George Washington.* Oxford University Press: London, 1940.

Stone, William L. *The Life and Times of Sir William Johnson, Bart.* J. Munsell: Albany, 1865.

Taylor, Alan. *American Colonies: The Settling of North America.* Penguin Books: New York, 2002.

Thayer, Henry O. *Sir William Phips: Adventurer and Statesman.* Maine Historical Society: Portland, 1927.

Thorpe, Francis N. *The Federal and State Constitutions: Colonial charters, and other organic laws of the states, territories, and colonies now or heretofore forming the United States of America.* Compiled and edited under the act of Congress of June 30, 1906, by Francis Newton Thorpe. Government Printing Office: Washington, DC, 1909.

Trumbull, James Russell. *History of Northampton, Massachusetts: From Its Settlement in 1654.* Press of Gazette Printing Co.: Northampton, MA, 1898–1902.

Ulrich, Laurel Thatcher. *Good Wives: Image and Reality in the Lives of Women in Northern New England 1650–1750.* Vintage Books: New York, 1991.

Vaughn, Alden T., and Edward W. Clark, eds. *Puritans Among the Indians: Accounts of Captivity and Redemption 1676–1724.* Belknap Press: Cambridge, MA, 1981.

Wahlke, John C., ed. *The Causes of the American Revolution.* D. C. Heath & Co.: Boston, 1962.

Warden, G. B. *Boston 1689–1776.* Little, Brown & Co.: Boston, 1970.

Wells, William V. *The Life and Public Service of Samuel Adams.* Little, Brown & Co.: Boston, 1865.

Williams, Basil. *The Whig Supremacy, 1714–1760.* Clarendon Press: Oxford, 1997.

Wood, William. *The Great Fortress: A Chronicle of Louisbourg, 1720–1760.* Glasgow Brook & Co.: Toronto, 1920.

Woodfine, Philip. *Britannia's Glories: The Walpole Ministry and the 1739 War with Spain.* Royal Historical Society: London, 1998.

Wrong, George M., ed. "Louisbourg in 1745: The Anonymous 'Lettre d'un Habitant de Louisbourg.'" *University of Toronto Studies, History* (Toronto), 2nd ser., I (1897): 1–74.

ARTICLES

Ames, Ellis. "Expedition Against Cartagena." *Proceedings of the Massachusetts Historical Society* XVIII (March 1881): 364–378.

Anderson, F. W. "Why Did New Englanders Make Bad Soldiers?: Contractual Principles and Military Conduct During the Seven Years' War." *William and Mary Quarterly,* 3rd ser., XXXVIII, no. 1 (January 1981): 396–417.

Balcom, B. A. "The Siege of 1745." Published on the Fortress of Louisbourg Web site. http://www.fortress.uccb.ns.ca.

————. "*La Renommee* and the Defense of Louisbourg, 1745." Draft 6 of unpublished manuscript supplied by the author, June 2002.

Bolton, Herbert E. "The Epic of Greater America." *American Historical Review* 38, no. 3 (April 1933): 448–474.

Buffington, Arthur H. "The Canada Expedition of 1746, Its Relation to British Politics." *American Historical Review* XLV (October 1939–July 1940). Macmillan Company: New York.

Chapin, Howard M. "New England Vessels in the Expedition Against Louisbourg, 1745." *New England Historical and Genealogical Register* (Boston) LXXVII (1923).

Clark, Dora Mae. "The Impressment of Seamen in the American Colonies." In *Essays in Colonial History Presented to Charles McLean Andrews by His Students.* Books for Libraries Press, Inc.: Freeport, NY, 1966.

Cooper, J. I. "Lawrence Washington: A Neglected Older Brother." *History Today* (August 1978): 516–521.

Donovan, Kenneth. " 'Good for Anything': Slaves Among the New Englanders and British at Louisbourg." Unpublished manuscript provided by the author, May 9, 2000.

Giddings, Daniel. "Journal Kept by Lieut. Daniel Giddings of Ipswich During the Expedition Against Cape Breton in 1744–5." *Historical Collections of the Essex Institute* XLVIII, no. 4 (October 1912): 293–304.

Goold, William. "Col. William Vaughn of Matinicus and Damariscotta." *Collections of the Maine Historical Society* VIII (1881).

Grahame, Allen. "Inflation: the Value of the Pound, 1750–2002." House of Commons Library, research paper 03/82, November 11, 2003.

Greer, Alan. "Soldiers of Isle Royale, 1720–45." *History and Archaeology* (Parks Canada, Ottawa) 28 (1979).

Harkness, Albert, Jr. "Americanism and Jenkins' Ear." *Mississippi Valley Historical Review* XXXVII, no. 1 (June 1950).

Hoyt, Albert H. "Pepperrell Papers, with Sketches of Lt. Gen. The Honorable James St. Clair, and Admiral Sir Charles Knowles, Bart." *New England Historical and Genealogical Register* (Boston) XXVIII (1874): 451–466.

Hudson, Charles. "Louisbourg Soldiers." *New England Historical and Genealogical Register* (Boston) XXIV (1870): 367–380; and XXV (1871): 249–269.

Janvier, Thomas A. "Greenwich Village." *Harper's New Monthly Magazine* LXXXVII, no. DXIX (August 1893): 339–355.

Jones, E. Alfred. "The American Regiment in the Cartagena Expedition." *Virginia Magazine of History and Biography* XXX, no. 1 (January 1922): 1–20.

Lanning, John T. "The American Colonies in the Preliminaries of the War of Jenkins' Ear." *Georgia Historical Quarterly* XI (1927): 129–155 and 191–215.

Lax, John, and William Pencak. "The Knowles Riot and the Crisis of the 1740s in Massachusetts." In Donald Fleming and Bernard Bailyn, eds. *Perspectives in American History*, vol. X. Charles Warren Center for Studies in American History, Harvard University: Cambridge, MA, 1976, pp. 163–214.

Leach, Douglas Edward. "Brothers in Arms?: Anglo-American Friction at Louisbourg, 1745–1746." *Massachusetts Historical Society Proceedings* 89 (1977): 36–54.

Lemisch, Jesse. "Jack Tar in the Streets: Merchant Seamen in the Politics of Revolutionary America." *William and Mary Quarterly*, 3rd ser., XXV, no. 3 (July 1968).

Linebaugh, Peter, and Marcus Rediker. "The Many Headed Hydra, Sailors, Slaves and the Atlantic Working Class in the Eighteenth Century." *Journal of Historical Sociology* 3, no. 3 (September 1990): 225–252.

Maier, Pauline. "Coming to Terms with Samuel Adams." *American Historical Review* 81, no. 1 (February 1976): 12–37.

Martz, Louis L. "Smollett and the Expedition to Cartagena." *Publications of the Modern Language Association of America* LVI (1941): 428–446.

Noble, John. "Notes on the Libel Suit of *Knowles v. Douglass* in the Superior Court of Judicature." *Publications of the Colonial Society of Massachusetts* (Boston) III (1900): 213–239.

Parkman, Francis. "The Capture of Louisbourg by the New England Militia." *Atlantic Monthly*, issues of March, April, and May 1891.

Parks Canada / Louisbourg Institute. *A Louisbourg Primer.* An Introductory Manual for Staff at the Fortress of Louisbourg National Site, Parks Canada, 1991. http://fortress.uccb.ns.ca/Search/eprim.html.

Schutz, John A. "Succession Politics in Massachusetts, 1730–1741." *William and Mary Quarterly*, 3rd ser., XV, no. 4 (October 1958): 508–520.

Shy, John W. "A New Look at Colonial Militia." *William and Mary Quarterly,* 3rd ser., XX (1963): 175–185.

Sibley, John Langdon. "William Vaughn and William Tufts, Jr., at Louisbourg, 1745." *New England Historical and Genealogical Register* (Boston) XXV (1871): 376–377.

Smollett, Tobias. "An Account of the Expedition Against Carthagena." In *The Works of Tobias Smollett, M.D.,* vol. VIII, pp. 427–457.

Sosin, Jack M. "Louisbourg and the Peace of Aix-la-Chapelle, 1748." *William and Mary Quarterly,* 3rd ser., IV (1957): 516–535.

Storer, Malcom. "Admiral Vernon Medals, 1739–1742." *Massachusetts Historical Society Proceedings* (Boston) LII (April 1919).

Swanson, Alan. "American Privateering and Imperial Warfare, 1739–1748." *William and Mary Quarterly,* 3rd ser., XLII, no. 3 (July 1985).

Way, R. L., "The Chateau St. Louis, as Built 1720–1745." http://fortress .uccb.ns.ca/search/hco1_1.htm.

NEWSPAPERS AND MAGAZINES

Boston Evening Post, Boston: October 31, 1748; November 21, 1748; November 28, 1748; December 26, 1748; January 16, 1749; January 23, 1749.

Boston Gazette, Boston: March 23, 1741; May 18, 1741; June 29, 1741; July 6, 1741; August 31, 1741; September 28, 1741; October 5, 1741.

Boston Gazette or *Weekly Journal,* Boston: May 21, 1745; June 11, 1745; June 18, 1745; June 25, 1745; July 9, 1745; July 16, 1745; July 23, 1745; July 30, 1745; August 20, 1745; September 10, 1745; November 26, 1745; November 24, 1747; December 8, 1747; December 15, 1745; December 20, 1748; February 7, 1749.

Boston News-Letter, Boston: June 5–12, 1704; November 18–25, 1706; October 30–November 6, 1710; July 30–August 6, 1711; August 27–September 3, 1711; September 10–September 17, 1711; October 1–8, 1711; October 8–15, 1711; October 22–29, 1711; November 12–19, 1711.

Boston Weekly News-Letter, Boston: March 20, 1740; May 8, 1740; July 17, 1740; March 12, 1741; March 19, 1741; April 24, 1741; May 28, 1741; June 11, 1741; June 18, 1741; June 25, 1741; July 2, 1741; July 9, 1741; July 30, 1741; August 6, 1741; August 13, 1741; October 8, 1741; April 14, 1743; July 19, 1745; August 1, 1745; August 15, 1745; September 5, 1745; September 12, 1745; October 10, 1745; November 14, 1745; November 21, 1745; November 28, 1745; December 12, 1745; December 19, 1745; May 8, 1746; July 3, 1746; December 18, 1746; December 17, 1747; June 10,

1748; September 15, 1748; November 25, 1748; December 22, 1748;
   May 11, 1749.

Boston Weekly Post-Boy, Boston: July 8, 1745; July 14, 1745; July 22, 1745;
   July 29, 1745; September 26, 1748.

Daily Post, London: July 24, 1745.

Gentleman's Magazine, London: vol. XI, 1741; vol. XIV, 1744; vol. XV, 1745;
   vol. XVI, 1746.

Independent Advertiser, Boston: January 4, 1748; January 18, 1748; February
   8, 1748; February 29, 1748; March 14, 1748; March 28, 1748; April 4,
   1748; May 23, 1748; May, 30, 1748; June 20, 1748; June 27, 1748; July 4,
   1740; August 1, 1748; September 5, 1748; November 7, 1748; November
   14, 1748; December 26, 1748; January 2, 1749; January 23, 1749; February 20, 1749; March 20, 1749; July 31, 1749; August 28, 1749; September 11, 1749; September 25, 1749.

Maryland Gazette, Annapolis: June 7, 1745; June 21, 1745; June 28, 1745; July
   5, 1745; July 19, 1745; July 26, 1745; August 9, 1745; October 4, 1745.

New England Weekly Journal, Boston: May 26, 1741; June 9, 1741; June 16,
   1741; June 23, 1741; June 30, 1741; July 7, 1741; July 14, 1741.

New York Weekly Post-Boy, New York: July 22, 1745.

Pennsylvania Gazette, Philadelphia: December 20, 1748.

REFERENCE WORKS

Blanco, Richard L. *The American Revolution 1775–1783: An Encyclopedia.*
   Garland Publishing: New York, 1993.

Boatner, Mark Mayo, III. *Encyclopedia of the American Revolution.* David
   McKay Company: New York, 1966.

Dictionary of American Biography. C. Scribner's Sons: New York, 1928–1936.

English, John, gen. ed. *Dictionary of Canadian Biography Online.* Library
   and Archives Canada: Ottawa, 2006.

Lee, Sidney, ed. *Dictionary of National Biography.* Macmillan & Co.: New
   York, 1892.

Matthew, H. C. G., and Brian Harrison, eds. *Oxford Dictionary of National
   Biography.* Oxford University Press: New York, 2004.

Index

Illustrations are indicated by page numbers in *italics*.

A Note on the Author

J. Revell Carr is the author of *All Brave Sailors*. A former president and director of Mystic Seaport, America's leading maritime museum, he was also president of the Council of American Maritime Museums and the International Congress of Maritime Museums. He lives in Santa Fe, New Mexico.